Enterprise Zones

Enterprise Zones

CRITICAL POSITIONS ON

Star Trek

EDITED BY

Taylor Harrison,
Sarah Projansky, Kent A. Ono,
Elyce Rae Helford

WestviewPress
A Division of HarperCollins*Publishers*

Film Studies

Copyright © 1996 by Westview Press, A Division of HarperCollins Publishers, Inc.

Published in 1996 in the United States of America by Westview Press, 5500 Central Avenue, Boulder, Colorado 80301-2877, and in the United Kingdom by Westview Press, 12 Hid's Copse Road, Cumnor Hill, Oxford OX2 9JJ

Library of Congress Cataloging–in–Publication Data
Enterprise zones : critical positions on Star trek / edited by Taylor Harrison . . . [et al.].
     p.   cm. — (Film studies)
   Includes bibliographical references and index.
   ISBN 0-8133-2898-5 (hardcover). — ISBN 0-8133-2899-3
 (pbk.)
   1.   Star trek, the next generation (Television program)   2.   Star
trek (Television program)   I. Harrison, Taylor.   II.   Series: Film
studies   (Boulder, Colo.)
PN1992.77.S73E58   1996
791.45'72—dc20   96-20159
                                                            CIP

The paper used in this publication meets the requirements of the American National Standard for Permanence of Paper for Printed Library Materials Z39.48-1984.

10   9   8   7   6   5   4   3   2   1

Contents

Appendices

Appendix A
Interview with Henry Jenkins   259

Appendix B
A Selective Bibliography of Critical Work on *Star Trek*
279

Acknowledgments

As we near the end of this project, we are only now just beginning to realize exactly how many people helped us write this book. We would like to begin by thanking all of the contributors to this collection. The book could not have been completed without their continuing enthusiasm for the project, the seriousness with which they take their own writing, their patience with our sometimes picky editing habits, and their willingness to think about the many suggestions we offered to improve the essays we received. By "contributors" we mean both the authors whose work is presented in this book and the dozens of people whose essays are not published here. We cannot begin to say how much we learned about *Star Trek* from all of these essays. We were given an education about criticism, theory, and cultural studies we could not have received in classrooms or lecture halls, and we appreciate it deeply. The number of essays submitted to us shows just how many talented academic writers are engaged in making sense of the cultural phenomenon of *Star Trek*.

Though we are four separate individuals, we would nevertheless like to offer a collective expression of thanks to all those who gave helpful advice to each and/or all of us throughout the process, including those who read our prospectus, coached us along the way toward publication, helped us with difficult editing decisions, and provided us with intellectual and emotional support during the editing and writing process, both expected and unforeseen: Cassandra Amesely, Michelle Asakawa, Carole Blair, Chad Crouse, Bruce Gronbeck, Suzanne Jackson, Henry Jenkins, Brooks Landon, Pat McCutcheon, Tom Nakayama, Chris Peters (and the rest of the regular posters in the *Star Trek* Universe forum on the Iowa Student Computer Association BBS), Marnie Schroer, Ramona Liera-Schwichtenberg, Staci Steadman, and Leah R. Vande Berg. Our students at the University of California, Davis, the University of Iowa, and Middle Tennessee State University also helped us to think about this project and gave much appreciated support along the way.

We would especially like to thank Gordon Massman at Westview Press for his continuous support and enthusiasm throughout the process, even as Westview made its transition to becoming part of HarperCollins. Gordon's energetic spirit boosted our confidence and efforts toward completing the project. We would also like to thank Tom Benson, who reviewed the book for publication.

Janice Hocker Rushing gave us helpful advice about obtaining photographs for the book. Though we asked for permission to republish their pictures, Paramount Pictures made it very clear to us that (academic book or not) rights to publish even a small number of black and white photos would be economically prohibitive. Unfortunately, this results in a book limited in its ability to help readers understand fully the complexity of visual media.

Finally, we would like to thank *Cinema Journal* for permission to reprint with minor changes Ilsa Bick's (1996) essay "Boys in Space: *Star Trek*, Latency, and the Neverending Story," 35.2: 43-60; and *Extrapolation* for permission to reprint a revised version of Rhonda Wilcox's (1993) essay "Dating Data: Miscegenation in *Star Trek: The Next Generation*," 34.3: 265–277.

Taylor Harrison
Sarah Projansky
Kent A. Ono
Elyce Rae Helford

Enterprise Zones

Introduction

Star Trek[1] promises so much to so many. Its textual credos include Infinite Diversity in Infinite Combination (IDIC) and the Prime Directive, two formulas that offer simple, but misleading, answers to complex social and cultural problems such as hunger, sexism, racism, and homophobia. *Star Trek*'s visible attempts at ethnic and gender diversity (what we might call a *liberal chic*) superficially validate liberal perspectives on multiculturalism and feminism. *Star Trek*'s promises for a better future include more advanced technology, greater political efficiency, and abundant moral and social progress. These assurances rely on Science to meet all human (and most "alien") personal and social needs. Within this promised world, the oxymoronic "peaceful" military organization known as Starfleet promises democracy for the United Federation of Planets—the galactic United Nations—and a resolution to painful human events.

Not surprisingly, then, in early *Star Trek* history, critics and fans alike hailed the original *Star Trek* series (*ST*) as the first televised science fiction program to offer a positive view of the future. They credited *ST* with bringing the first mass female audience to the genre. They lauded it for featuring the first televised interracial kiss. Indeed, *Star Trek: The Next Generation* (*TNG*) even prophesied an end to the Cold War by declaring peace between Klingon and human cultures, offered the cyborg as a model for new constructions of human subjectivity, and elevated psychology to the status of a hard science by bringing a counselor to the bridge to join the likes of science, weapons, military, engineering, and communications specialists. It placed at least one woman, however short-lived, in the nontraditional role of Security Chief. And *Star Trek: Deep Space Nine* (*DS9*) and *Star Trek: Voyager* (*Voyager*) have finally put women and people of color at the top of the chain of command, at the top of *Star Trek*'s self-created hierarchy.

Star Trek's many promises have deeply and profoundly influenced its audiences. It has become almost impossible to envision a future that does not include warp drive, phasers, photon torpedoes, tricorders, communicators, and numerous other *Star Trek* military and scientific technologies. *Star Trek* invites viewers to imagine a future in which humans interact with aliens, amiably. For these reasons, we think it is imperative to analyze, as fully and critically as possible, what and how this textual "utopia" encourages and discourages us to think about how militarism, science, technology, and culture affect our present and future realities. Therefore, the purpose of *Enterprise Zones* is to critically address the complex representational nature and emblematic status of *Star Trek* in order to interrogate and challenge the ethical system *Star Trek* produces.

However, writing about television is no easy task. So, while we offer these critical analyses as evidence of our attempt to criticize and illuminate *Star Trek*'s textual world, we sometimes had difficulty with the most innocuous tasks. For instance, the unwieldiness of *Star Trek* has made our attempts at consistent references, definitions, and spellings within the *Star Trek* universe difficult. Because our book is not about celebrating or protecting the world of *Star Trek*, however, we hope our readers will forgive our sometimes brief and overtly subjective definitions of terms such as Prime Directive and citations of characters' ranks and roles. While we have assiduously attempted to follow the logics of the *Star Trek* world, we have deviated from that system at times as part of a larger political project. Our attempt at consistent use of characters' last names is a case in point. Whereas *TNG* episodes, novels, and reference books often refer to Counselor Lt. Commander Deanna Troi, Chief Engineer Lt. Commander Geordi La Forge, and Chief Medical Officer Commander Beverly Crusher as Deanna, Geordi, and Beverly, respectively, while simultaneously referring to Captain Jean-Luc Picard and First Officer Commander William Riker as Picard or Captain and Riker or Commander, respectively, we have attempted to resist this gender- and race-specific hierarchy by refusing the subtle distinctions these naming practices may imply. Thus, simply using the surnames Troi, La Forge, and Crusher becomes part of our collectively (self-)critical act.[2]

In part because of this textual and ideological complexity, and also because of its respective simplicity, just as you have something definitive to say about television (and have the words with which to say it), *it changes*. The elusive and ephemeral quality of television makes television criticism all the more difficult. By the time this book comes out, the world of television will already have changed significantly, and so will the texts that we and our contributors ostensibly take as our objects. The social imaginary landscape will have shifted. Television criticism books quickly appear outdated because they fail to address the narratives of the audience's recent memory, they no longer make sense within the sociopolitical climate in which the book appears, or they simply prove unable to direct attention to the complex televisual system always attempting to harness technology's power to create a new visual and aural aesthetic.

On the one hand, this odd, old-before-new quality of television criticism can work productively to denaturalize television's perpetual flow not only through the course of an evening's viewing and between the television and one's living space but also across the history of our lives. On the other hand, and on a more practical level, because this book might already appear somewhat out-of-date by the time it is published, we think it best to give a brief synoptic history of its development to mark what has—and what has not yet—been done. We began soliciting contributions for this book in spring 1993 after presenting papers on *Star Trek* at the 1993 Popular Culture Association Conference in New Orleans, Louisiana. At that time, *DS9* had just begun. Now, nearly three years later, *TNG*'s run has ended, we have seen the crossover film, *Star Trek: Generations* (1994), and the television series *Voyager* is in its second season. Thus, while our book is influenced by *DS9, Voyager,* and *Star Trek: Generations,* no chapter in this volume takes them as primary subject matter.

The essays collected for this volume are, quite simply, the clearest critical analyses we could find on the subject of *Star Trek* within the limited scope of a small collection. While they do not respond to every aspect of *Star Trek* or address all of the *Star Trek* texts available now, they do respond to the *Star Trek* phenomenon as a contemporary entity. As a result, these articles focus heavily on *TNG,* paying somewhat less attention to the films and *ST.* One could argue that much of the material collected here represents the first attempts at mature commentary on *TNG,* the most recent part of *Star Trek* to move from regular, frequent production to the realm of popular— which is to say, fannish—memory.

All of the writing we include is sensitive to the fact that *Star Trek* is much more than a television show. The *Star Trek* phenomenon includes not only the original series and three spin-offs but also six films, a televised cartoon, numerous reference and fictional books, comic books, conventions, articles, journals, newspapers, toys, one-liners, and many other mediated and multi-mediated texts. Although all television shows could be considered "cultural phenomena" in relation to audiences, *Star Trek*—because its very definition goes well beyond the television screen—is unique within the televisual world. It has greater longevity than *M.A.S.H.* It has a larger audience than *Dallas.* It is more popular than *The Cosby Show.* Moreover, it is the "bread and butter" of Paramount Pictures (to quote their own representatives), one of the largest U.S. media conglomerates; this link of economics and culture, more than anything else perhaps, makes *Star Trek* a cultural production worth criticizing.

Viewers, in general, do have a critical view that they constantly enact through daily cultural performances and through relationships with other people that are by nature politically, socially, and economically formed. We believe viewing itself is a critical act in which we all engage on a regular basis (avid viewers are very adept at recognizing televisual strategies—very often more adept than academic television critics). However, we do believe there is something unique about a commitment to spending hours and hours attempting to account for textual production, both through the close study of theoretical and critical texts about cultural objects and through close textual analysis of mediated texts. It is with this philosophy that we approach the study of *Star Trek,* a phenomenon that rhetorically configures a certain dynamic system of relations among subjects.

We began this project because we all had more than a casual investment in *Star Trek.* Each of us had watched the show in some form; we also had seen the movies and, further, had participated in other *Star Trek* activities such as fan writing, conventions, clubs, and conversations. It is important to note, however, that our activity as fans does not necessarily imply our celebration of the text. In fact, one could argue that there is a certain pleasure in performing criticism via cultural and social means. Taking the text and "poaching" it is, as Henry Jenkins[3] argues, a profoundly pleasurable experience that contains its own system of production and critical reflection.

Because we all have different *Star Trek* experiences, and because we all are very different subjects, the idea of collaboration represented a challenge to assembling this book. Our collectivity signifies more than the creation of a joint project, however; it is in fact a collaboration *against* the text, one to which each editor contributed differently but equally. Underlying this book is a strong philosophy that collaborative projects make academic life what it should be—a social process. Society often encourages narcissism, individual achievement, and social bonds formed only within the social unity of the family. Television encourages asocial viewing; market analysts repeatedly remind producers that viewers who consume commercial television by themselves are more susceptible to the lure of advertised products. Thus, the sights and sounds of the screen dominate our attention within an otherwise silent room. Similarly, the academy too often seems to encourage narcissistic writing—that is, writing within the confines of one's own mind and home or office. We have actively intervened to the contrary, and the collaborative process constantly provided new life and created a renewed sense of purpose as we went along. This book is more than the sum total of the individual labors of four editors and nine other contributors. *Enterprise Zones* exemplifies what a seemingly unwieldy group of people can do when they combine efforts and disciplines to work steadily (sometimes even efficiently) on a critical project.

Many other critics, including academic ones, have recognized the need to study *Star Trek,* and we have benefited from reading their work in the process of developing our own project. Although much critical work has been done on *Star Trek,* much of the scholarship available on the topic addresses the issue of fandom—largely because critical studies, since the mid- to late-1970s, has been engaged in the study of audiences as much as of texts. Audience studies have reacted productively to the hegemony of textual studies of the past, but the advent of poststructural, feminist, neocolonial, and cultural studies has thrown into question, once again, the relationship between audiences and texts. For our purposes, the intersection between these two is the springboard for this book. Therefore, not only do the chapters in this volume reflect an exacting critical scrutiny of texts, they are also interested in the *connections* between audiences and texts.

One issue often overlooked within television criticism is the fact that the critics of the text are themselves audience members. Thus, the critic, as subject, becomes a fruitful location at which to study the relationship of text to audience, as well as a site for the investigation of the importance of fandom (and its disavowal) within the academy. We would not have taken on this project were we not invested in the texts about which we and our contributors write—and we would not have *finished* this project had those texts not continued to speak to us in frustrating, revealing, pleasurable, and even terrifying ways.

Part One of the book, Centering Subjectivities, addresses specific *Star Trek* characters and the ways in which those characters frame meaning. *Star Trek*'s characters are perhaps its most visible sites or "zones" for contestation over meaning. The focus of this section brings to light many issues that narrative analysis alone misses. These chapters examine the intersections of gender, race, and sexuality within subjectivities produced by and across texts and the ways such intersections create, maintain, and negotiate oppression, social bodies, and reading pleasures.

Elyce Rae Helford investigates constructions of masculinity through a study of Kirk. She argues that reading the multiple and complex elements of Kirk's privileged masculine subjectivity is essential to feminist critical goals of envisioning possibilities for social change within patriarchy. Helford suggests that Kirk, whose role as a womanizer has been the main focus of feminist criticism of him, provides a productive site for exemplifying a broad-based feminist study that recognizes the complex construction of masculinity in all its guises while attending to asymmetries of power within a male-supremacist cultural paradigm.

In her study of *TNG* rape narratives, Sarah Projansky illustrates how the show uses feminist concepts of consent and choice, paradoxically, to rearticulate patriarchal authority in relation to the colonialist project inferred by the Prime Directive. Projansky argues that in these narratives Troi's body is her only voice. The narrative tension between this speaking body and Federation rationality undermines Troi's authority on contemporary feminist issues. Simultaneously, *TNG* defines the villainous rapist as other-than-Federation, which justifies both the Prime Directive's assumption of Federation superiority and the *TNG* viewer's masculinist gaze.

Leah R. Vande Berg studies Worf's multiple representations within various episodes of *TNG*. She sees Worf as a liminal character—a character "betwixt and between" multiple subjectivities—and offers a way to read Worf's liminality and *TNG*'s attempt to assimilate him. Through bioessentialist discourse, humans incessantly call into question Worf's Klingon subjectivity and attempt to teach him how to act more like a "normal" human being. Vande Berg suggests, in part, that this representation of species, culture, and nationality in the twenty-fourth century metaphorically references race and racism in the present.

In the final chapter of Part One, Rhonda V. Wilcox analyzes the displacement of contemporary race issues onto Data, particularly as they concern the representation of African Americans. *TNG* offers Data as a character who yearns to be human. The show presents him as engaged in a struggle for human rights and self-knowledge on the borders between slavery and freedom, emotionless isolation and forbidden sexuality. His subjectivity is constantly in question, always in transition to a more appealing form for both his human counterparts and himself, yet never quite reaching his desire. Data is a figure, then, who both articulates and perpetuates the representation of racial difference and hierarchy.

Each of the chapters in Part One highlights the role of subjectivity in constructing particular cultural relations. Each takes the construction of characters as emblematic of larger processes at work. The character is itself part of the larger system of meaning within the text, and the studies within this section explain how that system continues to function through the bodies and subjectivities of liminal characters.

Part Two, Manufacturing Hegemonies, focuses on the way *Star Trek* reconstructs hegemonic systems of modernism, capitalism, and colonialism. This entails an interrogation of *Star Trek*'s representation of social and political power. The chapters in this section address processes of governing and the construction of idealized and naturalized control. The authors of these chapters suggest that *Star Trek* "manufactures" hegemonic relations anew through television's fictional narratives.

Katrina G. Boyd examines the issue of radical difference in *TNG* and the way *Star Trek* reconstructs a contemporary world in the likeness of Western modernism. The show represents the twenty-fourth century's goals as markedly similar to those of the nineteenth century: progress, perfection, individualism. Through its focus on a nineteenth-century utopian notion of progress, Boyd suggests that *TNG* attempts to assimilate difference, even the most radical difference it can imagine—the cy/Borg.

In the second chapter of Part Two, Amelie Hastie studies the way fashion and style operate on *TNG* to mediate audience understandings of social power. She emphasizes the role of hegemony and the assimilation of the physical and social body through critical study of the fashioning of the bodies of Troi and the Borg. Fashion on *TNG*, she suggests, mediates both gender and the relationship between the individual and the collective.

Steven F. Collins argues that *TNG* constructs a utopia filled with individualism and perfection. Yet, *TNG*'s simultaneous focus on militarism creates a tension that is always resolved in favor of order and hierarchy over individualism and self-actualization. This hierarchy, Collins argues, parallels contemporary trilateralism—an alliance between major capitalist states—and this presents a dominant ideology of order, hegemonic structures that ironically wish for, but never fully realize, democracy.

In the final chapter of Part Two, Kent A. Ono argues that *Star Trek* pretends colonialism was something that happened only in the past. While *Star Trek* relies on a successful colonialist system, it continuously denies the ways the text benefits from and reproduces such a system. The very premise of the show is ethnographic exploration of other cultures; many times, this means a fatal exploration. Through a close analysis of the *TNG* episode "The High Ground," Ono argues that *Star Trek* systematically constructs a neo-colonialist world that domesticates terrorism via representations of race and gender.

This second section addresses the way *Star Trek*, while pretending to be politically progressive, continues to reify new hegemonic forms in the shape of hegemonies of the past. These chapters show how, through this continual reprocessing of hegemonies, *Star Trek* maintains an oppressive political system.

Part Three, Producing Pleasures, addresses both modern and postmodern constructions of the changing interstices of pleasure and pain in relation to *Star Trek*'s televisual texts. These chapters focus on how the pleasures of *Star Trek* rely upon suppression, repression, and regression.

Ilsa J. Bick studies numerous episodes of *ST* as well as the *Star Trek* films to argue that *Star Trek* produces pleasures by referencing the latency period of youthful masculinity. Through the metanarrative of latency, Bick conducts a psychoanalytic study of the fantasies *Star Trek* represents for young boys and the way the text promises a fantastic reunion with the primal mother. This fantasy, an illusion of continuity, enables an escape from present social realities.

Evan Haffner studies the film *Star Trek VI: The Undiscovered Country*, arguing that the creation and ultimate destruction of a symbol of evil—General Chang, the "anal father"—while temporarily enabling homosexual enjoyment, maintains heterosexuality as the text's preemptive sexual possibility. Haffner sees this progression as necessarily postmodern and attempts to theorize pleasure at the nexus of paternal power.

Marleen S. Barr argues that the final episode of *The Next generation*—"All Good Things . . . "—epitomizes feminist struggles to balance the pleasures of nostalgia with the painful struggles for social change for contemporary U.S. women. She reads *TNG* as occupying a mediating space between loss of past fantasies (exemplified by the death of Jacqueline Kennedy Onassis) and future potentialities (as seen in the birth of such series as *Lois and Clark: The New Adventures of Superman* and *Dr. Quinn, Medicine Woman*).

Finally, Taylor Harrison investigates, through a study of the figure of the cyborg and its relation to Picard in *TNG*, how *Star Trek* creates a world wherein the process of mourning as an affective response to death is always deferred. She argues that *TNG*'s continual, rapid retreat from this necessarily fraught remembering emblematizes the show's preferred way of dealing with cultural anxieties.

These chapters all assert that *Star Trek* texts are well able to bear the weight of complex thought; indeed, these texts stimulate difficult questions and the search for equally difficult answers. That these questions and answers concern pleasure raises the stakes of the inquiry, and the chapters in this section recognize the dangers (and rewards) of playing such a difficult game. The pleasures of *Star Trek*, while often described, are rarely investigated.

The book closes with two appendices. In Appendix I, Taylor Harrison talks to Henry Jenkins about his role vis-à-vis fan studies and *Star Trek*. She and Jenkins discuss, among other things, such topics as academic investment in popular cultural texts, the place and role of fandom in the academy, and how gender impacts ethnographic practices. In Appendix II, we provide a selective bibliography of the critical work available on *Star Trek*.

Notes

1. Throughout this book, we will use *Star Trek* to designate the cultural phenomenon associated with its various textual productions. *ST* refers to the original series. *TNG* refers to *Star Trek: The Next Generation*. *DS9* refers to *Star Trek: Deep Space Nine*. *Voyager* refers to *Star Trek: Voyager*.

2. For readers who are relatively unfamiliar with *Star Trek* or who simply would like more information than we provide here, we suggest Hal Schuster and Wendy Rathbone's (1994) reference book *Trek: The Unauthorized A-Z* (New York: HarperCollins).

3. See both Taylor Harrison's interview with Henry Jenkins in this volume and Jenkins's book (1992) *Textual Poachers: Television Fans and Participatory Culture* (New York: Routledge).

Part One

Centering Subjectivities

1

"A Part of Myself No Man Should Ever See"

Reading Captain Kirk's Multiple Masculinities

ELYCE RAE HELFORD

That the original *Star Trek (ST)* is sexist hardly needs articulation. Feminist critics attack the stereotypical femininity of the series's women, the oversexualization or demonization of the few competent female characters, and the exoticization of women of color (Blair 1977, 1983; Cranny-Francis 1985; Lalli 1990; Selley 1986; Tetreault 1984; Wilcox 1992). It is easy to conclude that *ST*'s "reputation for progressiveness is due more to its suggestion of a future society devoted to equal rights than to what was portrayed in the show. In other words, the supposed sexual equality of the Federation was left largely to viewers' imaginations" (Lalli 1990, 41). Support for this argument emerges not only through critiques of *ST*'s undeveloped and objectified female characters but also through the actions and attitudes of the series's white male protagonist, Captain James T. Kirk. There is little critical support for reading Kirk as anything other than an oppressive patriarch bent on conquering the galaxy and sexually dominating all the young and "beautiful" women he encounters in the process. Even his name is unambiguously masculine, comprised as it is of two male given names. Kirk is best known to feminist critics as "a man who can rarely keep his hands off the nubile human and humanoid women he encounters" (Tetreault 1984, 121); "the archetypal wanderer, lovin' 'em and leavin' 'em from one end of the Milky Way to the other" (Blair 1983, 293); and "the footloose, carefree adventurer, the James Bond of interstellar travel" (Cranny-Francis 1985, 274). These critiques emphasize Kirk's ultramasculine persona and particularly highlight his aggressive sexuality. Understanding Kirk from this perspective demands special attention to the asymmetrical power distribution in his encounters with women. As Anne Cranny-Francis states, "these interactions are invariably those of aggression and passivity, dominance and submission. . . . In other words, Kirk's relationships with female characters signify a stereotypical male role, which is just as inflexible and non-reflexive as his political and social role" (276). Kirk is here entirely defined by a static hypermasculine sexuality which is reinforced by its function within a patriarchal social system.[1] A list of the names of the numerous women Kirk desires, pursues, possesses, or is pursued by during the 79 *ST* episodes adds substantive support for reading Kirk as a virile (hetero)sexual magnet and domineering womanizer: the unnamed "little blonde lab technician" whom Lt. Commander Gary Mitchell "aimed" at Kirk during their days at Starfleet Academy and whom Kirk claims he "almost married" (mentioned in "Where No Man Has Gone Before"); Eve McHuron ("Mudd's Women"); Yeoman Janice Rand (whom an aggressive "half" of Kirk attempts to rape in "The Enemy Within"); Andrea the android ("What Are Little Girls Made Of?"); Dr. Helen Noel ("Dagger of the Mind"); the adolescent Miri ("Miri"); Lenore Karidian ("The Conscience of the King"); Lt. Areel Shaw ("Court-Martial"); Edith Keeler ("The City on the Edge of Forever"); Sylvia ("Catspaw"); First Officer/Science Officer Commander Spock's betrothed T'Pring ("Amok Time"); Lt. Marlena Moreau ("Mirror, Mirror"); Dr. Janet Wallace ("The Deadly Years"); Nona ("A Private Little War"); Shahna ("The Gamesters of Triskelion"); Kelinda ("By Any Other Name"); Thalassa ("Return to Tomorrow"); Elaan ("Elaan of Troyius"); Miramanee ("The Paradise Syndrome"); Communications Officer Lt. Uhura (forced to kiss Kirk in "Plato's Stepchildren"); Deela, Queen of Scalos ("Wink of an Eye"); Marta ("Whom Gods Destroy"); Odona ("The Mark of Gideon"); Vanna the Troglyte ("The Cloudminders"); Rayna Kapec, another android ("Requiem for Methuselah"); and Dr. Janice Lester ("Turnabout Intruder").

In light of such data, constructing an argument that attempts to contradict, or at least complicate, the dominant critical perspective on Kirk should not be easy. And, in the context of a feminist agenda, constructing such an argument may not even be desirable. Nevertheless, the following pages will exemplify a feminist critical practice aimed at detailed interrogation of the masculine. I argue that the figure we call "Kirk" is made up of multiple masculinities through which he variously appears as stereotypical patriarch, feminized man, and a more complex patriarchal subject of gender play—a figure who reveals masculine and feminine as constructs that bear no relationship to the biological male or female other than that which we ascribe for sociopolitical reasons, even as he retains traditional political dominance.

Feminism and Masculinity Studies

Such a reexamination of Kirk is not intended as an apology for or a rationalization of *ST*'s obvious sexism. Problematizing Kirk's masculinity can be an instructive feminist project, as long as we do not seek to reconstruct the character himself as feminist. Before proceeding to textual analysis, however, this claim should perhaps be earned. To take Kirk as a primary object of feminist critical inquiry may bring to mind significant theoretical questions: What are the terms under which it may be productive for feminists to examine men and masculinity? What is to be gained for women in patriarchy by focusing our critical attention on representations of men, especially men with racial and class privilege? What could be lost? Attempts to address such questions may result in a predictable double bind for the feminist critic: If we study men and masculinity, we have the opportunity to challenge simplistic and misleading constructions of gender and patriarchy as a unified and unassailable force; however, if we turn our attentions away from women as our primary subject of study, we literally and symbolically return our scholarship to the nonfeminist focus that we have fought to challenge.

This double bind is easily seen in the rhetoric of recent scholarship on the subject of masculinity studies. Antony Easthope (1990), for example, in *What a Man's Gotta Do: The Masculine Myth in Popular Culture*, plainly asserts, "It is time to try to speak about masculinity, about what it is and how it works" (1).[2] His criticism proceeds from the assumption that

> To be male in modern society is to benefit from being installed, willy nilly, in a position of power. No liberal moralizing or glib attitudinizing can change that reality. Social change is necessary and a precondition of such change is an attempt to *understand* masculinity, to make it visible. (7)

Yet Easthope does not see his project and its political goals as necessarily aligned with feminism:

> Feminist and gay accounts have begun to make masculinity visible. But, written from a position outside and against masculinity, they too often treat masculinity as a source of oppression. Ironically, this is just how masculinity has always wanted to be treated—as the origin for everything, the light we all need to see by, the air we all have to breathe. The task of analyzing masculinity and explaining how it works has been overlooked. (2)

Easthope's limiting stereotypes of feminism and gay studies are problematic; however, traditional readings of Kirk—such as those offered by Karin Blair (1983), Cranny-Francis (1985), Mary Ann Tetreault (1984), and Clyde Wilcox (1992)—do serve to validate his concerns. To stop at a simple statement of oppressiveness, to fail to examine both the form and function of masculinity as well as the full complexity of patriarchal masculinities, also does an injustice to feminist critical efforts. Only by fully examining masculinity can we see men and patriarchy as fragmented social constructions.

In *Feminism Without Women: Cultural Criticism in a "Postfeminist" Age*, Tania Modleski (1991) presents the dangers of neglecting to address masculinity as a site of oppression while affirming the need to understand masculinity through feminist textual analysis. Studies of masculinity that do not focus on oppression, she argues, may deny the power imbalance between men and women within patriarchal culture, emphasizing the burden of masculine roles for men while ignoring the simultaneous privileges men may receive, often whether they "fit" the masculine stereotypes or not. This kind of masculinity study may "tacitly assume and promote a liberal notion of the formal equality of men and women" (6) while simultaneously ignoring the fact that women, as a whole, are far from achieving real economic and political equality with men.[3] Feminist critics interested in understanding privileged masculinity must therefore find ways to avoid rendering women invisible through such studies (thereby endorsing the authority we seek to challenge) and to emphasize the asymmetry of power distribution. Modleski suggests that the textual criticism she has found most useful on this subject "is the kind that analyzes male power, male hegemony, with a concern for the effects of this power *on the female subject* and with an awareness of how frequently male subjectivity works to appropriate 'femininity' while oppressing women" (7). Her model asks feminists to study privileged masculinity only when direct acknowledgment of women's oppression is a primary goal. Such a model examines textual representations that work to disavow male power and hegemony; however, it does not lament a privileged masculinity "in crisis" (Bly 1990) and thereby deny the continued dominance of privileged men in U.S. culture and their possession of a power that they can, at times, deny or disown but from which they benefit, nevertheless.[4]

Though working from different subject positions and critical perspectives, Modleski and Easthope both suggest that treating masculinity as a unified oppressive force may limit feminists' abilities to conceptualize real social change. By condemning Kirk as solely an exemplification of patriarchal might that does not require further investigation, we fortify his representational power as such. Ultimately, as Easthope suggests, if social change is our primary goal, "a precondition of such change is an attempt to *understand* masculinity, to make it visible" (7). In the following pages, I will attempt to make Kirk's masculinity "visible" by examining three versions or fragments of his gendered identity—intended to be suggestive but by no means exhaustive—as addressed in three *ST* episodes: "Turnabout Intruder," "Amok Time," and "The Enemy Within."

Hypermasculinity and "Turnabout Intruder"

The final episode of *ST* is perhaps its most notorious. In "Turnabout Intruder," Kirk is forced to swap "life essences" with Dr. Janice Lester, a former lover who is jealous of his power. Through the transfer, Lester is able to take over as captain of the Enterprise, a feat she was never able to accomplish before. Her rationale for stealing Kirk's body is made plain when she spits back to Kirk a sexist Starfleet policy never articulated in *ST* until this episode: "Your world of starship captains does not admit women." Concluding a series with so clearly masculinist an episode does much to validate feminist attacks on *ST*, as well as portraits of Kirk as the essence of hypermasculinity.

From the first scene, we see the rigid boundaries of masculine and feminine behavior on which the episode is constructed, as well as rationalizations for linking gendered traits with biological sex. Just after the transfer is made, Lester must carry through her plan to murder her body (with Kirk's "life essence" in it); however, she is unable to do so. Despite the claim she later makes to her partner-in-crime and former lover, Dr. Coleman, that she seeks only Kirk's power, here she reveals a lingering affection for Kirk and an inability to act decisively. Women, as represented by Lester, lack control over their emotions, which implicitly validates Starfleet's prohibition on women captains. An inability to murder would be highly commendable in a less militaristic and patriarchal social system, but Lester's sympathy for Kirk can only be a weakness in this context.

Feminine traits such as Lester's indecisiveness are also linked with female biology in this episode. When Kirk explains to his male cohorts why he ended his relationship with Lester, he calmly asserts, "Her hatred of her own womanhood made life with her impossible." He does not address the social conditions that would lead to such self-hatred; instead, he blames her for her own oppression. Both Kirk and Lester affirm the fact of biology as destiny. After having swapped bodies with Kirk, Lester looks down upon her own unconscious form and says, "Now you know the indignity of being a woman."

Turning this episode from misogynist to feminist would take little more than the separation of gender from sex and the acknowledgment of sexism within Starfleet policy.[5] But the episode instead focuses on Lester's immoral occupation of Kirk's body and how Kirk will get her out of it. It takes some time for the crew to realize that Kirk is not Kirk after he returns to the ship from the planet on which Lester carried out the transfer. During this interim, we as viewers are treated to femininity as portrayed by a man and masculinity by a woman. "Kirk" (Lester in Kirk's body) saunters about the ship, filing "his" nails and snapping at the crew. "He" is highly emotional, refuses to take advice from others, and uses violence to control the outbursts of "Lester" (Kirk in Lester's body), who is brought aboard the ship after Lester (as Kirk) is unable to kill "her," allegedly suffering from radiation sickness. Meanwhile, Kirk (as Lester), having figured out what must have happened, remains calm and rational and develops a plan to free himself from this intolerable condition. The plan entails a mindmeld with Spock, which cannot take place until Kirk (as Lester) escapes from sickbay;

"she" accomplishes this by manipulating Head Nurse Christine Chapel with convincing "girl talk."

Spock eventually learns the unbelievable truth of "life entity transfer," and the rest of the (primarily male) crew becomes suspicious of their increasingly irrational captain. Stereotypically masculine and feminine behavior continues in a hearing during which Lester (as Kirk) sets up the arrest of Kirk (as Lester) and Spock on charges of mutiny. Kirk (as Lester) remains calm and cool throughout the hearing, engaging in stereotypically masculine displays, such as sitting with "her" legs wide apart and smirking as Lester (as Kirk) betrays unmistakable feminine behavior through feigned maternalistic expressions of concern for the health of "Lester" that eventually become shrill accusations of betrayal, accompanied by fist-pounding and demands for the death penalty.

After Lester's (as Kirk) emotionally charged outbursts during the hearing, a recess is called to consider a final vote. In the hall outside, Chief Engineer Lt. Commander Montgomery Scott ("Scotty") reveals his confusion to Senior Medical Officer Lt. Commander Leonard McCoy: "I've seen the captain feverish, sick, drunk, delirious, terrified, overjoyed, boiling mad. But, up to now, I have never seen him red-faced with hysteria." His label could not be more appropriate. Lester (as Kirk) is a "hysteric" in the traditional language through which Freud defined the term: a woman who can also be a man.[6] She wants to hold the rank of captain in Starfleet, an organization in which the male subject is taken as norm; so she must become a "man." The resulting "hysteria," labeled as a feminine reaction and character trait by Scott, is part of the assumptions that govern the construction of gender in the episode for all characters. In this context, Tom Lalli's (1990) claim that "Turnabout Intruder" is an episode that "dramatizes the credo, 'a feminist is just a woman who wants to be a man'" (52) is particularly apt.

When Scott and McCoy return to the chamber for the vote, Lester (as Kirk) reveals that "he" has recorded their discussion. As "he" reveals that Scott and McCoy are also in mutiny, "his" extreme emotions momentarily break the life-entity transfer, but it is not until the entire crew rebels, refusing to take any orders from the "man" they know is not their captain, that the transfer is permanently broken, and Lester and Kirk return to their original bodies.

The break suggests that the power of Kirk's confident masculinity wins out over Lester's necessarily hysterical (feminine and female) consciousness. This is highlighted when we see Kirk regain his strength of body and mind immediately upon returning to his body, while Lester collapses into Coleman's arms, crying and moaning, "I want him dead, I want him dead"; then whining, "Now I'll never get to be the captain." Coleman offers to care for Lester, claiming she is once again the woman he loves (childlike and dependent), while Kirk concludes (both the episode and the series) with the haunting line, "Her life could have been as rich as any woman's, if only . . . "

Analyzing how we might respond to Kirk's perspective on Lester's (and all women's) relationship to a patriarchy that was supposed to have been transcended in this "utopic" representation of the twenty-third century, and how we might interpret his final line, helps us to understand the implications of the construction of gender in this episode. "Her life could have been as rich as any woman's, if only . . . she had realized her inadequacy to become a ship's captain"? or "if only . . . she had accepted the patriarchal tradition and tried to live within its boundaries"? Any way we complete the sentence reveals that a woman's power is finite. "If only . . . Starfleet realized the error of its ways" is not an interpretation the episode encourages us to contemplate.

Although Kirk's closing line clearly illustrates a traditional, masculinist construction of gender, the original script ending—different from the televised ending—is also noteworthy in this context: "The original story ended with a homophobic scene in which Kirk worries that his manhood may have been contaminated by Janice Lester. He knows that all is well when he finds himself gazing appreciatively at a female yeoman" (Lalli 1990, 52). Lalli is right to address Kirk's homophobia here, but sexual desire is not the captain's only concern. Fear of "contamination" reveals a horror at the thought of the femininity he witnessed from outside his body somehow taking up residence inside him. Kirk is threatened by the idea that Lester's emotional instability has invaded and permanently affected his rational, competence. Only comfort in his former (hetero)sexist gaze confirms the return of his purely masculine identity.

In addition, the body of Kirk with the mind of Janice Lester reveals a great deal about this episode's claims regarding the central elements of manhood and womanhood. In Kirk's male body, Lester's femininity is set into relief. Actor William Shatner must convince us that he is no longer male but female, with all the psychological and cultural implications that biological label can carry. Being overly emotional and irrational are the two primary characteristics that reveal Kirk's switched gender to the other (male) crewmembers. To these, general feminine attributes are added, including superficial behaviors such as sitting cross-legged, walking with a lilt, filing fingernails, and pursing lips.

One useful strategy for analyzing the constructions of masculinity and femininity within this episode is to examine their connections to binary oppositional thought. This is especially relevant in the context of the "split self" motif exemplified by both "Turnabout Intruder" and "The Enemy Within."[7] In "Sorties," Hélène Cixous (1989) argues, "Thought has always worked through opposition. . . . If we read or speak, the same thread or double braid is leading us throughout literature, philosophy, criticism, centuries of representation and reflection" (101). In terms of gender within a patriarchal culture, Cixous goes on to remind us that "all ... pairs of oppositions are *couples.*" And she asks, "Does that mean something? Is the fact that Logocentrism subjects thought—all concepts, codes and values— to a binary system related to 'the' couple, man/woman?" (102). For Cixous, the answer is a resounding "yes," and her conclusion leads her to examine the ways in which the feminine is devalued within all oppositional pairs, resulting in a "universal battlefield" of masculine domination that destroys the disempowered term, the female or the feminine, at every artic- ulation—just as Kirk destroys Lester to regain his body and his command.

Cixous begins "Sorties" with the question "Where is she?" followed by a list of binary oppositions that identify and separate masculine and feminine traits and roles (head/heart, for example). If we use Cixous's opening ques- tion for interpretation of the gender politics of "Turnabout Intruder," we see the oppositional attributes of Kirk (in Lester's body) and Lester (in Kirk's body) reinforce a conventional masculine/feminine dichotomy:

KIRK	LESTER
(in Lester's body)	*(in Kirk's body)*
Rational	Irrational
Competent	Incompetent
Compassionate	Cruel

Because the traits reverse so precisely as the characters move from imper- sonation to "natural" gendered behaviors, the episode argues for an essen- tialism that actively resists challenging gender stereotypes.

One moment in this episode, however, can be read productively as a break in the hypermasculinity so carefully established for Kirk, indicating that even in an episode that relies heavily on gender stereotypes we can find moments that challenge totalizing readings. When Kirk and Lester switch bodies, neither spends much time exploring what it is like to be in the body of the opposite sex. The episode ignores the sexual implications of the transfer, such as becoming accustomed to different sexual organs or consid- ering the issue of sexual orientation, with the exception of one easily missed homoerotic moment late in the episode when Lester (in Kirk's body) uses "feminine wiles" to assure Coleman's continued support. When Lester real- izes the crew is beginning to suspect that their captain is not quite "him- self," she runs to Coleman, to persuade him to murder Kirk in her body. She tries rationally to persuade Coleman that he is already a murderer, hav- ing helped her to kill off the rest of their research party on the planet below before Kirk and company arrived. When this does not work, she turns to Coleman's love for and sexual attraction to her, begging "do it for me" in a compelling and intimate voice. Though Lester's behavior is clearly stereo- typically feminine, the moment is subversive when we attend to the fact that it is Shatner, a male actor, actually cooing in Coleman's ear.

The Feminized Man and "Amok Time"

If "Turnabout Intruder" represents an extreme and rigidly simplistic take on masculinity, "Amok Time" provides an example of a tempered and more complex version. In "Amok Time," we see potential sites for reading Kirk and Spock through images of gender balance and a more feminized masculinity. Although Kirk does not fully embody the figure of the "feminized man" as I will presently define it, the episode does invite a reading that sees Kirk as more feminized.

Psychoanalytic (Freudian and Jungian) readings comprise a significant portion of *Star Trek* scholarship (Blair 1977, 1979, 1983; Ellington and Critelli 1983; Greenberg 1984; Penley 1991b; Roth 1987).[8] More generally, psychoanalysis provides a useful model for analyzing masculinity within popular culture. Easthope (1990), for example, relies on Freudian theory to define the "masculine ego":

> At present in the dominant myth the masculine ego is imagined as closing itself off completely, maintaining total defence. To be unified it must be masculine all the way through and so the feminine will always appear as something other or different and so a security risk. When it is in the external world outside the self the feminine will be a lovely enemy for whom desire triumphs over narcissistic anxiety. But when the feminine seems to have infiltrated within, as it must do because of the bisexual nature of every individual, it threatens the whole castle and must be savagely suppressed. Either way, since defence is attack, the more the "I" strives to be total master, the more aggression it releases. (42–43)

This reading articulates well the central conflict of "Turnabout Intruder," as Kirk's "masculine ego" must fight to regain control of his body from the feminine/female infiltration of Lester. Yet conceptions of masculinity are not limited to this model. The figure of the "feminized man" is another relevant type for analyses of textual representations of masculinity: He acknowledges the feminine within him without yielding any real power to women. Christopher Newfield identifies the process of "male feminization" as ushering in a movement away from the tyranny of male supremacy and toward the alleged "consensus" of liberal hegemony (quoted in Modleski 1991, 7). Modleski reads this process as men's efforts to "deal with the threat of female power by incorporating it" (7).

ST scholarship rarely reads Kirk as feminized and, when it does, it does so solely within a Jungian framework. Jane Elizabeth Ellington and Joseph W. Critelli (1983), for example, read Kirk through Jungian psychological types, emphasizing intuition (over sensation) as his "superior [perceptual] function" or preferred process of collecting information (242–244), a function more common among women than men (Ewen 1993, 103). Although in *Meaning in* Star Trek, Blair (1977) reads Kirk symbolically through Jung as the (masculine) focal point or center for the Enterprise as *mandala*—a feminine symbol of wholeness (20–23)—in "The Garden in the Machine: The Why of *Star Trek*" (1979), she also offers a less archetypal reading of Kirk as feminized:

> [T]he character of Kirk overlaps with the dedicated man of action, the traditional ship's captain, while at the same time adding something new. He is at home with his emotions and can be almost moved to tears. Something new has been added to the categories of the past in order that we can move beyond them. (311)[9]

That Kirk has a feminine side certainly adds "something new" to feminist readings of the character, especially as a response to gender representations in "Turnabout Intruder." To argue that this feminine side may help us reach "beyond" the "categories of the past," however, is more problematic.

The focus on the gendered nature of oppositional thought that is central to the psychoanalytic criticism of Easthope, Ellington and Critelli, and Blair provides a helpful framework through which to read masculinity not only in "Turnabout Intruder" but in many other *ST* episodes as well. "Amok Time," in particular, provides a clear example of the feminized man in the character of Spock, as well as in the relationship between Kirk and Spock, which feminizes Kirk.

In "Amok Time," Spock undergoes *pon farr,* a biological mating drive that compels him to return to his home planet of Vulcan to "marry." The depth of the bond between Kirk and Spock is exemplified throughout this episode, from Kirk's decision to go against Starfleet orders and divert the Enterprise from its current mission in order to take Spock home, to his willingness to risk death in battle to keep Spock from being killed by another opponent. After dealing with the shock of learning that Spock is not only betrothed but also under the influence of extremely powerful hormonal drives (which cause him to demonstrate feminine traits such as vulnerability, dependence, and irrationality), Kirk takes his first officer to Vulcan, only to find that Spock's bride, T'Pring, rejects him. She chooses the right of challenge, which demands that Spock engage in a battle with a champion of her choice, and selects Kirk. Kirk's enthusiastic willingness to fight—not for T'Pring, but to ensure that Spock is not hurt or killed by another man—is tempered when he learns that the fight will be to the death; but his bond with Spock wins out. McCoy gives Kirk a neural paralyzing hypo-spray that enables Kirk to simulate death midway through the combat; this sets up Spock's highly emotional response to Kirk's apparent resurrection aboard ship at the end of the episode and makes the depth of affection between the two men even more plain. The homoerotic implications of their relationship in this episode serve to challenge the dominant views of Kirk as rigidly masculine.[10]

In addition to showing the intensity of the relationship between Kirk and Spock, "Amok Time" feminizes Kirk and especially Spock through emphasis on biologized forces. Spock's deep sorrow over Kirk's apparent death, for example, proves stronger than his need to bond with T'Pring, breaking the physiological hold of the *plak tow* (blood fever) in which Spock is immersed when he fights Kirk. More generally, the state of *pon farr* links Spock with female hormonal cycles. As Blair (1983) describes it, *pon farr* is the Vulcan "equivalent of the sexual heat usually associated with female animals" (295).

K/S fiction—fan writing that depicts Kirk and Spock as lovers—often uses *pon farr* as a plot device. Constance Penley (1991a) offers a feminist interpretation of this tendency:

> I think the fans relish these stories, in part, because they like the idea of men too being subjected to a hormonal cycle, and indeed their version of Spock's pre-*pon farr* and *plak tow* symptoms are wickedly and humorously made to parallel those of PMS and menstruation, in a playful and transgressive leveling of the biological playing field. Another nice touch is that Kirk, because he is empathically bonded with the Vulcan through the mind link [a permanent condition known as the "bond" in K/S fiction], does not have to be told when Spock is getting ready to go into *pon farr* or how he is feeling; in fact, he often shares Spock's symptoms. (158)

According to Penley's perspective, K/S fiction can make "Amok Time" a source for reading not only Spock but also Kirk as feminized. Clearly, in the episode Spock is at the mercy of biological mating drives that can be interpreted as akin to women's hormonal cycles. Yet Kirk, too, can be read as sexually motivated to extricate Spock from his vow to T'Pring by engaging in the battle to win Spock, not T'Pring. And when this bond is exaggerated in K/S fiction, Kirk not only sympathizes, but empathizes, with Spock's version of PMS.

Because it is Spock who is most feminized in "Amok Time" through his hormonal cycles (and, arguably, throughout the series, through his subordinate role), it is easy and tempting to read Kirk as "husband" to Spock as "wife." Nevertheless, Patricia Frazer Lamb and Diana L. Veith (1986) in "Romantic Myth, Transcendence, and *Star Trek* Zines" claim that K/S fiction is based on a balance of power and gender qualities between Kirk and Spock. The authors provide an extensive table of masculine and feminine qualities that each possesses:

KIRK	SPOCK
"Feminine" qualities	*"Masculine" qualities*
Femininely "beautiful"	Masculinely rugged
Shorter, physically weaker	Taller, more powerful
Emotional	Logical
Intuitive	Rational
Sensuous, engages in much touching	Controlled, physically distant
Verbal	Reticent
Evokes powerful emotions from others	Keeps others at a distance
Sexually ready at all times	Sexually controlled (except during his Vulcan mating cycle)
Is undisputed leader, initiator of action	Needs to be led, follows Kirk into action
Is the "real" or "norm," always at home	Is the "alien" or "other," always the "outsider"
Is fulfilled prior to Spock, only with acceptance of the bond is he firmly united with Spock	Is fulfilled only with Kirk; felt one-sided fidelity to Kirk even before the bond
Spock complements his "at-homeness"	Needs Kirk for full identity
Is sexually promiscuous (bond assures his fidelity)	A virgin until marriage, he exhibits absolute monogamy after marriage
Is usually the seducer	Is usually seduced, but once unleashed, his sexuality is very powerful (243)

Certain gendered characteristics in this list may seem exaggerated to audience members whose conceptualizations of Kirk and Spock differ from those of Lamb and Veith. For example, Leonard Nimoy's tall but lean frame hardly suggests "ruggedness" to all viewers; and while Spock may attempt to be entirely logical most of the time, he continuously struggles with the (feminine) emotions he stifles. Similarly, Kirk may not seem "femininely 'beautiful'" to all audiences, nor is he entirely intuitive. The significance of Lamb and Veith's list to my project, however, lies in the authors' acknowledgment that Kirk and Spock's possession of both masculine and feminine traits simultaneously maintains rigid binary distinctions between masculinity and femininity. The limitation for problematizing constructions of gender here is that, although *pon farr* as a device may well "level" the "biological playing field" (Penley 1991a, 158), it cannot help us to envision a new arena for gender play.[11] The feminized Kirk of "Amok Time" (read through K/S) is clearly more complex than the hypermasculine Kirk of "Turnabout Intruder," but we have not reached "beyond" the gendered categories of the past (as Blair [1979] would have it); the boundaries have merely been blurred a little.

Gender Play and "The Enemy Within"

Like "Turnabout Intruder," "The Enemy Within" also uses the split-character motif. Rather than swapped identities, however, in "The Enemy Within" Kirk is split into two halves, both of whom are functioning individuals with different personalities and agendas. In this episode we see two sides to Kirk—not masculine and feminine halves, as might be expected, but halves that complicate gendered traits in a way that challenges the link between biology and culture and the view of Kirk as purely masculine.

When a transporter malfunction divides Kirk, both Spock and McCoy respond to his two selves as "good" and "evil" halves (though I will refer to them as Kirk 1 and Kirk 2), respectively. The crew identifies Kirk 1 (the "good" half) as the captain, while they disrespect, attack, and imprison Kirk 2 (the "evil" half or "dark side"). And Kirk 2 immediately exhibits hypermasculine traits as he attempts to rape Yeoman Rand in her quarters. She shouts to another crewmember outside her cabin to "Call Mr. Spock!" (suggesting her awareness of the strength of the bond between Kirk and Spock?), but only clawing Kirk 2's face stops the attack.

When Kirk 1 hears of this attack, he is calm and rational, showing another side of masculinity (developed in more depth in "Turnabout Intruder"). Rand is confused when she is confronted by Kirk 1, who has no scratch upon his face to verify her accusation of attempted rape. She is dismissed, without any explanation of or comfort for the attack she faced, thus establishing one area of limitation in the episode's representation of gender. Yet the fact that the rapist and his accuser are both Kirk serves to establish a forum for challenging gendered behavior in this episode. The representation of the issue of rape turns to a more blatant sexism at the end of the episode, however, when Spock, evoking traditional rape myths, "teases" Rand about the attack. When she brings him a document to sign, he asks her, with a smirk, if she did not think the "impostor" had some "interesting qualities." Spock can be read as sympathetic with Kirk 2 here, seemingly validating the desirability of his hypermasculine attitudes about the possession of women's bodies and perhaps indicating a homoerotic attraction to the man who wields the power, though Spock will overtly reject Kirk 2's perspectives throughout the rest of the episode, arguing that he is irrational, overly aggressive, and unfit for command.

In addition to the victim/criminal opposition (as the innocent Kirk 1 is accused of Kirk 2's attempted rape), the two Kirks suggest additional oppositions, such as rational/irrational and gentle/violent. To this is added compassionate/cruel when Kirk 1 is greatly disturbed to learn that Kirk 2 has sabotaged the transporter controls thus making it impossible to return the remaining members of the away team (of which Kirk was a member before being split upon his return to the ship) from the surface of a planet whose temperature can drop significantly below freezing overnight. When he discovers that there is a second and more malevolent "Kirk" on board, Kirk 1 decides to inform the crew. Before he can do so, however, he is quickly and sharply reprimanded by Spock: "You're the captain of the ship. You haven't the right to be vulnerable in the eyes of the crew. You can't afford the luxury of being anything less than perfect. If you do, they lose faith and you lose command." The gender implications of this statement are clear. Vulnerability, a traditionally feminine attribute, is a quality a captain must not show. Kirk 1 immediately recognizes the truth of Spock's words and asks to be told if he "slips" again. The concept of the "slip" becomes significant in the episode, for it is through the experience of "imperfect" decisions that Kirk 1 realizes the splitting process has caused him to lose a trait he calls his "strength of will."

As Kirk 1 becomes increasingly weak, Kirk 2 grows stronger and irrationally assumes he can exist without his other half. He is, nevertheless, eventually captured and strapped into a bed in sickbay. As Kirk 1 looks at his suffering twin, Spock observes:

> We have here an unusual opportunity to appraise the human mind, or to examine, in Earth terms, the roles of good and evil in a man: his negative side—which you call hostility, lust, violence—and his positive side—which Earth people express as compassion, love, tenderness. . . . And what is it that makes one man an exceptional leader? We see here indications that it is his negative side which makes him strong. That his "evil" side, if you will, properly controlled and disciplined, is vital to his strength. Your negative side removed from you the power of command begins to elude you.

Although the two are discussed as "halves," Spock also labels them "good" and "evil." Kirk 1 is unhesitatingly given the status of the "real" captain. If these are halves, the first Kirk is clearly dominant. Yet despite his dominance, he is apprehensive (indicating another "slip"?). McCoy attempts to help by reminding his friend and captain, "You're no different from anyone else. We all have our darker side. We need it. It's half of what we are." But this does not help much, for Kirk 1 knows that his command ability resides largely within this "evil" half.

To McCoy's words, Spock adds another theory, which he directs to Kirk 1: "You have [the] goodness, . . . the intelligence, the logic. And perhaps that's where man's essential courage comes from. For, you see, he was afraid, and you weren't." Though perhaps not afraid, Kirk 1 is certainly distraught. He must debate whether or not to risk an attempt at reunion in the recently repaired transporter. He needs to see that the transporter is functioning normally so he can return his nearly-dead away team from the freezing planet on which they are still stranded. He needs to become whole again so that he can command. But his will is weak; he cannot decide what to do. Almost in tears, wracked with pain, he calls out, "Help me . . . somebody make the decision." But when Spock asks him if he is relinquishing command, the masculine ego regains control and Kirk 1, accompanied by swelling melodramatic music and the opening notes of the series' theme, confidently asserts, "No. No, I'm not."

After a skirmish in sickbay and again on the bridge, the two Kirks are eventually successfully reunited. However, the reunified Kirk's sympathy for his evil half seems entirely and instantly lost when he is put back together. As he thanks Spock for his help "from both of us," he adds: "The impostor is back where he belongs. Let's forget him."

An examination of binary thought in "The Enemy Within" can begin with the title. The image of a split between "good" and "evil" in every individual is as common as horror icons Jekyll and Hyde and the Wolfman; the suggestion that the "evil" part is inseparable from the "good" is as familiar as the Judeo-Christian concept of original sin. Yet the ways in which attributes and characteristics line up under the oppositions of "good" and "evil" in this episode are far less simple in terms of gender than in "Turnabout Intruder."

Returning again to Cixous's question "Where is she?" we can compose the following list of gendered oppositions for the two Kirks of "The Enemy Within":

KIRK 1	KIRK 2
Good	Evil
Gentle	Violent
Rational	Irrational
Compassionate	Cruel
Nurturing	Demanding
Courageous	Afraid
Incompetent	Competent

Most significant in this list, when compared to Cixous's list or the one I developed for "Turnabout Intruder," is that the traits do not line up neatly under traditional categories of masculine and feminine. While masculine stereotypes include qualities from the "good" side, such as rationality and courage, they do not generally include nurturance. Similarly, to be irrational and afraid may be considered traditionally feminine, but to be violent is not. Competence, the power to make decisions and command, is within the same "half" as irrationality and destructiveness. How can this be reconciled?

As previously mentioned, despite the fact that Kirk 1 feels he is losing control as the episode progresses, the crew responds to him as their captain during the period of the split. Spock and McCoy never even attempt to speak to Kirk 2. This behavior, as well as frequent reference to Kirk 2 as an "impostor," suggest that the "evil" half is less "Kirk" than the "good." While the quality of decisiveness may reside in the "evil" half, whatever it is that makes Kirk the recognizable captain is represented by his "good" half. The quality that makes Kirk competent in "The Enemy Within" is described as will or decisiveness, which Kirk 1 begins to lose as soon as he is split. Although Kirk 2 is physically stronger and more aggressive than Kirk 1, these are not the qualities that Spock labels as essential for command. Instead, Spock values Kirk's ability to make clear, effective decisions—a masculine trait, according to Starfleet. Since this quality resides in Kirk's "evil" half, logically it should be this half that is the "masculine" in the gendering of the oppositions.

In the end, it is not possible to divide Kirk completely or easily into masculine and feminine halves in this episode. The feminine (as represented by what I am calling Kirk's "good" half) is not what might be expected. "She" is both nurturing and courageous, rational yet emotional. The crew responds to this half as their captain once the split is made. The violent rapist, despite the fact that he may have the decision-making power that makes a captain a captain, is evidently but a small part of James T. Kirk. Ultimately, the "evil" half is, as Kirk himself proclaims when reunified, "a part of myself no man should ever see." But, by seeing this "part," we also see the breakdown of the hypermasculine self.

"The Enemy Within" illustrates an important resistance to simple constructions of masculinity in Kirk through the theme of the split self. The two Kirks effectively destabilize a viewer's ease with the idea that to be overly aggressive is acceptable in men. The episode refutes the suggestion that feminine qualities (such as nurturance and compassion) are unsuitable for individuals in positions of power. It challenges the vision of Kirk solely as the overconfident and ultramasculine commander so condemned by feminist critics. And it reveals that there is no necessary connection between traits we label "masculine" and "feminine" and biological sex. However, though the episode refutes essentialism, the circumstances of Kirk's split and reunification do not necessitate a reexamination of social roles or power distribution. Spock can still make rape fantasy jokes; Kirk can "forget" his other half. Certainly, the need to "forget" or repress awareness of the complexity of his own masculinity (and the fact that Spock and McCoy saw this complexity) offers a symptomatic space for a feminist psychoanalytic reading of the episode; yet even the most gender-complex Kirk is still a white male who upholds Starfleet's patriarchal status quo. This fragment, then, is worthy of study not because it reveals a feminist version of Kirk that we can isolate and celebrate but because, when examined in the context of previous scholarship on Kirk or representations of masculinity more generally, it illustrates that even the most hypermasculine man exists only as a fragment of a necessarily more complex identity.

Conclusion

Ultimately, this study is not intended to argue that an episode such as "The Enemy Within" rights the sexist wrongs of an episode such as "Turnabout Intruder." Likewise, it is not intended to disprove feminist readings of Kirk as domineering sexist patriarch, to find and applaud a progressive "side" to Kirk, or the like. Simply examining the complexity of Kirk's masculinity is not necessarily a significant move toward social change; however, the first step toward enacting change is envisioning the possibilities for such change. Feminist textual analysis of masculinity enables us to envision points of attack for creating a more just and egalitarian society through the narratives we create. And such study is particularly significant when the text under scrutiny makes claims to represent an egalitarian future that it does not earn. By contrast, then, models that resist careful readings of masculinity are ultimately antithetical to a feminist agenda. As Andrew Ross (1992) puts it:

> To see men as a universally exploitative class, to see male sexuality as a uniformly violent force, is to accept at face value only our (as men) most reactionary fantasies of power and to reduce the prospects of change to the occasional glimpse of chinks in a vast and formidable male armor. (219)

As we have seen, though Kirk's exploitativeness and his aggressive, even violent, sexuality are undeniably a part of his character, they are only a part. If a primary goal of feminist cultural critics is to work for social change through textual study, it is far more productive (and accurate) to read masculinity as complex and fragmented than to attack what we (must) first construct as an impenetrable fortress.

Notes

This chapter has been through multiple revisions. Its earliest incarnation was a paper entitled "Captain Kirk and Gender Identity in *Star Trek*," presented at the 1992 Meeting of the Popular Culture Association. A revised version appeared in a chapter of my dissertation. I would like to thank my coeditors and Chad Crouse for reading multiple drafts of the most recently and substantially revised version of this chapter. I am grateful to Middle Tennessee State University's Faculty Research Program, which provided me with financial support for the completion of this work.

1. Discourses outside academia affirm, as well, that Kirk is aptly and completely defined by ultramasculine traits. Fan critic Pamela Rose (1990), for example, addresses ST's gender inequality by comparing Kirk's work to that of the ship's female crewmembers: Women "seem to spend most of their time passing coffee and carrying fuel reports for the Captain to sign—when he gets time after saving the galaxy" (22). William Shatner, who plays Kirk, has repeatedly supported sexist readings of Kirk. During an interview included on the 1975 LP Inside Star Trek, for example, Gene Roddenberry asks Shatner why he thinks Kirk needs a different love interest every week; Shatner laughingly replies, "He uses up the old one!" And comedian Tom Rhodes (in a 1991 stand-up routine aired repeatedly on Comedy Central) reads the series through a metaphor of the suburban nuclear family, where Kirk-the-father "sits in front of a giant TV screen telling everybody else what to do."

2. Easthope uses the terms "male" and "masculinity" without racial or class qualifiers which makes it clear that his primary object of study is the middle-class white male. It is to avoid such misrepresentation through generalization that I have chosen to use the phrase "privileged masculinity" in this study to distinguish middle-class white masculinities from the masculinities of minoritized men.

3. All men, of course, do not benefit equally under patriarchy; men lose privilege and suffer increasing oppression as they manifest deviations from established, privileged norms—in terms of race, class, sexual orientation, physical ability, religion, and other determinants of identity.

4. I am attempting to establish a contrast here between arguments that examine masculinity in order to fortify male power within a patriarchal culture that is being "lost" to feminist gains (e.g., Robert Bly's [1990] Iron John: A Book About Men) and arguments that examine masculinity in order to challenge the patriarchal status quo and create a more egalitarian society (e.g., Modleski's [1991] Feminism Without Women). Yet not all texts that analyze masculinity fit neatly into this simple dichotomy. Even texts sympathetic to feminist goals and perspectives may hesitate to address the degree to which men as a class have been responsible for maintaining systemic relations (albeit differentially according to race, sexual orientation, and so on). In their introduction to Out of Bounds: Male Writers and Gender(ed) Criticism, for example, editors Laura Claridge and Elizabeth Langland (1990) reveal that their collection was originally to be titled "Male Feminist Voices" (4), but the editors changed their reference and focus to "gender," at least in part because there "are men more innocent of the power politics of 'patriarchy' than some women; there are men as resistant to it, as confined by its assumptions, as women, who at least can take comfort in being empowered by marginalization" (8). Such a claim would be supportable from a feminist perspective, were it not for the fact that the "more innocent" men to whom Claridge and Langland refer are not men who experience some form of minoritization. Although they acknowledge that "patriarchy, as a term of power, encompasses issues of class and race as well as gender" (13), they do not consider these or other determinants necessarily relevant to what can make a man "more innocent" than a woman in terms of manipulation of patriarchal power. The result is a statement that seems to blame women for their

own oppression and frees men from responsibility for their privileges. This is made even more clear in the conclusion to the authors' introduction, where they state, "We all, of course, are implicated in the damage that gender expectations do, and at the most sophisticated, delicate, dangerous nexus of that damage the origins and culpability become less clear than feminist theory has sometimes allowed" (20). To be sure, women must take responsibility for the degree to which they participate in their own disempowerment through identification with patriarchal norms; however, to assert that feminist theory has not "allowed" certain knowledge, at any time, ignores the reality that feminist theory is always written from a disempowered position relative to dominant (white masculine) theory and ideology. Such a statement accords an inaccurate amount and kind of power to feminists, only to attack them for its possession.

5. Indeed, Edward Whetmore (1981) argues that even without a shift in focus the episode can be read as feminist: "Despite its almost medieval notion of 'a woman's place,' it is easy to walk away from 'Turnabout Intruder' thinking that it advocates feminism. For some, it certainly must create a sympathetic feeling for the sex role limitations that will apparently continue to constrain women—even in the future time of *Star Trek*" (159). Whetmore seems to suggest that "Turnabout Intruder" depicts sexism in order to critique it; this would be more clearly supportable if the episode placed less emphasis on biological essentialism. As Arthur Asa Berger (1981) asserts in a personal response to Whetmore's argument: "I'm not sure, now, whether Janet [Lester]'s self-hatred was caused by disappointed love, penis envy, depression, menstrual cramps, destructive self-images of women in our society, or some combination of the above" (163).

6. Alice Jardine's (1985) reading of hysteria as a key concept within psychoanalysis sheds important light on this moment in "Turnabout Intruder": "Within [the] strange gap between the female bodies at the inceptions of psychoanalysis and the male subject taken as its norm, and especially within the resultant syntax, lies the power (and, for some, the faults) of psychoanalysis itself. 'The hysteric is a woman who can also be a man' becomes, in a hallucinatory conceptual leap, the very definition of hysteria as an object of psychoanalytic knowledge. Through this gap, itself hysterical, slipped the confusion between women and [the construct] 'woman,' a confusion which in turn generated a perpetual oscillation that has never been able to move beyond its first contradictory articulation" (160).

7. This motif has been used in episodes of all the *Star Trek* series. In addition to "Turnabout Intruder" and "The Enemy Within," "Mirror, Mirror" is perhaps the most gender-significant split-self *ST* episode. Most recently, the first season *Star Trek: Voyager* episode "Faces," in which half-human/half-Klingon Chief Engineer B'Elanna Torres is divided into gender- and race-significant halves by an alien species seeking a cure to a plague-like disease, seems to borrow heavily for its study of subjectivity from "The Enemy Within."

8. Also see Ilsa J. Bick's chapter, "Boys in Space," in this volume.

9. It is interesting to note Blair's multiple published perspectives on Kirk. To her, he is *mandala* focal point (1977), feminized man (1979) and, in "Sex and *Star Trek*" (1983), a one-dimensional seeker of "adolescent" sexual relationships (293). Though the most simplistic and stereotypical reading is published last of the three, Blair's changing perspective offers evidence of what I read as the complexity of Kirk's masculinity.

10. April Selley (1986) develops in some depth Kirk and Spock's dependence on and love for one another; however, she stops short of identifying the sexual suggestiveness in their efforts to "consistently [rescue] each other from the romantic Dark Lady" (95), to "resist restrictive marriages with women in episodes which allow them to prove their loyalty to one another" (97), and, by *Star Trek II: The Wrath of Khan* (1982), to reserve their most intense emotions for each other (98).

11. Although Penley (1991a) does not claim that K/S creates radical gender play, she does read the feminization of Kirk and Spock in this fiction as politically transformative (in opposition to the readings of feminization by Newfield [quoted in Modleski 1991] and Modleski [1991]). She asserts: "Kirk and Spock *are* sensitive in the slash [K/S] stories, as well as kind, strong, thoughtful, and humorous, but their being 'sensitive' carries with it none of the associations of wimpiness or smug self-congratulation it does in the present day. Only in the future, it seems, will it be possible to conceive that yielding phallic power does not result in psychical castration or a demand to be praised extravagantly for having yielded that power" (156). I would challenge this reading. Although they may "yield power" within their relationship, in most K/S stories with which I am familiar, Kirk and Spock retain their positions of power within Starfleet's military hierarchy, request no changes in Federation politics or policies, and hide their sexual relationship and feminization from all or most of the crew.

References

Berger, Arthur Asa. 1981. "A Personal Response to Whetmore's 'A Female Captain's Enterprise.'" In *Future Females: A Critical Anthology.* Ed. Marleen S. Barr. Bowling Green, OH: Bowling Green State U Popular P. 162–163.

Blair, Karin. 1977. *Meaning in* Star Trek. Chambersburg, PA: Anima Books.

_____. 1979. "The Garden in the Machine: The Why of *Star Trek.*" *Journal of Popular Culture* 13.2: 310–320.

_____. 1983. "Sex and *Star Trek.*" *Science-Fiction Studies* 10.2: 292–297.

Bly, Robert. 1990. *Iron John: A Book About Men.* Reading, MA: Addison-Wesley.

Cixous, Hélène. 1989. "Sorties: Out and Out: Attacks/Ways Out/Forays." In *The Feminist Reader: Essays in Gender and the Politics of Literary Criticism.* Ed. Catherine Belsey and Jane Moore. New York: Basil Blackwell Publications. 101–116.

Claridge, Laura, and Elizabeth Langland. 1990. *Out of Bounds: Male Writers and Gender(ed) Criticism.* Amherst, MA: U of Massachusetts P.

Cranny-Francis, Anne. 1985. "Sexuality and Sex-Role Stereotyping in *Star Trek.*" *Science-Fiction Studies* 12.3: 274–284.

Easthope, Antony. 1990. *What a Man's Gotta Do: The Masculine Myth in Popular Culture.* Boston: Unwin Hyman.

Ellington, Jane Elizabeth, and Joseph W. Critelli. 1983. "Analysis of a Modern Myth: The *Star Trek* Series." *Extrapolation* 24.3: 241–250.

Ewen, Robert B. 1993. *An Introduction to Theories of Personality.* 4th ed. Hillsdale, NJ: Lawrence Erlbaum Associates.

Greenberg, Harvey R. 1984. "In Search of Spock: A Psychoanalytic Inquiry." *The Journal of Popular Film and Television* 12.2: 52–65.

Jardine, Alice A. 1985. *Gynesis: Configurations of Woman and Modernity.* Ithaca: Cornell U P.

Lalli, Tom. 1990. "Same Sexism, New Generation." In *The Best of TREK #15.* Ed. Walter Irwin and G. B. Love. New York: Penguin. 39–67.

Lamb, Patricia Frazer, and Diana L. Veith. 1986. "Romantic Myth, Transcendence, and *Star Trek* Zines." In *Erotic Universe: Sexuality and Fantastic Literature.* Ed. Donald Palumbo. New York: Greenwood P. 235–255.

Modleski, Tania. 1991. *Feminism Without Women: Culture and Criticism in a "Postfeminist" Age.* New York: Routledge.

Penley, Constance. 1991a. "Brownian Motion: Women, Tactics, and Technology." In *Technoculture.* Ed. Constance Penley and Andrew Ross. Minneapolis: U Minnesota P. 135–161.

———. 1991b. "Feminism, Psychoanalysis and the Study of Popular Culture." In *Cultural Studies.* Ed. Lawrence Grossberg, Cary Nelson, and Paula Treichler. New York: Routledge. 479–500.

Rose, Pamela. 1990. "Women in the Federation." In *The Best of the Best of TREK.* Ed. Walter Irwin and G. B. Love. New York: Penguin. 21–26.

Ross, Andrew. 1992. "Wet, Dark, and Low, Eco-Man Evolves from Eco-Woman." *Boundary 2* 19.2: 204–232.

Roth, Lane. 1987. "Death and Rebirth in *Star Trek II: The Wrath of Khan.*" *Extrapolation* 28.2: 159–166.

Selley, April. 1986. "'I Have Been, and Ever Shall Be, Your Friend': *Star Trek, The Deerslayer* and the American Romance." *Journal of Popular Culture* 20.1: 89–104.

Tetreault, Mary Ann. 1984. "The Trouble with *Star Trek.*" *Minerva: The Journal of Women in the Military* 24.2: 119–129.

Whetmore, Edward. 1981. "A Female Captain's Enterprise: The Implications of *Star Trek*'s 'Turnabout Intruder.'" In *Future Females: A Critical Anthology.* Ed. Marleen S. Barr. Bowling Green, OH: Bowling Green State U Popular P. 157–161.

Wilcox, Clyde. 1992. "To Boldly Return Where Others Have Gone Before: Cultural Change and the Old and New *Star Treks.*" *Extrapolation* 33.1: 88–100.

2

When the Body Speaks

Deanna Troi's Tenuous Authority and the Rationalization of Federation Superiority in *Star Trek: The Next Generation* Rape Narratives

SARAH PROJANSKY

In the *Star Trek: The Next Generation (TNG)* episode "Violations," Captain Jean-Luc Picard claims that rape no longer takes place in his twenty-fourth-century world. Whereas other cultures and species in the *Star Trek* universe continue to engage in violent sexual acts, humans, as Picard puts it, have "evolved." The members of the Enterprise crew live in a society in which the messy problems of rape and sexism (not to mention hunger, poverty, and most crime) no longer exist. As a badge of having already achieved this social utopia, the Federation's Prime Directive out-laws interference in the internal affairs of other (read: less-evolved) species and cultures. This paternalistic isolationism, however, creates a paradox that the Enterprise's ethnographic mission "to go where no one has gone before" heightens. The socially evolved Federation tries to avoid influenc-ing other cultures directly, even while it must have some form of contact with them in order to amass as much knowledge about those other cultures as possible, affirming its own superiority over them in the process. This paradox often leads to (only sometimes) thinly veiled rescue missions that test the boundaries of the Prime Directive.

So in "Where No One Has Gone Before," for instance, while flashbacks of running from rape gangs on her childhood home haunt Security Chief Lt. Tasha Yar, she also has flashbacks of the Federation rescuing her; figures in red, yellow, and blue suits whisk her off her devastated planet. The paternalistic rescue of the helpless woman/child in this image (which defines Yar's faithful dedication to protecting Picard and his ship[1] and in fact leads to her career in military security) also evokes the cultural mythol-ogy of the U.S. soldiers doling out chocolate bars to survivors of the Hiroshima and Nagasaki bombings and liberating Nazi concentration camp survivors, many of whom, like Yar, endured rape. Time and again

TNG links the quest for knowledge and social expansion in the Enterprise's mission and in the Federation's Prime Directive to rescue missions that are like the one Yar experiences as a child, rescue missions rooted in U.S. neo-colonialist[2] ideology that illustrate the superiority of Federation technology, government, military, and culture.

That the Federation saves Yar from a life of never-ending rape, specifi-cally, is not surprising, given the history of cultural representations linking war, colonialism, and rape: from U.S. propaganda posters during World War II in which a dark-skinned Japanese soldier carries away a lily-white, naked woman on his back;[3] to 1950s westerns like *The Searchers* (1956), a film in which rape and murder justify Ethan Edwards's (John Wayne) decade-long personal war against Native Americans; to the book *Against Our Will*, in which Susan Brownmiller (1975) offers an influential feminist analysis of rape as a military weapon; to the film *Casualties of War* (1989), in which the narrative refigures the soldier rapist (Sean Penn) as a member of the U.S. military while simultaneously maintaining the U.S. national identity of the savior-soldier (Michael J. Fox); to the most recent spate of cover stories and books about Bosnia in which rape functions as a fate worse than war itself.[4] Each of these narratives, as part of a cultural meta-narrative about war, needs rape in order to define the United States collec-tively as a neocolonialist rescuer (whether soldier or feminist). In *TNG*, the Federation citizen represents a new and improved version of this U.S. savior citizen; the Federation citizen is a post-nationalist, post-sexist, and post-racist soldier-feminist.

The two *TNG* episodes in which Counselor Lt. Commander Deanna Troi is raped, "The Child" and "Violations," do not refer to military might and neocolonialism as explicitly as do a variety of other *Star Trek* episodes, including "Where No One Has Gone Before," which explicitly defines Yar's rape-survivor identity. Nonetheless, these two episodes do participate in *Star Trek*'s idealization of Federation neocolonialism. Thus, I begin this chapter with a brief discussion of Yar's childhood rescue in order to suggest that Troi's experience of rape can profitably be read in the context of *TNG*'s larger neocolonialist narrative. Specifically, I will argue that both characters' rape experiences are on a continuum that uses repre-sentations of rape to justify the paradoxical Prime Directive. Concom-itantly, *TNG* evokes feminist ideals of "choice," "consent," and women's "self-determination" in response to rape in order to confirm the superior-ity of the Federation's evolved social status. Finally, *TNG* is able to sustain the paradoxical Prime Directive by representing these feminist ideals ambivalently, which in turn allows *TNG* ultimately to abandon them in favor of paternalistic militarism.

Narrative analysis will show that "The Child" and "Violations" invoke choice and consent in order to portray Troi as an authority on rape. Yet her authority is not equivalent to the Federation's authority on rationality, technology, culture, and, by extension, rape. As Dana Cloud (1992) argues in relation to the television series *Spenser: For Hire,* rather than being polysemic and opening up a multitude of possible meanings, television texts can be ambivalent, representing two possibly contradictory meanings but ultimately valuing one over the other. Specifically, in these *TNG* episodes, while Troi has authority *and* Picard has authority, while the Prime Directive insists on noninterference *and* the Enterprise's mission calls for cultural exchange, the text ultimately values the latter over the former in each case. The show undermines Troi's authority and her voice, both of which are located specifically—and only—in a bioessentially feminine body. In the end, the members of the Enterprise crew, headed by Picard, know better than Troi what rape is and how best to respond to it. And it is their obsession with exploring Others that guides them toward the truth Troi's body unintentionally masks. Although Picard religiously evokes "choice" and "consent" as natural rights in his twenty-fourth-century society, the particular structures of the rape narratives simultaneously naturalize his and the Federation's superiority over both women and other species. In short, *TNG* renders choice, consent, and women's embodied voices ineffectual and silent and then fills that silence with the voice of Federation superiority.

Essentializing Women's Bodily Authority: Choice and Consent

Choice

In "The Child," a small point of light, which later calls itself a "life-force-entity," encounters the Enterprise (a fellow explorer) and, being "curious," decides that the best way to learn about these people is to live as one. In order to do this from start to finish, the entity needs a female body to inhabit as an incubator until it is born in humanoid form. As the point of light travels through the halls and sleeping quarters of the Enterprise, it pauses and hovers above a sleeping crew member. The camera, low and tight to the man's chest, and the bright light the entity generates within the diegesis both emphasize thick hair on the bare chest, highlighting the body's maleness. The entity leaves. In the next shot, the background music changes from quick and playful to slow and eerie as the entity enters another darkened room. The camera pans with the point of light as it approaches the foot of a bed, linking the spectator with the entity as it investigates the sex of this particular body. The camera continues to track with the light as it moves under the covers and slowly up toward the torso of the sleeping body. Up until this point the body is sexless, but as the person rolls over, the light disappears and the camera continues its path toward the face, revealing Troi tossing and turning, as if experiencing a nightmare. Suddenly, Troi sits up in distress; the camera cuts to a close-up that reveals sweat running down her face.[5]

Although neither Troi nor any other member of the crew ever explicitly names this experience a rape, the point of light enters her body and impregnates her without her consent. Despite being asleep at the time, Troi is aware of the "unlawful entry."[6] As she puts it while trying to make sense of her immaculate conception: "Last night, while I slept, something which I can only describe as a presence entered my body." The fact that the pregnancy results from a rape is relatively unimportant to the crew and to Troi; they focus their attention, instead, on whether or not to abort the fetus. In this episode, rape is merely a catalyst for negotiating another social issue central to feminist activism: abortion.[7] Not surprisingly, the episode initially illustrates the twenty-fourth century's enlightened insistence on a woman's right to choose. In the process, however, the ambivalent text links Troi's choice to her bodily femininity, thus privileging abstract social enlightenment over an individual woman('s body). Troi's body speaks for her but, as an empty signifying shell, necessarily speaks against the greater social good the right to choose supposedly protects. In short, Troi's body, a metaphor for the absent woman, loses the right to choose because it makes the wrong choice.

After the lead-in, during which the entity rapes and impregnates Troi, Picard searches out the newly arrived Chief Medical Officer Dr. Katherine Pulaski. Angry with her for neglecting to report to the captain when she boarded the ship, Picard quickly discovers that she is already hard at work, conferring with Troi about her unexpected pregnancy. Picard immediately revises his negative opinion of the new doctor. This lapse in Picard's authority and his willingness to accept it once he realizes Pulaski is working for the ship's safety rather than against Picard's leadership articulate the collusion between medical and military knowledges that pervade *Star Trek* generally and work to bio-essentialize Troi's identity in this episode in particular. As Picard approaches the two women, he begins to chastise Pulaski until she interrupts him by saying: "Sit down, Captain. You better listen to this." The camera pans down from Picard's face to a close-up of Troi sitting in silence. Still silent, Troi looks toward Picard and then back toward Pulaski. While Pulaski's dialogue implies that something needs to be said, Troi's grim physical expression, combined with nondiegetic music, melodramatically communicates the seriousness of the situation.

In the next scene, her silent body continues to speak. Troi sits alone at the very end of the conference table, and several empty chairs and a wide-angle lens emphasize her separation from the others. Throughout the scene she stares straight ahead or down at the table surface while Picard, First Officer Commander William Riker, Lt. Commander Data, Security Chief Lt. Worf, and Pulaski discuss the unusual speed with which her fetus is growing. According to Pulaski, the fetus's gestation period will be thirty-six hours, rather than the nine or ten months common to humans and Betazoids, respectively.[8] Picard informs the group that their "purpose here is to determine what is to be done about this through discussion." Emphasizing the complexity of the situation and acknowledging the possibility and legal availability of abortion in the twenty-fourth century (at least for rape victims), Picard calls for discussion. Troi, however, does not participate in this decision as "ship's counselor." Her silence, isolation, and bowed head, in this and the previous scene, in fact may suggest that she feels some guilt for her unexpected pregnancy and that as a result she has no right to participate in the discussion as either counselor or the body in question. When Pulaski starts showing pictures of the fetus, however, if Troi was feeling guilt before, she now clearly begins to feel maternal love. Her newfound obsession with the fetus further distances her from the discussion about her possible abortion. Her distance from the deliberations no longer signifies possible wrongdoing but instead emphasizes her bodily identity as a reproducing woman.

As Pulaski shows moving images of the fetus and declares that it is half-human/half-Betazoid, in identical proportion to Troi herself (the physical fetus is literally an extension of Troi's body alone), Troi is drawn into communion with herself/her fetus. A close-up of the fetus, framed so that the amniotic sac and umbilical cord are not visible, emphasizes "baby-like" characteristics. Ribs, fingers, toes, and a distinct face are visible as the fetus moves rhythmically, presumably in response to Troi's heartbeat. Despite the fact that these are images Pulaski says she recorded earlier and that a careful viewer can identify them as a few seconds of images repeated over and over again, a shot of Troi shows her looking toward the screen and then down at her stomach, drawing an explicit connection between the image on the screen and what is happening in her own body.[9] The camera pans down her body and reveals her hand on her stomach before panning back up to her face, signaling Troi's emotional point of view. Simultaneously, she hears the voices of the crew, which begin to distort, signaling Troi's point of audition. Troi refrains from offering her opinion about abortion though she is both a pregnant woman and the ship's counselor; instead, she retreats into a solipsistic interaction with the fetus. At this moment, her body consumes her; she becomes her body.

The intensity of Troi's experience "speaks" her inevitable decision to carry the fetus to term. When she comes out of her reverie, she announces her body's decision: "Captain, do whatever you feel is necessary to protect the ship and the crew, but know this, I'm going to have this baby." This statement encapsulates the text's ambivalence; it insists on Troi's right to choose but simultaneously sacrifices her role as crewmember (counselor), linking her access to choice, instead, to her biological identity (reproducing female). She is not interested in the captain's protection; nor is she willing to participate in rational, democratic discussion about the implications of her unusual pregnancy. Rather, she is simply the pregnant female body—the object of discussion. Thus, when Picard replies: "Then it seems that the discussion is over," he affirms a woman's "right to choose"; confirms Troi's new identity as body rather than full-fledged crewmember; and reasserts his unilateral authority over women's rights, women's bodies, the ship as a whole, and the fetus/life-force-entity itself.

Elspeth Probyn (1993) has coined the term "choiceoisie" to signify the way in which popular culture represents feminism as enabling "choices" but then represents women's ideal choice as a return to the traditional roles of mother and/or wife. She writes: "Rather than in the hands of the woman choosing, choice in some situations is represented as already having been made, always and already chosen. In other words, the active quality of choosing is replaced by a plethora of nouns, of choices made" (285).[10] In Troi's case, while Picard insists on Troi's control of her own body, he does so only in relation to her right to choose motherhood. Despite Pulaski's deliberate use of the term "fetus"—a supposedly pro-choice tactic—the framing of the mobile fetus with which Troi seems to communicate is, like pro-life representations, cropped and magnified to signify "babyness." As Celeste Condit (1990) argues, the use of hyperbole (through framing and enlargement) to transform a fetus into a "baby" in pro-life images tends to have more emotionally persuasive power than the deliberate verbal use of de-emotionalized terms like "fetus" in pro-choice discourse. Melodramatic images may not make arguments, she suggests, but they certainly can limit options through persuasion. This episode constructs choiceoisie by locating Troi's authority in her body and making that seem natural. She gains authority when she speaks about reproduction or motherhood. Yet, as we shall see, her decision to have the child endangers the crew and even undermines this tenuous bodily authority. Her body, the source of her authority, ultimately betrays her and those who depend on her innate knowledge. She makes the only choice she can make (given her identity as feminine body), but (given her identity as feminine body) it is the wrong choice.

Consent

When Troi is raped during the episode "Violations," the narrative again privileges Troi's perspective on rape (this time the characters explicitly name her experience "rape") but then constrains her voice and her authority in her body—a body that inevitably makes bad decisions. Furthermore, as in "The Child," her body causes the rape in the first place. In "The Child," the life-force-entity chooses her because she is biologically female. In "Violations," the rapist chooses her because, as he says: "You're so lovely. . . . Why do you have to be so lovely? So nice?" Her body, it seems, encourages rape in both instances, which further undermines her right either to choose or to consent.

In "Violations," the Enterprise transports three Ullians—a father, Tarmin; an adult son, Jev; and a mother, Inad.[11] The Ullians are members of a telepathic species who conduct anthropological research on other cultures by helping people recover long-forgotten memories. Although all three Ullians are friendly and respectful, demonstrating their amiability by helping botanist Keiko Ishikawa O'Brien relive a pleasant memory of her grandmother, Jev soon attacks Troi telepathically, forcing her to remember a forgotten sexual encounter in which Riker pressures her both physically (he holds her down and kisses her even after she says "no" and pushes him away) and emotionally (he refers to their former love affair and calls her by their Betazoid love name—Imzadi) to have sex. During this nightmare-like memory sequence, Jev replaces Riker, continues the attack, and even plays two roles—as attacker and as spectator—in order to watch himself raping Troi. Thus, Jev forces Troi to recover her repressed memory of Riker's (attempted) rape and rapes her metaphorically twice more, first by entering her mind without her consent and then by taking the place of the rapist in the memory.

After this triple rape, Troi falls into a coma. Silenced again by rape, her body speaks the violation through a change in physical state. The coma, however, unlike the pregnancy in "The Child," renders Troi absolutely silent. Thus the bulk of the narrative takes place without her. While Troi is unconscious and they do not even have access to her embodied authority, Picard, Riker, Chief Medical Officer Commander Beverly Crusher, Chief Engineer Lt. Commander Geordi La Forge, and Data attempt to discover the cause of her coma. In the process, they return again and again to the issue of consent, emphasizing the absolute sanctity of each individual's right to consent or to refuse to consent, which illustrates the twenty-fourth century's support of feminist ideals.

The very first scene, in fact, raises the issue of consent. Tarmin begins to probe Crusher's memory without her permission. He interprets her as thinking about her first kiss and says he can help her remember the entire experience. Crusher remains reticent, not necessarily because of Tarmin's reference to a sexual memory, but, like most of the rest of the crew, because she is uncomfortable with the entire concept of memory probes.[12] Jev, however, seizes upon Tarmin's sexual comment and draws attention back to Crusher's lack of consent:

J: Father, you know you're not supposed to probe someone's memory unless they've given you permission.

T: You are right. But sometimes, with a beautiful woman, I cannot help myself.

Like Picard insisting on Troi's right to choose (motherhood) in "The Child," Jev foregrounds the (sexual) threat that the Ullians' telepathic skills represent in order to insist on the need for full sexual consent at all times. In each case, the characters paradoxically use their insistence that a woman has a right to control her own body in order to rationalize their coercive practices against women.

As the episode progresses, it rationalizes masculine coercion by separating consent from the specific sexual threat in the opening scene and thus from the issue of rape per se.[13] For example, during a dinner party, Crusher and Tarmin both pressure Picard to have his memory probed. Eventually, Inad stops the exchange by reminding Tarmin that "We mustn't influence people. We must let them come to us willingly." Consent, initially a reference to both a woman's right during a sexual encounter (Tarmin's reference to Crusher's first kiss) and feminist ideals, now becomes, more generally, an innate human(oid) right. This intermediary move enables a final shift in the meaning of consent in the episode when Picard transfers the right to give or deny consent from the person whose memory is being probed (i.e., the potential victim) to the Ullians, the suspected villains. As the search for the cause of Troi's coma progresses, Picard repeatedly asks the Ullians for their "consent" to be questioned, physically examined, and ultimately confined to quarters. Picard's sensitivity to the issue of coercive relationships, as presented here, serves to assure us that continuing characters on the show do not coerce or pressure others into consenting. Each time Picard asks the Ullians to consent, they respond with increased outrage at Picard's request. By the end of the episode, Jev and Inad refuse to consent to confinement and, instead, insist on their right to defend themselves. By this point, the episode has reversed the meaning of the legal term "consent." While consent continues to evoke an awareness of feminism, the narrative eventually uses that awareness against women.

Later in the episode, after Troi has come out of her coma and Jev has invoked his right not to consent (to confinement), Jev asks that Picard allow him to defend himself by helping Troi remember what happened to her right before she fell into a coma. Again articulating his unconditional support of Troi's right to control her own body after it has been violated, Picard says to Troi: "Counselor, I want to reiterate, if you have any doubts whatsoever about this procedure, you don't have to go through with it." Like Troi's right to choose in "The Child," however, this right to give or deny consent can lead in only one direction. Because she cannot remember what happened to her—why she "is so frightened"—she has no choice (according to the narrative trajectory) but to submit to the process of re-remembering her recovered traumatic memory, this time for public scrutiny.

While Picard listens to Troi's embodied voice remembering the memory, Jev makes that voice lie. Picard places authority in Troi at this moment, accepting the woman's interpretation of her rape, but Jev is able to make

Troi mis-remember his father invading her memory, rather than Jev, himself. Troi has complete authority to name the rapist, but she betrays herself by remembering the wrong man. Thus, while the episode insists on the right to consent and on the authority of the woman's perspective on rape, neither work in Troi's favor. Not only by making a false accusation of rape but by doing so unintentionally, Troi illustrates once again woman's inability to provide irrefutable evidence of rape—at least within the logical confines of a masculinist text.

Responding to the Feminine Body's Voice: Rationality and Militarism

Rationality ·

Despite Picard's belief in Troi's (false) accusation of Tarmin, La Forge and Data continue to use logic to pursue the (true) villain. Although the narrative locates the authority to name the rapist in Troi's body/memory, a rational process ultimately leads to the discovery of the rapist. In fact, the bulk of the episode focuses on the developing investigative process as it shifts from Riker to Crusher to La Forge and Data. Riker begins the process of discovery by questioning Jev, the last person to see Troi before she falls into a coma. Calling Troi's coma a "mystery," Riker asks Jev to consent to a medical examination. He says Dr. Crusher "is just trying to eliminate the possibility that one of you might be carrying an organism that was harmful to Troi. I'm not implying that you did anything intentional. I'm just trying to get to the bottom of the mystery." Of course, Jev did do something intentionally, as Riker suspects (despite his denial).[14] In order to thwart the process of discovery, Jev forces both Riker and Crusher to remember painful memories. And, like Troi, Riker and Crusher fall into silent comas. Neither of their memories, however, are sexual in nature. Riker remembers the death of a crewmember for which he feels responsible, and Crusher remembers viewing her husband's body after his death. While Jev may take some sadistic pleasure in producing unpleasant memories that cause people to fall into comas, Jev's focus is on hiding his villainy from Riker and Crusher. Troi's coma, the only one to result entirely from Jev's sadistic sexual pleasure, functions as the major mystery of the episode.

While Jev wanders the ship after Troi (mistakenly) absolves him of guilt, La Forge and Data continue to use logic to discover that he is the villain, which allows them to arrive just in time to rescue Troi from another attack. First, La Forge and Data check all the unexplained comas on planets visited by the Ullians, only to discover that they are not similar to Troi's coma. Faced with a null set, they begin checking all the explained comas on planets visited by the Ullians, assuming that the doctors on those planets would not have been as skilled as Crusher in determining that although Troi's coma looks like "Yrizine syndrome," it is not. Finally, they determine that misdiagnosed Yrizine syndrome occurred on two planets where Tarmin, the (falsely) accused rapist, was not present but Jev was. As a result, they solve the mystery and capture the villain, just as he is about to rape Troi again, both mentally and physically. The rational process, predicated on the assumption that Crusher, as a Federation-trained scientist, has superior diagnostic skills to all other doctors, responds to and gently corrects Troi's mistaken embodied voice.

Medical rationality also supersedes Troi's embodied voice in "The Child." Not surprisingly, Troi's bodily decision to continue her pregnancy in "The Child," like her bodily identification of Tarmin as the villain in "Violations," turns out to be a mistake. Although the child that results from Troi's pregnancy, Ian, is well-behaved and sweet, his rapid growth rate ultimately does endanger the rest of the crew by causing an extremely dangerous plasma plague on board to grow in tandem with Ian's body. Together, the plasma plague and Ian (the extension of Troi's body) threaten the effectivity of the plague's containment field and endanger the life of the entire crew. Troi's authoritative body, it seems, is dangerous.

After the birth, Troi continues to fawn over her child. While the Enterprise crew secures the plasma plague within the containment field, Troi orders soup from the replicator and comforts her son when he burns his finger. In one scene, for example, Troi walks toward Ian smiling broadly. As she passes the door to her quarters, the door chimes and her distinct smile changes to a frown as Picard and Pulaski enter. Her body yet again speaks her emotions and links her to Ian (an extension of her body) rather than to the Enterprise.

Picard and Pulaski are friendly to Troi and Ian, but their underlying purpose is to get Ian to tell them his reason for boarding the Enterprise. In response Troi protects her "eight-year-old," human/Betazoid son. While Picard and Pulaski discuss the fact that Ian intentionally burns himself in order to experience the sensation of physical pain and to induce tears, Troi draws Ian to her chest in a close-up that emphasizes their physical connectedness. Despite the fact that Ian talks about himself as an entity investigating another species, Troi continues to treat him like a human/Betazoid child. For example, after Ian burns himself and begins to cry, he says in surprise: "My face is wet." Troi, rather than explaining the principle of tears to the ever-curious Ian/life-force-entity, simply wipes Ian's face and says: "Is that better, sweetheart?"

Regardless of Troi's myopic focus on performing motherhood, the plasma plague begins its threatening growth. While La Forge and Pulaski attempt to discover why the plague is growing, the life-force-entity solves the mystery when it announces to Troi that Ian's own rapid growth rate is causing the change in the plasma plague and that the life-force-entity must allow its bodily form (Ian) to die in order to save the ship. Troi, however, is only concerned with her son's impending death. She calls Pulaski to her quarters "Now!" and demands: "You must save him." Ian, however, is more conscious of the threat he represents. Ian, the physical body that came from Troi's body, purposefully dies and dissolves, and the life-force-entity's original form—a point of light—replaces him. After briefly resting in Troi's hands and communicating with her telepathically, the life-force-entity exits through the wall of the ship, leaving the Enterprise intact and Troi in tears.

Militarism

Troi (inevitably) chooses motherhood over abortion, but within the narrative logic of the episode, the choice is the wrong choice after all. This mistake, in turn, creates the ship's need for stronger security. Although the rational process assures the absolute truth of the material world and undermines the truth spoken through the body of a woman in both of these episodes, the importance of military defense—even before rational truth replaces woman's truth—is also central to each episode. In each case, Worf, as the head of security, represents this need for defense. For example, while Riker, Worf, and Data debate whether or not to abort Troi's fetus in "The Child," Worf articulates perhaps the most brutal argument and is the only crewmember to speak (a form of) the word "abortion."

W: Captain, obviously the pregnancy must be terminated. For the safety of the ship and the crew.

R: Worf, you can't assume the intent was belligerent.

W: That is the safest assumption.

D: Captain, this is a life form. Not to allow it to develop naturally would deny us the opportunity to study it.

W: If the fetus is aborted, laboratory analysis is still possible.

While Riker insists that the intent of a fetus is relevant and Data holds firm to his belief that the scientific pursuit of knowledge is paramount, Worf makes what turns out to be an accurate assumption: The life form is dangerous. Worf's viewpoint does not win out, however, because Picard insists on the (temporary) authority of the embodied woman's voice. Troi's decision to carry the fetus to term, in fact, also benefits Riker's paternalistic masculinity and Data's curious rationality. Thus, as the narrative begins, it isolates the militarism Worf represents only to develop in such a way that military security becomes an absolute necessity, not for its own sake, as Worf suggests, but for the sake of rational masculinity.

As it develops, the episode repeatedly draws attention to Worf's presence. For example, when Troi declares that "it's time," Data immediately calls for security. As a result, Troi and Pulaski change from smiling about the impending birth to frowning about what they consider to be unnecessary and intrusive security. Once in the delivery room, several close-ups show Worf watching the delivery from the back of the room. After the child is born and appears to be a harmless humanoid infant, Pulaski takes the time to dismiss Worf, who turns his back and leaves the room.

This emphasis on military security, like the emphasis on choice and consent, is a mark of ambivalence in the text. By repeatedly dismissing Worf's myopic concern with security (in this episode as well as many others) and then ultimately confirming his suspicions, the narrative supports woman's embodied voice in order, paradoxically, to dismiss it in favor of military concerns. Yet, because the text dismisses Worf's perspective along the way and couples militarism with rationality, Worf's presence is only a foil that enables the text to use medical rationality to shift authority away from Troi and toward the Federation's neocolonialist attitude toward women and other cultures and species. In both "The Child" and "Violations," in fact, Worf's security abilities are useless against the non-humanoid and telepathic, respectively, life form threats.

Worf does not explicitly address the threat the Ullians pose to the crew in "Violations," but he nonetheless is present during the scene in which Troi agrees to let Jev help her re-remember the events that led to her coma. The Ullians, in fact, insist on Picard and Troi's right to have security present. Positioned again in the back of the room, standing at attention with a phaser attached to his hip, Worf silently watches Troi as she begins to re-remember. The irony here, as in "The Child," is that the kind of military might that Worf represents is absolutely useless against telepathy and the physical effects of the plasma's rapid growth rate. Thus, whereas *TNG* uses Worf to represent a particular military perspective, this perspective cannot be the totality of the Federation's superiority. In other words, although the Enterprise is inevitably more powerful than all the other ships it encounters[15] and Worf is inevitably right that whatever new life force they meet has the potential to cause them harm, like Troi's embodied voice, Worf's myopic focus on military might cannot take Picard's place as the patriarch at the head of a military, economic, *and* cultural neocolonialist superpower.

Identifying the Villain: Federation Superiority

The superiority of the Federation in relation to the Ullians is clear throughout "Violations." Because the audience knows Jev is the villain from the beginning and because he overtly intends the harm he causes, he clearly functions as an example of an evil that humans and their Federation allies have eliminated in the twenty-fourth century. *TNG* needs to insist on this difference between Self and Other in order to prevent the contradictions in the philosophy and application of the Prime Directive from becoming exposed for what they are. Episodes in which humans, rather than aliens, do violate social rules contribute to this differentiation. A comparison of Jev's (alien) villainy and Lt. (junior grade) Reg Barclay's[16] (Federation) redemption is instructive here. In "Hollow Pursuits," when the crew discovers Barclay has been writing holodeck programs in which he is the captain of the ship and Troi and Crusher stand around half undressed, beckoning to him in constant sexual readiness, the crew does not punish Barclay for objectifying women; they cure him. They must cure him so as not to undermine the Federation authority Barclay represents. The fact that the holodeck is a representational technology absolves Barclay of responsibility for using (a representation of) Troi's body against her will. Because Troi considers her virtual body to be distinct from her physical body, she is able to maintain her role as ship's counselor in this episode rather than to collapse into her body as she does when aliens violate her. Thus, rather than accusing Barclay of physical and mental assault, she begins teaching him how to make friends with other people on the ship and how to develop self-confidence. Whereas Troi uses *mok'ba,* Klingon martial arts, to hold Jev off when he attacks her physically and mentally at the end of "Violations," she uses therapy to redeem Barclay.

Given the parallels between the diegetic holodeck and the television text in terms of representation, when Troi and the narrative absolve Barclay of guilt for looking at women without their consent they also absolve the spectator of any responsibility for objectifying women's bodies in virtual ("Hollow Pursuits"), mental ("Violations"), or actual ("The Child") rape scenes.[17] In *TNG,* the representation of villainous aliens not only places violence elsewhere, outside the utopic twenty-fourth-century Federation culture, but also naturalizes the recuperation of the occasional Federation member (potentially standing in for the spectator) who simply makes a mistake. In other words, whereas one might argue that Barclay's use of the holodeck to force (the images of) Troi and Crusher to have sexual contact with him is a form of sexual assault, the *TNG* textual system uses the distinction between Jev (who represents all aliens) and Barclay (who represents the Federation) to position the locus of violence elsewhere. Jev and Tarmin's identities as members of an alien telepathic species make them "always-already" rapists (Tarmin simply controls his impulses better than Jev does); in contrast, when Barclay rapes, his status as Federation citizen defines his actions as inappropriate but forgivable and reformable. In Barclay's case, the logic of the show dictates that "boys will be boys."

In "The Child," however, the matter is slightly more complicated. Unlike Jev, "Ian" is not intentionally villainous. Rather, his natural curiosity has troubling side effects. Like *TNG*'s character the immortal Q, he is more advanced than the Federation. He is able to control other life forms' bodies, to exist in space without a planetary environment, to travel at the speed of light without any technological instruments, and to enter and leave the Enterprise at will, despite the complex technological security systems on the ship. But, also like Q, his curiosity about humanoid life forms can cause destruction. The fact that, unlike Q, he does not know he will cause distress does not change the outcome of his actions.

The irony here is important. Whereas the Enterprise's mission is clearly grounded in curiosity ("to go where no one has gone before"), *TNG* naturalizes self-serving curiosity by repeatedly defining the curiosity of other species as problematic. Thus, when "lesser developed" species request technological help from the Enterprise, the Prime Directive makes it impossible for the Enterprise crew to reveal their secrets. Simultaneously, however, the Enterprise, as the more advanced community, is free to engage in Federation curiosity (without intervention). For example, when a Federation observation station on a technologically unsophisticated planet suddenly malfunctions, the problem is not that the Federation has been spying but that the inhabitants of the planet might discover that the Federation has been spying ("Who Watches the Watchers"). Similarly, when more "highly developed" species like Q and "Ian" express interest in the Enterprise crew, they are rejected or destroyed, which in turn naturalizes the view that the Federation is superior, even to "advanced" species. Flanked on both sides by less- and more-developed species, the Federation emerges as unique, enabling the show to embrace the ambivalence in the Federation's Prime Directive and the Enterprise's mission to explore. When rape functions as the fulcrum of this ambivalence, it provides an ideal ground, given its cultural link to both feminism and war, on which to build a hegemonically ambivalent neocolonialist text.

Conclusion

Rape narratives on *TNG* not only reflect an ambivalence about women's bodies and feminism, they also function symbiotically with the neocolonialist system itself. The use of rape in particular, whether defined as such (as in "Violations") or merely alluded to (as in "The Child"), works so well because it provides *TNG* with an opportunity to articulate support for feminist ideals like "consent" and "choice" while simultaneously separating those ideals from women per se and using them as marks of human(oid) rights that often justify government intervention. In the process, the text invalidates women's experience by grounding women's knowledge in the body, which it then opposes to logical rationality and protects with militarism. That Troi speaks through her body so explicitly in the two episodes examined here—and that her body is mistaken in each case as being dependable for adjudicating truth claims—provides *Star Trek* with "evidence" of both the short-sightedness of feminism and the need for government control not only over other cultures but over the bodies of all women.

I want to end by rereading the rape in "Violations," this time focusing on a villain other than the alien Jev. After all, Troi remembers that Riker raped her at some point in the past. Although she has repressed this memory, Jev, at least temporarily, forces her to recover the experience. I think it is safe to assume that the show's "bible" does not explicitly state that Riker is a rapist. One possible reading of the text, in fact, is that Jev plants the entire memory and that Riker never actually assaulted Troi. I feel it is safe to assume, again, that this is the reading Troi and Riker, themselves, have of the entire incident. Yet, the possibility that Riker did/might rape Troi contributes to the narrative's ambivalence about Troi's perspective on rape, which in turn supports *TNG*'s general project of justifying neocolonialism. In short, whether Riker ever actually "attempted" to rape Troi is irrelevant. Either way, Troi's embodied voice is suspect and in need of protection; she simply cannot win. A brief discussion of three scenes in "Violations" will illustrate this point.

When Troi begins to remember this incident, she is immediately distressed. Shots of her frowning, ordering hot chocolate (a generic cure-all for Troi throughout the series) from the replicator, sitting tentatively on the edge of her bed, and finally gasping and drawing back as though someone is touching her, are all intercut with the shots of her memory. And each of these signs of distress *precedes* Jev's replacement of Riker. In other words, Troi is distressed initially, not because she is having a memory and not because Jev has entered her mind, but because she is having a bad memory about Riker. In the memory shots, as well, Riker pursues her relentlessly. Extreme close-ups show his hand displacing the skin on her bare arm and pushing her to the floor. When he kisses her, she pushes him away. In one shot, he enters the frame above her, blocking her path of escape up off the floor.

T: Imzadi, we can't. Not when we're serving on the same ship.

R: Have you stopped thinking about us? Just answer that. . . . I can't stop thinking about you.

T: Will, don't.

Both Troi and the text as a whole, however, must repress knowledge of this rape. When Troi begins the process of re-remembering the experience with Jev's help, the memory is altered (by Jev? by Troi?), not only because Jev replaces himself with his father but also because Troi *smiles* when she realizes she was thinking of Riker. Thus, while the text initially acknowledges the element of coercion in the relationship between Riker and Troi on the series generally, by the end of the episode Troi re-represses that knowledge, transforming her earlier distress (one that was intense enough to arouse her desire for chocolate) into a temporarily pleasant experience that allows her to think of the sexual tension between herself and Riker positively. In other words, Troi redeems Riker implicitly, much as she redeems Barclay explicitly. Riker's character is generally defined as a "lady-killer," and he distinctly ogles a woman early in "Violations" while the crew is sharing a meal with the Ullians ("boys will be boys"), but the text ultimately accepts this element of his character when Troi represses the more violent expression of Riker's desire for her. At the end of "Violations" Picard says, in some attempt at paternalistic comfort for the Ullians (read: spectator):

> Earth was once a violent planet, too. At times the chaos threatened the very fabric of life. But like you, we evolved. We found better ways to handle our conflicts. But I think no one can deny that the seed of violence remains within each of us. We must recognize that because that violence is capable of consuming each of us, as it consumed your son.

Although Riker, unlike Jev, is not consumed by his sexually violent tendencies, when the text is read as I have suggested here, he represents the "seed" to which Picard refers. Ultimately, *TNG* suggests, because that seed exists even in the utopic twenty-fourth-century Federation culture, government control and distrust of women's embodied voices is (un)ambivalently necessary.

Notes

1. Ensign Ro Laren has a similar devotion to Picard (although not to the Federation) that is also grounded in his savior/father function (see the episode "Ensign Ro"). In "Preemptive Strike," Ro transfers her devotion to a paternal Maquis figure who also "saves" her—this time from the Federation.

2. For a fuller discussion of the neocolonialist nature of *TNG*, see Kent A. Ono, "Domesticating Terrorism: A Neocolonial Economy of *Différance,*" in this volume.

3. See Michael Renov (1989), "Advertising/Photojournalism/Cinema: The Shifting Rhetoric of Forties Female Representation," for a cogent discussion of the relationship between this propaganda poster and other objectified images of women during World War II.

4. See, for example, the cover stories in *Newsweek* (Post 4 Jan. 1993) and *Ms.* (MacKinnon July/Aug. 1993), and Alexandra Stiglmayer's (1994) edited collection, *Mass Rape: The War Against Women in Bosnia-Herzegovina.* The *Ms.* cover, ironically, is the most sensationalist, declaring: "EXCLUSIVE! New testimony from the rape/death camps reveals *sexual atrocities* being used as pornography . . . "

5. This image of a distressed sweaty woman waking from a fitful sleep is common to televisual representations of rape, usually in post-rape nightmares. See, for example, the television movie *Settle the Score* (1989) and various episodes of the television series *Melrose Place.*

6. I intend this oblique reference to the film *Unlawful Entry* (1992)—another (threat of) rape narrative.

7. Rape frequently generates narratives about other struggles over women's voice and body, functioning as an absent presence that legitimates narrative tensions between different perspectives without demanding attention to rape as an issue per se. See Lynn A. Higgins and Brenda R. Silver's (1991) edited collection *Rape and Representation* for a series of essays that explore the structured absence of rape even within rape narratives.

8. In addition to the life force's ability to accelerate gestation, it is able to protect Troi's body from the physical effects pregnancy—especially an accelerated pregnancy—would have. In this way, the show represents the effects of rape as painless. Various members of the crew repeatedly ask Troi how she feels, but she never experiences any pain—even during the birth process.

9. The televisual manipulation of this image is an extension of the manipulation of fetus images in the anti-choice/pro-life propaganda film *The Silent Scream*, in various television ads in which happy women gaze lovingly at moving ultrasounds, and in the ultrasound photos pregnant women sometimes now carry, presumably in anticipation of future baby pictures. Recently, while waiting in an airport, I observed a pregnant woman poring over several ultrasound photos. Was she studying them for some evidence of humanness? Was she, like Troi, using this technology to heighten her connection to the fetus growing inside her? Whatever her intent, she and her photos, like the *TNG* episode "The Child," signify the cultural use of image technology to create the formula fetus=baby that challenges the feminist demand that all women have the legal and moral right to choose to abort a fetus they are carrying.

10. See also Probyn's (1991) earlier article "New Traditionalism and Post-Feminism: TV Does the Home."

11. The show never names Inad as the mother; however, her only role is to protect and exist in relation to the men. She never engages in telepathy herself, nor does she ever appear in a scene without one of the two men.

12. In a later scene, Worf articulates the crew's general position more forcefully when he says: "Klingons do not allow themselves to be [pause] probed!" His veiled homophobia is the exact opposite of Keiko's distinct pleasure while experiencing a memory probe in the opening scene. Worf's and Keiko's responses to the memory probe in this episode represent cultural stereotypes (to which other episodes also contribute) of the hypermasculine African American man and the demure, sexually available Asian/Asian American woman, respectively. See Leah R. Vande Berg, "Liminality: Worf as Metonymic Signifier of Racial, Cultural, and National Differences," in this volume for an inter-episode reading of Worf's character as a metaphor for African American identity and culture. She develops this reading by analyzing narrative, character, and the actor's (Michael Dorn) raced identity.

13. In the terms of the text, rape is not necessarily sexual. At the end of the episode, when Tarmin specifically calls Troi's attack a rape, he simultaneously calls later nonsexual attacks on Riker and Crusher rapes as well. Thus, the episode both acknowledges the specific sexual threat in rape and then uses that acknowledgment, paradoxically, to deny the specificity of women's experience of sexual threats.

14. While Riker questions Jev in the guise of his role as first officer, each man's combative style, Riker's excessively protective attitude toward Troi, and his medical-

ization of Jev's threat (could the organism Riker suspects Jev is carrying be a metaphor for AIDS?) suggest Riker feels a bit like a jilted lover. The spectator's omniscient knowledge that Jev has literally replaced Riker as sexual partner/assailant in Troi's mind lends support to this interpretation. I will return to the implications of Riker's role as Troi's former lover in the conclusion of this chapter.

15. Except, of course, the Borg ships. See Katrina G. Boyd, "Cyborgs in Utopia: The Problem of Radical Difference in *Star Trek: The Next Generation*," and Taylor Harrison, "Weaving the Cyborg Shroud: Mourning and Deferral in *Star Trek: The Next Generation*," both in this collection, for detailed discussions of the relationship between the Borg and the Federation.

16. Barclay is the shy and socially awkward young engineer on the Enterprise, first introduced during the third season in "Hollow Pursuits."

17. The film *The Accused* (1988) develops a similar distinction between good and bad looking during rape scenes in order to absolve the spectator of responsibility for watching rape scenes. See Susan Jeffords (1994), *Hard Bodies: Hollywood Masculinity in the Reagan Era.*

References

Brownmiller, Susan. 1975. *Against Our Will: Men, Women and Rape.* New York: Bantam Books.

Cloud, Dana L. 1992. "The Limits of Interpretation: Ambivalence and the Stereotype in *Spenser: For Hire.*" *Critical Studies in Mass Communication* 9.4: 311–324.

Condit, Celeste Michelle. 1990. *Decoding Abortion Rhetoric: Communicating Social Change.* Chicago: U of Illinois P.

Higgins, Lynn A., and Brenda R. Silver, eds. 1991. *Rape and Representation.* New York: Columbia U P.

Jeffords, Susan. 1994. *Hard Bodies: Hollywood Masculinity in the Reagan Era.* New Brunswick, NJ: Rutgers U P.

MacKinnon, Catharine A. July/Aug. 1993. "Turning Rape into Pornography: Postmodern Genocide." Cover Story. *Ms.*: 24–30.

Post, Tom. 4 Jan. 1993. "A Pattern of Rape: War Crimes in Bosnia." Cover Story. *Newsweek*: 32–36.

Probyn, Elspeth. 1990. "New Traditionalism and Post-Feminism: TV Does the Home." *Screen* 31.2: 147–159.

———.1993. "Choosing Choice: Images of Sexuality and 'Choiceoisie' in Popular Culture." In *Negotiating at the Margins: The Gendered Discourses of Power and Resistance.* Ed. Sue Fisher and Kathy Davis. New Brunswick, NJ: Rutgers U P. 278–294.

Renov, Michael. 1989. "Advertising/Photojournalism/Cinema: The Shifting Rhetoric of Forties Female Representation." *Quarterly Review of Film and Video* 11.1: 1–21.

Stiglmayer, Alexandra, ed. 1994. *Mass Rape: The War against Women in Bosnia-Herzegovina.* Trans. Marion Faber. Lincoln, NE: U of Nebraska P.

3

Liminality

Worf as Metonymic Signifier of Racial, Cultural, and National Differences

LEAH R. VANDE BERG

In her elegy to *Star Trek: The Next Generation (TNG)*, science fiction writer Ursula K. Le Guin (1995) writes:

> Worf (Michael Dorn) was my first love. That voice, Richter 6.5—that forehead—those dark, worried eyes—those ethical problems. The glimpses of Klingon dynastic struggles were like Shakespeare's plays about the kings of England, full of quarrels and treachery and kinfolk at each other's throats. . . . Worf, caught between two worlds, was a powerful figure, tragic. (125)

Security Chief Lt. Worf is indeed a tragic character who struggles with his liminal status as the only Klingon officer in Starfleet. "Liminality" is cultural anthropologist Victor Turner's (1974) term for the social position or state of being "betwixt and between" social status positions (232), and it is a term that describes the character Worf throughout the entire *TNG* series.

During the series's first-season episode, "Heart of Glory," for example, when the Enterprise discovers that three Klingons they rescued from an exploding ship are renegades that the Klingon Empire wants returned for trial, Captain Jean-Luc Picard indicates verbally and by his actions that he is fully cognizant of Worf's feeling of liminality as both Klingon and Starfleet officer. At one point, Picard tells Worf directly, "Lieutenant, I am not unmindful of the mixed feelings you must have about this incident." Again, later in that episode Picard comments to First Officer Commander William Riker about Worf: "He must be torn. These are his people." Meanwhile, the two surviving renegade Klingons play on Worf's feelings of liminality by saying to him: "What is it like for the hunted to lie down with the prey? Have they tamed you or have you always been docile? . . . Being among these humans has sucked the Klingon heart out of you. . . . I don't care what you look like, you are no Klingon!" These comments reflect both Worf's function in the series as the site where cultural, national, and racial/species identities and tensions intersect and the painful lessons he and *TNG* viewers persistently are taught over the course of the series about how difference is disciplined not through mutual appreciation of cultural difference but rather through cultural assimilation. Furthermore, the comment "I don't care what you look like, you are no Klingon!" illustrates not only the link the series makes between race/species and culture/nationality but also Worf's liminal position as being somewhere "betwixt and between" Klingon and Starfleet identities.

Worf's liminality does make him, as Le Guin's quote indicates, a powerful, tragic figure. Indeed, Worf's persona—the emblematic brave, honorable loner who struggles alone to find a midpoint between total cultural assimilation and anachronistically fierce racial/species pride and loyalty to his cultural beliefs—is part of his character's and the series's appeal for Le Guin. According to Le Guin (1995), "On the Enterprise, we see the difference of racial and alien types, gender difference handicaps, apparent deformities, all accepted simply as different ways of being human. . . . This is what science fiction does best. It challenges our idea of what we see as like ourselves. It increases our sense of kinship" (125). Many *TNG* fans, like G. Harry Stine (1988), agree with her. Stine's review of *TNG* argues that "along with the obvious technological progress that has taken place in 78 years, social progress is also evident. The best example of this is a bridge officer of a race portrayed as the archenemy of the Federation 78 years before. He is Lieutenant Worf, a Klingon" (164).

Like Le Guin and Stine, I, too, have been a fan of the series, but I disagree with their unrelievedly laudatory views of *TNG*—particularly in regard to the series's treatment of the character of Worf. Le Guin (1995) echoes the intent of *TNG*'s creators when she writes "the continuing mission of the starship Enterprise has been to take us out of the smog of fear and hate into an open space where difference is opportunity, and justice matters, and you can still see the stars" (125). However, my own close textual analysis of the twenty-five episodes[1] that feature storylines involving the character Worf indicates that the only route the series provides out of the smog of hate and fear of difference is cultural assimilation.

In this chapter, I use Turner's (1974) concept of liminality to analyze several powerful episodes featuring Worf in order to illustrate how the series's treatment of Worf models the colonialist process of enculturation, the disciplining of difference to conform to an ideology which sees itself as the ideal and Worf as "other"—as a liminal being in need of "civilization." Turner's concept of liminality provides a useful tool with which we can examine selected encounters between Worf and those who wish to assimilate him, one which enables us to see that Worf's character functions as a powerful dramatic site wherein the discourses of cultural imperialism/nationalism, race/species, and patriarchal gender intersect. A brief review of Worf's narrative construction will provide background before we proceed to the analysis of several illustrative episodes.

Worf as a Liminoid Character: An Overview

Worf, son of Mogh, was born on the Klingon Homeworld in 2340 and accompanied his parents to the Khitomer Outpost in 2346; his younger brother, Kurn, was left with close friends since this was expected to be a short tour of duty. However, in a brutal Romulan attack on the outpost later that year, 4,000 Klingons, including Worf's parents, were killed. The U.S.S. Intrepid responded to the outpost's distress call but was too late. A human engineer on the Intrepid, Sergeny Rozhenko, rescued Worf. Sergeny and his wife, Helena, adopted Worf and raised him, along with their biological son, Nikolai, as their own because it was believed that Worf had no remaining family on the Klingon Homeworld.

As Worf's "human parents" explain to Chief Engineer Lt. Commander Geordi La Forge and Guinan, the bartender, in "Family," Worf had a difficult childhood, in part because there were no other Klingons with which he could interact. Nevertheless, Worf successfully entered Starfleet Academy, graduated, was commissioned as a lieutenant, and served as flight control officer aboard the U.S.S. Enterprise until being promoted to chief of security and full lieutenant after the death of Security Chief Lt. Tasha Yar. As Picard reminds Worf on a number of occasions (e.g., "Redemption: Part I"), being the only Klingon ever to graduate from Starfleet Academy and to serve as a Starfleet officer gives Worf a "singular distinction." However, another word for this singularity is liminality—a sense of always being betwixt and between human and Klingon culture.

Worf potently confronts his liminal status when Klingon officer Captain Kurn comes aboard the Enterprise in an officer exchange program (the counterpart to Riker's Klingon officer exchange in "Code of Honor") and reveals that he is the younger Klingon brother Worf never knew he had (because Kurn was raised by their father's friend Lorgh and was not told of his true parentage until he reached the Age of Ascension). Kurn informs Worf that Duras, the son of Ja'rod and a member of a politically powerful family as well as a member of the Klingon High Council, has made accusations before the Klingon High Council that their father was the traitor who caused the Khitomer massacre. With Picard's approval, Worf, Kurn, and Picard return to the Klingon Homeworld to challenge these accusations, knowing that the penalty for failing to disprove them is death.

To the amazement of Worf and Picard, Klingon High Council leader K'mpec is already aware of the evidence Picard and the Enterprise uncover, evidence that proves that Duras's father and not Worf's was the traitor who caused the Khitomer massacre. K'mpec explains, however, that prior to the ritual challenge, the High Council had decided that rather than publicly acknowledge the truth and risk a Klingon civil war because of the power of Duras's family, they would take the politically safer and expedient course by accepting the false charges that the Duras family brought against Worf.

When Picard makes it clear that he will not allow either Worf or his brother to die to protect this lie, even if it results in the destruction of the Federation/Klingon alliance, Worf suggests a compromise: He will accept discommendation, a Klingon ritual shaming in which the person who receives the discommendation is treated as a pariah by other Klingons and the discommended person's family is disgraced for seven generations. In return, Kurn's life is spared and his true identity is hidden until such future time when Worf and Kurn may decide to take other action.

The discommendation is a truly remarkable extension of his liminality, for once Worf agrees to accept discommendation he is no longer betwixt and between being a Klingon expatriot and a Starfleet token minority; instead, he is betwixt and between being a disgraced outcast with whom no self-respecting Klingon will associate and a Starfleet token minority. On several subsequent occasions when the Enterprise encounters Klingon vessels and officers, these Klingons refuse even to speak to Worf because he is a *pahtk,* a disgraced outcast. Meanwhile, his loyalty as a Starfleet officer is at times still suspect. One result, as we learn in "Redemption: Part I" when Guinan seeks Worf out on the holodeck where he is target shooting, is that Worf no longer feels like laughing.

Several years after Worf's discommendation, K'mpec discovers that he is being poisoned and sends special Federation Ambassador K'Ehleyr to ask Picard to meet with him. Ambassador K'Ehleyr is a bi-species (half-Klingon, half-human) emissary. Six years earlier she had helped Worf successfully handle a touchy situation involving the reawakening of a Klingon warbird that had been frozen in time for seventy-five years. When K'Ehleyr arrives, Worf discovers for the first time that their liaison six years earlier resulted in a son, Alexander Rozhenko.

While K'Ehleyr and Worf begin to negotiate their family identities, she uncovers evidence that Duras had falsified the charge against Worf's father (evidence that Picard and Worf had sworn to K'mpec they would keep secret to prevent civil war), and Duras murders her. In accordance with Klingon tradition, Worf avenges the death of his mate by challenging and killing Duras. Shortly thereafter, Klingon civil war erupts and Worf briefly resigns his commission to fight with his brother Kurn on Gowron's (Duras's rival) side. With Picard's indirect help, Gowron succeeds in winning the war. In return for Worf's support, Gowron gives Worf and Kurn back their family name and honor, and Worf returns to Starfleet.

Although the return of his Klingon family's good name was "a symbolic birth or reincorporation into society" (Turner 1984, 53), Worf nonetheless remains a liminal character throughout the remainder of the series, his actions indicating that he is "betwixt and between" cultures—no longer fully Klingon in attitudes, beliefs, and values and yet not fully part of the dominant humanoid Starfleet culture either. Among these actions are his struggles in raising his bi-species son, Alexander. During the final season, Worf and Counselor Lt. Commander Deanna Troi develop an intimate sexual relationship, and in the series's tentative finale, "All Good Things . . . ," we learn that Worf's friendship with Riker was ruined by Worf's relationship with Troi, and that Troi had since died. The finale also indicates that Worf returns to Qo'noS (the central planet of the Klingon Empire), serves as a member of the Klingon High Council, and retires from that position to become governor of one of the states on the Klingon Homeworld.

With this background on Worf's shifting liminal status, we can proceed to a detailed analysis of several episodes to illustrate how the series's treatment of Worf and his liminality can be read as a colonialist narrative in which Worf is continuously "civilized" and enculturated into the human-dominated Federation culture. The remainder of the chapter examines the series's conflation of race with species and nation with culture and discusses how the experiences of expatriation and paternity teach Worf, and invite viewers, to learn lessons about the disciplining of difference and enculturation.

Intersections of Race and Species, Culture and Nationality

TNG would have viewers believe that in the twenty-fourth-century Federation world there is no "racism" or "race consciousness."[2] However, as a closer analysis of the series's episodes indicates, racial tensions, differences, and issues have not disappeared; they have merely been transformed into species differences. In *TNG,* species has become a metaphor for race, as the series' treatment of the character of Worf indicates.

For example, when Worf tries to explain to Picard why he feels called to leave the Federation to fight Gowron on his birth world, he asserts the view many patriots and freedom fighters have expressed—that love of one's home world is part of one's soul: "I was rescued from Khitomer by humans. Raised and loved by humans. Spent most of my life around humans. Fought beside them. But I was born Klingon. My heart is of that world. *I do hear the cry of the warrior.* I belong with my people" ("Redemption: Part I").

Worf's use of "world" as a metaphor that encompasses culture, national origin, and species leaves open two possible readings of the text. First, because Worf left the Klingon Homeworld as a five-year-old boy and subsequently was raised by humans on other planets, the text suggests that race/species is a powerful bioessentialist force and a source of inescapable "wild animal" traits—love of the "smell of the hunt," the "taste of blood"—and that Worf's desire to join the other Klingon warriors is a "natural," primordial (i.e., bioessentialist) response: ontogeny recapitulates phylogeny. And yet the text also suggests that being Klingon is as much cultural as it is biological. For example, Worf's human mother tells Guinan that as a boy Worf read everything he could find about Klingons and Klingon traditions, history, legends, and culture ("Family"). Furthermore, in "Birthright" both Worf and the viewers discover that his distrust of Romulans is a learned—not autonomic—biological response. Whether biological or cultural, however, Worf's Klingon identity is always essential.

Somewhere Betwixt the Charybdis of Nature and the Scylla of Culture

As the only Klingon officer in the Federation, Worf faces constant yet unstated demands to prove himself both to his fellow Federation officers and to other Klingons with whom he comes into contact. Doubts about Worf's loyalty as a result of his species and bicultural identity are the focus of the first-season episode "Heart of Glory." This glimpse into Worf's liminality occurs when the Enterprise rescues three Klingons from a damaged Talarian freighter in the Romulan Neutral Zone. Picard assigns Worf to escort Captain Korris and Konmel, who were uninjured, to their quarters while their severely injured comrade Kunivas is transported to sickbay.

Once inside their guest quarters, Korris and Konmel immediately begin taunting, challenging, and testing Worf. They sneeringly ask him, "Tell me, what is it like for the hunted to lie down with the prey? Have they tamed you or have you always been docile? Does it make you gentle? Has it filled your heart with peace? Do glorious battles no longer inspire your dreams?" Worf's controlled response is to ask them why they are mocking him and trying to rouse him to anger. Korris and Konmel then tell Worf that they hate the Federation-Klingon Alliance and want to help other Klingons to return to the true Klingon warrior spirit that they believe has been lost through the alliance with the Federation. They talk of the magnificent battles they could fight if they commanded the Enterprise, because, unlike Worf, their "instincts have not been dulled by living among civilized men." Worf responds that perhaps their dreams of glory belong in the past and adds that, as a Klingon, of course "those feelings are still a part of me, but I control them. They do not rule me."[3] At this Korris shakes his head disapprovingly. However, he stops mocking and begins to compliment Worf even as he rejects the possibility of a Klingon truly fitting into the human-dominated world of Starfleet and the Federation: "Yes. To fit in the humans demand that you change the one thing that you cannot change. But because you cannot, you do not. That, too, is the mark of a warrior. You said I mock you. I do not. I salute you."

When the three men are called to sickbay because Kunivas is dying, as Korris holds Kunivas's eyes open, Worf joins them in howling the Klingon death cry; Picard and Chief Medical Officer Commander Beverly Crusher look on in astonishment. Subsequently, Picard returns to the bridge, where his questions and tone in discussing the death scene he has just witnessed subtly but clearly convey a supercilious attitude toward Klingons. Picard tells Riker and Lt. Commander Data that watching Worf "howling was like looking at a man I had never known." Data's response suggests that Picard's reaction may be a function of his unfamiliarity with the ritual; to the best of Data's knowledge this was the first time that outsiders had ever witnessed the Klingon death ritual. However, Picard's follow-up question clearly indicates that he views this cultural ritual as a primitive, animalistic one: "I can understand their looking into a dying man's eyes, but the howling?" The cultural imperialism in Picard's query entirely misses Data, whose objective response is to provide an explanation that indicates that this expression is a direct outgrowth of their religious beliefs: "They are warning the dead, sir, 'Beware! A Klingon warrior is about to arrive!'"

Concomitantly, at the request of Korris and Konmel, Worf takes them on a tour of the ship. As he does so, a Klingon Defense Force cruiser approaches the Enterprise; its captain explains that Korris and Konmel are renegades who hijacked the Talarian freighter and that their comrade was injured when the three of them used the commandeered freighter to attack and destroy the Klingon ship sent to capture them. The Klingon captain asks Picard to turn them over to him, and Picard agrees to do so. However, rather than calling Worf and telling him to arrest Korris and Konmel, Picard sends then-Security Chief Yar and three security officers to take them into custody.

Yar and the security contingent catch up with Worf and the two Klingon guests in a corridor. As Yar informs Korris and Konmel that they are under arrest, a civilian female and a small child step out of a door and into the hallway. The little girl walks over to Korris, who picks her up. Yar immediately taps her com badge and announces to Picard that they may have a hostage situation. Korris, however, merely looks at Yar, silently hands the child to Worf, and he and Konmel peaceably accompany the guards down the hall to their quarters.

Yar calls Picard and cancels the alert, and then, sighing, turns to Worf and comments that she had been afraid that they were going to have a hostage situation on their hands. To this Worf disdainfully responds, "That is not our way. Cowards take hostages. Klingons do not." In using the words "our way" to explain to Yar why her presumption indicates her ignorance of Klingon culture, Worf clearly acknowledges his pride in his identity as a Klingon. Although the text leaves open the possibility that Picard avoided calling upon Worf to take the Klingons into custody out of fear that they might overpower Worf and use his weapons to commandeer the ship, Picard's previous comments about the Klingon death howl—and the defensive tone of Worf's response to Yar's assumption that Klingons would use defenseless children as hostages—suggests another reading of this scene. Specifically, Worf's words and tone suggest that Worf sees Picard's action as an indication that his liminal status raises doubts about his loyalty to Starfleet when he is around other Klingons. A subsequent scene on the bridge clearly confirms that this is indeed Picard's concern.

In this scene, Worf returns to the bridge immediately following the arrest of Korris and Konmel, at which time Picard tells him that the commander of the Klingon ship has requested the return of the renegades and is ready for their transfer. When Worf responds that they certainly will be tried and executed and asks Picard if there are any other options, Picard replies that he sees none, but that he is "not unmindful of the mixed feelings you must have about this incident." As Worf returns to his post on the upper level of the bridge, Riker and Picard have the following *sotto voce* conversation on the lower level of the bridge, less than twenty feet away from Worf:

R: He seems to be handling this quite well, sir.

P: So far. He must be torn. These are his people.

The "so far" and "his people" expressions by Picard, the series's primary spokesperson, reflect doubts about Worf's loyalty that clearly are a result of his species difference from Picard and the other human-dominated Starfleet officers. Indeed, Picard's comments display a form of what Stuart Hall (1990) terms inferential racism: "those apparently naturalized representations of events and situations relating to race, whether 'factual' or 'fictional,' which have racist premises and propositions inscribed in them as a set of unquestioned assumptions" (13). That is, Picard's comment is racist because he assumes that Worf automatically would feel the pull of both cultures whenever there is a disagreement between Klingons and the Federation rather than assuming that Worf might or might not feel seriously torn depending upon the situation. Additionally, it is important to note that Picard and Riker, although they lower their voices while exchanging these observations, are speaking about Worf in his presence as if he is not there and making patronizing assumptions about his feelings. Only low-status, marginalized social groups—children, criminals, medical patients, and ethnic minorities in a racist society—are first made objects of scrutiny and then talked about in their presence (*sotto voce* or not) as if they are not there. That Worf is treated this way by the ship's captain and first officer provides another indicator that species is a metaphor for race on *TNG*. And protestations by Picard that "the Enterprise crew has representatives from thirteen planets. They all have their different beliefs and customs and I respect them all" ("Reunion") to the contrary, there is an underlying, pervasive species discrimination reflective of U.S. racism on *TNG*.

When Korris and Konmel subsequently create a weapon and escape from their quarters, Worf resolves the dilemma Riker and Picard assume he has by redefining his silent passivity on the bridge (and in the Federation generally) as a mark of his Klingon identity rather than of his enculturated Federation identity. Konmel is killed, but Korris flees to engineering, where Worf confronts him. Korris tries to talk Worf into escaping with him to fight glorious battles, but Worf declines, explaining: "You look for battles in the wrong place. The true test of a warrior is not without, it is within. Here [tapping his heart] is where we meet the challenge. It is the weaknesses in here a warrior must overcome." After Korris refuses to put down the phaser, Worf shoots him, performs the Klingon death ritual, and later reports to the captain of the Klingon defense cruiser that the Klingons died well; they died with their heads unbowed, as proud—not broken, resigned shadows—of their warrior selves.

The narrative invites implicit metaphorical parallels between Klingons and stereotypes of Native American warriors, Japanese samurai warriors, and kamikaze soldiers, all of honor and duty are valued more than life itself. Thus, when the narrative characterizes the overwhelming sense of pride, honor, duty, and revenge of the renegade Klingons as uncivilized relics of a violent, primitive culture, the viewer is invited to extend those deprecatory comparisons to Native American and Japanese cultural values and traditions. Furthermore, because Worf is played by the 6 foot 3 inch African American actor Michael Dorn, Worf's liminality also metonymically signifies the ongoing tensions in contemporary African American/ Euro-American race relations.

Expatriation and Liminality

The pervasive condescension of most Starfleet humanoids toward Klingons and Klingon culture is reaffirmed, albeit with a subtle ironic twist, in the second-season episode "The Icarus Factor" through a comment linking the episode's two plotlines. In the first storyline Riker's father, Kyle, boards the Enterprise as a civilian strategist assigned to brief Riker on the new ship, the Aries, whose command he has been offered. After Riker rejects his father's attempt at reconciliation of their fifteen-year hostility, the two eventually confront their feelings of anger and rejection by "duking it out" in an anbo-jyutsu combat. The second storyline begins with Acting Ensign Wesley Crusher, Data, and La Forge walking down the hallway, talking:

W: You try talking to him, Geordi. I'm telling you, he's not normal for Worf.

D: There is, of course, a genetic predisposition to hostility among all Klingons. But Worf is unusually out of sorts.

La F: Come on, he's never been much on charm.

W: Well, whatever is troubling him, I think we should try to help. He is our friend.

This short interchange illustrates both the series's ongoing species stereotyping and its strategic attempts to defuse stereotypes. The comments indicate that although La Forge, Wesley, and Data have come to regard themselves as Worf's friends, they nonetheless regard his temperament—which in a human might be characterized as a brusque, or pointedly business-like style of communication ("not much on charm")—not as a personality quirk but as a species shortcoming. In fact, Data contextualizes Worf's typically difficult temperament, which they all agree is currently more exaggerated than usual, as endemic to his species. This is important because having the android Data, who is an "objective machine," express this bioessentialism "naturalizes" this species stereotype and confirms the pervasive and enduring nature of Worf's liminal status.

After their conversation, Wesley investigates and discovers, as he tells the other three, that the cause of Worf's testiness is that "Worf is feeling spiritually and culturally isolated" because it is the tenth anniversary of an important Klingon ritual. As Wesley explains, to move to the next level of spiritual development, Worf needs to celebrate the anniversary of his Ascension, and to do this he needs both Klingon warriors and his family to be present in a ceremonial chamber. Wesley goes on to explain to them that the ritual begins with the Klingon warrior celebrant proclaiming his innermost feelings: "Today I am a warrior. I must show you my heart. I travel the river of blood." He then walks between two lines of Klingon warriors who jab him with Klingon painsticks until he reaches his waiting family because "enduring pain and suffering is considered a Klingon spiritual test." To this La Forge responds, "You mean in order for Worf to celebrate this Ascension he has to be hurt and we have to witness this?" Despite La Forge's obvious repugnance at the ceremonial infliction of pain to arrive at spiritual growth, he joins Data, Wesley, and Chief Medical Officer Dr. Katherine Pulaski as Worf's family in the holodeck re-creation of the ceremony.

Although La Forge's comments reflect the series's dominant attitude of cultural superiority toward Klingons and their cultural traditions, the episode also provides one of several small but noteworthy ruptures in the series's overarching construction of the humanoid-dominated Federation as the cultural ideal against which all others are measured and almost all are found wanting. This occurs during a conversation between Pulaski and Troi; when Troi asks Pulaski if she is staying for the refreshments celebrating Worf's Ascension anniversary, Pulaski replies that after witnessing the anniversary rite on the holodeck she does not feel like eating. She adds,

"I'm just glad humans have progressed beyond the need for such barbaric display." Troi immediately challenges this: "Have they? Riker and his father are in the gymnasium, about to engage in a barbarism of their own." Although Pulaski acknowledges the childishness of this human father and son's resorting to a fighting match to outgrow the stage of anger and resentment they have been locked into for fifteen years, that small moment of irony and self-reflexivity is inadequate to counter the series's overriding cultural imperialist attitude.

Worf's friends help him to reduce temporarily his feelings of cultural and spiritual isolation, but his liminality intensifies when he voluntarily accepts discommendation as the price of both preventing a Klingon civil war and saving his brother's life by hiding his identity. Worf's liminal status does not change after Gowron's installation as the new leader of the Klingon High Council, nor does it disappear when Worf chooses to give up his commission to fight at Gowron's side in the Klingon civil war.

As Worf is packing to leave Starfleet and join Gowron's fight against Duras's forces, Picard comes to Worf's quarters for a private farewell:

> Being the only Klingon ever to serve in Starfleet gave you a singular distinction. But I felt that what was unique about you was your humanity, compassion, generosity, fairness. You took the best qualities of humanity and made them part of you. The result was a man who I was proud to call one of my officers!

Worf (and no doubt the audience) accepts these words as the compliment the narrative indicates Picard intended them to be; nonetheless, Picard's comments provide yet another example of the series's pervasive inferential racism in the guise of "speciesism." Picard's words provide a lesson in liminality and enculturation: Worf is the perfect token Klingon, a "model minority," because although he has lived among Federation humanoids, adopted their (superior) values, and more or less learned to fit in, he has never forgotten his place—never lost sight of the fact that even though he had taken "the best qualities of humanity and made them part of" himself, he remained "singular" as the only one of "his kind" ever to serve in Starfleet. The lesson is that those who are "different" must always change themselves to meet the needs of the dominant culture.

Similarly, Worf's liminal status with other Klingons does not improve much when he leaves Starfleet to fight with Gowron. Although his expertise and his potential influence in gaining needed Federation military assistance are welcomed, Worf's fellow Klingons regard him with suspicion because he has lived almost his entire life among humans, been raised and educated by humans, and still works with humans. Over and over they challenge Worf's commitment to Klingon culture. Even his brother Kurn acerbically comments, "Perhaps your human values have clouded your judgment!" ("Sins of the Father").

In fact, the only way for Worf to prove to his fellow Klingons that he is both biologically and culturally Klingon is by fighting, killing, or bravely enduring torture. Worf does meet these tests by avenging the murder of his mate K'Ehleyr by Duras (in "Reunion") and by fighting bravely and enduring torture during the Klingon civil war, which is won by Gowron with Federation assistance ("Redemption"). For this Gowron rewards him with the redemption of his family name, restitution of his family honor, and the life of Duras's adolescent son, Toral. As Gowron hands Worf the knife with which he is expected to slay Toral, Gowron states the dispositive Klingon law: "Worf, this child's family wrongly took your family name and your honor from you. In return I give his life to you."

Worf, however, responds by tossing the knife to the ground. Despite his brother Kurn's urging that "It's our way. It's the Klingon way," Worf refuses to kill Toral or to permit Kurn to kill him. As Worf explains, "I know [it is the Klingon way], but it is not my way. This boy has done me no harm and I will not kill him for the crimes of his family." He then requests and receives permission from Picard to resume his commission on the Enterprise. As he and Picard walk out of the High Council chamber together, Gowron pats the shoulder of the frustrated brother whom Worf leaves behind on the Klingon Homeworld.

Here again the Klingon cultural traditions, values, and norms (eye for an eye, even several generations later) are presented as primitive in contrast to the Federation's civility. Worf apparently has been sufficiently enculturated that he has come to accept Federation values (compassion, generosity, forgiveness—which Picard names as values that Worf had made a part of himself) as superior to the traditional Klingon values of justice, unsullied family honor, and social responsibility for other family members' actions. The episode's conclusion positions Worf's decision as the morally better, culturally superior choice. Viewers are also invited to see Worf's decision to return to the Federation—where he is not "a stranger in his home land" as he was on the Klingon Homeworld, but a "stranger in a strange land" (i.e., liminal)—as the courageous, fitting, and tragically necessary choice, given the "primitive" value hierarchy of the Klingon culture.

Worf and the Limen of Paternity

Liminality involves limens or thresholds. A limen is "a place and moment 'in and out of time,'" and, according to Turner (1974), for the individual the experience of crossing a limen is the cultural counterpart to "open-endedness in biological evolution" (197). In addition to accepting his commission and joining Starfleet, Worf also crosses the limen of paternity. As the series makes eminently clear, Klingon culture is a patriarchal one in which male identity is communicated through listing one's male progenitor.

"I am Worf, son of Mogh," is how Worf identifies himself (until his disc-ommendation) and how other Klingons identify him. Thus, it is not really surprising that when Worf first discovers he has a son, he displays the typical Klingon patriarchal, hegemonic masculine conceptualization of fatherhood in which the father is the ruler/educator whose responsibility is limited to "caring, loving, and nurturing children to become soldiers" (Harris 1992, 192). For example, in "Reunion," Worf demonstrates his traditional patriarchal Klingon perspective when he objects to K'Ehleyr that Alexander knows nothing of "our ways":

K: *Our* ways? You mean Klingon ways, don't you?

W: He *is* Klingon!

K: He is also *my son,* and I am half-human. He will find his *own* ways. Why the sudden concern? You won't even acknowledge that he is yours.

Vivian Sobchack (1991) argues that although at one time patriarchy and paternity were perceived as identical, more recently they have been at odds. According to Larry May and Robert A. Strikwerda (1992), this is because the image of the father as nurturer has challenged the traditional patriarchal image of the father—the towering "image of strength," "provider and arranger of all things in the public realm," and at home the adult whose "major responsibility is that of disciplinarian and secondarily one of role model for male children." That is, in contrast to the historical patriarchal ideals of fatherhood as either ruler or educator, the nurturant father displays "'receptivity, relatedness, and responsiveness' . . . fulfilling a responsibility to care for the other . . . over some appreciable period of time, the time necessary to bring the subject to some end state such as health or adulthood" (79).

Once Worf becomes a parent, we again see him struggle to retain traditional Klingon values and cultural traditions and once again to learn to discipline his cultural differences by choosing a course of action that affirms Federation human cultural values over Klingon traditions. In the fifth-

season episode "Ethics," Worf begins the process of discarding the patriarchal, traditional Klingon parental role of ruler/disciplinarian/warrior role model and replacing it with the more nurturing parental role typical of Federation parents such as Transporter Chief Lt. Miles O'Brien and botanist Keiko Ishikawa O'Brien, Crusher, and Worf's own adoptive parents, Sergeny and Helena Rozhenko.

In "Ethics," an explosion in one of the cargo bays paralyzes Worf from the waist down. Once Worf realizes this he asks Riker, as his friend, to help him commit Klingon ritual suicide because "when a Klingon can no longer stand and face his enemies as a warrior, when he becomes a burden to his friends and family, it is time for the *Hegh'bat*. . . . I will not live as an object of pity or shame. My life as a Klingon is over." Riker reads Klingon laws searching for a way to avoid doing this and discovers, as he tells Worf, that he cannot help Worf perform the ritual suicide because according to Klingon law his son, Alexander, must do it.

Initially, Worf refuses to see his son, which Troi explains to Alexander. Alexander responds by telling Troi, "This is part of that Klingon stuff, isn't it? My mother always said Klingons had a lot of dumb ideas about honor. . . . Well, it isn't very important to me. I don't care about being Klingon. I just want to see my father." Troi relates this to Worf and scolds him, saying: "All I care about at this moment is a little boy who's terrified he's going to lose his father. Maybe it's time you stopped lying here worrying about your honor and started thinking about someone else—like your son!" After some thought, Worf allows Troi to bring Alexander to see him. However, during the visit, Worf's arms give out and he falls from the standing position he felt he had to assume when he saw his son. He angrily orders Alexander to leave and resolves to go ahead with the suicide.

Concomitantly, Picard talks with Crusher about Worf. Crusher has refused to permit a visiting research physician, Dr. Toby Russell, to tell Worf about her experimental techniques for regenerating the kind of spinal and nerve damage he received because Worf could live, albeit as a paraplegic, without the experimental surgery, but with the surgery he would have less than a thirty-seven percent chance of survival.

C: Klingon or no there are some things I cannot fix. He will have to accept his condition.

P: Beverly, he cannot make the journey you are asking of him. You want him to go from contemplating suicide to accepting his condition and living with a disability. But it's too far, and the road between covers a lifetime of values and beliefs. He cannot do it, Beverly. But perhaps he can come part of the way. Perhaps he can be persuaded to forego the ritual in order to take the chance of regaining the kind of life he needs. A Klingon may not be good at accepting defeat, but he knows all about taking risks.

Here again, despite Picard's overt expressions of cultural tolerance and respect, it is clear he, Riker, and Crusher all regard Worf's Klingon culture as a primitive one and his beliefs, attitudes, values, and practices in need of change—specifically, replacement with those the dominant Federation culture accepts. The fact that Picard implies his attitude is more tolerant than Crusher's and grounds that attitude in "knowledge" of Klingon identity makes his attempts at enculturating Worf all the more insidious.

When Russell does tell Worf about her experimental genetronic replication surgery, Worf decides to undertake it. He calls Alexander to his bedside to explain that he has decided to break with tradition and undergo the operation rather than take his life according to Klingon custom. Through this decision, brought about in part by his experience of the limen of paternity, Worf embodies the enculturated identity Picard expects of him.

Worf initially appears to die, but his redundant Klingon anatomy eventually kicks in. Although he survives, he must retrain his nervous system through physical therapy. The final scene in the episode shows viewers that Worf indeed has exchanged the traditional patriarchal hegemonic masculine view of parenthood central to Klingon cultural tradition—a view that does not permit a male to show weakness, even to his son—for a liberated human/Federation view of masculinity in which fathers are nurturers who both give and seek help from their families. In this scene, Troi takes Alexander to see his father in the physical-therapy room, where Worf is learning to walk using handrails. Once again Worf's arms give out and he begins to fall, and again Troi stops Alexander from rushing to his father's aid; however, this time Worf responds, "It's all right, Counselor. I would appreciate some help from my son. We will work together." Worf's willingness to forego the Klingon suicide ritual and his willingness to allow his son to see him in a state of weakness and, more importantly, to help him, signifies that a substantial amount of colonialist enculturation has occurred.

Final Observations on Worf and TNG's Colonialist-Narrative of Enculturation

The previous diachronic analysis of Worf's liminality over the course of the series reveals that cultural imperialism—and not multiculturalism—is the dominant discursive position affirmed in *TNG*. Only when Worf demonstrates his increasing enculturation with, and adoption of, human values, attitudes, and behaviors does the human-dominated Enterprise crew begin to accept, trust, and value him as a Starfleet officer and friend. However, though he learns to discipline his differences and to conform to the dominant Federation culture, Worf is never quite accepted into that culture and never quite at ease with his enculturation or his estrangement from Klingon culture.

Using Turner's concept of liminality to analyze Worf's character enables us to interrogate what Constance Penley and Sharon Willis (1993) term the "politics of possibilities" (xix), which makes this and other science fiction series so engaging for so many. The result of that critical examination is that *TNG* can be read simultaneously as an open text through which viewers can interrogate certain social and cultural spaces and also, "irrespective of its superficially futurist stance," as another example of "mainstream male-oriented science fiction [that] has traditionally been a genre obsessed with nostalgia and conservation" (Armitt 1991, 2).

Turner's concept of liminality helps explain why for some fans being a Klingon like Worf is cool; Worf can be read as a twenty-fourth-century version of the western gunslinger hero—an oxymoronic but nostalgic innovation on the "lone man" of courage, bravery, and loyalty who willingly leaves everything and risks his life to do and to fight for what he believes is right. Some of these fans may see in Worf's Klingon liminality a similar situation to theirs and may identify their bicultural struggles with his bi-species ones. Some may see in Worf a liminality similar to but slightly more menacing than the "stage adolescents go through on their way to becoming responsible human beings" (Le Guin 1989, 228). And still other viewers may look at the series's treatment of Worf and see a colonialist narrative of enculturation, not a nostalgic science fiction series or a potentially liberating and oppositional postcolonialist narrative.

Despite the series's overt discursive characterization of this twenty-fourth-century Federation world as one in which there is no consciousness of racism, only multi-species tolerance and respect, my analysis of narratives featuring Worf belies this. Rather, in Worf's perduring liminality and the "civilizing the beast" narrative that his character metadiegetically enacts over the course of the series, *TNG* presents the contemporary social struggles in our multicultural society and a soberingly dystopian vision of the future. As this analysis has illustrated, Worf's Klingon "difference" metonymically signifies his racial/cultural/national difference, and his liminality metaphorically reflects the pervasive racism and cultural intolerance of our contemporary social world.

Despite their great diversity, one common feature of postcolonialist texts is that each "foregrounds a politics of opposition and struggle, and problematises the key relationship between centre and periphery," especially those differences having to do with racism, second languages, and political struggle (Mishra and Hodge 1993, 30, 41). These issues most assuredly pervade *TNG* episodes featuring Worf, but the relationship between the dominant Federation culture (here the colonizer) and Klingon culture (here Worf) is never seriously problematized on anything but a personal level for Worf. By foregrounding the personal dimension of Worf's struggles to come to terms with his bi-species identity as a Klingon warrior, Federation officer, and single parent, the series effectively exnominates both its pervasive militarism and the bioessentialist underpinnings of his representation and remains a colonialist narrative of enculturation. In the end, then, *TNG* goes where many colonialist narratives of enculturation have gone before; it just does so without stories about shooting elephants.

Notes

1. The twenty-five episodes analyzed for this chapter include the following (in chronological order within seasons): Season 1: "Heart of Glory"; Season 2: "The Icarus Factor," "The Emissary"; Season 3: "The Bonding," "Yesterday's Enterprise," "The Enemy," "Sins of the Father"; Season 4: "Family," "Reunion," "Redemption: Part I"; Season 5: "Redemption: Part II," "Disaster," "New Ground," "Ethics," "Cost of Living"; Season 6: "Birthright: Part I," "Birthright: Part II," "Rightful Heir"; Season 7: "Gambit: Part I," "Gambit: Part II," "Parallels," "Homeward," "Bloodlines," "Firstborn," "Eye of the Beholder," and "All Good Things . . . ".

2. Indeed, *Star Trek* creator Gene Roddenberry himself has commented that "It did not seem strange to me that I would use different races on the ship. . . . I had been in the Air Force and had traveled to foreign countries. Obviously these people handled themselves mentally as well as anyone else. . . . So, having not been taught that there is a pecking order in people, a superiority of race or culture, it was natural that my writing went that way." Furthermore, in response to an interviewer's query about Roddenberry's observation that "television is—a giant medium to sell products," Roddenberry replied, "Yes. Unfortunately, also to sell ideas—like that America is pure and decent and the rest of the world, depending upon its relative darkness, is less so." Thus, when he received some pressure from the network "to make *Star Trek* 'white people in space,'" Roddenberry's response was "if we don't have blacks and whites working together by the time our civilization catches up to the time frame the series is set in, there won't be any people. . . . Understand that *Star Trek* is more than just my political philosophy. It is my social philosophy, my racial philosophy, my overview on life and the human condition. . . . I also look forward to when we will contact other races and life forms" (Alexander 1991, 12–14).

3. Indeed, in "Gambit: Part II," the renegade Vulcan Talaria reassembles a banned weapon that kills by using people's own aggressive thoughts against them and that can be deflected by emptying one's mind of violent thoughts. When Picard, Riker, Worf, and two other Starfleet offers confront her, Picard tells them to empty their minds of all violent, aggressive thoughts as she points her weapon first at Worf and then at Picard. Both of them deflect the weapon, indicating that Worf indeed has learned to control the aggressive, bloodthirsty animus that Korris and Konmel suggest is the essence of Klingon nature.

References

Alexander, David. Mar./Apr. 1991. "The *Humanist* Interview: Gene Roddenberry—Writer, Producer, Philosopher, Humanist." *The Humanist*: 5–30, 38.

Armitt, Lucy, ed. 1991. *Where No Man Has Gone Before: Women and Science Fiction*. London: Routledge.

Hall, Stuart. 1990. "The Whites of Their Eyes: Racist Ideologies and the Media." In *The Media Reader*. Ed. Manuel Alvarado and John O. Thompson. London: BFI. 7–23.

Harris, Leonard. 1992. "Honor: Emasculation and Empowerment." In *Rethinking*

Masculinity: Philosophical Explorations in Light of Feminism. Ed. Larry May and Robert A. Strikwerda. Lanham: Little Adams. 209–220.

Le Guin, Ursula K. 1989. *Dancing at the Edge of the World.* London: Gollancz.

———. Spring 1995. "My Appointment with the Enterprise: An Appreciation." In *Star Trek: Four Generations of Stars, Stories, and Strange New Worlds. TV Guide Collector's Edition.* Radnor: News American Publications. 124–125.

May, Larry, and Robert A. Strikwerda. 1992. "Fatherhood and Nurturance." In *Rethinking Masculinity: Philosophical Explorations in Light of Feminism.* Ed. Larry May and Robert A. Strikwerda. Lanham: Little Adams. 75–94.

Mishra, Vijay, and Bob Hodge. 1993. "What is Post(-)colonialism?" In *Australian Cultural Studies: A Reader.* Ed. John Frow and Meaghan Morris. Urbana, IL: U of Illinois P. 30–46.

Penley, Constance, and Sharon Willis, eds. 1993. *Male Trouble.* Minneapolis: U of Minnesota P.

Sobchack, Vivian. 1991. "Child/Alien/Father: Patriarchal Crisis and Generic Exchange." In *Close Encounters: Film, Feminism, and Science Fiction.* Ed. Constance Penley, Elisabeth Lyon, Lynn Spigel, and Janet Bergstrom. Minneapolis: U of Minnesota P. 3–32.

Stine, G. Harry. Nov. 1988. "State of the Art: *Star Trek* Revisited." *Analog Science Fiction–Science Fact*: 158–167.

Turner, Victor. 1974. *Dramas, Fields, and Metaphors: Symbolic Action in Human Society.* Ithaca: Cornell U P.

———. 1984. "Liminality and the Performative Genres." In *Rite, Drama, Festival, Spectacle: Rehearsals toward a Theory of Cultural Performance.* Ed. John J. MacAloon. Philadelphia: Institute for the Study of Human Issues. 19–41.

4

Dating Data

Miscegenation in *Star Trek: The Next Generation*

RHONDA V. WILCOX

Long before *Star Trek: The Next Generation (TNG)* aired, Karin Blair (1983) reported "the reaction of the network executives when [*Star Trek* creator] Gene Roddenberry ... proposed a new show featuring a robot who was to make love to a human female." The executives asked, "Would you like your sister sleeping with one?" (293). *Star Trek*'s plots about the future often parallel contemporary sociopolitical issues; similarly, character interactions, including various nonhuman species, may be read as representing interactions among human ethnic groups. The epitome of such interactions comes with *TNG*'s android officer, Lt. Commander Data. The character should not be oversimplified: He is the locus of many different issues and themes. But certainly central is his representation of the oppressed, particularly African Americans. The android is far from an allegorically direct equivalent of African Americans; in fact, the character's ability to stand for many different ethnic groups (African American, Jewish, WASP) is part of its point. But clearly, through temporary enslavement, trials to determine his freedom, and threats to "sell his child down the river," Data's treatment resembles that given minorities. Like the half-alien First Officer/Science Officer Commander Spock of the original *Star Trek (ST)*, Data must struggle with prejudice. And like Spock, he is attractive to women who are drawn to the exotic. As in the traditional literature of miscegenation, the central character's search for Self takes place in the liminal territory of the encounter with the Other.[1] Data must move beyond definition as Other to definition of Self. And as even the etymology of the word "miscegenation"—mixed race—suggests, such definition of Self/Other is problematic.

One of the first qualities noticed and admired in *ST* was its racial and cultural integration. Communications Officer Lt. Uhura, a black woman, Helmsman Lt. Hikaru Sulu, an Asian American man, and Navigator Ensign Pavel Chekov, a Russian youth, were part of the bridge crew.[2]

TNG continues and expands this notion of idealistic inclusiveness, adding a representative of the physically disabled, the blind Chief Engineer Lt. Commander Geordi La Forge, and more major women characters, including Chief Medical Officer Commander Beverly Crusher. Within the Federation, conflict between races has given way to cooperation—in the phrase of the highly logical Vulcan species, "Infinite Diversity in Infinite Combination."

But if the bridge of the starship Enterprise displays an ideal of integration, conflict has not disappeared from the world of *Star Trek*: It has simply been displaced. Interracial and other social conflicts are represented by interactions between humans (for production reasons, but also with thematic implications, most members of the Federation are depicted as white humans) and aliens. The histories of *ST* and *TNG* include many such examples. Wm. Blake Tyrrell (1977) identifies two alien races, the noble but militaristic Romulans and the ferocious warrior Klingons, with the mythic U.S. West's Indians (712). In discussing *Star Trek*'s treatment of the twentieth-century arms race, David Buxton (1990) associates the Klingons with the Chinese and the Romulans with the Russians (68). Aside from these constant elements of the *Star Trek* universe, occasional encounters also highlight displaced twentieth-century sociopolitical concerns. Perhaps the most polemical use of an alien species comes in *ST*'s antiracist episode "Let That Be Your Last Battlefield," in which a planet's population is destroyed by centuries of hatred between two races—one of which is black on the left side and white on the right side, the other of which is black on the right and white on the left. *TNG* continues the displacement device, for example, with the introduction of the Ferengi species, who seem to represent 1980s greed in twenty-fourth-century space. Economically rapacious, sexist, and literally twisted (when Ferengi molecules move through their transportation beam, they zigzag), they are described as believing only in profit and free trade and follow the motto *caveat emptor* (see "The Last Outpost"). While the Ferengi are unpleasantly comic, a more deadly representation of the political Other comes with the Borg, part human, part machine, who declare that they "only wish to raise [the] quality of life for all species," promise a "new order," and don't mind obliterating all individualism to achieve it ("The Best of Both Worlds").

Within the Federation, however, economic and certainly racial problems are presented as a thing of the distant past. In her study of the "social construction of whiteness," Ruth Frankenberg (1993) posits three broad stages of U.S. racial attitudes: "essentialist racism" (based on the idea of inherent biological difference), "race-evasiveness" (based on the wishful thinking of selective "color-blindness"), and "race-cognizance" (based on a desire for equality grounded in an understanding of historically generated racial problems). Read on a surface level, *TNG*'s racial integration might be considered simply race-evasiveness, a naïve way of neutering social problems.

But the fact that the series is set four centuries in the future argues against such a reading; the implication is that such racial harmony may have taken a long time to achieve.[3] At the same time, the goal of its achievement is crucial to the series's agenda: Hence, African American actors, for example, are not used to represent African American oppression (that oppression being fictitiously past), yet the series shows itself to be cognizant of current racial difficulties through displacement. This displacement subtext denies the "formal closure on a Utopian terminus" of which Clyde Taylor (1989) accuses *Star Wars* (1977), among other "master narratives" (97).

Perhaps the most powerful recognition of such difficulties comes when the displacement acknowledges problems close to home—when conflict occurs within the Federation family. The most famous example is *ST*'s Spock, a half human, half Vulcan who has to endure prejudice in a predominantly human (translate "white") world, both as a Vulcan and as a "halfbreed" ("Balance of Terror," "What Are Little Girls Made Of?"). Patricia Frazer Lamb and Diana L. Veith (1986) point out that Spock and Captain James T. Kirk are "a science fiction variation on [Leslie] Fiedler's thesis: the white hero and his nonwhite male partner leave-escape-reject 'feminine' civilization to seek their destiny in the dangerous frontier"; they compare Spock to Fenimore Cooper's Chingachgook (238). Racism here is presented as speciesism. But with one *Star Trek* character, the displacement goes even further—from the difference between races to the difference between human and machine. The *TNG* character most like Spock is Data, the android second officer of the new Enterprise.

Data's similarity to Spock is such that Brent Spiner, the actor who portrays Data, has protested their identification, complaining that some fans look for Vulcan points on his ears ("Trekkie" 1991, 8). Both characters are precisely knowledgeable, highly logical, and enormously strong physically. These similarities prepare viewers to recognize another similarity—Data's inheritance of Spock's function of raising racial issues. And in a more general sense, the characters evoke the experience of alienation. Many viewers identify with that alienation (Greenberg 1984): In *ST*, Spock is the only Vulcan-human hybrid, and Data is introduced as the only android with a "positronic" brain, thus the only one accepted as a living being and a command officer in Starfleet. Data is the realization of Isaac Asimov's "dream of a positronic brain" ("Datalore"), a brain that would have consciousness and, potentially, feeling.[4] Data's brother, Lore, who feels emotion, appears three times but is believed killed at the end of his first appearance; he also disappears, mentally unstable, at the end of his second appearance and is shut down after the third, leaving Data again alone.

Spock and Data are quintessential representatives of the Other. It is no coincidence that they are both markedly unemotional, though in different ways. Spock represses his human emotions; Data searches for emotions he does not have. Both are musicians—Spock plays a Vulcan lyre, Data a violin—following an art that is theoretically mathematical but essentially emotional. Their quests to discover the proper role for emotion are inextricably tied to their quests for self-discovery.[5] Within Spock and Data, lack of emotion is a cause of alienation; in real life, it can also be a result. In each case, a modern dissociation from sensation emphasizes the sense of Otherness.

As an android, Data is part of a long tradition of symbolic representations of the Other. From *Metropolis* (1926) to *Blade Runner* (1982), androids have been presented in film as both sexual and social Other (Desser 1991, 112–115). They stand not only for forbidden sexual pleasure but also for subjugated classes of people. As Joseph Francavilla (1991) states:

> Contemporary science fiction's view of the android . . . as a persecuted being deprived of human rights may reflect our culture's projected guilt over the exploitation, conquest, enslavement, and extermination of other races and nationalities in history: the Aztec Indian, the American Indian, the African slaves, the Jews in World War II, and many more. (9)

Data fits squarely within this tradition.

In the *TNG* pilot, Data refers to human "prejudice"; and, as early as the first regular episode, *TNG* made clear Data's role as a representative of the oppressed. This episode, "The Naked Now," was used to establish characters' natures and relationships in overt similarity to the *ST* episode "The Naked Time." In both episodes the crew is affected by a mutated form of water that acts like alcohol and lowers inhibitions, thus allowing them to display their true natures in a dramatically convenient shortcut to character development.

In the first of many Shakespearean references in *TNG*, Shylock's famous speech in *The Merchant of Venice*, "Hath not a Jew eyes? . . . If you prick us, do we not bleed?" (1600, III, i, 51–56), becomes transmuted to a humorous confrontation between the drunken Data and the sober Captain Jean-Luc Picard (played by Shakespearean actor Patrick Stewart; Davis 1990, 3). Picard directly raises the question of Data's humanity:

P: Data . . . intoxication is a human condition. Your brain is different. It's not the same as . . .

D: [Interrupting] We are more alike than unalike, my dear captain. I have pores; humans have pores. I have fingerprints; humans have fingerprints. My chemical nutrients are like your blood. If you prick me, do I not [pause] leak?

Despite debate on the historical context of Shakespeare's words, Shylock's speech is widely accepted as a plea by an oppressed race for treatment as human, and Data's speech unquestionably performs the same function. As part of the character-establishing "Naked Now" episode, it can be taken as a keynote of his nature. The fact that Data's taking a pratfall follows this significant speech only underscores his humanity with humor—as is often done throughout the series.

TNG even more often compares Data's condition to that of African American slaves. It may seem absurd to propose as a representative of blackness the most pallid character ever to serve as a television series regular. One might contend that in the TNG liberal world view, a view that sees all humanity as one (but see the discussion above on race-evasiveness), the use of a very white male to represent the nature of blackness is predictably naïve. Data's coloration, however, dramatically enriches the series's racial discourse. Attempts in print to describe/name that color illuminate the subjective and culturally constructed nature of response to skin tone by their failure to agree: Data's color is variously identified as "golden" ("Trekkie" 1991, 8), "opalescent-gold" (Gerrold 1987, 8), and "chrome" (Carey 1988, 21), as well as, more frequently, simply "pale" (e.g. Lorrah 1989, 179). In "The Schizoid Man," Data is overtly and repeatedly compared to the Tin Man of *The Wizard of Oz* (for the first of many times in the series), a comparison that might guide interpretation of the skin tone; it is not a natural one (of which more later). White actor Brent Spiner wears makeup that presents him as paler than any normal "white"; he is "whiter than 'white,'" and his startling coloration is an ironic unvoiced commentary on the racial term "white."

Most importantly, perhaps, Data's skin tone is *marked*, purposely made noticeable. This marking naturally serves the dramatic function of identifying him as the android character; however, android characters in *ST* were presented without special complexion indicators (and they were uniformly played by white actors).[6] Clearly, the creators' choice to present Data as markedly different in skin color is not merely a matter of dramatic convenience. In the first TNG novel, Diane Carey (1988) describes First Officer Commander William Riker (who in this fiction is presented as "prejudiced" against Data and as later overcoming that prejudice) contemplating Data's color:

> For the hundredth time, Riker involuntarily wondered why anybody smart enough to create an android so intricate was too stupid to paint its face the *right color*. . . . If his builders filled it with human data—pardon the pun—somewhere in the download must have been information that the palette of human skin types didn't include chrome. It was as though they went out of the way to shape him like a human, then went even further out of the way to paste him with signs that said "Hey! I'm an android!" (21; emphasis added)

Richard Dyer (1989) and Ruth Frankenberg (1993) discuss in detail the *unmarked* nature of whiteness as it is represented in dominant cultural art; but here, Data's "whiteness" (itself, as noted above, an elusive category) is clearly *marked*. As Dyer (1989) says, "white power secures its dominance by seeming not to be anything in particular" (44); and as Frankenberg (1993) explains, "often . . . white stands for the position of racial 'neutrality,' or the racially unmarked category" (55). Data, in contrast (both ideologically and visually), invites the conscious viewer to consider whiteness as Other. His skin tone certainly marks him as a member of a minority. One might also argue that Data's "unreal" color means that he is of no single human race and can represent anyone dehumanized by references to his/her skin color. The African American references of the narrative join with the boundary issues Data's skin tone represents to create a character capable of standing for black or white. Data's treatment as dehumanized Other may subliminally suggest to white viewers, "It could happen to you." "Whiteness" is just as socially constructed a category as "blackness," and it could be just as marked. Do blacks see themselves viewed by whites in as startlingly unreal a fashion as Data is seen to be? Is Data's unreal whiteness the equivalent of the unreal blackness that constitutes many whites' "vision" of blacks? The character's whiteness may make it easier for white viewers to identify with the person being oppressed. At the same time, by avoiding the use of a black actor/character to play this role, *TNG* maintains the "race-transcending" goal of racial harmony, if not species harmony. Oppression of blacks is thus represented through an intellectual construct rather than represented with visceral force; that intellectual construct, when examined, is pregnant with implication.

Data is also clearly marked as Other through his language use, just as African Americans often are. Again, as with the skin color, the representational connections are far from simplistic. Data's conversational style can hardly be called funky.[7] Data, whose command of scientific terminology is extensive, has, like Spock, difficulty with colloquial English (e.g., terms such as "snoop" ["Encounter at Farpoint"] or human figures of speech such as "needle in a haystack" ["The Naked Now"]). But as Sander L. Gilman (1985) points out in his study of the stereotyping of blacks and Jews, language difference stigmatizes the outsider (178). Data's speech marks him as different, but that speech is also markedly intellectual, rational. Thus, if Data is accepted as, in part, a representation of the oppressed African American, that representation binds up within it an antistereotypical intellectual marker (cf., e.g., Dyer 1989, 49). But there are more clear-cut indicators of Data's connection to African American experience than coloration and language.

A good example of Data in the role of the oppressed black man comes in the second-season episode "The Measure of a Man," which presents an Enterprise variation on the Dred Scott case. Data, the creation of the missing and presumed dead Dr. Noonian Soong, is the only known positronic android, and his construction is something of a mystery. A Starfleet scientist appears with orders to disassemble Data for study. The scientist,

Commander Bruce Maddox, hopes to produce myriads of Datas with the purpose of their "acting as our hands and eyes in dangerous situations," his use of synecdoche emphasizing his view of Data as less than a person.[8] Data refuses disassembly on the grounds that Maddox's procedure will destroy his individuality: The facts of his memory will be preserved in a "core dump," but as Data puts it, "the substance, the flavor of the moment could be lost." Although Maddox finds in Data's quarters a copy of Shakespeare marked at the very appropriate passage, "When in disgrace with fortune and men's eyes/I all alone beweep my outcast state . . . ," he doubts Data can "fathom the meaning" and persists in his view of Data as subhuman. Ordered to submit to the procedure, Data attempts to escape by resigning from Starfleet, telling Maddox, "I am not under yours, nor anyone else's, command." But Maddox counters that as a machine, Data has no right to resign: He is the "property" of Starfleet.

A trial ensues in which Picard defends Data's rights in spite of his admittedly different nature. In Jean Lorrah's (1990) *TNG* novel *Metamorphosis*, a character remarks to Data, "I want to understand you as *you*, not some imitation humanoid" (13); or, in other terms, the representative of African Americans does not have to be imitation white to be human. It must be admitted that, visually, Data is just that: imitation white human. Should that image, however, be deconstructed as an indicator of an embedded problem or seen instead as a *recognition* of that problem, that way of seeing? In any case, Picard has trouble seeing how to construct a case for this very different person until he consults the wise Enterprise bartender Guinan, who makes clear that the "comfortable, easy euphemism: property" is being used to disguise the true issue: slavery. Guinan states:

> Consider that in the history of many worlds there have always been disposable creatures. They do the dirty work. They do the work no one else wants to do because it's too difficult or too hazardous. [Imagine] an army of Datas, all disposable. You don't have to think about their welfare, you don't think about how they feel. Whole generations of disposable people.

Armed with this understanding, Picard returns to the trial to ask, "Are you prepared to condemn him and all who come after him to servitude and slavery?" and thus secures, at least temporarily, Data's "freedom to explore [the] question" of his own nature.

One of the reasons Picard and the crew of the Enterprise champion Data is their protective response to his "childlike" nature. "You see things with the wonder of a child," says Security Chief Lt. Tasha Yar. Data begins life on the Enterprise quite unversed in human interactions. The android's frequent questions about human behavior recapitulate the experience of a human child being socialized. For instance, like a child fascinated by procreation, he pelts out a string of questions for the very briefly very pregnant Counselor Lt. Commander Deanna Troi: "Are you able to access his thought processes? Does he have thoughts? You are aware of him. Is he aware of you? When does that awareness begin?" ("The Child"). And his attempts to expand his language abilities recreate the linguistic development of a child, with sometimes similarly humorous errors. That childlike nature itself, however, participates in the stereotype of the subjugated class. Seeing someone as a child means, among other things, seeing that person as subject to control; as Gilman (1985) points out, part of the stereotyping of blacks is to see them as children (37, 113–114, 142). David Desser (1991) further notes that the attribution of these "child-like behaviors ... ha[s] the ideological and political consequence of dehumanizing the subjects" (116). If Data never moved beyond that childlike image, one might propose Uncle Tom as his literary ancestor; but Uncle Tom does not participate in miscegenation. As will be seen later, Data's character is not restrained to bland innocence.

A crucial element in Data's nature is his presumed emotionlessness, and this supposed lack of feeling corresponds to his potential status as a slave. Historically, one rationalization for the poor treatment of the underclass is that their feelings are not as sensitive as those of the dominant class (Berzon 1978, 22). Dr. Katherine Pulaski, Chief Medical Officer during the second season, frequently challenges Data in terms of his machine nature, expressing scorn for his supposed insensitivity (Pulaski departs after one season; see Wilcox 1991, 55). In their first encounter, for example, Data objects to her "call[ing] him out of his name" (see Angelou 1969, 61), and she expresses doubt that there can be "a circuit for bruised feelings" ("The Child").

Nowhere is the correlation of emotionlessness with slavery more apparent than in the third-season episode "The Offspring," in which Data's child is, in effect, to be sold down the river. Data's first problem is the creation of a child at all: With Dr. Soong missing, no one knows how to reproduce a positronic brain. Data therefore secretly uses patterns of his own neural pathways to create another positronic android—"a new life out of his own being," as Troi observes, and one which Data regards as a child: He teaches the new android to call him "father." (Note that the title, "The Offspring," in contrast with "The Child," uses a term that does not necessarily indicate a human.) Though Data has declared on repeated occasions that he has no feelings, he, the being named for facts, chooses to name his child "Lal"— the Hindi word for "Beloved." When Picard chastises Data for engaging in this experiment without getting permission, Data replies, "I have not observed anyone else on board consulting you about their procreation, Captain." Picard gradually comes to see Data's point of view, but Starfleet headquarters does not. Like slave owners, the admiralty believe they have at least as much interest in the child as does the parent. In fact, they tell

Data and Picard that Lal is to be taken away, and Admiral Haftel sneers at Picard's suggestion that the experience would be traumatic: "Are we talking about breaking up a family? Isn't that a rather sentimental attitude about androids?" As James Kinney (1985) says, in the literature of miscegenation, "whites fail to understand that blacks share the same human feelings. . . . The lack of feeling allows the sale of [family members]" (80).[9]

Ironically, Lal's most interesting characteristic is that she does begin to develop human feelings in a way that puts her on the borderline between android and human. In fact, Lal is a representation of that essentially liminal character, the tragic mulatto, the product of miscegenation, the character between black and white (see Berzon 1978, 13–14 on the "marginality of the mulatto"). When Data creates his child, he allows her to make many choices about her own nature: She chooses her own sex and species (for example, she considers being a Klingon male). But one choice he makes for her: her skin color. Data enables Lal to "pass" as a human by giving her what he terms "more realistic skin and eye color than my own."[10] (Although he once changes skin tone for a spy mission ["Unification"], Data does not himself consider "passing" through modified skin color—perhaps, in effect, a type of racial assertiveness.) In a scene that provides a possible explanation for some of Data's own behavior, he also teaches Lal to "supplement her innate android behavior with simulated human responses" such as blinking—"passing" through actions as well as appearance. Lal is so successful that she is even involved in a brief, humorous flirtation with Riker, the Enterprise's first officer and resident Romeo, who has been away on leave and is stunned to learn that Lal is Data's daughter.

But like the typical tragic mulatto, Lal is not long for this world. Standard patterns of the tragic mulatto story involve the beautiful young mulatto woman being sold down the river and/or dying in the agony of the realization of her mulatto nature, either by suicide or some mysterious wasting illness.[11] Picard arranges for meetings between the androids and Admiral Haftel to convince him that they should not be separated, but the admiral does not want to keep her at her father's side; he wants to put her in her place. When she declares that he does not respect her father, Haftel replies, "I don't think your father has taught you selective judgment in the verbalization of your own thoughts. That is a skill we will help you develop." She must learn to talk nice to the white folks, and to teach her a lesson, the admiral will take her away from her father.[12] Data declares that he will not volunteer to give her up, and Picard vows to fight the order, reminding Haftel of Data's trial for his rights. However, the issue is rendered moot. Lal, in reaction to the climactic events, discovers fear: she experiences human emotion. The onset of emotion—certified by Troi, who can sense others' emotions—means that Lal has combined within herself the human and the android. She feels not only fear of the admiral but love for her father. Like the tragic mulatto, however, she cannot stand the shock of the knowledge of her own true nature and thus undergoes "total system failure."

As in the standard tragic mulatto story, Lal's character is made less threatening by being made female.[13] (A more rebellious male type of tragic mulatto [see Berzon 1978, 225] is found in Data's brother Lore, an unstable character who feels emotion but violently rejects humanity/whites). Females are also traditionally regarded as the depository of emotion, a pattern that clearly operates here. Lal (love), a female, is the Other to the male Data (knowledge), the unemotional father, as every child is both Other and Self to the parent. The issue of self-exploration through embracing the Other is brought up in an unusual way at the end of the episode "The Offspring." Those familiar with the *Star Trek* movies will know that at the point of death Spock transfers his katra, his "living spirit," his soul and memories, into the mind of his comrade, Senior Medical Officer Commander Leonard McCoy (*Star Trek III: The Search for Spock* [1984]). At the end of "The Offspring," after Lal's death, Data tells his sorrowing comrades, "I thank you for your sympathy, but—she is here [pointing to his head]. Her presence so enriched my life that I could not allow her to pass into oblivion. So I incorporated her programs back into my own. I have transferred her memories to me." This transfer is the android version of the passing of the *katra*, a highly spiritual experience. Because Lal had achieved emotion, one is left wondering whether the transfer might eventuate in some effect on Data.[14] In any case, this memory transfer is another step in Data's search to answer the question that his trial judge phrased: "Does Data have a soul?" This spiritual search is tied closely to the question of Data's status as a person, which is in turn tied to his representation of the racial Other.

The mulatto character's attempt to grapple with Self and Other is also represented at length in the two-part "Descent," the first part of which is the sixth-season-ending cliff-hanger. *TNG*, although much more unified than most television series, is still written by a variety of authors; and the writers of "Descent" present Data in a more condescending fashion than do any others. Whereas the first part of the episode is often moving, its next-season conclusion—perhaps as much for reasons of quick plot resolution as anything else—is atypically dehumanized in an uncritical fashion. In "Descent," the rebellious tragic mulatto android Lore takes on the role of racist demagogue, planning to destroy the Federation's "biological organisms," humanity—that is, whites. The episode is saturated with references to evolution, from the title on. It seems to propound what Dyer (1989) terms "evolutionism, the idea of a path of progress already followed by whites, but in this case open to all human beings. . . . [S]uch evolutionism raises the possibility of blacks becoming like whites" (51), or, in this case, of androids becoming like humans. That agenda, however, does not become obvious until the second part of the episode. The episode begins with a scene of Data playing poker with holographic images of three of history's greatest minds, including the real Dr. Stephen Hawking; poker has been, since *ST,* a sign of the intuitive nature of humanity (see Kirk versus Spock in "The Corbomite Maneuver"), and Data here cites it as "a useful forum for exploring the different facets of humanity," a humanity it is his goal to join. In the next scene Data apparently comes closer to doing so when he unequivocally displays strong emotion for the first time: As an immensely powerful cyborg warrior, a Borg, attempts to choke him to death, Data defends himself with fury. The measure of humanization accorded this response is clear in Data's sudden accession of colloquial, non-android speech (cf. Gilman 1985): "I got angry," he says in close-up.

For Data, such an event is the occasion for immediate self-examination, and he takes himself off duty in a fruitless attempt to research and recreate the emotion he felt in the presence of the Borg. Up until this point, the episode, in its endowment of Data with the humane mystery of emotion, is a powerful and optimistic, even if somewhat frightening, representation of the possibility of Data's recognition of human nature within himself. "Perhaps," he says to his friend La Forge, "I have *evolved* to the point where emotion is within my grasp" (emphasis added). Other episodes (discussed previously and later) advance the idea that Data already *has* emotions (i.e., humanity), unrecognized. But with the capture of the Borg warrior, we are shown the imprisoned Borg, Krosus, controlling Data emotionally through a green radiation emitted from his cyberarm. Although the source of Data's original emotionalism is ambiguous (was it provided by the Borg he battled? Perhaps, but Data was identified only during the course of that battle), Krosus is certainly emotionally manipulating Data by the time they secretly leave the Enterprise together, Data thus rejecting humanity/whites.

Data's marked whiteness and its complex of meanings has been discussed earlier; even whiter are those bearers of death, the Borg.[15] The Borg begin fictional life as a condemnation of white policies of "assimilation" (their term). In the well-known two-part episode "The Best of Both Worlds," they attempt to take over the Federation's various humanities, declaring every individual difference "irrelevant" and killing thousands in a grotesque attempt, as they put it, to "raise the quality of life," a harsh parody of white assimilationist and colonialist practices and an implicit endorsement of "race-cognizance" by contrast. In "Descent," however, their political significance has changed. Here, the Borg have become the disenfranchised underclass. In an earlier episode ("I, Borg"), a young Borg has been helped to self-awareness and individuality by La Forge, who has named him Hugh, simply a re-pronunciation of "you," the Other in relation to the I. Hugh has returned to the Borg collective in order to prevent their wreaking vengeance on the Enterprise, and in doing so he has conveyed to the other Borg, who are mentally joined, his sense of individuality—as the Enterprise personnel hoped he would. As Picard reports (in "Descent") to an authoritarian Starfleet admiral, "When Hugh was separated from the Borg collective, he began to grow—to *evolve* into something other than an automaton. He became a person. When that happened, I felt I had no choice but to respect his rights as an individual." Picard's position here is clearly endorsed, in opposition to that of the authoritarian admiral (a nasty female), who simply wants the Borg destroyed.

But freedom for this underclass, this episode suggests, is dangerous. With their new sense of individuality, their new "rights," the Borg become confused and fall under the sway of Lore, the android who, like Lal, unquestionably feels emotions and, therefore, is on the borderline of being human. In fact, Lore has (in an earlier episode) stolen a computer chip from his and Data's "father," Dr. Soong—a chip meant to give Data emotions, and with which Lore now controls Data along with this rebellious group of the Borg. Lore is presented as a charismatic and angry leader who fancies himself a prophet of pain, crudely evoking stereotypes of Malcolm X, and the Borg are displayed as misguided rabble; we see them muttering furiously and incoherently in large crowd scenes.[16] As Hugh, who refuses to join Lore (and yet leads his own literally underground group), later explains to Riker and Security Chief Lt. Worf, "You probably can't imagine what it's like to be so lost and frightened that you will listen to any voice that promises change." Lore's promise is of a future in which "the reign of biological life forms is coming to an end"; the control of the white power structure is to be ended, and, to that end, Lore espouses violence. Indeed, he demands it of Data, to prove his commitment to the cause. At this point, the borderline nature of the Borg themselves—half human, half machine—comes to the fore as Lore offers them "the promise of becoming a superior race—of becoming fully artificial." Lore, the mulatto figure, offers an appeal to racial purity.[17] But the Borg with the fully articulated voice, Hugh, rejects Lore's rabble-rousing; though he resents the situation in which the Enterprise has left his fellows, he is at last reluctantly willing to help the Federation interlopers for the sake of his individual, personal friendship with Geordi La Forge. The model for racial relationships is clear: the members of the underclass are to forgive the mistakes of the power structure and work with its representatives; the violent separatist is to be condemned.

Data is the figure on the border between the power structure and the separatists. Early in the show, Krosus asks Data, "If it meant that you could feel emotions again . . . would you kill Geordi?" And Data answers yes; he is willing to achieve emotions, the marker of humanity and freedom, "by any means necessary" (Malcolm X's words; Data's meaning). But instead of choosing independently, Data is shown as being acted upon, first by Lore and Krosus, then by La Forge and Picard. Lore disengages Data's "ethical program" (hence Data's willingness to use "any means necessary"; he has no conscience, we are being told), then uses Dr. Soong's chip to manipulate

Data with "negative emotions" such as anger. But in an even more dismaying mechanistic recuperation of Data, Picard and La Forge correct his behavior by the emission of a "Cadian pulse" from a stolen Borg part. The "pulse" is used to "reboot" Data's "ethical program." Despite the drug-like temptation of the emotions flowing from the chip, once Data's ethical program ("in essence . . . [his] conscience") is mechanically reactivated, Data refuses Lore's plans. But the refusal comes as the consequence of Data's passively receiving the emissions arranged by his traditional authority group. Data's major action is to deactivate Lore.

Furthermore, in first shooting down Lore, Data damages the emotional programming chip. Lore has earlier taunted Data by withdrawing some of the emotions flowing to him, the demagogue denying the subordinate his freedom. But in the last scene of the episode, Data denies himself. He starts to destroy the damaged chip so that he will never again risk harming his friend La Forge. La Forge, for his part, refuses to let Data destroy the chip, his chance at emotions, humanity, freedom, his "life-long dream." We have moved from the speeches of Malcolm X to those of Dr. Martin Luther King, Jr., from separatism to integration. But Dr. King, of course, condemned those who recommended interminable patience in the struggle to achieve that dream, whereas La Forge's final words present an unequivocal endorsement of painfully slow "evolutionism": he hands the damaged chip back to Data with the words, "Maybe. Someday. When you're ready."

The racialized discourse in which *TNG* participates is not uniformly legible; the mulatto figure, for example, is generally divorced from sexual generation. Though Lal displays many characteristics of the mulatto, she is made less threatening not only by being made female but also by being born asexually. For the android Data, procreation and sexual relationships with females are not physically related; yet both in their separate ways dramatize the confrontation of borders implicit in the construct "miscegenation." The depiction of Data's sexual relationships with females, however, is ultimately the most empowering presentation of miscegenation associated with the character. This empowerment may result partly from the fact that in the sexual context the series seems to acknowledge the problems (rather than, as it occasionally does elsewhere, attempting to overlook them, e.g. by "gentling" Data as infantile), and partly because the subject matter may impel or draw the pertinent episodes to deal with the character as an adult human.

The depictions of Data's relationships with women highlight his qualities as Other. Responses to these relationships can be seen as a litmus test of the progressiveness of the characters involved. When, for example, a young woman on an endangered planet is attracted to Data, the planet's leader, Gosheven, calls him her "toy," a "walking calculator" ("Ensigns of Command"). She responds to his denigrations of Data by declaring that she has no such "silly prejudice"—yet, in her first action on the screen, before even speaking to Data, she "test[s his] reflexes." The immense strength of androids is a trait they share with the stereotype of the slave, who is treated as an animal, a sexual beast.[18] When she and Data try to convince the population to oppose their leader's plans, Gosheven accuses Data of being a trouble-maker and, in effect, lynches him: he goes outside the community's professed standards to shoot and apparently kill Data, his justification being that he has "merely shut down a machine." Jane Gaines (1989) cites turn-of-the-century black novelist Pauline Hopkins on the widely held view that the specious fear of rape was used as an excuse for "lynching [which] was instituted to crush the manhood of the enfranchised black" (23–24); Data and those who agree with him are specifically disenfranchised by the dictatorial Gosheven, who refuses their political input. As lynching might result for the black man accused of kissing a white woman, Data is seemingly murdered after an alliance with a human woman who has kissed him; in both cases the ultimate goal is for the killer to retain political control.

Data does not normally pursue women but is pursued by them. In "The Schizoid Man," however, Data's mind and body are usurped by a dying cyberneticist, Dr. Ira Graves. Graves's posthumous pursuit, through Data, of the woman he loves brings into relief the connections made between Data's android nature and the stereotype of black sexual power and bestiality. The stereotype held by the grossly bigoted Graves is thus condemned by the episode. Graves, in the body of Data, tells his beloved, "I can love you now. The way I always wanted to. It was not right before. I was too old for you. Too weak. Now I can be everything you want me to be." The woman responds not with love for Graves or concern for Data but with revulsion at the idea of the machine. Suddenly realizing her perspective, the scientist in the body of Data is aghast; and when he next confronts Picard, his own revulsion shows in his comment: "I can hear you coming, Captain. My ears are better than the average dog's, you know." Graves has considered Data as less than human; so, for that matter, has he considered women (he declares, "Women aren't people"). In an allusion repeated throughout the series, Graves whistles the Tin Man's song "If I Only Had a Heart" in mockery of Data; he assumes that he merely needs to deposit his heart in Data's soulless body. Instead, two personalities reside in the schizoid man. And Graves, the dead white male who has rendered Data unconscious and become the dominant personality, is less successful as a person than Data: He misuses Data's great strength even to the point of physically harming his love object. Realizing her pain and his own failure, he finally accepts that, as Picard states, "No being is so important that he can usurp the rights of another."

Whereas outsiders frequently respond to relations between Data and women in terms of simple miscegenational stereotypes, his standing within the Enterprise crew is a more complicated matter. The central sexual relationship for Data is with Yar. Data delivers his reference to

Shylock's "Hath not a Jew eyes" speech in "The Naked Now" soon after
he and Yar make love, at Yar's invitation. Yar, the security chief of the starship, is a slender, beautiful woman with short blonde hair. Under the influence of an infectious intoxicant, she tells Data of her abandonment as a
child and her pursuit by rape gangs—her treatment as an object by other
humans. Now she asks for "gentleness, and joy, and love—from you, Data.
You are fully functional, aren't you?" Data's at first solemn then smiling
response, also under the influence of the intoxicant, shows a pleasure to be
found in none of his other relationships with women. As Gilman (1985)
points out, "Human sexuality, given its strong biological basis, not unnatu-
rally is often perceived as out of control of the self" (24). Hence, Data's
encounter with Yar seems more human because of his intoxication, his
being out of control. The happy pratfall mentioned earlier presents, in sympathetic fashion, a proudly postcoital Data cheerfully falling down drunk.

   The circumstances would seem to suggest that Data has more of feeling
than he himself is aware of—as many Enterprise characters suggest from
time to time, including Crusher, who "find[s it] hard to believe" Data does
not love Lal ("The Offspring"). Furthermore, the idea that Data is *really*
unemotional—really less than human—is constantly undermined by the
quiet expressiveness of actor Brent Spiner. Data's experience with Yar is a
pivotal one. She knows him and wants him for exactly what he is. It is also
true that when sobriety returns, Yar informs Data that "it never happened," and indeed never refers to the incident again. "The Naked Now"
establishes sexual pairings for other members of the crew as well (Crusher
with Picard, Riker with Troi)—and, in the well-known television tradition
of "sexual tension," none of these relationships is openly pursued.
Furthermore, Yar's repudiation of Data may be considered simply the result
of professional insecurity, especially given that Yar is a young female security chief. But her vehemence might also result from embarrassment at having a relationship with an android, that is, a member of another race.
Despite her denial of the relationship, however, viewers schooled in *ST*'s
precedent of "The Naked Time" would assume that "The Naked Now"
lays bare the true nature of the relationship between Data and Yar.

   When Yar dies in the line of duty, her posthumous holographic message
to her crewmates is constructed as a series of brief assessments of the essential natures of her friends: She declares that Data is "more human than any
of us" ("Skin of Evil").[19] Data is left standing in contemplation after the
others slowly depart the funeral, his lonely figure the final image in the
episode of Yar's death. From this point on Yar assumes the status of a
Petrarchan heroine in the life of the supposedly unfeeling android. She is
raised—or reduced—to the level of icon (Wilcox 1991, 62). Though she is
dead, her inspiring image appears at moments of conflict, especially those
moments that involve questions of miscegenation and personhood. In "The
Schizoid Man," Yar's picture is part of a psychological test that determines

the true Data as a separate nature from the invading Dr. Graves. In "The Measure of a Man," the sonnet "When in disgrace with fortune and men's eyes" is discovered in Data's quarters immediately after Data privately contemplates a small holographic image of Yar. Of course, the loudly unspoken lines of the sonnet are "Haply I think on thee . . . / For thy sweet love remembered such wealth brings / That then I scorn to change my state with kings" (Shakespeare, 1609). In fact, it is Yar's death that qualifies her for Petrarchan status; she has become literally unattainable, in perfect parallel to Data's often-expressed desire to become human. But his relationship with her repeatedly serves to confirm his essential personhood. Later in the same episode, during Data's trial, Picard asks why Data carries the portrait of Yar and no other. When after some urging Data explains, "She was special to me. We were . . . intimate," the judge's face reveals obvious shock. As Kinney (1985) states, "Miscegenation can be viewed as the ultimate manifestation of equality" (159); and in this trial to prove that Data is more than subhuman his relationship with Yar is significant evidence.

The implications of Data's coloration create an interesting effect in this context. Gaines (1989) points out

> that, since a black male character is not allowed the position of control occupied by a white male character, race could be a factor in the construction of cinematic language. More work on looking and racial taboos might determine whether or not mainstream cinema can offer the male spectator the pleasure of looking at a white female character via the gaze of a black male character. (24)

More than any other episode, "The Measure of a Man" presents Data as standing for African Americans; yet we *see* a white face contemplating Yar's blonde beauty. One might argue that the idea of "miscegenation . . . as . . . equality" of races is thus pictorially weakened. In contrast, Michele Wallace (1990), quoting Eldridge Cleaver's *Soul on Ice* ("I know that the white man made the white woman the symbol of freedom"), expresses a black feminist's distaste for black male desire for the white woman (23). Had an African American actor portrayed Data, his focus on the blonde Yar might call up the disapproval of those who share Wallace's view. So *TNG*'s representation of the miscegenational relationship between Data and Yar imagistically spares viewers the cause of Wallace's complaint. Perhaps this concatenation of image (Data as white) and narrative symbology (Data as African American) makes it easier, in theory, for viewers of various leanings to converge (accepting relationship with Other).

The image of Yar appears indirectly in the episode "In Theory," wherein Data unsuccessfully attempts to pursue a romance. The issue of miscegenation is touched upon lightly, though the theme of objectification versus per-

sonhood is central to the episode. A young lieutenant who has been working with Data gives him, as he informs Guinan with a wonderfully ambiguous modifier, "a passionate kiss in the torpedo bay." Data, with typical
naïvete, consults all his friends to decide on his response, and in this
humorous segment, the serious idea of the difficulty of an interracial relationship is implied. The psychologist Troi reminds him that being friends
with a human is much easier than pursuing a romance, and again, the parallel with black-white relationships is clear. However, unlike some nonregu-
lar characters, the regulars on *TNG* endorse Data's relationship with a
human, the consensus being that he and the woman, Ensign Jenna D'sora,
have the right to choose the risk.

Unfortunately, Data's relationship with D'sora does not work: As she confesses at the end of the episode, she is following a pattern of seeking out a certain type of man—an unemotional one. She has treated Data as an object in a
way that men and women often do, and he attempts to live up to her expectations rather than simply being himself. Not surprisingly, Data's inhuman
responses are humorously and painfully highlighted in the episode. He programs his responses to D'sora from his study of literature, though Troi tells
him, "Ultimately Jenna will care for you for who you are—not what you imi-
tate out of a book." But Data bases the relationship on imitation, even going
so far as to echo D'sora's perky vocal tone on occasion. And any man who
has ever used a prefabricated line is rendered ridiculous by Data's artificial
suavity: "Darling, you remain as aesthetically pleasing as the first day we
met. I believe I am the most fortunate sentient in this sector of the galaxy."
This reification of romance, however, is as much a human as an android trait:
D'sora, too, has been programmed to see the relationship in a stereotypical
way. She is no more genuinely relating to the Other than is Data. From the
beginning of the episode, where D'sora sees the explosions of a scientific
experiment as "fireworks,"[20] to the end, when Data blows out the candle for
their uneaten "romantic" dinner, stereotypical images are exposed.

The episode's adventure plot, which (as often happens in *TNG*) parallels
and explicates the plot of personal relationships, also undercuts the
romance.[21] "In Theory" depicts a mysterious force causing increasingly
larger disruptions on the Enterprise. Picard humorously suggests that there
may be a poltergeist, a playful spirit, and the audience is shown the walls to
Data's quarters temporarily dissolving as D'sora passes by. Is the mysterious force somehow connected with the woman who attempts to bring to
Data the force of love? The theoretically unfeeling Data is the only officer
who keeps a pet—a cat, a symbol of animal passion, who is released (escaping from Data's quarters) because of the mysterious force and is repeatedly
referred to during Data's encounters with D'sora, including a plot-turning
kiss. Will Data's metaphorical walls be breached? No, the disruptions are
caused by "dark matter" creating what Data describes as "gaps in the fabric of . . . space." D'sora has no secret force, and in fact the whole episode

has been devoted to the discovery of emptiness, whether in space or human relationships.

If D'sora has objectified Data by pursuing her standard male object—the replacement for her missing father—Data seems to have made the same poignant mistake. In a relationship based on imitation, D'sora is an imitation Tasha Yar. Like Yar, D'sora is a slim blonde. For much of the episode, she wears her long hair in a fashion that makes it appear as short as Yar's; she tells of the loss of her father as Yar has described her abandonment; she even briefly commands Yar's bridge station. In his quest for human nature, Data pursues the image of the unattainable woman. While Data protests that he has no "human emotions" (note the adjective), the effect of the episode is to make him seem more human even in his failure to relate, especially in the context of the intervening image of Yar. Although on the surface it may seem that the relationship fails because it is the equivalent to an interracial encounter, it may instead fail because Data is more human than even he realizes.[22] And a successful relationship is not found in external characteristics—blonde, beautiful, white.

The image of Yar appears more directly in "The Most Toys," an episode in which Data is temporarily enslaved. A shady intergalactic merchant, Kevas Fazio, arranges to have Data apparently blown up so that the Enterprise crew will suspect nothing when Fazio secretly traps Data for his private museum of unique collectibles. Here Data has become not a sex object but an art object—again, however, property. The collector uses both physical and psychological torture, turning Data's highest ideals into a tool to enslave him; Fazio forces Data to cooperate by threatening to kill Varya, a woman whom the collector has owned for fourteen years, and who, like Data, is stigmatized, in her case by scars.[23] But Data's resistance inspires Varya to attempt to escape, and she forms an alliance with the android. Meanwhile, on the Enterprise, Data's best friend La Forge—played by LeVar Burton, the star of *Roots* and so an extratextual allusion to slavery in himself—is dissatisfied with the record of Data's death and slowly discovers the truth. As Data and Varya attempt to escape, Fazio kills Varya and warns Data that he will only kill someone else every time Data tries to regain his freedom. While Data holds a gun on him, Fazio taunts the android with his lack of free will—though Data can shoot in self-defense, he is programmed by his creator with "fundamental respect for all living beings"[24]—so Fazio believes Data will neither shoot him nor choose freedom at the cost of other lives:

> Their blood will be on your hands, too, just like poor Varya's. Your only alternative [to slavery], Data, is to fire. Murder me. If only you could feel rage over Varya's death. If only you could feel the need for revenge, then maybe you could fire. But you're just an android. You can't feel anything, can you?

The firing of the gun becomes a symbol of the expression of passion. Data has once before helplessly watched a woman be killed: Tasha Yar. The connection is made when La Forge finds the holograph of Yar among the supposedly dead Data's effects. In the episode of Yar's death, the normally pacifistic Data says to her killer, "I think you should be destroyed." Now, with Fazio, Data says, "I cannot permit this to continue." Data fires on Fazio.

The episode does not conclude, however, with a simple phallic explosion, a shoot-em-up solution. At the instant Data fires, the Enterprise, which has arrived at La Forge's urging, transports Data back; the transporter chief disarms the weapon in transport. The ideal world of the Enterprise intervenes to prevent the consequences of Data's action. But Data not only fires, he lies about it—though Data is usually as honest as a Vulcan: "Perhaps something happened during transport," he says, which is certainly true, but hardly the truth. In this speech to Riker, a representative of the white male power structure, Data equivocates, maintaining the privacy of an experience that his friend, the first officer, might not understand and for which Data might be condemned by Starfleet legalities. The border between African American private lives and the dominant culture is here evoked. One must also wonder whether Data lies again in the episode's closing scene. He goes to the Enterprise brig to visit Fazio, who tells him, "Our roles are reversed. . . . I'm in a cage. . . . It must give you great pleasure." Data replies, "No, sir, it does not. I do not feel pleasure. I am only an android." The echo of Fazio's taunt, "You're just an android," provides a chillingly ambiguous conclusion. What was Data's motive for visiting the imprisoned Fazio? Does the final scene display Data's tragic confrontation with his own inability to feel? Did Data act with pure logic, to reduce the number of deaths? Or does the Yar-Varya parallel imply some kind of unrecognized emotional involvement? In his denial of emotion, does Data lie to Fazio, or to himself, or to no one?

The episode suggests Data's Adamic fall from innocence to sin in response to a woman and the devilish Fazio.[25] But Data's fall, like Adam's, brings him closer to the realm of ordinary human existence. To use Cornel West's (1993) term, Data has here claimed "the freedom to err" (3). He is no simple child or sinless creature. This presentation of what might be called a "Fortunate Fall" (because of its implication that Data is fully human) is in clear contrast to the name and structure of the episode titled "Descent," in which Data must recover from his fall, his descent, to recapture childlike innocence, untainted by adult sin or sexuality, by even a hint of miscegenation. Furthermore, Data's fall in "The Most Toys" establishes his free will in spite of his creator's ordained plan. The ethical dilemma results in his going beyond the predictable limits of his programming. Thus Data's normal virtue is shown to be more than mere programming; it is also the result of experience and choice. Here he chooses his own freedom over the life of the unequivocally evil slave owner Fazio. As consistently happens in the presence of Yar's image, Data's human rights are reasserted.

Still, Data's child self-destructs; Data's violence dissipates in transport; Data's lover ascends into the empyrean (a.k.a. the Romulan Empire):[26] The ultimate confrontation is always avoided. It might seem that the series practices the evasions of traditional literary miscegenation: the mulatto conveniently dies, the violence is self-directed, the acceptable interracial lover must be foreign, an alien, of course (Kinney 1985, 41). But Data's character has a nontraditional element that, instead of avoiding the conflict, deepens it. Given Data's inhuman android calm, the mere possibility of the arousal of emotion in him implies the seriousness of the cause— whether it is the injustice of Fazio or the inspiration of Yar.

The character of Data is a complex and multiply signifying creation. Elements of his nature taken to represent not racial concerns but dehumanization in general—treating others as machine rather than human—may have generated the comment reported by Brent Spiner that Data "is becoming more and more human, but Gene [Roddenberry] says he'll never make it. . . . He is a character who makes a journey" ("Trekkie" 1991, 8), a quest for truer humanity shared by many *Star Trek* viewers. That journey, however, when applied not strictly to Data as Machine Other but also to Data as Racial Other, has been represented in some episodes (notably in "Descent") as a condescending, slow-paced "evolutionism." But the construction of the *TNG* world—placing Data's struggles in the context of equality already achieved for those such as his black friend La Forge and the multiple implications of Data's coloration showing the potential for whiteness marked as Other even while alluding to blackness—prevent a simple "evolutionist" interpretation of the text overall. Furthermore, the actor's careful reading of the character, necessarily providing emotional nuance, suggests the idea of a person who, though emotionally cool, is only perceived as unemotional (by himself as well as others), rather than being truly emotionless, inhuman, unfree. The ethical chiaroscuro accorded the character of Data in episodes such as "The Most Toys" resists the condescension of the traditional miscegenation paradigm. And because the ability to embrace the Other (*Star Trek*'s essential credo) means the ability to become wholly Self, the choice to combine with Data paradoxically means resistance to dehumanization no less than Data's choice to combine with "humanity." But in television's perpetuity, Data stands forever poised on the margin, trapped in the transporter beam as he fires across the line from slavery to freedom, from emotionless isolation to forbidden sexual union.

Notes

Adapted from material previously published in *Extrapolation* and *The Mid-Atlantic Almanack*.

1. See Sander L. Gilman (1985, 126), Mary V. Dearborn (1986, 4, 102, 158), and Judith R. Berzon (1978, 218–235) on the search for identity in the literature of miscegenation.

2. Chekov was "expressly added in the second season" to improve the picture of "the happy human family in miniature" (Buxton 1990, 67).

3. Cf. Cornel West's (1993) term "race-transcending *prophets*" (42; emphasis added).

4. See Asimov's (1950) *I, Robot* with its master-slave relationships.

5. On the Spock/Data parallel, see Rhonda V. Wilcox (1991, 54–55).

6. One exception to the lack of special complexion indicators is the death-white pallor (cf. Dyer 1989, 59–63) for white actor Ted Cassidy (known for his role as Lurch in *The Addams Family* series) in the *ST* episode "What Are Little Girls Made Of?" His character's rebellion from servitude forecasts themes for Data.

7. See Michele Wallace (1990) on black language as deconstruction.

8. Maddox is associated with the Daystrom Institute—a name that *Star Trek* fans would connect with the creator of the M–5 computer in the *ST* episode "The Ultimate Computer." The computer attempts to take over Kirk's Enterprise and goes mad in the process. The reference is both ominous and ironic—ominous for Data because of Daystrom's failure with the experimental computer mind, and ironic because the *TNG* episode will defend the individuality of Data's unique machine brain rather than destroy it. Data's daughter Lal is later threatened with being sent to the Daystrom Annex ("The Offspring").

9. See also Gilman (1985, 202).

10. See Dearborn (1986, 155) and Kinney (1985, 117) on the "ambivalence" and "agony," respectively, of passing in miscegenation literature. On passing in general, see Berzon (1978, 141–159).

11. These patterns are discussed by Berzon (1978, 5, 99–100, 102, 104), Dearborn (1986, 140), and Kinney (1985, 10, 28, 30, 63–64, 96, 108, 117).

12. Mary Prince (1831), in her nineteenth-century narrative *The History of Mary Prince, A West Indian Slave*, details the Byzantine excuses advanced by white slave owners, when challenged, for the separation of slave families (passim, esp. 208–214, 217, 220–224).

13. Berzon (1978) points out that "the tragic mulatto is usually a woman" (99).

14. The question of memories as a basis of personhood has already been touched on in "The Measure of a Man." The *ST* episode "Requiem for Methuselah" presents in abbreviated form the calculated bringing of an android, Reena, to emotional life. This android also dies as a result of gaining emotion (see Blair 1983, 292–293). In the *ST* episode "What Are Little Girls Made Of?" two androids who seem to have just learned emotions die pressing a phaser during their first kiss.

15. See Dyer (1989) on the whiteness of the *Night of the Living Dead* (1968) zombies (59–63).

16. Cf. Dyer's (1989) discussion of the Mau-Mau meeting in *Simba* (1955, 49–51).

17. Cf. West (1993, 103) on Malcolm X's white grandparent.

18. Judith B. Kerman (1991, 22). On blacks as sexual beasts, see Lawrence J. Friedman (1970, 109), Gilman (1985, 83), and Kinney (1985, 151, 166–168, 172, 176–177).

19. Cf. Kirk's eulogy of Spock: "Of all the souls I have encountered in my travels, his was the most human" (*Star Trek II: The Wrath of Khan* [1982]). The funeral setting for both remarks emphasizes the seriousness of the assessments.

20. Cf. the "much-imitated fireworks scene" of *To Catch a Thief* (1955) (Maltin 1986, 1004).

21. On *TNG*, adventure plots parallel personal plots; see Wilcox (1991, 59–60).

22. Lorrah (1989, 1990, respectively) in her *TNG* novels *Survivors* and *Metamorphosis* investigates the relationship between Yar and Data as a humanistic encounter of beings who have trouble accepting their own natures. In her interpretation, Data unquestionably has emotions (see, e.g., 1989, 27), though his different nature is also maintained—in essence, a "race-cognizant" interpretation (see, e.g., 1990, 13). I wish here to note, without attempting to investigate fully, the interrelatedness of *Star Trek*'s various-media texts; cf. Jane Feuer (1992) on multiplicity and hierarchy of texts in "Reading *Dynasty.*"

23. Cf. Irwin Katz's 1981 discussion of blacks and the disabled (esp. 2–5).

24. Cf. Asimov's (1950) First Law of Robotics: "A robot may not injure a human being or, through inaction, allow a human being to come to harm" (frontispiece).

25. Varya testifies to Fazio's unadulterated evil, saying: "He has no moral problems [i.e., scruples] at all"; he is shown to be greedy, sadistic, murderous, and extremely untruthful—a "father of lies," i.e., a devil.

26. Beginning with the end of the fourth season ("The Minds [sic] Eye," "Redemption"), Denise Crosby appears as the Romulan commander Sela, claiming to be, as a result of a time distortion ("Yesterday's Enterprise"), the daughter of the dead Tasha Yar. To this new version of Yar, Data becomes a nemesis ("Redemption," "Unification"); traditionally, such a relationship in drama is often transmuted to romance. In either case, Data is pointedly made Yar/Sela's Other.

References

Angelou, Maya. 1969. *I Know Why the Caged Bird Sings*. New York: Random.

Asimov, Isaac. 1950. *I, Robot*. New York: Gnome P.

Berzon, Judith R. 1978. *Neither White nor Black: The Mulatto Character in American Fiction*. New York: New York U P.

Blair, Karin. 1983. "Sex and *Star Trek*." *Science-Fiction Studies* 10.2: 292–297.

Buxton, David. 1990. *From* The Avengers *to* Miami Vice: *Form and Ideology in Television Series*. Manchester, NY: Manchester U P.

Carey, Diane. 1988. *Ghost Ship*. New York: Pocket.

Davis, Ivor. 25 Nov. 1990. "Patrick Stewart Boldly Goes Where No Man Has Gone Before." *Macon Telegraph*: TV Teletime 3+.

Dearborn, Mary V. 1986. *Pocahontas's Daughters: Gender and Ethnicity in American Culture*. New York: Oxford U P.

Desser, David. 1991. "Race, Space, and Class: The Politics of the SF Film from *Metropolis* to *Blade Runner."* In *Retrofitting* Blade Runner: *Issues in Ridley Scott's* Blade Runner *and Philip K. Dick's* Do Androids Dream of Electric Sheep? Ed. Judith B. Kerman. Bowling Green, OH: Bowling Green State U Popular P. 110–123.

Dyer, Richard. 1989. "White." *Screen* 29.4: 44–64.

Feuer, Jane. 1992. "Reading *Dynasty*: Television and Reception Theory." In *Classical Hollywood Narrative: The Paradigm Wars.* Ed. Jane Gaines. Durham, NC: Duke U P. 274–293.

Francavilla, Joseph. 1991. "The Android as Doppelganger." In *Retrofitting* Blade Runner: *Issues in Ridley Scott's* Blade Runner *and Philip K. Dick's* Do Androids Dream of Electric Sheep? Ed. Judith B. Kerman. Bowling Green, OH: Bowling Green State U Popular P. 4–15.

Frankenberg, Ruth. 1993. *White Women, Race Matters: The Social Construction of Whiteness.* Minneapolis: U of Minnesota P.

Friedman, Lawrence J. 1970. *The White Savage: Racial Fantasies in the Postbellum South.* Englewood Cliffs, NJ: Prentice.

Gaines, Jane. 1989. "White Privilege and Looking Relations: Race and Gender in Feminist Film Theory." *Screen* 29.4: 12–27.

Gerrold, David. 1987. *Encounter at Farpoint.* New York: Pocket.

Gilman, Sander L. 1985. *Difference and Pathology: Stereotypes of Sexuality, Race, and Madness.* Ithaca: Cornell U P.

Greenberg, Harvey. 1984. "In Search of Spock: A Psychoanalytic Inquiry." *Journal of Popular Film and Television* 12.2: 53–65.

Katz, Irwin. 1981. *Stigma: A Social Psychological Analysis.* Hillsdale, NJ: Lawrence Erlbaum.

Kerman, Judith B. 1991. "Technology and Politics in the *Blade Runner* Dystopia." *Retrofitting* Blade Runner: *Issues in Ridley Scott's* Blade Runner *and Philip K. Dick's* Do Androids Dream of Electric Sheep? Ed. Judith B. Kerman. Bowling Green, OH: Bowling Green State U Popular P. 16–24.

Kinney, James. 1985. *Amalgamation! Race, Sex, and Rhetoric in the Nineteenth-Century American Novel.* Contributions in Afro-American Studies, No. 90. Westport, CT: Greenwood.

Lamb, Patricia Frazer, and Diana L. Veith. 1986. "Romantic Myth, Transcendence, and *Star Trek* Zines." In *Erotic Universe: Sexuality and Fantastic Literature.* Ed. Donald Palumbo. New York: Greenwood. 235–255.

Lorrah, Jean. 1989. *Survivors.* New York: Pocket.

———. 1990. *Metamorphosis.* New York: Pocket.

Maltin, Leonard. 1986. *Leonard Maltin's TV Movies and Video Guide.* New York: Signet.

Prince, Mary. 1831. "The History of Mary Prince, A West Indian Slave." In *The Classic Slave Narratives.* Ed. Henry Louis Gates, Jr. New York: Mentor/Penguin, 1987. 183–242.

Shakespeare, William. 1600. *The Merchant of Venice.* Ed. Brents Stirling. In *William Shakespeare: The Complete Works.* The Pelican Text. Rev. ed. Ed. Alfred Harbage. New York: Viking, 1969. 211–242.

———. 1609. Sonnet 29. *Shakespeare's Sonnets.* Ed. Douglas Bush. In *William Shakespeare: The Complete Works.* The Pelican Text. Rev. ed. Ed. Alfred Harbage. New York: Viking, 1969. 1458.

Taylor, Clyde. 1989. "The Master Text and the Jeddi [sic] Doctrine." *Screen* 29.4: 96–104.

"Trekkie: Spock He's Not, Data Either: *Next Generation* Actor Loves the Human Aspects of His Android Character." 4 Aug. 1991. *Atlanta Journal/Constitution*: TV Week 8.

Tyrrell, Wm. Blake. 1977. "*Star Trek* as Myth and Television as Mythmaker." *Journal of Popular Culture* 10.4: 711–719.

Wallace, Michele. 1990. *Invisibility Blues: From Pop to Theory*. London: Verso.

West, Cornel. 1993. *Race Matters*. Boston: Beacon.

Wilcox, Rhonda V. 1991. "Shifting Roles and Synthetic Women in *Star Trek: The Next Generation*." *Studies in Popular Culture* 13.2: 53–65.

Part Two

Manufacturing
Hegemonies

Cyborgs in Utopia

The Problem of Radical Difference in
Star Trek: The Next Generation

KATRINA G. BOYD

> I wonder if the Emperor Honorius watching the
> Visigoths coming over the seventh hill truly realized
> the Roman Empire was about to fall. . . . Will this be
> the end of our civilization?
> —**Picard, contemplating an impending Borg attack**[1]

The cyborg alien invaders, the Borg, pose an extreme narrative danger because they embody a postmodern vision of radical difference that threatens to exceed the bounds of *Star Trek: The Next Generation*'s *(TNG)* utopian future, circumscribed as it is by nineteenth-century humanist assumptions. *TNG* constructs its utopian future by drawing on a nineteenth-century faith in progress, human perfectibility, and expanding frontiers. At least within the Federation, technology, social planning, and the march of history have triumphed over poverty, injustice, and alienation. From a postmodern vantage point, this vision of continuous technological progress leading to a unified utopian state has turned out to be, as Fredric Jameson (1982) suggests in "Progress versus Utopia," "merely the future of one moment of what is now our own past" (151). *TNG*'s utopia depends on a particular constellation of concepts—progress, perfection, and social harmony—that all revolve around essentialist definitions of the self and of human nature. Because these essentialist notions efface differences between peoples, classes, and genders, *TNG* has difficulty addressing contemporary issues of radical difference.

The nexus of meanings hovering around the idea of "utopia" and *TNG*'s complex relationship to those meanings make this show particularly appropriate for an ideological approach. "Utopia," in its narrow sense, is associated with the creation of alternative social systems, whether they are to serve as imagined spaces for a comparative critique of contemporary societies or as blueprints for social change. *TNG* adopts the particularly nineteenth-century concept of utopia, based on "the eradication of conflict, crime and misery, and the creation of social harmony" (Goodwin 1978, 2). In a broader sense, "utopia" is related to more abstract longings for something different, with "the sense that things could be better, that something other than what is can be imagined and maybe realized" (Dyer 1977, 177). Richard Dyer (1977) has suggested that the appeal of all entertainment lies in the way it offers "utopian solutions" to real needs and social longings created by capitalist society, providing images of abundance, energy, and community to counter actual problems of scarcity, exhaustion, and fragmentation. But entertainment also delimits what constitutes "legitimate needs," containing utopian longing within an ideological framework (183–184). *TNG* not only has the utopian appeal characteristic of "entertainment" in general but is also utopian in the narrow sense of the term. In *TNG* the marvels of technology suggest an atmosphere of plenty, the adventurous exploration of space creates excitement, and the crew forms a harmonious community. In short, *TNG* attempts to deal with contemporary issues, using the type of estrangement typical of science fiction, but does so largely within the confines of a modified nineteenth-century utopian imagination.

Tom Moylan (1986) suggests that the literary utopias of the 1970s and 1980s are widely recognized as more open and less totalizing than their nineteenth-century predecessors: "In preserving the expression of otherness and radical difference, the critical utopias of recent years hold open the activity of the utopian imagination while also being fully aware that the figures of any one utopian society are doomed to ideological closure and compromise" (36). From these utopias, Donna Haraway (1985) draws the image of the cyborg to use as a metaphor for a fragmentary, "postmodernist identity" constructed out of "otherness, difference, and specificity" (155). Recognizing that the "social and historical constitution [of] gender, race and class cannot provide the basis for belief in 'essential' unity," Haraway conceives of a "cyborg world" with its "permanently partial identities and contradictory standpoints" (154–155). The cyborg confounds the boundary between human and machine, subverting the dualisms of Western colonial culture, such as male/female, mind/body, culture/nature, and whole/part. Although *TNG* explicitly deals with many of the concepts involved in the "new" postmodern "networks" that Haraway discusses, the transformations that the Borg undergo during their six appearances on the show reveal the difficulty of representing radical difference in a humanist utopia dependent on nineteenth-century essentialist notions of the "self" and human nature.

In this chapter I will first examine *TNG*'s complex relation to the nineteenth century in terms of direct references and appropriations. Next, I will consider how *TNG* centers its utopia on a nineteenth-century essentialist definition of human nature, building that utopia on faith in perfection, progress, social evolution, and free will. I will demonstrate how this utopian vision relates to *TNG*'s multiculturalist attitude, which ultimately downplays differences by suggesting that they are superficial and only mask fundamental similarities. Having explained how *TNG* typically deals with the "other," I will then proceed to consider how the problem of radical difference is engaged directly when the Enterprise encounters the Borg. Although *TNG*'s Borg are a far cry from Haraway's cyborgs, they are still a considerable threat to the show's humanist utopia.

Back to the Future: Recuperating the Nineteenth-Century Imagination

In an era when liberal humanism is continuously under attack by the far right, *TNG* strikes a careful balance between its acceptance of other cultures and a recuperation of our own cultural past. Captain Jean-Luc Picard's pseudo-Victorian fantasy of a happy home life as *paterfamilias* in the motion picture *Star Trek: Generations* (1994) is a recent example of *TNG*'s obsession with the nineteenth century. *TNG* makes many references to nineteenth-century figures (Mark Twain, William James, Charles Dickens) and characters (Sherlock Holmes, Cyrano de Bergerac, Scrooge). These overt references are reinforced by the show's championing of a humanist perspective originating in the late nineteenth century, even when dealing with the twentieth century. For example, in "Descent: Part I," when Lt. Commander Data plays cards with holograms of Isaac Newton, Albert Einstein, and contemporary physicist Stephen Hawking, the scene is in keeping with a nineteenth-century view that a series of Great Minds create continual progress in the sciences and that Great Men generate history. The show also presents education in the nineteenth-century humanist mold. We learn that Starfleet Academy supports the humanities in ways even contemporary universities no longer do, requiring the study of Latin and ancient philosophies.[2] *TNG* actually presents culture as less problematic than it has been in recent years. The overall impression is that high culture won out over low/mass culture. The canon is intact again and cultural artifacts give a neutral, timeless, unproblematic representation of what it means to be human. As Picard tells Data, "You are here to learn about the human condition and there is no better way of doing that than by embracing Shakespeare" ("The Defector"). Besides coinciding with the 1980s backlash against multicultural curricula,[3] *TNG*'s overt references to nineteenth-century cultural attitudes point toward the show's attempt to reclaim the humanist imagination of that period from charges of complicity in oppressive practices.

The two-part episode "Time's Arrow" nicely reveals *TNG*'s complicated relationship to the nineteenth century. The episode simultaneously pays homage to the ideals of the period while reconstructing the past to fit a utopian future. The action-adventure plot still leaves time for Samuel Clemens to muse about the nature of "Man" and the possibility of progress at a literary *salon* in late nineteenth-century San Francisco. Twain discusses the discoveries of geology that suggest the insignificance of Man with respect to both the age of Earth and the number of planets in the universe. As an alien visiting Earth in disguise, Guinan voices the more optimistic view that humanity is special, even if not "unique." Although this is supposedly a young Guinan, unaware that she will eventually work alongside humans as the bartender on the Enterprise, her statements carry special weight because we know her fate and humanity's. Twain's doubts, however, are assuaged neither by this encounter nor by meeting those Enterprise crewmembers who have traveled into the past. Twain continuously proclaims his fears about progress. When he actually ventures into the future he is full of questions about Starfleet's technological advances and its moral position. He accuses the Enterprise of being a ship of "military conquest" and remarks that its claim to be a "vessel of exploration" in search of "new worlds" echoes the words of past conquerors. Seeing an alien crew member walk by, Twain assumes that the "blue skinned fellow" has been captured as a slave. Counselor Lt. Commander Deanna Troi explains:

Tr: He is one of the thousands of species that we have encountered. We live in a peaceful Federation with most of them. The people you see are here by *choice*.

Tw: So there are a privileged few who serve on these ships, living in luxury and wanting for nothing. But what about everybody else? What about the poor? You ignore them.

Tr: Poverty was eliminated on Earth a long time ago and a lot of other things disappeared with it: hopelessness, despair, cruelty.

Tw: Young lady, I come from a time when men achieve power and wealth by standing on the backs of the poor, where prejudice and intolerance are commonplace and power is an end unto itself, and you are telling me that isn't how it is anymore?

Tr: [Nodding] That's right.

Despite the vagueness of Troi's explanation, Twain apparently loses all his fears about technological progress, colonialist expansion, and economic domination.

The utopian context of *TNG* allows the show to acknowledge past racial and class inequities while maintaining that these problems can be solved through progress. These references to the troubled past work as "inocula-tions," to use Roland Barthes's (1972) term,⁴ by holding out the promise that the issues of the past (and the present) will eventually be solved by the same system that engendered them. *TNG* emphasizes progress but largely removes economics from the picture, both by indicating that economic inequality has been wiped out and by suggesting that technology has been harnessed to provide for all needs (most notably in the form of replicators capable of creating matter out of energy). Although trade and exchange are sometimes mentioned, they are rarely part of Federation motivations (unless they are intervening for a needy third party, as in the episode "Symbiosis"). Most often, economic concerns are displaced onto non-Federation aliens such as the Ferengi. In *TNG*, the Federation, freed from the types of economic considerations that lead to nineteenth-century expansionism, explores the "new frontier" as a champion of free will and self-determination for all cultures.

The irony of Twain's encounter with the Enterprise's crew comes in large measure from the idea that the utopian future of *TNG* is represented as more optimistic about progress and the destiny of "Mankind" than this nineteenth-century figure. Although Twain's comments bring up the issues of racism, slavery, and conquest, the show cannot bring itself to represent the very inequities to which Twain alludes. The nineteenth-century scenes do not address the issue of race, or gender inequality for that matter. Although Guinan masquerades before salon guests as an African American woman, there is no mention of race. Indeed, as "Madame Guinan," she is the guest of honor. Also, Twain's dialogue about conquerors, in which he specifically names the Spanish, Dutch, and Portuguese, conspicuously leaves out the British and French (the two national identities with which Picard is most strongly associated). What the show does emphasize is the cultural heritage of the nineteenth century, as we meet not only Mark Twain but also Jack London. Even in acknowledging the past and celebrat-ing Western culture, the show takes great pains to distance itself from cer-tain aspects of that culture: conquest, colonialism, class distinction, racial discrimination, and exploitation.

The Road to Utopia: Progress, Perfection, and "Human" Nature

"Time's Arrow" upholds, and even exaggerates, the nineteenth-century faith in "progress" by downplaying the negative, exploitative connotations that term has come to have. But to understand how *TNG* makes use of its humanist heritage, we need to look more closely at the nineteenth-century utopian imagination. As products of the late nineteenth century, most "modern" utopias are rooted in a rationalism that confirms "mankind's" ability to understand and control the world. Whatever future these utopias propose, they emphasize the ability to discern the most reasonable course and to implement it in a totalizing way. They are strongly influenced by concepts revolving around the idea of progress combined with a "necessary" historical development, of evolution moving toward an ascertainable *telos*. Barbara Goodwin (1978) asserts that the nineteenth-century utopians

> were materialists, naturalists, perfectibilists and neo-Newtonians: they believed in material causes of social events, believed that society and men were natural objects to be studied by methods analogous to those of the natural sciences, believed in human perfectibility, and longed to unearth a principle of universal harmony operating in society with the efficiency and totality of Newtonian attraction. (11)

She suggests that the nineteenth-century emphasis on harmony, which tends to present utopia as a "self-sufficient, integrated, conflict-free social system," cannot be part of a "general" definition of utopia. The "transcendent vision of social harmony" was made possible in the nineteenth century by a belief in "the human capacity for improvement and perfection" (Goodwin 1978, 8–10).

For nineteenth-century thinkers such as Matthew Arnold (1869), the seemingly static concept of "perfection" is held in tension with the more dynamic idea of "progress" and change: "Not a having and a resting, but a growing and becoming is the character of perfection as culture conceives it" (48). *TNG* maintains the same type of tension between progress and perfection both in its narrative structure, which juxtaposes the Enterprise's adventurous travels through space with the relatively static setting on board the ship, and through its rhetoric, which stresses constant improvement in the context of an "ideal society." The utopian myth—as in the myth of the American frontier—of infinite abundance makes possible *TNG*'s emphasis on striving for individual perfection. Picard tells us: "A lot has changed in the past 300 years. People are no longer obsessed with the accumulation of things. We've eliminated hunger, want, the need for possessions. We've grown out of our infancy. ... The challenge ... is to improve yourself, to enrich yourself" ("The Neutral Zone"). Human agency and self-determination are strongly tied to social interaction and responsibility. The Enterprise crew dedicates itself to peaceful scientific exploration and altruistic provision of humanitarian aid. In the show's own terms, the Federation's mission is not one of colonialist expansion; rather, the crew's literal journey to the outer reaches of space is also a figurative one toward both social and individual human perfection.

The concept of human perfectibility is rooted in an essentialist definition of human nature. In Arnold's (1869) terms, the essence of human nature, or "the best self," is "not manifold, and vulgar, and unstable, and contentious, and ever-varying, but one, and noble, and secure, and peaceful, and *the same for all mankind*" (204; emphasis added). The concept of a universal human nature combined with the ideal of conflict-free social harmony tends toward valorizing dominant culture. *TNG* always emphasizes humanity in general, but as in nineteenth-century humanism, the term "human" is in many ways conflated with a concept of Western Man. As Ernesto Laclau and Chantal Mouffe (1985) suggest, it is not humanist values themselves that are the problem, but the way they can be perverted "through equivalential articulation with other values, and [restricted] to certain categories of the population—the property owning class, for example, or the male population" (117). They remind us that "in colonial countries, the equivalence between 'rights of Man' and 'European values' was a frequent and effective form of discursively constructing the acceptability of imperialist domination" (116). They call for a recognition that "Man" is a discursively constructed subject position that should be analyzed to show the historical conditions of its emergence, "enabling us to struggle more efficiently, and without illusions, in defense of humanist values" (117). *TNG* takes up the commendable task of celebrating humanist values without adequately investigating the status that Western Man has historically been given in the humanist concept of history.

Laclau and Mouffe (1985) also note that the rationalist and empiricist attributes of human individuals include "the view of the subject as an agent both rational and transparent to itself; the supposed unity and homogeneity of the ensemble of its positions; and the conception of the subject as the origin and basis of social relations" (115). In *TNG,* the agency of the humanist, holistic self is limited neither by Marxist concepts nor by psychoanalytic theory. The possibility of free will and agency is stressed above and beyond social, economic, political, and psychological forces. As one of the show's most developed characters, Picard is virtually an ideal subject in these terms: supremely rational, self-aware, self-motivated, and able to make choices.

Picard, with his constant references to Western history and culture and his status as the most perfect and progressive human on the show, serves as the voice of reason and exemplifies the show's privileging of Western, patriarchal culture as a universal standard. Picard, an amateur archeologist, is an enthusiastic student of alien cultures and languages, but his overpowering characteristic is his staunch defense of human (read Western European) culture. His character makes the show's liberal humanism less threatening by emphasizing that openness to other cultures will neither displace male authority nor significantly alter its character. More like a scholar than a military leader, Picard is generally able to make his crew (and most alien groups they encounter) set aside their own biases and see things his way. Compared to the more exotic nonhumans serving on his crew, Picard's French heritage becomes a rather "neutral" background. Whereas other officers sometimes have conflicts with Federation policy because of their own cultural heritage (Security Chief Lt. Worf, Ensign Ro Laren), Picard rarely does. His own conflicts with Starfleet come from personal conviction rather than cultural baggage. Consider, for example, when Picard defends Data's right to keep his android creation, Lal: "There are times when men of good conscience cannot blindly follow orders. Order a man to surrender his child to the State. Not while I'm his captain" ("The Offspring"). His respect for the rights of individuals distracts from his actual position of authority.

TNG balances individual free will against faith in a type of "historical necessity" or "social evolutionism." Utopias project social evolution into the future, and the social sciences developing in the nineteenth century used this concept to account for the development of other cultures: "Social evolutionism entails a law of progress that allows us to know our past through the present of others, to know the present of others through our own past, and to know their future through our own present" (Lutz and Collins 1993, 239–240). Although there are many varieties of social evolutionism, these views "share a common basic structure: stages of human social organization are passed on the way to a specific goal—a goal synonymous with the contemporary Western social system" (240). Obviously, this type of explanation emphasizes the inevitability of these changes, often shifting attention away from other factors, such as colonialism. In *TNG*, the Prime Directive crystallizes the Federation's social evolutionist stance.

The "Prime Directive," which restricts the Federation and its Starfleet officers from interfering in the "natural" development of another culture, not only implies noninterference but also confirms the law of progress. The Prime Directive enacts the show's fundamental conflict between a belief in the exercise of free will and self-determination and the existence of some necessary, natural pattern of development, which "common sense" tells us involves unending technological and moral progress. In "Who Watches the Watchers," for example, members of a society whom the Federation has classified as proto-Vulcan and in the Bronze Age of development witness the advanced technological capabilities of the Enterprise crew. Picard is forced to explain the concept of technological progress to convince the Mintakans that he is not a supernatural being. In the course of his discussions with the leader of the planet, he concurs that the inhabitants of her planet will also achieve space flight one day. In this episode, as in many others involving the Prime Directive, "natural development" becomes a shorthand for a particular kind of progress. The Prime Directive is often used to counteract the negative connotations associated with interference in "underdeveloped" areas: forced economic change and cultural imperialism. Although the Prime Directive can be seen as protecting the autonomy of other cultures, it is also used to imply that all cultures, if left to their own devices, will "progress" toward the Federation ideal.

As Laclau and Mouffe (1985) suggest, the type of rationalism that presents "history and society as intelligible totalities constituted around conceptually explicable laws" is prevalent in both left- and right-wing discourse of the nineteenth century. Both depend on a concept of "History in the singular" and "universal" subjects (2–3). It is because *TNG* holds up the law of progress as an observable natural phenomenon that movement toward the ideal of a harmonious utopia is possible. Laclau and Mouffe (1985) assert that, in the twentieth century, the Left's faith in Revolution has been shaken by the actual failure of communist governments and by theoretical shifts, such as the complication of the category of "class" by considerations of race and gender. Likewise, the "liberal-conservative camp" has been worried by the "crisis of governability" revolving around issues of diversity and by the limits to continued "progress," as pointed up by environmental crises (1–2). *TNG* upholds the rationalist attitude with a return to faith in progress and social evolutionism. Because the show maintains the ideas of both a rational, self-determining individual and a "natural" pattern of development, it suggests that culture (or rather Western culture) is not based on domination but on consent and on common sense.

Consent Formation: Coercion, Consensus, and Hegemony

In the utopian context of *TNG*, in which economic and social unrest have largely been conquered, the Federation never coerces anyone to join it but rather leaves that decision up to the newly encountered civilization. Compared to hostile forces struggling for domination and exploitation (the capitalistic Ferengi, the imperialistic Romulans, and the totalitarian Borg), the Federation, with its Prime Directive of noninterference, seems the best answer. These alien groups exemplify what Gramsci calls "direct domination" by using the coercive military and legal power of the state to rule, rather than "leading" through the process of hegemony which involves gaining "active assent from allies and passive assent from other classes and groups." To gain "leadership" a group must "articulate a worldview that accommodates a broad range of interests, not merely the leading group's interest" (Condit 1994, 206–207). Laclau and Mouffe emphasize that consent is gained, not from the rational self of humanism, but from interpellated subjects such that it can be considered somewhat illegitimate, since it becomes "coercion in a more sophisticated guise" (Condit 1994, 207). *TNG* has no difficulty portraying direct domination, but given the essentialist definition of the self with an emphasis on reason and free will, the show can only account for Starfleet's leadership by suggesting the legitimacy of its worldview and the naturalness of its supremacy. Starfleet wins out by virtue of consensus to a worldview that, though clearly of a liberal bent, contemporary dominant ideology can easily recuperate.

The Enterprise mirrors an idealized version of U.S. society as seemingly classless, culturally open, and harmonious. Several factors shift attention away from the hierarchical structure of Starfleet itself, making the running of the Enterprise seem to be consensus-based rather than militaristic. There is little conflict between the ordinary crewmembers and the officers, and, because technology has made harsh physical labor unnecessary, there is little visible difference in their jobs. Everyone is a high-tech, white-collar worker living in comfortable surroundings and has equal opportunities for advancement in a meritocracy. Although the crew of the Enterprise is multicultural and the signs of "diversity" are often pointedly on display in crew quarters, the crew's ability to reach agreements easily emphasizes group unity and the legitimacy of Starfleet policy. Starfleet, with its regulation uniforms and official language ("Federation Standard," otherwise known as English), comes to represent a neutral norm of behavior.

Despite the proliferation of various alien groups in *TNG*, the emphasis on and display of the unique attributes of each race/culture simultaneously works to reinforce the self-contained identity of each group and the existence of a universal nature. Although some episodes, such as "Darmok," feature aliens whose language and culture remain fairly opaque,[5] most alien cultures are portrayed as readily understandable and easily classifiable. *TNG* depends on a classical humanism, which postulates that "in scratching the history of men a little, the relativity of their institutions or the superficial diversity of their skins . . ., one very quickly reaches the solid rock of a universal human nature" (Barthes 1972, 101). Barthes's consideration of "The Great Family of Man" exhibition in *Mythologies* illustrates the way in which "otherness" can be used to confirm the existence of an essential "human nature" when he explains the myth of the human community:

> This myth functions in two stages: first the difference between human morphologies is asserted, exoticism is insistently stressed, the infinite variations of the species, the diversity in skins, skulls and customs are made manifest, the image of Babel is complacently projected over that of the world. Then, from this pluralism, a type of unity is magically produced: man is born, works, laughs and dies everywhere in the same way; and if there still remains in these actions some ethnic peculiarity, at least one hints that there is underlying each one an identical "nature," that their diversity is

only formal and does not belie the existence of a common mould. Of course this means postulating a human essence... (100)

In the context of *TNG,* this same process is used with exotic aliens standing in for the terrestrial Other.

Not only does *TNG* construct both individuals and alien groups in ways that reinforce the idea of a "humanoid essence," it also ties their characteristics to a particular nineteenth-century model of progress exemplified by Auguste Comte. As Leslie Sklair (1970) explains, Comte suggests that there is a necessary relation between three types of progress: "Practical progress ... whose agency is Activity, Theoretical progress whose agency is Intellect, and Moral progress whose agency is Feeling" (37). Although all these types of progress are seen as interconnected, Comte judges moral progress to be most important, proclaiming "Feeling is not only the essential spring of true progress, but also its main end, since our Moral amelioration is of much more importance, public as well as private, than any advance in either Speculation or Action" (Comte, quoted in Sklair 1970, 37). *TNG* takes the same stance, showing humans as almost the only group that sees the importance of all three types of progress.

To a large extent, the predominance of one of these sets of characteristics identifies each officer. In *TNG,* First Officer Commander William Riker looks for practical solutions, whereas Data, the android, expounds on theory. The female characters—Chief Medical Officer Commander Beverly Crusher, Troi, and Guinan—tend toward emotional and moralizing responses to problems. In the context of this utopia, Picard is generally shown as basing his actions on a mastery of both reason and emotion. As a result, *TNG* never truly considers radical difference: Though each crew member possesses "unique" attributes (often associated with their cultural group), these only help in creating a "whole" crew that always works in harmony to attain continuous technological and moral progress. The ease of "consensus" appears to be the product of the logic of the situation, rather than of the processes of hegemony.

If human development is always marked by the necessary conjunction of practical, theoretical, and moral progress, the fatal flaw of most alien "races" encountered by the Enterprise is a failure to balance these three spheres. Warlike Klingons have an overabundance of "feeling"; Ferengi tradesmen pursue pointless economic activity; Vulcans struggle with repressed emotions, and so on. Even Q, an apparently omnipotent being, is represented as inferior on the grounds that he lacks the appropriate moral compunction for his actions. Like Q, many of the enemy alien groups are characterized by an overindulgence in selfish goals. The largest threat to both the tenets of the show and to the Federation itself, however, has been the Borg, who are initially without emotion, representing a nightmare vision of technological progress from which the concept of a self has been eliminated.

The Borg episodes, then, raise a number of questions about "natural development" and "human nature," maintained by *Star Trek* as a whole.

Cyborgs and the Problem of Radical Difference

In "Progress versus Utopia," Jameson (1982) suggests that the "utopian imagination" or "the imagination of otherness and radical difference" has become atrophied so that "setting forth for the unknown, [this imagination] finds itself irrevocably mired in the all-too familiar, and thereby becomes unexpectedly transformed into a contemplation of our own absolute limits" (153). As we have seen, *TNG*'s utopian vision remains confined by the nineteenth-century humanist imagination. If Starfleet is ultimately characterized by extreme homogeneity, with each crew member acting as part of a team pursuing naturalized goals, the Borg represent the show's nightmare vision of hegemony-as-assimilation, leaving no room for essence or agency. The show's repression of the importance of gender, class, and other factors in favor of a bourgeois individualist vision of human identity and homogeneity comes back with a vengeance when the Borg invade the universe of *TNG*.

Haraway (1985) points to the way that postmodernist, feminist science fiction attempts to deal with contemporary society by confronting what she terms the "new networks" (characterized by Simulation, postmodernism, Cyborg citizenship, Optimization, and Artificial Intelligence). Although *TNG* explicitly deals with many of the concepts involved in these "new networks," it is firmly rooted in the humanist models of the "old hierarchical dominations" (reliant on Representation, realism, Public/Private, Perfection, and Mind) (161–162). Perhaps the best way to illustrate this is to consider *TNG*'s own mechanical man, Data.

As an android, Data has the potential to threaten any essentialist conception of human nature or the self. But Data is constantly used as the resident "professor of the humanities."[6] He is not modeled after the cyborgs of contemporary science fiction or the mass-produced robots of the early twentieth century; rather, he is analogous to the artificial beings of the nineteenth century who were "still conceptualized as individuals, unique artifacts with a personal relationship to their maker. . . . They were essentially craft products—experimental prototypes or customized luxury goods" (Wollen 1989, 50).[7] Data is characterized as a "unique" individual. Whether he is deemed to be particularly human (due to his altruism) or to lack human qualities (emotion, for example), such considerations predominantly reinforce the humanist concept that there is a real, universal human nature. Indeed, Data's self-professed goal is to constantly strive to become more human, although he knows he will never fully realize his aim. His is the humanist drive toward "perfection" rather than the cyborg call for "optimization."

Already a storehouse of cultural knowledge, Data frequently pursues his quest by studying high-culture artifacts of the West and dabbling in artistic endeavors including painting, playing the violin, and acting. Data is able to work well with the crew because, although he may miss some of the nuances of human culture, their goals are fully integrated into his circuitry. Data chooses to suppress his difference in order to reach toward the transcendent human ideal.

Haraway's (1985) cyborgs are not based on this view of the automaton as a self-contained, self-motivated, idealized representation of human identity. Rather, the cyborgs of feminist, postmodern science fiction represent "contradictory permanently unclosed constructions of personal and collective selves" that must replace various humanist, essentialist models of the self (157). As boundary transgressors, Haraway's cyborgs "make very problematic the statuses of man or woman, human, artefact, member of a race, individual entity, or body" (178). Because of its appropriation of nineteenth-century humanist models, *TNG* generally strives to reinforce the boundaries—between male and female, human and machine, nature and culture—that its subject matter often initially seems to put into question. Whereas Haraway views cyborgs as offering the possibility of conceptual liberation, such postmodern fragmentation is incredibly threatening to the humanist universe of *TNG*. Cyborgs, with their interchangeable parts and interlocking circuitry, counter the image of the holistic self possessed of a consistent identity. *Star Trek*'s cyborgs are severed from utopian, revolutionary, postmodern possibilities. Instead, they fulfill Haraway's alternate vision of cyborgs as representing the "final imposition of a grid of control on the planet" (154).

In the first three episodes dedicated to the Borg, "Q Who," "The Best of Both Worlds: Part I," and "The Best of Both Worlds: Part II," the Borg are described as neither male nor female and as organic beings so fully integrated into the technological "whole" and controlled by a "group mind" that they do not even register as individuals.[8] These episodes establish the Borg as entirely alien and as lacking the possibility of individual self-determination (the most essential human characteristic on the show). Whereas Data's circuitry remains safely contained within a human form, Borg costuming combines human bodies with painfully visible apparatuses—added mechanical limbs, external electronic circuitry, and independently moving parts—showing the interdependence of machine and organism. Featured primarily in low-angle, long to medium shots, the zombie-like Borg are visually threatening. In the context of *Star Trek*, cyborgs are not associated with "patriarchal capitalism" but with a 1950s nightmare of communism as envisioned in the original *Invasion of the Body Snatchers* (1956). Like the "body snatchers," who were organic beings from outer space, the Borg promise "better quality of life" but demand the sacrifice of individuality and emotion. They promise "optimization" through effective use of component parts, rather than perfection of individuals through an improved understanding of the transcendent ideal of human nature.

The Borg also function as a projection of *TNG's* own emphasis on colonization and the assimilation of other cultures into a social structure based on what Haraway (1985) calls the "logic of appropriation, incorporation, and taxonomic identification" (157). Haraway suggests that anticolonialist discourse dissolves "the 'West' and its highest product—the one who is not animal, barbarian, or woman: man, that is, the author of a cosmos called history" (156). *TNG,* in creating a fictional future of infinite scientific progress, firmly seeks to maintain Western man as the center of that cosmos. Those who are female or alien in some way are merely possessed of some supplementary quality that they must choose either to use in support of Federation goals or to suppress in order to take up their position in Starfleet. How many times has Picard lectured Crusher about her tendency to disregard the Prime Directive for overly emotional reasons or chastised Worf for acting on Klingon motivations? Although Picard is usually portrayed as open to other perspectives, the show emphasizes the idea of consensus without problematizing the grounds for such a consensus.

The Borg threaten the annihilation of difference through assimilation. In "The Best of Both Worlds: Part I," the Borg, having now learned to recognize Picard as a leader, choose to "assimilate" him to serve as their spokesperson in confronting the "archaic," "authority driven" cultures he represents and that they plan to conquer.

B: (multiple voices) Captain Jean-Luc Picard, you lead the strongest ship in the Federation fleet. You speak for your people.

P: I have nothing to say to you, and I will resist you with my last ounce of strength.

B: Strength is irrelevant. Resistance is futile. We wish to improve ourselves. We will add your biological and technological distinctiveness to our own. Your culture will adapt to service ours.

P: Impossible! My culture is based on freedom and self-determination.

B: Freedom is irrelevant. Self-determination is irrelevant. You must comply.

Even the "universal translator" is no help, since the Borg, unlike other *TNG* aliens, do not accept the same basic terms as the Federation. Whereas *TNG* insists that the knowing subject can control unconscious impulses as well as social, political, and technological forces, the Borg represent the fear that these impulses can overwhelm the individual.

The Borg's assimilation of Picard literalizes their threat to the concept of human agency. Pierced by invasive wiring and overtaken by mechanical modifications, Picard is physically transformed into "Locutus of Borg" and forced to collaborate with the enemy. Yet Picard does not simply disappear into the Borg collective, rather he becomes their figurehead and the personification of the Borg threat. Much of Locutus's dialogue actually parallels the kinds of statements Picard might make when encountering new civilizations as a representative of the Federation ("We mean you no harm," "We only wish to improve quality of life"). But, as the Borg do not allow any room for choice and free will, these statements imply forcible coercion rather than voluntary consensus. The Borg draw on Picard's knowledge and experience to destroy Federation ships against his will. They are defeated eventually because the humans work in individual guerrilla units and because Picard, having overcome his Borg programming, suggests a way to destroy them. The ending works not only to reestablish Picard in his position of command and nullify the Borg threat but also to reaffirm the possibility of human agency.

In attempting to create a new and convincing villain by drawing on recent science fiction, *TNG* may have found a greater threat than it bargained for. Even stripped of postmodern formal techniques, transformed into totalitarian monsters, and projected into the utopian realm of *TNG*, the Borg, in their first three appearances, retain a disturbing quality that suggests the limitations of the Western humanist concepts so basic to *TNG*. Whereas most episodes have a firm resolution, "The Best of Both Worlds: Part II" ends with Picard in his office, in command but still oddly disturbed by his encounter. Considering the power of the cyborgs to transgress the boundaries that are fundamental to the show's fragile utopia, conceived of as a universe dominated by rational human agents pursuing the goals of Western culture without being aware of their complicity in hegemony, Picard seems justified in stating that "no defense may be adequate against this enemy."

In the fourth episode about the Borg, "I, Borg," *TNG* finds that its best defense against the enemy is to redefine it. When the Enterprise discovers a Borg shipwreck, the lone survivor is identified as "a male adolescent." Even in this opening sequence, the Borg lose some of their previous defining characteristics, as they are apparently no longer "both male and female." Visually, this Borg is also more appealing than his predecessors; fairly close shots frequently individualize him. Although Picard agrees to bring the Borg on board for "humanitarian reasons," the captain soon reveals that his actual intention is to use him to destroy the Borg collective. Picard's combative stance in this episode toward both the Borg and his fellow officers is rather atypical. His usual impassioned defense of virtually all life forms is replaced by an emotional tirade on the Borg's status as completely alien and unredeemable: "Because it has been given a name by a member of my crew doesn't mean it's not a Borg. Because it is young doesn't mean it's innocent. It is what it is. In spite of efforts to turn it into some kind of pet, I will not alter my plans." Picard, however, changes his mind once he becomes convinced that the Borg, now called Hugh, has gained a sense of his own individuality. To test Hugh's loyalty, Picard again assumes the role of "Locutus of Borg" and orders Hugh to help him assimilate the crew of the Enterprise. The dialogue is almost a word-for-word recreation of the scene of Picard's initial capture by the Borg, but now Picard is repeating the Borg slogan "Resistance is futile," and Hugh provides the "human voice": "Resistance is not futile. Some have escaped." Picard is stunned when the Borg refers to himself in the first-person singular saying, "I will not assist you." When Picard counters, "But you are Borg," the Borg replies, "No, I am Hugh." In Picard's eyes the Borg becomes "human" in the moment that he acknowledges an identity outside the collective.

Picard decides that it will no longer be necessary to introduce a virus into Hugh that would destroy the Borg collective. Rather, Hugh's memory will be left intact so that contact with his newfound feelings of individuality might change the Borg. Picard ponders that

> perhaps, in that short time before they purge his memory, the sense of individuality which he has gained with us might be transmitted through the entire Borg collective, every one of the Borg being given the opportunity to experience the feeling of . . . of . . . singularity. Perhaps that's the most pernicious program of all; the knowledge of self being spread throughout the collective in that brief moment might alter them forever.

Picard describes the sense of "self" as a virus that will efface the collective consciousness of the Borg, making room for the transition to hegemonic consensus. In this episode, the Borg threat is diminished as their characteristics are redefined, as "otherness is reduced to sameness" (Barthes 1972, 151).

Various effects of giving the Borg a sense of individuality are followed up in the two-part sixth-season cliff-hanger "Descent." We learn that the Borg have, in fact, gained a sense of individuality through their contact with Hugh and that they now act on emotional impulses. The motivations of the Borg are no longer grounded in an entirely alien world view; instead they stem from emotional desires (from "human nature"). Unfortunately, because a group of Borg has fallen under the sway of Data's sadistic twin, Lore, they are rampaging through the galaxy destroying remote Federation outposts. These Borg retain the same basic costume as their predecessors, but they are now capable of moving swiftly, taking individual actions, and acting on emotion. They are no longer interested in assimilating alien cultures and technologies, only in destroying inferior life forms. Whereas the androgynous Borg were "like nothing you [had] ever seen before" in "Q Who," in "Descent" they are overtly compared to other vicious alien groups (the Klingons, the Ferengi). The Borg are transformed into fascists, with Lore convincing them that they will become a "master race." They have simultaneously become more "human" because they now conceive of themselves as individuals and more evil because their fascistic dystopia leaves no room whatsoever for difference. They have been integrated into the *Star Trek* cosmology, for they have added a sense of self and agency to their mastery of practical and theoretical progress. But, because their ability to "feel" is not appropriately linked to a capacity for moral judgment, they are enemies of the Federation.

In "Descent: Part II," however, Hugh demonstrates that he has retained the moral sense he gained on the Enterprise. At first he blames the crew for the problems of his people (the destruction of his culture because of the introduction of their concept of the individual). Hugh, however, does eventually come to the rescue of the Starfleet officers, freeing the Borg from Lore's control and allowing room for speculation that he will become the new Borg leader. It is clear that, in these six episodes, the Borg have been put back on the "natural" path for any alien group in *TNG*. They have gained the capacity for free will and self-determination and are ready to make continued progress in practical, theoretical, and moral realms. Before you know it, they may *choose* to join the Federation.

Conclusion

Having eliminated economics and other structuring factors, *TNG* builds its utopia on the foundations of nineteenth-century notions of progress and infinite human potential. Continuous human progress is made possible by the actions of human agents but is also tied to a natural pattern of development. The show's constant emphasis on the idea of progress allows it to acknowledge past inequities, but only in order to stress humanity's ability to overcome them. Although the show ostensibly celebrates diversity with its multicultural crew, its reliance on an essentialist definition of human nature not only downplays the importance of psychological and social factors in general, but also serves to suppress issues of class, race, and gender. In defining the characteristics of the Enterprise crew and the alien groups they encounter, the show admits diversity and acknowledges history, but does so always with an eye toward finding "neutral" ground. The evolution of the Borg shows this tendency toward eliminating the problem of radical difference. Just as Arnold (1869) contends that the "best self" is "not manifold, and vulgar, and unstable, and contentious, and ever-varying, but one, and noble, and secure, and peaceful and the same for all mankind" (204), so *TNG* promotes an essentialist view of human nature that favors consent and harmony rather than recognizing the inevitability of difference.

Notes

1. "The Best of Both Worlds: Part I."
2. In "The Game," Picard speaks in Latin to Starfleet Cadet Wesley Crusher.
3. In fact, the show began the same year E. D. Hirsch, Jr.'s (1987) book *Cultural Literacy: What Every American Needs to Know* was published.
4. In *Mythologies*, Barthes (1972) explains the strategy of admitting the "accidental evils" of a particular institution: "One immunizes the contents of the collective imagination by means of a small inoculation of acknowledged evil; one thus protects it against the risk of a generalized subversion. This *liberal* treatment would not have been possible only a hundred years ago" (150).
5. Eventually, Picard does manage to learn the narratively metaphoric language of the alien species well enough to communicate. The melodramatic *pathos* of the episode rests on the fact that this progress comes too late.
6. Q uses this phrase disparagingly in "Déjà Q."
7. Data is often overtly compared to figures originating in the nineteenth century, such as Pinocchio and the Tin Man.
8. These characteristics are explicitly stated in "Q Who."

References

Arnold, Matthew. 1869. *Culture and Anarchy*. Ed. J. Dover Wilson. Cambridge: Cambridge U P, 1932, 1990.

Barthes, Roland. 1972. *Mythologies*. Trans. Annette Lavers. New York: The Noonday P.

Condit, Celeste Michelle. 1994. "Hegemony in a Mass-Mediated Society: Concordance about Reproductive Technologies." *Critical Studies in Mass Communication* 11: 205–230.

Dyer, Richard. 1977. "Entertainment and Utopia." *Movie* 24: 2–13. Rpt. in *Genre: The Musical*. Ed. Rick Altman. Boston: Routledge and Kegan Paul, 1981. 175–189.

Goodwin, Barbara. 1978. *Social Science and Utopia: Nineteenth-Century Models of Social Harmony*. Atlantic Highlands, NJ: Humanities P.

Haraway, Donna. 1985. "Manifesto for Cyborgs: Science, Technology, and Socialist Feminism in the 1980s." *Socialist Review* 80: 65–108. Rpt. as "A Cyborg Manifesto: Science, Technology, and Socialist-Feminism in the Late Twentieth Century" in *Simians, Cyborgs, and Women: The Reinvention of Nature*. New York: Routledge, 1991. 149–181.

Hirsch, E. D. Jr. 1987. *Cultural Literacy: What Every American Needs to Know*. Boston: Houghton Miffin.

Jameson, Fredric. 1982. "Progress versus Utopia; or, Can We Imagine the Future?" *Science-Fiction Studies* 9: 147–158.

Laclau, Ernesto, and Chantal Mouffe. 1985. *Hegemony and Socialist Strategy: Towards a Radical Democratic Politics*. London: Verso.

Lutz, Catherine A., and Jane L. Collins. 1993. *Reading* National Geographic. Chicago: U of Chicago P.

Moylan, Tom. 1986. *Demand the Impossible: Science Fiction and the Utopian Imagination*. New York: Methuen.

Sklair, Leslie. 1970. *The Sociology of Progress*. London: Routledge and Kegan Paul.

Wollen, Peter. 1989. "Cinema/Americanism/the Robot." *New Formations* 8: 7–34. Rpt. in *Modernity and Mass Culture*. Ed. James Naremore and Patrick Brantlinger. Bloomington: Indiana U P. 42–69.

6

A Fabricated Space

Assimilating the Individual on
Star Trek: The Next Generation

AMELIE HASTIE

In "Conundrum," a 1992 episode of *Star Trek: The Next Generation (TNG)*, an alien comes aboard ship and forces the crewmembers to lose (or "suppress," as Captain Jean-Luc Picard hypothesizes) their identities in order to engage them in a war between his and another species.[1] Thus, members of the crew must rediscover who they are and what they are doing. First, they attempt to locate the leader of the ship; in order to do so, they check one another's uniforms. Looking at the pips on his and Picard's collar, First Officer Commander William Riker announces, "It looks like you're the leader." Security Chief Lt. Worf, however, speaks up, indicating his warrior sash (obviously maintaining his "instincts," if not his identity[2]): "Perhaps we should not jump to conclusions. I am decorated as well." He then takes control of the ship—propelling it toward war—until the crew is able to access personnel records and realize that Picard is the captain of the starship. By the end of the episode, when the alien is revealed, the Enterprise is able to return to its goal of exploration rather than war (which is represented as antithetical to the starship's mission).

Particularly significant about the scene above is the crewmembers' dependence on costume markers to ascertain positions of power aboard the ship. As the crew is costumed uniformly, Riker and Worf each look for the member who is decorated differently from the others. Contrary to conventional wisdom, fashion, at this point, is clearly not only a women's concern. Indeed, this mark of "individuality" in the midst of an otherwise uniform collectivity identifies positions of control on the Enterprise. As Quentin Bell (1976) proclaims in *On Human Finery*, "Fashion for those who live within its empire is a force of tremendous and incalculable power" (62).[3]

Part of its power, I would contend, lies in the fact that fashion, like the unconscious, is not structured only like a language, but also like *parole*, or speech.[4] Leslie Rabine (1994), in her essay "A Woman's Two Bodies: Fashion Magazines,

Consumerism, and Feminism," also notes this relation: "Critics of fashion have analyzed clothing as a language, incessantly communicating messages about its wearers" (59). Jane Gaines (1990) underscores the importance of fashion in visual narratives and its connection to language in her analysis of fashion in silent film. Considering the rules of economics in cinematic (and televisual) narratives, Gaines understandably claims that in silent film "in the absence of sound [costume] was seen as a substitute for speech" (188). With the advent of sound film (and television), costume is no longer a substitute for speech; rather, it provides an additional commentary. Thus, "the rules of costume and typage that the dress should place a character quickly and efficiently, identifying her in one symbolic sweep" (188), which Gaines indicates in relation to silent film, are still in play. In the case of "Conundrum," costume is clearly understood as an accurate mark of identities of power and control. I open with this scene, then, in order to begin demarcating certain links (and spaces) I shall be exploring throughout this chapter—between individuality and collectivity, uniforms and uniformity, gender and display—and to mark fashion as an important rather than trivial space for exploration, particularly in how fashion "places" Counselor Lt. Commander Deanna Troi on the Enterprise.[5]

If fashion is a "language," Rabine (1994) insists that we must be prepared to ask the following: "[W]ho speaks this language, to whom is it addressed, what does it mean, and how are its meanings established and transformed?" (59). These questions seem particularly relevant in the case of Troi. When she first appeared on the show attired in low-cut bodices and short skirts, I found her a throwback to the original series. This regression seemed somewhat surprising in the context of the new series's attempt to correct other wrongs of the past: changing the opening voice-over to declare the starship's mission more inclusive ("to go where no *one* has gone before") and adding more central female characters in positions of relative power (including Troi and Chief Medical Officer Commander Beverly Crusher). At the same time, however, Troi's empathic abilities on the show appear often patently absurd—nothing more than a masquerade, a ruse.[6] Over the course of the series, Troi's empathic powers and her costumes become less excessive, and in 1992, five years into the series, she finally is ordered to put on a standard uniform by the substitute Captain Edward Jellico. This change, and those that led up to it, begs the questions of who wants whom to wear what and why.

To begin to answer these questions, I shall trace the change in Troi's costume. In doing so, I will look at two other extreme wardrobe changes that occur on either side of her shift into regulation uniform—one that seems to realize a "hyperfemininity" of sorts and the other that seems to represent if not a "hypermasculinity" at least a "hyperuniformity." I focus primarily on Troi as a subject of fashion precisely because she goes through significant and repeated changes of costume that largely identify changes in her character in the plot of the series.[7] To uncover the effects of Troi's wardrobe changes, I will compare her position to one seemingly in stark contrast to hers: that of the Borg Collective. At a glance, the two are indeed in opposition. Where the two meet, however, is at an ideological address; each, I will argue, represents *TNG*'s enterprise(s) of "assimilation."[8] Importantly, the very notion of assimilation is linked to fashion; the *American Heritage Dictionary* (1978) definition of the latter is the "prevalent custom or practice among a group, usually following a convention of polite society or mass culture." Crucially inherent in this definition—and in its root *factio*, "a making"—"fashion" is both to construct and to follow a mode of behavior, style, and so on—in a sense, then, to *assimilate*. In posing questions concerning the relation of fashion to the representation of Troi on the show—is she fashionable? or is she unfashionable? must she be made fashionable?—I hope to illustrate that these questions produce further inquiries concerning subjectivity, gender, and the relations between individuality and collectivity. In turn, such inquiries elucidate ideological interests of *TNG*, television, and, certainly, fashion itself. In other words, I would like to show how fashion reveals the "character," or ideological "identity," of *TNG* and in the process helps to elucidate the "character" of the television industry from which it springs.

Answering questions concerning fashion, of course, cannot be so simple, as the very notion of fashion appears to rest on two seemingly contradictory principles: to be fashionable, one must be able to "stand out," to assert her or his individuality, for instance (as do Worf and Picard in "Conundrum"); at the same time, what might be defined as "fashionable" (what allows the individual to "stand out," fashionably) is often predicated on a matter of collective taste, a matter of convention, a matter—as Bell (1976) would put it—of "tyrannical democracy." Thus, to be fashionable is to be able to "stand out" and "fit in" simultaneously. Georg Simmel (1971) similarly describes the way that fashion unites a class through isolating it from another: "Two social tendencies are essential to the establishment of fashion, namely, the need of union on the one hand and the need of isolation on the other" (301). (Importantly, however, on *TNG* fashion is often used not necessarily to distinguish between classes but between species[9] and, at least in the case of Troi and the bartender Guinan, genders.)

This odd spatial dissymmetry (being at once both "out" and "in," being "isolated" yet "united"), then, stands for a prominent contradiction of fashion: the most fashionable appear both as an "individual" and as part of a "collective." At the same time, the spatial dissymmetry of fashion offers an interesting response to further questions about gender, sexuality, and performance that have also been articulated spatially through the concept of "masquerade." In particular, this concept highlights a tension between proximity and distance. As Mary Ann Doane (1991) theorizes, masquerade is predicated on a process of distancing oneself from, for instance, a conventional representation of femininity. As she says, "The masquerade, in flaunting femininity, holds it at a distance" (25). At the same time, since this flaunting also consists of a corporeal (and often material) display, masquerade seems to hold a very proximate relation to the woman doing the flaunting. Thus femininity, as registered by dress, must hold a proximate relation to a woman in order for her to "hold it at a distance."

Both fashion and masquerade, then, seem to mediate between two disparate positions through the "space" of an individual woman's body. In fact, the very materiality of fashion—which is, of course, the material of clothing itself—offers a contradictory, or perhaps mediating, spatial function. Fashion can be visible through clothes; thus, fashion can be recognized at a distance. At the same time, fashion has a clear tactile relation to the body (we can feel clothing against our bodies—in a sense, then, we can *feel* fashion); thus, fashion also can be recognized at a very close proximity. Moreover, fashion is not only relegated to costume (changes) on the body but to changes *to* the body as well, including relatively superficial hairstyle and facial make-up modifications and other, more substantial, physical alterations. Indeed, in *TNG*, contradictions both of proximity and distance as well as individuality and collectivity are played out *on* Troi's body—visually, tactilely, and ideologically.

Such contradictions between notions of individuality and collectivity are particularly elucidated in a 1992 episode entitled "I, Borg." The plot of this episode does not directly involve Troi, but the issues it does invoke (even, peripherally, those concerning fashion) clearly inform an analysis of her position. Certainly differences between her and the Borg abound. Most importantly, in spite of the fact that she is only half-human, Troi seems to represent all that is "human"[10] for the viewers (or more specifically, all that is *woman*): She repeatedly reveals her empathic and affective powers as well as her feminine body. The Borg, in contrast, represents (almost) all that is machine: It is strictly affectless and hides most of its humanoid characteristics with mechanical parts. Costume and body, then, are collapsed on individual Borg members; unlike Lt. Commander Data, an android who is fashioned as human, Borg humanoid bodies are fashioned into identical machines. A growing organism that is part humanoid-part machine and made of hundreds or thousands of bodies, the Borg feeds on entire civilizations in order to assimilate them. It takes humans and "regenerates" (or refashions) them to become part of the human-machine collective. Those on the Enterprise, therefore, understand the Borg as a monstrous "community of one" engaged in repeated acts of genocide. Through its discourse on the fashioning of a Borg member's "individuality," however, "I, Borg" can usefully inform how Troi's own "assimilation" is fashioned, and, thus, how similar contradictions between individuality and collectivity (as well as proximity and distance) are played out on her in subsequent episodes.

In this significant episode, the Enterprise takes aboard a dying member of the Borg in order to revive and return him to the place where he was found. When the Borg member, "Three-of-Five" (as he is designated), boards the ship, the crew institutes a plan to insert a kind of "virus" into his neurosystem so that it might infect the whole Borg's neuronetwork and thus destroy it. However, throughout the show, various crew members are stricken with attacks of conscience and begin to worry about the "ethics" involved in this seemingly humanitarian act of genocide (one of the many contradictions with which this episode is riddled). Those working with Three-of-Five feel as if they come to "know" him; indeed, they even name, or *re*name him. In a particularly striking scene, Chief Engineer Lt. Commander Geordi La Forge and Crusher decide on a name for him. Three-of-Five asks La Forge and Crusher what their "designations" are:

C: I'm Beverly, he's Geordi and you . . .

T-o-F: You . . .

C: You . . .

LaF: No, no wait a minute, that's it—Hugh.

T-o-F: You.

LaF: No, not you—Hugh.

T-o-F: Hugh . . .

C: Okay, now I'm Beverly,

LaF: I'm Geordi,

T-o-F: We are Hugh.

Indicated by the Borg member's insistent use of "we," the tension between collective and individual identity is very much alive. At the same time, the proximity between "You" and "Hugh" should be lost on no one; indeed, "you" is the explicit origin of Three-of-Five's new name. On the one hand, the designation of "you" distances[11] the Borg member from La Forge and Crusher—a distance the Borg member maintains through his emphasis on the collective "we." On the other hand, the designation of Three-of-Five as Hugh/you is the first step toward his assimilation on board the Enterprise.

Over time, through parroting the words of Crusher, La Forge, and Guinan, Hugh becomes like the members of the Enterprise. For instance, when he comments that, unlike the Borg ship, the Enterprise is quiet—he can hear no "voices" on board—Crusher interprets his remarks: "I think what you are saying is that you are lonely." Later, La Forge convinces Guinan to speak with Hugh. She is understandably hesitant to do so, as the Borg almost annihilated her people. Guinan's subsequent conversation with Hugh is thus doubly significant in the process of Hugh's transformation. First, throughout "I, Borg," Guinan is able to tell the story of "her people's" resistance to the Borg—a story that not only places Guinan in relation to the Borg but also further delineates an understanding of species/race on the series. It is unclear exactly who "her people" are; indeed her "people," or (according to the logic of the series) her "species," seem comprehensible primarily in terms of what viewers would see as "racial" markers. For instance, Guinan's usual costume—brightly colored, widely-fitted floor-length gowns—points to her cultural and racial "makeup." Resembling stereotypical African dress, Guinan's gowns thus help to code her story as one analogous to the "diaspora" of Africans who were "assimilated" and then "regenerated" as slaves in the United States.[12] Her people, she tells us, were scattered throughout the galaxy after the Borg came for them, and they no longer have a "home." Second, and at least as important, her story presents Hugh with the opportunity both to repeat Crusher's statement to him and to appropriate Guinan's own words: "What you are saying is that you are lonely. You have no others, you have no home. We are also lonely."

In spite of the fact that Hugh continues to evoke the collective in the first-person plural, this exchange proves to Guinan that Hugh does seem to be an individual. Her recognition of his subjectivity is particularly important in light of Guinan's own subjectivity; she is clearly the only person aboard the Enterprise who was assmiliated neither by the Borg (her people resisted) nor by the Federation. Working on the Enterprise as the bartender in Ten-Forward, she is, as far as we can tell, the only adult person on board who is not a Federation crewmember. She also, then, does not have to dress in standard Federation uniform but wears instead her flamboyant gowns, which vary from episode to episode and which identify her as displaced from the Federation. (Interestingly, Guinan's similarity to Troi in terms of wardrobe is further extended in terms of occupation; as La Forge points out in "I, Borg," what Guinan "does best" is "listen.") As one who has doubly resisted assimilation, then, Guinan's own subsequent transformation during this episode—from being completely unwilling to talk to Hugh to being sympathetic to his plight as an "individual"—makes Hugh's transformation that much more significant.

Hugh's fabricated similarity to La Forge, Guinan, and other Enterprise crewmembers extends to a conversation with Picard. A couple of seasons prior to "I, Borg," a two-part episode entitled "The Best of Both Worlds" aired in which Picard was taken captive by the Borg in order to begin an assimilation of the entire crew of the Enterprise. Successfully assimilated by the Borg (at least temporarily), Picard became "Locutus of Borg." Masquerading as a member of Hugh's collective in this scene, he thus dons the Locutus persona when he meets with Hugh in an attempt to find that Hugh has, in fact, not lost his identification as a member of the Borg—to find that he has not abandoned the Borg collective and become the "individual" that other crewmembers report he has. To test his allegiance to the collective, Locutus/Picard demands that Hugh help him assimilate the starship. Hugh refuses. "I will not," he says. "Yes, you will," demands Locutus/Picard, "You are Borg." "No," the Borg member asserts, "I am Hugh." In a sense this exchange echoes Emile Benveniste's (1971) assertion that subjectivity is constituted by the ability to say "I" and "you." As Benveniste claims:

> Consciousness of self is only possible if it is experienced by contrast. I use *I* only when I am speaking to someone who will be a *you* in my address. It is this condition of dialogue that is constitutive of *person,* for it implies that reciprocally, *I* becomes *you* in the address of one who in his turn designates himself as *I.* (224–225)

Hugh's final enunciation of himself as "I" both marks him as an individual subject and links him to Picard, closing the distance between them. In the previously illustrated connection between "Hugh" and "you," his assertion "I am Hugh" thereby stresses the reciprocity that Benveniste describes. Hugh is not only an individual, but he is one like "you"—in this case, like Picard, who recognizes these connections.[13] Through this incident he also recognizes a change in Hugh. "He seems to be a fully realized individual," he declares. Considering this "realization" (on the part of both Hugh and Picard), the crewmembers then decide that they must offer Hugh sanctuary with them. (We might wonder if he will trade in his cyborgian drag for Federation garb: will his body be refashioned to reflect this alteration of identity?) Given a choice to stay aboard the Enterprise or rejoin the Borg, however, Hugh sacrifices himself as an "individual." "I am one, and you are many" is his justification. Ultimately, then, his own "individuality" is exchanged for the collective that the Enterprise represents. In his final statement to Picard, he declares, "I will not forget that I am Hugh."[14]

Whereas Picard and the rest of the crew recognize this change as a mark of Hugh's burgeoning "individuality," the change can also be read as simply a new assimilation; in other words, Hugh has become the newest member of the collective the starship Enterprise. By naming his identity "I am Hugh," the threat of assimilation by the Borg ("we are you") is exchanged for the benevolent assimilation of the Enterprise ("I am [like] you"). Inevitably, then, at the end of the show the crew, led by Picard, abandons the original plan to kill the Borg through a computer virus but plants another (masked) virus in its place: the concept of individuality. As this concept is anomalous to the Borg's collective identity, it too will "destroy" the Borg as a collective. In a debate concerning the ethics of giving Hugh an

identity and then taking it away from him, Picard ruminates on the import
of Hugh's new-found identity and pronounces, "Perhaps that's the most
pernicious program of all: the knowledge of self being spread throughout
the collective." Of course, the starship crew uncritically qualifies this pernicious act not as one of "assimilation" (to become more like the starship),
nor as one of genocide, but instead as one of "resurrection": They are
merely attempting to reconstruct (or deconstruct) the Borg back into individuals. This "exchangeable truth" is reminiscent of Jean Baudrillard's
(1983) concept of the proof of the real by the imaginary; only in *contrast* to
the Borg does the Enterprise understand an otherwise genocidal act as
humanitarian, as just individualizing. The starship crew here "forgets" its
own identity as also a collective one (a collectivity of individuals).

These notions of individuality and collectivity also have significant bearing on Troi's fashion changes. Until December 1992, Troi was the only
crewmember of the Enterprise who did not appear in regulation uniform. A
number of members wear accoutrements over their uniforms—Worf has his
Klingon warrior sash, Crusher wears what looks like a color-coordinated
lab coat, Ensign Ro Laren wears Bajoran ear jewelry, and Picard has a
unique jacket. These accoutrements primarily help to establish national or
"federal" identities.[15] Troi's difference from the others, by contrast, illustrates a double marking of her species and gender. The two interestingly
meet in the figure of her mother, Lwaxana, who is Betazoid (Deanna's
father was human).[16] As a Betazoid empath, Lwaxana appears particularly
prone to fashion and whimsy. Indeed, empathy and fashion are significantly
related: to be empathic is to *feel* like another, to be fashionable is, at least in
part, to *dress* or *act* like another. Lwaxana's particular fashion, however,
lines up more on the side of *haute couture,* which is accessible only to a
small fashionable few, thus allowing her to position herself squarely in the
isolated/united space that Simmel (1971) delineates for fashion.[17] Troi's
own fashion sense, though less excessive, seems to come from her mother's
side and is, then, simultaneously associated with gender (feminine) and
species (Betazoid).

Because of the marked difference of her outfits, Troi's costumes appear to
be the only ones that have been contested outside of the show. In 1988,
People magazine ran a short interview with Marina Sirtis, the actor who
plays Troi. Typically focusing on fashion and romance concerning the
actress and character, the article reads:

> [H]er revealing costume, in the words of supervising producer Rick
> Berman, made Marina look like a "cross between a cheerleader and
> a waitress at Denny's"—and caused some consternation among the
> show's female fans. This season's costume, says Sirtis, "is much
> sleeker, and we lost the cleavage. I got so many letters last season
> about my cleavage. It seemed to be a hot topic of discussion among

Trekkies. To get a cleavage like that, you have to wear a certain bra. Nobody's boobs do that without help. I think a lot of women felt I wasn't doing my bit for women's lib by wearing that. So I'm glad it's gone. Besides, my body looks better in the new costume." (Kaufman and Alexander, 121)

These remarks have bearing on two important points: (1) the audience presumably didn't find Troi's costume "appropriate"; and (2) Sirtis herself is markedly ambivalent about the role of her dress in the series. In "Costume and Narrative," Gaines (1990) discusses the concept of "appropriate" costuming:

> "Appropriate" costuming for character is rather like the value of fidelity in literary-film adaptation. It depends on creating the impression of "rightness" by striving for exact connotative equivalence for items drawn from relatively unlike systems. Frequent use of such combinations of a couple of items establishes the rule or code, and eventually this coding becomes "naturalized." (191)

Sirtis points out that the audience did not feel that her original costume was "appropriate"—not necessarily, however, for the character Troi exactly, but for the assumed (or desired) "character" of the series. In a program such as *TNG*, she seems to be saying, the audience expects a nod to feminism or "women's lib." Moreover, Sirtis's own ambivalence about her display on the show is striking; she simultaneously asserts that she is happy to be no longer highlighting her bosom, and she also asserts that the new costume "makes her body look better." Offering a further contradiction to this position, Sirtis elsewhere (at a *Star Trek* convention in Milwaukee, 1993) contends that once she got the special "regulation bra" (as she calls it), all the other women on the show asked for it, too, suggesting that it is precisely the bra that makes one's body "look better." Furthermore, her description in *People* is not entirely accurate; although she may have lost *some* cleavage, she did not lose it all.[18]

Cleavage aside, Troi's outfits are clearly distinct from the rest of the Enterprise crewmembers' costumes, even though they are usually in some way coordinated with other members' uniforms, through either color or *some* resemblance in style. And indeed, I imagine it is this very coordination with Starfleet garb that motivates the flamboyant Lwaxana to refer to Troi's clothing as "drab." This "drabness," however, is offset by variety: Troi is the only member who changes "uniforms" throughout single episodes (for instance, she appears in two different pantsuits in "I, Borg").[19] In the last seasons of the show, her changes in uniform signify an alternate reality or time, but at other times (as in the case of "I, Borg"), her changes appear to represent nothing more than whim or fancy, or, perhaps, her "individuality" (one possibly based on whim or fancy). Indeed, as Gaines (1990) notes, in early film, aspiring screenwriters were told, "So much of character is told in one's manner of wearing clothes." Thus,

> Clothes and mannerisms ... are not vehicles for conveying the sense of a "real" person nor are they elements utilized in the craft of character construction, they are "truths" told about a person. Character writing here depends on an idea that real selves (rather than types) can be studied by reading appearance signs which are communicated in public. (185)

In the case of *TNG*, costume tells a "truth" about Troi concerning her relation to the ideological structure of the Enterprise. Indeed, her changing costumes help to communicate the "character" of the starship itself and the social space from which it springs.

Significant within this social space is the fact that Troi's "individuality," depicted by her dress, is sexually coded. Until "Chain of Command: Part I," Troi's fashion—through style and color—highlighted her gender and, conventionally, what might be seen as her sexual and "feminine" allure. In an episode originally aired in the fall of 1992, "Man of the People," Troi's "femininity" as marked by her costumes is taken to an extreme. In this episode, Starfleet Ambassador Olcar temporarily boards the Enterprise on his way to mediate peace negotiations between two warring nations. He arrives with his seemingly aged mother who repeatedly accuses Troi of being attracted to Olcar. Noting these "disturbing encounters," Troi tells Riker: "The feelings I sense from her are malevolent, they're evil." And as we begin to see, this evil is markedly sexual.

After the mother dies, Olcar asks Troi to perform a "funeral meditation" with him, claiming he needs her because she's an empath. During this "meditation ceremony," in which Troi repeats Olcar's words, Olcar transfers energy through two identical crystals to Troi which, as we later learn, allows him to use her as a receptacle for his "darker thoughts and unwanted emotions." Following the ceremony, the "malevolent feelings" of Olcar's mother (which we know in retrospect to be Olcar's own malevolent thoughts) are transferred to Troi. The repetition within the meditation ceremony, and the further repetition of the malicious behavior that follows the ceremony, represents Troi's process of assimilation to become a representation of malevolent feminine behavior. She begins to change psychologically and physically. She also begins to change her clothes—to an excessive degree. Soon after the energy transfer, in fact, we see Troi hold up a number of very nonregulation outfits (not unlike Lwaxana's fashions) against her body in front of a mirror and uncharacteristically—indeed, malevolently—order the computer to cancel all of her appointments before noon.

When we next see her, she is in the Enterprise gym, dressed in her white exercise suit, again in front of a mirror. The mirror behind her in turn reveals multiple images of her as she begins to touch herself—moving her hands across her breasts, over her hair and face—and then as she loosens her clothes. This figurative "loosening" of her clothes continues throughout the episode; when we next see her she is wrapped in a high-neck but extremely tight-fitting white gown accentuating her breasts even more clearly than her usual nonstandard uniforms and so displaying her "loosening" of Starfleet regulation. Following this scene, Troi appears sporting a Cruella de Ville dye job (perhaps further accentuating her new-found malevolence) and wearing a black gown that appears to move to another extreme (from white to black, tight-fitting to draped, cleavage covered to cleavage revealed). Data's observation that "Counselor Troi has altered her appearance" thus seems as understated as Troi's gown is overstated.

Within this episode, Troi's behavior consistently parallels her change in wardrobe. Dressed to kill, she repeatedly attempts to seduce Olcar and Riker. Olcar refuses her on the basis that their relationship "cannot be like that." Riker, in contrast, at first appears interested but flees her room when her sexual desire becomes evidently "malevolent"; as she whispers "You want me, don't you?" Troi scratches Riker's face and he flees her quarters.[20] However, this libidinous fashion show is soon discontinued. In the next scene, Troi resurfaces in her maroon V-neck pantsuit; indicating that age and sexuality are not compatible she has, moreover, visibly aged and become increasingly desperate. Furthermore, Olcar's initial decision to use Troi as a receptacle has backfired. Indeed, her empathic powers seem to have speeded up this process of aging, making her transformation much more obvious to others on the Enterprise; as Olcar says, surprised, "Usually my receptacles last for years." When Troi next sees Olcar, her transformation has gone full circle: Aged and desperate, she virtually echoes the words of his former receptacle—now revealed as another prematurely aged victim—warning the young woman accompanying Olcar to stay away from him.

When Picard learns how Olcar has been using Troi (and other women), he is, understandably, furious. Olcar insists that Picard examine the "broader canvas" in order to recognize that Troi is just one individual whose life is being exchanged for thousands of people who would die if Olcar could not remain calm and so properly negotiate peace between warring nations. Picard, however, says that the fact that Olcar is "unwilling to shoulder the burden of unpleasant emotions" is no reason to brutalize Troi. What Picard finds important is both that Troi is being used without having agreed to sacrifice herself (unlike, say, Hugh) and that Olcar is not sacrificing one person for thousands but one person for only one other person—Olcar himself.

After the energy link between Olcar and Troi is finally destroyed (and Troi does have to be temporarily killed to do it, so she is, albeit briefly, sacrificed for herself), Olcar's "dark thoughts" are channeled back into him immediately—and with a vengeance. Significantly, his malevolent behavior appears in marked contrast to that of Troi and his former receptacle. When *he* "shoulders the burden" of his own dark thoughts, his malevolence is played out solely in terms of violence; when a *woman* (Troi or his first receptacle) "shoulders this burden" the malevolence is played out primarily in terms of female heterosexuality gone haywire (which in part is also violent). This opposition between masculine and feminine display is fairly typical of *TNG*'s representations of men and women, which otherwise have undergone, at least, a facelift.[21] Moreover, as Troi's malicious sexual behavior is an assault on the bodies of others, the "darker thoughts" Olcar channels into her are an assault on her own body. Her peculiar and excessive wardrobe changes signify—if only metaphorically—this visual and tactile assault. As Gaines (1990) would say, her changes in costume "place [her] quickly and efficiently, identifying her in one symbolic sweep" (188).

Thus, when Troi is finally regenerated, her "normal" body inevitably returns to her "normal" outfit. However, although normal (and normalized) by the end of this episode (particularly in contrast to the other outfits she models during her transformation), Troi's unique rendering of Starfleet uniforms is not tolerated for much longer. Indeed, perhaps this episode exposed too much of the repressed of ideology, made too explicit the link between fashion and gender, fashion and the individual/collective, and so required a reeling in. A couple of months after the first airing of "Man of the People," "Chain of Command" aired. Although, like "Conundrum," it examines relations of power aboard the ship and thus includes some examination of Troi's position on the Enterprise, this episode is not directly about Troi. Rather, it focuses on two plots: a change in command when Jellico replaces Picard on board the Enterprise, and Picard's subsequent psychological and corporeal torture by a Cardassian captor.

A common structuring device in several episodes, when Troi first appears in this episode she is wearing her maroon-colored V-neck, whereas in her next appearance she is dressed in the lavender pantsuit. And later in the episode, when Jellico meets with Troi individually, he makes the notorious command: "By the way, I prefer a certain formality on the bridge. I'd appreciate it if you wore a standard uniform when you're on duty." With Troi's change in wardrobe comes a change in designation. Looking like an officer (with her pips now visible, signifying her rank[22]), Jellico now designates her as an officer: "Lt. Commander Troi" as opposed to "Counselor Troi." Thus, the language of the military (which Jellico clearly speaks and represents) demands both uniform designations and designation by uniforms. And, although Picard resumes command at the end of "Chain of Command: Part II," Troi remains in the standard uniform (though she resumes her title of "Counselor," both illustrating Picard's tendency to "speak" a more civilian—or "civilized"—language than the hard-boiled Jellico and perhaps also indicating Troi's "place" on the starship, which is marked not in terms of military designation but rather in terms of a "feminized" profession[23]). In fact, with the exception of alternate realities and dreams (both waking and sleeping), she does not change back into her old clothes until the final episode of the series, "All Good Things ... ," in which she appears in her lavender pantsuit at the end of the show.[24] While she otherwise never returns to her previous wardrobe, however, Troi does significantly change costumes in the final episode I will discuss—"Face of the Enemy"—in which she is biologically and fashionably altered to become a Romulan.[25]

Romulans are known for their cloaking devices. Making their ships invisible, these devices allow the Romulans to travel through space undetected. In what appears to be a refashioning of an original *Star Trek (ST)* episode (another common structuring device for *TNG),* members of the Romulan resistance, here led by a man named N'Vek, kidnap Troi. They then effectively "cloak" her as a Romulan ambassador who has been killed so that Troi can take her place (the Borg might call this an act of "regeneration").[26] Mirroring many elements of the other episodes I have discussed, in this episode Troi loses her identity as Counselor Troi and is forced to masquerade as Major Rakal of the Tal Shiar, the Romulan secret mission organization. In "Face of the Enemy" the process of Troi's Romulan assimilation is continually documented through her parroting of Romulan "language." Masquerade, via costume (and, in this case, surgical operation as well), like the acquisition of language, requires repetition of an existing style. Troi's Romulan name, for instance—emphasized when she speaks as "I" (and this episode might have been entitled, "I, Romulan")—like her wearing of the Romulan uniform, provides Troi with a mobile identity.[27] So, when Troi first meets N'Vek, he orders her to repeat exactly what he says to the commander of the Romulan ship she is traveling on: "Commander Toreth will want to know your mission. Tell her nothing. Simply instruct her to head to the Kalab Center, heading 102, mark 4. ... Repeat it." At first resistant, Troi eventually repeats, "Heading 102, mark 4" for N'vek and then later for Commander Toreth.

Perhaps due to her empathic powers, Troi becomes more and more adept at the role of a Romulan as the episode continues.[28] In fact, one of her most stunning performances as a Romulan occurs when she is alone with N'Vek. After N'Vek addresses her as "Counselor" (and not Major Rakal) Troi begins this diatribe:

> We're not playing it your way anymore, N'Vek. I have been kidnapped, surgically altered, put in danger. I've gone along with all your plans, now you are going to listen to me. You find a way to let

the Enterprise track us, or I will go to Toreth and tell her I've discovered you're a traitor. I'll have you ejected into space. Is that
clear, Subcommander?

It seems here, as in the case of "Man of the People," that because Troi is
an empath she is particularly easily assimilated—in this case to become the
tough-talking, hard-hitting member of the asexual (which we might read
as "masculine") Romulan species, a species whose uniformity is starkly
delineated by hairstyle and clothing (taking on a masculine, or, perhaps,
"butch," aesthetic).

The scheme is, of course, relatively successful, and Troi manages the masquerade well. When Troi is returned to the Enterprise, Crusher is able to
return Troi to her original state. Crusher asks, "How does it feel to have
your own face back?" Troi's polite reply—"Just right, thank you"—shows
that she is both biologically and psychologically regenerated. However, as
Picard tells her, N'Vek did not survive; he sacrificed himself both for Troi
and for other members of the Romulan collective resistance. Once again,
the individual exists in an ambiguous (and ambivalent) relation to the
group. In fact, the uniformity presented by the resistance is necessary to
give the appearance of a collectivity of Romulans aboard Toreth and
N'vek's ship. In this case, uniformity is clearly a ruse, as members like
N'vek (and, temporarily, like Troi) must masquerade as loyal Romulans in
order to carry through a successful underground mission. The fact that difference exists in the Romulan collective cannot be detected aboard this
ship, though this difference is essential to the ideology of humanism that
TNG wants to articulate.

Many of the themes that circle through these three episodes on which I
have focused are both directly and indirectly related to questions concerning fashion. For instance, each one involves the motif of repetition, echoing
part of the very definition of fashion (to "follow"). To become an individual, Three-of-Five repeats La Forge's, Guinan's, and Crusher's words. To
become a proper receptacle for Olcar, Troi both repeats the funeral meditation Olcar chants and then the malicious words of Olcar's former receptacle. And to become (temporarily) assimilated as a Romulan, Troi repeats
N'vek's commands to the commander of the ship and then repeats—or par-
rots—Romulan behavior. Each episode also includes the theme of an individual sacrifice for the collective: Three-of-Five insists on sacrificing himself
for La Forge and the rest of the Enterprise; Troi is almost (unwittingly) sacrificed, allegedly for the warring peoples between whom Olcar is mediating;
and N'Vek sacrifices himself for Troi and the Romulan resistance movement.[29] And all of these episodes in one way or another are about war.

In fact, considering these themes of sacrifice and of battle, Troi's prominent fashion changes seem a result or an incident somehow indicative of

war—war, at least, between an individual and collective identity. Certainly, her change into regulation uniform is indicative of the military organization that Starfleet represents: all members must exhibit a uniformity. This indication is, interestingly, very much in line with fashion's often metaphorical connection with the military. In a brief seasonal fashion review, for instance, Ingrid Sischy (1993) made the somewhat customary comment that "fashion is war" (85).[30] Although she was referring to *runway* "skirmishes," I find her observation relevant here, for, I would say, a war of fashion—both ideological and tactile—is played out on Troi's body. In "Man of the People" and "Face of the Enemy" her body is biologically altered at best and brutalized at worst; with her corporeal changes come, of course, her changes in dress. But in "Chain of Command," Jellico simply orders Troi to change her uniform. Indeed, through this intervention by Jellico, the extreme imbalances of Troi's fashions—the excessive sexual garb that precedes it and the butch costume of the Romulan that follows it—seem to reach an equilibrium, or find "an exchangeable truth" (Baudrillard 1983), in her wearing of the Starfleet standard uniform. In other words, after her body has been ravaged as a "receptacle" in "Man of the People" and later as a Romulan in "Face of the Enemy," we hardly notice that Troi has been successfully assimilated into the uniform Enterprise "collective."

"Costume," says Roland Barthes (1972), "should be an argument" (46). I would extend this to say that "fashion is an argument," one that debates the two contradictory (or, metaphorically, warring) spaces, in Simmel's (1971) words, of isolation and union. And while fashion is an argument, television is an argument as well, an argument not unlike fashion. Although fashion might be said to assimilate individuals into a collective spectacle, television requires the assimilation of individual viewers into a collective (or familial) audience. One way to do this is to create a collective spectacle. Thus the "dialogue" between the television spectacle and the television audience is based not on a reciprocity of "I" and "you" (as Benveniste notes in the case of language and as Christian Metz recognizes in the language of film), but on a reciprocity of "we" and a collective "you." As Mimi White (1992) and others have pointed out, television is designed to conform to the desires and positions of a heterogeneous viewing audience, "allowing for the orchestration of a variety of issues, voices, positions and messages" (190). This orchestration, however, is often purely a fabrication, for as White points out: "In striving to represent itself as a totality that speaks for and to us all, the medium inevitably raises issues and points to values and ideas that are problematic or disruptive and that cannot be neatly or easily subsumed in general social consensus" (192). Contradictions, like the contradictory space of fashion itself, inevitably arise. *TNG* mediates a particularly interesting set of contradictions. Within the narrative itself, the enterprise of the Enterprise is itself in question. The series constantly attempts to represent the enterprise of the starship as purely exploratory and thus tries to conceal its actual tie to the military (Starfleet) and to war (as it effectively does in "Conundrum"). *TNG* narratives also manage temporal contradictions in that many of the narratives of the show actually reveal that *TNG*'s future is, in fact, present.

Furthermore, while it could be understood as an "alternative" show (it is syndicated; it is known for its cult following; it often provides unusually complicated story lines; etc.), it might also be understood as a "mainstream" show as well (it has been valorized by *TV Guide*; its stars appear in magazines such as *People*; and its storylines are often uncomplicatedly resolved). Attempting to locate itself within a heterogeneous viewing space—with an appeal to both a "cult" and mainstream audience—*TNG* seeks an impossible ground for itself. In other words, these contradictory positions arise—and are possibly eliminated—when individual viewers conform to become part of a familial (or "collective") identity that television posits. So, as it does attempt to appeal to a larger, more mainstream audience (and it has been clearly successful in this attempt, for it is the most popular hour-length show in syndication ever), its enterprise to maintain a position as an "alternative" show becomes increasingly difficult. Indeed, perhaps its position as an alternative show is itself a kind of ruse. (Even an "alternative" show requires a collectivity of viewers.) As is the case with television, the very debate concerning fashion's own contradictions might also be exposed as a ruse, for in fashion, individuals are often assimilated into a collectivity. (Union actually overrides isolation.) As I remarked previously, Saussure (1966) distinguishes between *langue* (language) and *parole* (speech), noting that speech is "both a social product of the faculty of speech and a collection of necessary conventions that have been adopted by a social body to permit individuals to exercise that faculty." Speech, and I would argue fashion (like television), are already bound to the "social." Thus, an individual neither speaks nor dresses outside of some sort of collective order; indeed, Saussure declares, speech "belongs both to the individual and to society" (9). Thus, Troi's initial "individuality," coded by costume, figures her as an individual purely in sexual terms—she stands out as the only crewmember in eroticized garb. At the same time, the apparent eroticism of her costumes stems from a "collection of necessary conventions" that recognize women's "individuality" as sexual beings.

As Rabine (1994) has deftly pointed out, we must ask who speaks the language of fashion and to whom it is addressed. With regard to Deanna Troi on *TNG*, we must note that her dress—"spoken" simultaneously by "Troi" and the "social" world of the Enterprise (a microcosm of television itself)—addresses, or places, her squarely within the spatial dissymmetry of fashion. She stands out on the Enterprise but is placed within its collective control, as markedly when she is transformed in "Man of the People" as when she is dressed in regulation uniform in "Chain of Command." This seeming contradiction of being at once an individual and part of a collective is particularly contained when her individual body itself is fashioned (either figuratively or literally) into the collective. In fact, at this point, the fashioning of a body no longer allows a masquerade, a play between spaces, because the distance necessary for masquerade no longer exists (if a distance existed in the first place) between the body and its gender display. Thus, the fashion "addressed" to and in Troi reveals less about the character wearing it than about the character of the social space in which she is wearing it. Moreover, Troi's fashion helps to reveal that her individuality itself, like Hugh's—sacrificed in the end for the collective—may indeed have been a ruse all along.

Notes

Many thanks to Lynne Joyrich for her support of this original essay and for her valuable suggestions toward revision. I would also like to thank my old friend Max for his perceptive comments about Troi's costume, Herbert Blau for leading me to important critical sources on fashion, and the editors of this volume for pushing me to improve this essay. My special appreciation goes to Aline Akelis for her sustained insights about *TNG* and for her invaluable friendship.

1. I would like to thank Lisa Cohen for reminding me of this important episode after I presented a version of this chapter at the 1994 Console-ing Passions Conference in Tucson, Arizona.

2. The notion of "instinct" plays an important role in this episode. In the opening scene, after beating Data at a game of chess, Troi tells Data that the game is not based purely on logic but on instinct as well. In this episode, Worf's "instinct" is—not surprisingly—represented as warring. This "instinct," moreover, is draped across his body in the form of his warrior sash. Perhaps it is this secondary instinct toward fashion, or "decoration," that brings him and Troi together by the series' end.

3. Although I would take issue with Bell's tendency to see fashion as liberatory or oppressive, I do find his national metaphors about fashion insightful.

4. I am referring to the distinction Ferdinand de Saussure (1966) lays out in *Course in General Linguistics.* Language, he says, "is a self-contained whole and principle of classification." Human speech, on the other hand, "is both a social product of the faculty of speech and a collection of necessary conventions that have been adopted by a social body to permit individuals to exercise that faculty. Taken as a whole, speech is many-sided and heterogeneous; straddling several areas simultaneously—physical, physiological, and psychological—it belongs both to the individual and to society; we cannot put it into any category of human facts, for we cannot discover its unity" (9). I will return to Saussure's simultaneous invocation of the individual and society later.

5. In a sense, then, what I want to do is reconsider Virginia Woolf's (1929) infamous words: "[I]t is the masculine values that prevail. Speaking crudely, football

and sport are 'important'; the worship of fashion, the buying of clothes 'trivial.' And these values are inevitably transferred from life to fiction. This is an important book, the critic assumes, because it deals with war. This is an insignificant book because it deals with the feelings of women in a drawing room" (77). In other words, I would like to ask how the worship of fashion is not antithetical, but *related*, to what Woolf here terms "masculine values," and how fashion, as so many have characterized it, is a kind of "war" itself.

6. I will not be examining Troi's occupation in depth here, though clearly it is related to questions of fashion and gender identity. Indeed, her empathic powers seem both to make her susceptible to fashion and allow her to be a good counselor. For an in-depth exploration of her occupational role, see Lynne Joyrich's (1996) "Feminist Enterprise? *Star Trek: The Next Generation* and the Occupation of Femininity." Analyzing "the way in which she personifies the professionalization of femininity itself," Joyrich declares: "Deanna is valued more for her ability simply to sense feelings and incite them in others than for anything she might do in an actual office; employed for her pure emotive capabilities, she embodies rather than performs work per se" (64). This embodiment of her work, I argue, is evident in her bodily representation revealed and enhanced by costume.

7. As Rabine (1994) declares, "Women of fashion become the 'speaking' subjects of a symbolic system which inseparably entangles signs of oppression and liberation within the images of the fashionable feminine body" (60). Again, I am not entirely interested in focusing on the binary of liberation versus oppression, but it is an important binary to keep in mind, as it is often used to describe the "powers" of fashion.

8. I will be understanding "assimilation" as it is defined through episodes pertaining to the Borg, though I also will be using this same definition to critique the process of "assimilation" enacted by those on the Enterprise. To those on the Enterprise, assimilation means that one's cultural or national identity will be subsumed (and thus erased) by the new dominant order.

9. "Species" on *TNG*, I would contend, stands in for race. I will thus use the term "species" throughout this paper, but I would agree with Anna McCarthy (1992) that "[s]pecies it seems, can only be understood according to the existing terms which designate race" (4). Through its attention only to "species," the series superficially erases questions of race *within* the diegesis. At the same time, the tension between particular species and even the identifying characteristics of some species are pointedly informed by race issues outside of the diegesis. The series thus purports to eliminate race as part of its humanist, utopic project, but its often obvious exchange of "species" for "race" in its narratives reveals the impossibility of erasing questions of race altogether from the sort of social commentary *TNG* attempts.

10. Troi's empathic abilities, marked as a characteristic of the Betazoid species, work to prove that the humanism *TNG* wants to advocate is universal. Such a logic is repeated (and exceeded) in the representation of Data, the android who is more "human" than any other member of the ship.

11. This scene seems to lend itself to an analysis in terms of the concept of the Other. The designation of the Borg member as "you" seems related to an attempt by Crusher and La Forge to "other" him. However, to recognize it as such is also problematic. The act of indicating an Other is traditionally performed by those with a "dominant" identity. At the same time, the recognition of having been identified as

Other has been a significant step for those who have been dominated (people of color, women, nonheterosexuals, etc.). The very recognition—and at times, the appropriation—of this identity thus becomes a strategic act. Since the Borg is attempting to become the dominant order in the space in which Starfleet also travels, it is not in the conventional position of an Other. To name it (even just one member, a concept already troubled) as such is to allow it a strategic position of marginalization usually reserved for the dominated rather than the dominating. Clearly, those on the Enterprise wish to see the Borg as something "other" than they, but, as I will show, they are also similar—similar precisely in terms of their desire toward "dominance." (This similarity would be most emphatically denied by members of the Enterprise and, I think, makers of the show.) In a sense, this difference/similarity does underlie the concept of otherness. For instance, Trinh T. Minh-ha (1986/1987) describes the "gestures" of the "Inappropriate/d Other" as follows: "that of affirming 'I am like you' while pointing insistently to the difference; and that of reminding 'I am different' while unsettling every definition of otherness arrived at" (9). But considering the position of the Borg—and, indeed, noting the fact that here Trinh is describing the gestures of non-white women—I would still maintain that this concept is relatively inappropriate in this case.

12. Significantly, as far as I can tell, all of the Borg members are white.

13. This declaration interestingly resembles that by a young woman who is found to possess the powers of the Q two seasons after "I, Borg." She also is given the chance to stay aboard the Enterprise as a human or take on the powers of the Q. Unable to resist her omnipotence when a planet is threatened, she inevitably (and naturally) chooses the latter. Explaining this choice to Picard, she states simply, "I am Q." Having already proven that she is like the other humans aboard the Enterprise ("I am you"), this statement seems to indicate that she will use the powers of "Q" as would "you."

14. And these words seem to have come true when, in a later episode, many members of the Borg, at the bidding of Data's brother Lore, seem to have become "individuals" of a sort, ones who collectively break with the Borg and join Lore in order to fight the Federation. Hugh, in fact, is torn between helping the Federation and helping the Borg members.

15. Worf's, Ro's, and others' racial and national identities are further underscored by the use of makeup, a direct fashioning of the body. In her essay "Making Faces," Kathy Peiss (1990) explores the relationship of the cosmetics industry to the formation of feminine and racial identities. She says, "Whatever the class and race of cosmetics consumers, all segments of the industry in their advertising and marketing reshaped the relationship between appearance and feminine identity by promoting the externalization of the gendered self, a process much in tune with the cosmetics industry" (157). Although not directly benefiting the cosmetics industry, the use of makeup on *TNG* works to produce not merely feminine (and, indeed, often masculine) but also "naturalized" species, or by extension, racial identities. Clearly an entirely different essay could describe the effects of makeup as a fashioning of identities on the series. McCarthy (1992), for instance, touches on this in "Displacing Difference."

16. In "Encounter at Farpoint: Part I," Troi states that she is only half-Betazoid, declaring, "My father was a Starfleet officer." Starfleet, here, seems to be a species in and of itself; in opposition to the Betazoid species, moreover, it seems to be a human

one. This detail belies *Star Trek*'s enterprise to incorporate racial difference (through species variation) into the Federation.

17. Significantly, however, Lwaxana's most excessive costuming is her wedding "dress": for a Betazoid wedding, the two partners appear wearing nothing at all.

18. Indeed, the cleavage merely shifted. What she did lose, however, was the display of her legs.

19. In some episodes, other characters do change from uniforms to civilian clothes and vice versa.

20. She appears to have been successful, however, in seducing a young cadet she picks up in the elevator.

21. As I noted earlier, this "facelift" would include the change in the voice-over that opens the show as well as the inclusion of more women in the series. These changes have been primarily superficial, as the series remains dependent on traditional notions of femininity as identifying markers for women and also on conventional oppositions between femininity and masculinity. One important exception to these traditional dualisms would be Ro, a female character who is often involved in complicated plots that explore her national, rather than only gender or romantic, identity. Some episodes about Crusher also examine her identity as a doctor.

22. This change in appearance was necessary before Troi could take the bridge officer's test: i.e., before she could be fully assimilated into the (masculine) Federation and in the process leave behind even more of her mixed-species identity—her use of empathy rather than authority, love rather than violence.

23. See Joyrich (1996).

24. Indeed, in alternate realities and dream states, Troi's clothes are often used to mark both time and fantasy.

25. Bemoaning the fact that most of Troi's narratives have been romances, Marina Sirtis has claimed that this was her favorite episode, since she was kidnapped not because she was a woman but because she was an empath (Logan 1994).

26. In an original *ST* episode, Senior Medical Officer Lt. Commander Leonard McCoy alters Captain James T. Kirk to look like a Romulan, while First Officer/Science Officer Commander Spock is "wooed" by a Romulan (female) commander. Interestingly, in "Face of the Enemy" these two "masquerades" are conflated in Troi's performance as a Romulan (she is biologically altered, and she must act unlike herself). Also interesting is a scene in the *ST* episode in which the female commander whispers her name to Spock. "How incongruous for a soldier," he responds. "If you give me a moment I will transform myself into a woman," she tells him in return. With the exception of Troi's necessary retransformation at the end, such a similar transformation seems neither possible nor necessary on *TNG*. The original episode also notes the similarity between Vulcans and Romulans, while it simultaneously stresses the necessity for humans to look distinct from either species and conflates species and race. At the end of the show, McCoy suggests Kirk return to sickbay so that he can perform the corrective surgery. "Do you want to go through life looking like your first officer?" he asks.

27. To Benveniste (1971), "I" presents some mobility in subjectivity, as one becomes a subject at the moment one utters "I." As he says, "[T]here is no other criterion and no other expression by which to indicate 'the time at which one *is:*' except take it as 'the

time at which one *is speaking*.' This is the eternally 'present' moment . . . " (227). Uttering "I" dressed as a Romulan, Troi (temporarily) *is* a Romulan.

28. This adaptation of the Romulan persona also seems to presage the "assimilation" of Troi as a bridge officer.

29. In "Chain of Command," as well, during his torture, Picard is given the option to leave the Cardassian torture chamber and return to his ship. However, the Cardassian torturer tells him that they will instead turn to Crusher for "information." Unwilling to allow Crusher to be tortured, Picard decides to stay with the Cardassian.

30. Indeed, changes in fashion are often referred to as battles or skirmishes. In J. C. Flugel's (1950) influential *Psychology of Clothes*, he notes: "And indeed 'the battle of the skirts' [that] has already been christened by the press, is (at the time these lines are written), far from being ended" (165). He continues this metaphor on his own when he says, "There is even some possibility of the opposition becoming organised. . . . The moment is undoubtedly a thrilling one for the student of dress; and if the psychologist and sociologist can spare a little time from their graver preoccupations, the struggle now taking place in fashion may be well worth their contemplation, for the interesting lesson that it offers of skillful leadership in a cause of doubtful popularity" (165–166).

References

Barthes, Roland. 1972. "The Diseases of Costume." In *Critical Essays*. Trans. Richard Howard. Evanston, IL: Northwestern U P.

Baudrillard, Jean. 1983. *Simulations*. Trans. Paul Patton, Paul Foss, and Philip Beitchman. New York: Semiotext(e).

Bell, Quentin. 1976. *On Human Finery*. London: Hogarth P.

Benveniste, Emile. 1971. *Problems in General Linguistics*. Trans. Mary Elizabeth Meek. Coral Gables, FL: U of Miami P.

Doane, Mary Ann. 1991. *Femmes Fatales: Feminism, Psychoanalysis and Film Theory*. New York: Routledge.

Flugel, J. C. 1950. *Psychology of Clothes*. London: Hogarth P.

Gaines, Jane. 1990. "Costume and Narrative: How Dress Tells the Woman's Story." In *Fabrications*. Ed. Jane Gaines and Charlotte Herzog. New York: Routledge. 180–211.

Joyrich, Lynne. 1996. "Feminist Enterprise? *Star Trek: The Next Generation* and the Occupation of Femininity." *Cinema Journal* 35.2: 61–84.

Kaufman, Joanne, and Michael Alexander. 12 Dec. 1988. "For *Star Trek*'s Marina Sirtis, Love Is on the Launching Pad." *People*: 121–122.

Logan, Michael. 14 May 1994. "The Magnificent Seven." *TV Guide*: 14.

McCarthy, Anna. May 1992. "Displacing Difference: Species as Race in Science Fiction Television of the Bush Era." Society for Cinema Studies Conference. Pittsburgh, PA.

Peiss, Kathy. 1990. "Making Faces: The Cosmetics Industry and the Cultural Construction of Gender, 1890–1930." *Genders* 7: 143–169.

Rabine, Leslie. 1994. "A Woman's Two Bodies: Fashion Magazines, Consumerism, and Feminism." In *On Fashion*. Ed. Shari Benstock and Suzanne Ferriss. New Brunswick, NJ: Rutgers U P. 59–75.

de Saussure, Ferdinand. 1966. *Course in General Linguistics*. Trans. Wade Baskin. New York: McGraw-Hill.

Simmel, Georg. 1971. *On Individuality and Social Forms: Selected Writings*. Ed. Donald Levine. Chicago: U of Chicago P.

Sischy, Ingrid. 8 Nov. 1993. "All about Women: Down the Runways." *The New Yorker*: 82–87.

Trinh T. Minh-ha. 1986/1987. "Introduction" to "She, the Inappropriate/d Other." *Discourse* 8: 3–10.

White, Mimi. 1992. "Ideological Analysis and Television." In *Channels of Discourse, Reassembled: Television and Contemporary Criticism*. Ed. Robert C. Allen. Chapel Hill, NC: U of North Carolina P. 161–202.

Woolf, Virginia. 1929. *A Room of One's Own*. New York: Harcourt Brace Jovanovich.

7

"For the Greater Good"

Trilateralism and Hegemony in *Star Trek: The Next Generation*

STEVEN F. COLLINS

Recently, a Norwegian exchange student attempted to explain to me her bewilderment regarding *Star Trek: The Next Generation*'s (*TNG*) popularity in the United States. Norwegians, she claimed, generally find the television series "stupid." Although she struggled to articulate exactly why she reached this conclusion, one argument she was able to express concerned the entire science fiction motif of *TNG*: "starships" exploring the universe and technology eliminating basic human needs are conceptually as alien to her rural, pastoral native culture as a Cardassian might be to an Earthbound human. Because the assumptions behind *TNG* had no connection to her real life, the fantasy of the series did not interest her.

My conversation with this student serves to remind me that *TNG* is a television series created to reflect the interests and values of a specific culture. That is, when Captain Jean-Luc Picard speaks of space as "the final frontier," that the mission of the Enterprise is to "boldly go where no one has gone before," this French character, played by an English actor, speaks with a distinctly "American" voice. As cultural critic Anne Norton (1993) argues,

> Americans look—adventurously, aggressively, evangelically, arrogantly—at boundaries as frontiers. This is a nation extending over land, across oceans, into space; acquiring more territory, more power, more influence, more people, more cultures; transgressing the boundaries of time with those of space; extending itself into past and future; acquiring more histories; comprehending more; making more futures accessible. (174)

TNG's narrative is constructed from the values and interests that define the cultural history of the United States and is an accessible future where the characteristics Norton describe become successfully actualized in human practice. In *TNG*, "America" has become the world—indeed, the galaxy. The exchange student's distance from the series may lie in the fact that *TNG* is more than a popular speculation about the future; it is a document of contemporary U.S. ideology.

This chapter will focus on the ideology of *TNG*. Specifically, my goal is to conduct a critique of *TNG* "not to find unadulterated truth or unbridled manipulation 'beneath' or 'behind' a given text or system of representation, but to understand how a particular system of representation offers *us* a way of knowing or experiencing the world" (White 1987, 141). *TNG* presents a U.S., utopian vision of a future where contemporary values of equality, individualism, and self-actualization are ostensibly realized. *TNG*'s twenty-fourth century is a future where technology fulfills all material desires and needs. No longer concerned with the banalities of day-to-day existence, humans and nonhumans work collectively to gain knowledge from the wonders of the cosmos.

In the first two sections of this chapter, I will describe *TNG*'s utopian gestures toward the actualization of modern, "liberal" values: self-actualization, individual egalitarianism, self-determination, and democracy. Through gestures such as these, mass culture serves not only to fulfill utopian desires but also to repress them through the same structures. Additionally, I examine the militaristic interests defended by Starfleet and the inevitable tension that occurs when those dominant interests contradict the liberal *telos* of *TNG*. These contradictions will provide the focus of the third section. The Enterprise is a site of individualism and self-actualization; it is also a site of order, rank, and hierarchy. Thus, *TNG* is structured around very real struggles between such competing values as individualism and hegemony, liberty and order, democracy and governability. And despite the "fantasy" of *TNG*'s utopian self-determination, whenever the interests of "the individual" and the interests of Starfleet come into conflict, Starfleet wins.

In the final two sections of the chapter I will argue that the hegemonic interests of Starfleet in *TNG* parallel those of contemporary *trilateralism*, which Stephen Gill (1990) defines as "the project of developing an organic (or relatively permanent) alliance between the major capitalist states, with the aim of promoting (or sustaining) a stable form of world order which is congenial to their dominant interests. More specifically, this involves a commitment to a more-or-less liberal international economic order" (1). I will argue that the strategies Starfleet uses to interact with other dominant powers in the universe reflect the contemporary hegemonic interests of trilateralism in *TNG*. More importantly, whereas *TNG* purports to advocate a clear commitment to egalitarian democracy, it instead serves to legitimate an ideology that constrains democracy in favor of the "governability" of human beings. Finally, I argue that by defining human rights through the security of international capitalism, *TNG* perpetuates an oppressive cultural imperialism.

Reification, Utopia, and Liberal Ideology

In the conclusion of *Republic of Signs,* Norton (1993) makes this observation about U.S. culture:

> The American passion for expansion—from the Atlantic to the Pacific, to new frontiers, "where no one has gone before"—is allied to a passion to extend ourselves in time. . . . There is never enough. . . . Against satisfaction, [U.S.] popular culture speaks of desire: the desire for more things, more knowledge, more forms of self, more time, more power, more rights, more justice. (173)

Norton here implies two arguments: first, that U.S. popular culture defines the present by glorifying the past and speculating on the future; second, that U.S. popular culture identifies *desires* instead of recognizing *possessions.* Science fiction texts realize this expansive desire by constructing ideological commitments of the present in speculative utopian futures, safe from the interruptions of present-day realities. Certainly, this function of science fiction can have positive utility. Marleen S. Barr (1987), for example, notes a feminist potential of speculative fiction: "Because [speculative fiction] writers are not hindered by the constraints of patriarchal social reality, they can imagine presently impossible possibilities for women. Their genre is ideally suited for exploring the potential of women's changing roles" (xi).

TNG constructs a utopian "liberal" text that identifies "self-expression and self-discovery with liberation . . . predicated on the notion of an autonomous self, an independent will that [individuals can] discover within" (Norton 1993, 159). Although "liberal" and the corresponding "liberalism" are certainly complex and broadly defined terms, for the purposes of this chapter I refer to "liberalism" simply as the political philosophy of modernism. For example, Janice Peck (1994) offers the following definition:

> Liberalism is based on a belief in the primacy and autonomy of the individual. . . . Capitalism is viewed as the natural result and extension of this essentialized individualism, and society as an aggregate of such individuals pursuing their interests. The ability to engage in this pursuit without constraint constitutes individuals' rights, and equality becomes the condition in which all individuals have equal access to the means to pursue their private ends. (94)

Thus, the utopian future of *TNG* offers an opportunity to imagine the possibilities of liberal goals and values: self-actualization and self-determination, without external interference.

As Frederic Jameson argues, however, the positive potential of mass culture can be counterproductive: through satisfying the desire for change, the realization of the need for change can be repressed. In "Reification and Utopia in Mass Culture," Jameson (1979/1980) states that "all contemporary works of art ... have as their underlying impulse ... our deepest fantasies about the nature of social life, both as we live it now, and as we feel in our bones it ought rather to be lived" (147). Jameson's emphasis on the normative functions of art suggests that art cannot be an end in itself but rather becomes a means to an end through its commodification (131). Thus, mass culture serves as a locale for the complex reification of contemporary attitudes and values: we experience our fantasies for social life through the construction of utopian ideals, and it is through the constant repetition of those ideals that our faith in their actualization is entrenched. The ideology of mass culture depends on utopian elements as a kind of "fantasy bribe" through which people may be promised the things they desire, without ever actually obtaining them (144). Television is ideological precisely because it offers a "particular construction of the world" in this manner (White 1987, 146). Referring to the psychoanalysis of Norman Holland, Jameson (1979/1980) explains:

> To rewrite the concept of a management of desire in social terms now allows us to think repression and wish-fulfillment together within the unity of a single mechanism, which gives and takes alike in a kind of psychic compromise or horse-trading, which strategically arouses fantasy content within careful symbolic containment structures which defuse it, gratifying intolerable, unrealizable, properly imperishable desires only to the degree to which they can again be laid to rest. (141)

We can therefore "conceive how (commercial) works of art can possibly be said to 'manipulate' their publics" (141). The key to Jameson's argument in ideological terms rests with the "management of desire" in mass culture. As commercial products, television and other works of mass culture are constructed in particular ways according to particular interests. The management of how a text is constructed thereby imbues that text with a particular ideology.

Utopian Gestures

At first glance, *TNG* offers the positive potential for a utopian future: the twenty-fourth century where there is no poverty, no inequality, no material wants. The universe of the future is one where idealistic images of contemporary liberal values become actualized everywhere: reason reigns over passion; science rules over mysticism; technology is an unqualified good; the "progress" of the human subject is a given. Indeed, these very values are codified in the Articles of Federation (AOF) that govern Starfleet and guide *Star Trek* as a whole. Michael Calvin McGee (1980) writes that "ideology in practice is a political language, preserved in rhetorical documents . . . characterized by slogans, a vocabulary of 'ideographs' easily mistaken for the technical terminology of political philosophy" (5). The Preamble to the AOF, for example, is saturated with liberal "ideographs": "the dignity and worth of the intelligent life-form person"; "equal rights of male and female and of planetary social systems large and small"; "establish . . . justice and mutual respect"; "promote social progress . . . in larger freedom"; "practice benevolent tolerance and live together in peace"; promote "the economic and social advancement of all intelligent life-forms" (Joseph 1986, n. pg.). The terminology of the *Star Trek* "constitution," therefore, establishes a liberal ideology.

Episodes of *TNG* amply represent the AOF's utopian liberalism. In "Encounter at Farpoint," *TNG*'s first episode, the omnipotent Q places Picard and the Enterprise crew on trial for the crimes of humanity to prove Q's claims that humans are "a dangerous, savage, child race." Picard's response to Q's initial challenge establishes Picard's ideological ground: "I agree we still were . . . four hundred years ago. . . . But even [then] we had already started to make rapid progress." When Q rebuts that human history is the "same old story" of murder and conquest, Picard asserts that "the same old story is the one we're meeting now: self-righteous life forms who are eager—not to learn—but to prosecute, to judge anything they can't understand or won't tolerate." Picard establishes the "progress" of humanity to a point where injustice has disappeared, where altruism and fairness exist instead of "self-righteousness" and prejudice, where the categorical imperative is to learn about others instead of to dominate them. Thus, from the first episode, *TNG* establishes a view of itself as already-actualized perfected liberalism.

TNG's commitment to the use of technology for the progress of individual self-actualization further expresses this reification of liberal values and society. Norton (1993) states that liberal society "value[s], in practice, not only the useful products of the mind but inventions that serve the senses" (172). Technology is, therefore, an inherent good, a tool used for the benefit of humanity. Specifically embodied through the Enterprise, "technology" is as much a character on *TNG* as Picard, First Officer Commander William Riker, or Counselor Lt. Commander Deanna Troi.[1] In *TNG*, technology is the tool with which the crew of the Enterprise solves the unknowns of the universe; as such, especially through the ship/computer dialectic, it becomes a metonym for the entire crew and their liberal desire to investigate the unknown and gain knowledge from it. The very name of the ship itself—Enterprise—indicates an ideological resonance with the integrity of liberal-capitalist values. Unsurprisingly, the majority of the plots on *TNG* involve threats to the integrity of the vessel by various life forms or situations. Because the entire crew lives *within* the Enterprise, any threat to the ship becomes a threat to each individual member: the crew depends on technology for their very existence. Lt. Commander Data is an actualized embodiment of this merging of technology and the liberal self (in contrast with the Borg, a merging of technology with a totalitarian self). With Data, technology is self-actualized: an artificial life form, he is nonetheless regarded as a "sentient being," is given his own living quarters, and actively pursues becoming "more human." By successfully solving whatever problem exists by episode's end, *TNG* reifies the individual's control over the autonomous self; indeed, through the interdependence between technology and crew, the Enterprise *becomes* the liberal autonomous self.

Reification and Contradictions of Liberalism

Despite utopian gestures toward a fully democratic liberalism, in practice *TNG* exhibits contradictions within its utopian vision. Mimi White (1987) stresses that in television "there is a range of intersecting, and at times even contradictory, meanings through the course of programming offering some things for most people, a regulated latitude of ideological positions" (160). In *TNG*, these contradictory ideologies present themselves as a tension between individualism and rank, between democracy and hierarchy. Specifically, *TNG* contradicts its purported ideals when it comes to issues of gender and individual autonomy. For example, regardless of its claim to "reaffirm faith . . . [in] the equal rights of male and female" (Joseph 1986, n. pg.), *TNG* dictates a paternalistic and patriarchal ideology. One case where this patriarchal ideology is most evident is in the relationship between Picard and (former Ensign and now) Lt. Ro Laren, particularly in the episode "Preemptive Strike."

    The character of Ro, among others, represents the tension that arises when the liberal goal of individual autonomy clashes with the more hegemonic interests of Starfleet and military hierarchy. Ro is an outsider—a Bajoran rebel orphaned by prior Cardassian genocide—who has been given a "second chance" by joining Starfleet and assuming the "discipline" that accompanies her commission. Central to Ro's "progress" in Starfleet is Picard, who assumes a role as father figure to her. Picard respects Ro's abilities and has high expectations for her; in return, Ro demonstrates a deep sense of loyalty to Picard. Near the beginning of "Preemptive Strike," Ro tells Picard: "Without you, my life would be a very different one right now."

    In the episode, the Enterprise assumes a mission to infiltrate and expose an underground group of Bajoran rebels, the Maquis, who employ guerrilla tactics against the Cardassians. The revolutionary tactics of the Maquis threaten to disrupt a peace treaty that exists between the Federation and Cardassia; thus, Ro is recruited to become a double agent with the Maquis and to facilitate their capture in order to protect the greater interests of Starfleet. Ro accepts her assignment, largely due to her daughter-like rela-tionship with Picard: she tells him, "There is one good reason to take this mission—to validate *your* faith in me."

It quickly becomes apparent in "Preemptive Strike," however, that Ro's duty to Picard and Starfleet cannot so easily outweigh her own identification with the Maquis. After her acceptance in a Maquis enclave, Ro develops a relationship with a competing father figure, Macias, who clearly reminds Ro of her own deceased father. The "success" of Ro's mission thereby becomes caught between two polarized ideologies: on the one hand, her identification with Macias and the Maquis as a Bajoran and a victim of the Cardassians pulls her toward assisting a Maquis offensive strike; on the other hand, her duty to Picard and Starfleet demands that she betray and sabotage the Maquis. Ro's double bind lies at the root of her identity, a predicament made all the more unpleasant in that it is defined through men and paternal relationships. Ro must essentially choose between being a daughter of Bajor or a daughter of Starfleet. In either case, her decision rests on her role not as an *autonomous* individual but as a *subordinate* one.

One scene in particular demonstrates the inherent patriarchy of "Preemptive Strike." Near the episode's climax, Ro's crisis of duty becomes such that Picard is required to meet with her in person. To remain under-cover, Picard meets with Ro in a local bar, where he negotiates her loyalty to Starfleet as if he were negotiating the price of a prostitute. Retreating to a distant table, the two whisper to each other from close proximity, pre-tending to be prostitute and client. Ro informs Picard, "By this time you should be negotiating my price"; Picard places some money on the table. Ro admits that she no longer knows where she stands between Starfleet and the Maquis, and the following dialogue results:

R: Sir, I don't want to let you down. I swear that I don't.

P: This has nothing to do with me. This is about you. If you back out now, you'll throw away everything you've worked for. We're committed to this mission; now, my question for you is, "Can you carry out your orders?" I could put you before a board of inquiry for having lied to me about this operation. I will certainly have you court-martialed if you sabotage it. Now it's your decision.

R: I'll carry out my orders, sir.

P: I feel it necessary to have Commander Riker go back with you. He can pose as a relative. I just want to make sure that nothing happens to obstruct this mission. [Stands up.] I'm sorry, I don't have that kind of money.

Picard's comments frame Ro in a number of problematic positions. First, the juxtaposition between the success of the mission and prostitution places Ro in an incestuous relationship with her father figure, Picard. And in a move eerily reminiscent of an abusive father, Picard places the burden of responsibility on Ro-the-daughter rather than assume it himself. Second, the prostitution motif suggests that Ro's relationship to Starfleet is strictly in economic terms as *property*; Ro's autonomy at the cost of Starfleet's interests is a price Picard finds "too high." Finally, Ro's honesty convinces Picard that she *can no longer be trusted,* whereby he assigns Riker to keep her under surveillance. In all three cases, Ro is placed in a subordinate position to the paternal order, and her decision is framed solely in terms of her position in the patriarchy. When Ro eventually decides to desert Starfleet and join the Maquis permanently, she is compelled to apologize to Picard for it. Following her decision, Ro is no longer seen in the episode; instead, the focus is on the emotional response of loss and betrayal seen in the face of Picard, thereby granting him a favored position. In "Preemptive Strike," Ro as an autonomous individual does not exist; rather, she is portrayed solely as a means to the Starfleet end, embodied by the paternalistic Picard.

In addition to the contradictions between liberal autonomy and hierarchy in *TNG*, tension exists between the values of liberal egalitarianism and Starfleet's hegemonic interests. That is, although *TNG* plays lip service to democracy, it is deemed that "too much democracy" is a condition to be avoided at all costs. For example, in "Encounter at Farpoint," even while he is arguing with Q about the progress of human beings and asserting their liberal principles, Picard is ordering and controlling his crew's actions. Similarly, the connection between technology and the individual on board the Enterprise dictates a tension between individual will and collective responsibility. Through its metonymic function, the Enterprise designates each individual member as a cog in the greater organic machine. Any loss of "control" on behalf of an individual crew member, therefore, becomes an impediment to the overall efficiency of the machine and threatens the integrity of the Enterprise itself. One example of this can be found in the episode "The Naked Now," which functions to demonstrate further a competing ideology to self-determination in *TNG* of order and hierarchy.

In "The Naked Now," the Enterprise investigates a Federation ship whose crewmembers are all dead. The Enterprise crew becomes infected by a disease that causes them (including Data) to act as if they are extremely intoxicated. On the other ship, the intoxicating symptoms of the disease grew so strong that the crew died by irrational acts, such as lowering temperature controls to well below freezing and blowing out air hatches. As the intoxication spreads on the Enterprise, individual control amongst the crew diminishes to the point where the ship is threatened by a similar "anarchy" of radically individual wills; concomitantly, a nearby star collapses and ejects matter on a collision course with the Enterprise. This episode demonstrates how a loss of individual control directly threatens the efficiency, and thus the integrity, of the collective machine. More important, however, it shows a situation where absolute self-determination directly threatens *order*. Ideologically, "free will" is encoded as "death"; "rank-and-file" is encoded as "life."

In one scene from "The Naked Now," the crewmembers of the Enterprise—while intoxicated—cast aside their respective ranks, thereby becoming true "equals" and further normalizing this ideological tension. Crewmembers interact in ways not normally expected: duty and insubordination are moot, and the ship essentially becomes the site for one big party. In the most telling breakdown of established order and hierarchy, young Wesley Crusher gains control of the ship in engineering. As a result of Wesley's action, the less infected crewmembers are unable to steer the Enterprise away from the approaching debris. Thus, a still-"rational" Picard attempts to persuade Wesley to restore order to the ship:

P: You will now return control of this vessel to the bridge, *where it belongs,* at once.

W: I'm sorry, sir. Why don't you just tell me what you want done, and I'll do it.

P: Because, *ship's captains control their own vessels, young man!* (emphasis added)

Picard's conclusion contains a dual message. On the one hand, Picard argues that Wesley is not qualified to be captain and should, therefore, restore control, because Wesley is not "in control" of the vessel. On the other hand, Picard disciplines Wesley in order to encourage him to think that *only he* (Picard) is the captain, that only captains control vessels, and that *only* captains have the privilege of destroying them. Wesley is in violation of rank, and it is *this* act that threatens the ship. Wesley, however, breaks communication, control is not reestablished, and Picard eventually becomes as intoxicated as the rest of the crew. In the end, Data and Wesley sufficiently "regain their collective senses" of duty to resume efficiency and save the Enterprise from destruction by excessive individual desires.

"The Naked Now" represents the breakdown of liberal values because of the relaxation of established hierarchy and order. Put another way, the collapse of the desired liberal ideology stems from the existence of *too much* democracy—too much egalitarianism and individuality. The utopian actualization of liberalism is carried to its most radical extreme; as a result, the ideology of "self-determination" becomes *dangerous*. What saves the Enterprise is the status quo: ordered discipline established through rank. Thus, the interpersonal dynamics of the crew become polarized into competing ideologies: "free will" versus "law-and-order." In this context, the liberal ideology is valued only when constrained by the boundaries of dominant interests. *TNG*'s constructed situation justifies repression of human individuality. As Jameson (1979/1980) argues,

> Mass culture entertain[s] relations of repression with the fundamental social anxieties and concerns, hopes and blind spots, ideological antinomies and fantasies of disaster, which are [its] raw material; . . . mass culture represses . . . by the narrative construction of imaginary resolutions and by the projection of an optical illusion of social harmony. (141)

In other words, by using order to resolve scenarios of disaster *assisted by too much equality,* and by showing the social harmony of a future utopia achieved through order first and *equality second, TNG* effectively perpetuates strategies of repression. A "moral" of "The Naked Now" may read: Don't rock the boat. In the next section, I will argue that *TNG* is positioned in the particular hegemony of contemporary *trilateralism,* instead of promoting the "promise" of liberal autonomy and democracy, the show reflects the trilateralists' "crisis of democracy." *TNG* may value liberal ideology as an ideal, but it considers it dangerous if actually fulfilled.

Trilateralism, the Crisis of Democracy, and Hegemony

Trilateralism, as I use it here, is the ideology espoused by the Trilateral Commission, a select group of several hundred business executives, politicians, and diplomats whose "purpose is to engineer an enduring partnership among the ruling classes of North America, Western Europe, and Japan—hence the term 'trilateral'—in order to safeguard the interests of Western capitalism in an explosive world" (Sklar 1980, 2). A late–Cold War formulation, like *TNG,* trilateralism at first appears grounded in liberal theories and values. Gill (1990) cites public trilateral commission statements from the early 1970s to the 1980s as featuring "normative commitments to the liberty of the individual, representative government, the market economy, 'an international order that encourages efficiency and equity through specialization and trade,' and 'an international political order based on national self-determination and evolution'" (198). Nevertheless, trilateralism approaches the liberal individual exclusively through international economic stability; trilateralism advocates the need for an "international economic order," indicative of what Gill describes as an increasing trend toward "the transnationalisation of the state" (1). "Representative government" and "national self-determination," in fact, become defined as the "evolution" toward Western capitalism. For example, an early-1980s trilateralist report argues "that demands for a New International Economic Order should be taken seriously and steps should be taken to integrate newly industrialising nations into the international order, by engaging Third World nations more actively in international economic institutions" (Gill 1990, 201). In short, trilateralism develops a cooptative methodology for "collective management [strategies] such as 'international regimes' (in trade, money, arms control, etc.) which help mediate the relationship between states and also non-state actors" (Gill 1990, 200).

It should be noted that trilateralism does not actually function as a concrete and unanimously approved set of dictums and policies: Gill observes that "The aim of fostering a practical Trilateral consensus is a very difficult, sometimes impossible, objective" (201). Additionally, the Trilateral Commission is not an official governing body, although its members certainly include very powerful government actors. Instead, trilateralism can be viewed specifically as an ideology, one that reflects the hegemonic interests of the world's corporate elite and continues to gain material progress after the end of the Cold War. Critic Jerry Mander (1991) argues:

> As "market economics" broke out in Eastern Europe, the World Bank, the International Monetary Fund (IMF), and the Japanese Overseas Development Bank, among others, began pressuring Third World countries to mold their economies to Western development models. Worldwide homogenization was thereby accelerated. The old Trilateral Commission model of a *one world economy* . . . was finally achievable. Based on unlimited industrial production, the free flow of resources and labor, unlimited commodity consumption, and continuous ever-increasing exploitation of nature, it posited that all countries would arrive at a conceptual agreement on what the world economy should be and collaborate on attaining that common aim. (378)

The initial response of George Bush, himself a member of the Trilateral Commission, to the 1991 Iraqi takeover of Kuwaiti oil as a threat to "our way of life" and "the new world order" indicates the pervasiveness of the trilateral ideology today (Mander 1991, 377–378). The decision of Iraq to pursue its own "national self-determination" in favor of the "international economic order" thus quickly resulted in the U.S. War against Iraq of 1990–1991.

This is not to say that *TNG* functions overtly as trilateralist propaganda. The series is, however, imbued with a strong trilateralist theme. As ideology, trilateralism projects its own utopian vision of the future: "Trilateralists look forward to a . . . postnational age in which [Western] social, economic, and political values are transformed into universal values,

... a *world economy* in which all national economies beat to the rhythm of transnational corporate capitalism" (Sklar 1980, 21–24). This hegemonic outlook is situated in the context of *TNG*: In the twenty-fourth century, nation-states no longer exist on Earth, and the Federation of United Planets serves as a strategic and economic alliance. Even though money supposedly no longer exists in *TNG*, issues of "free trade" and the exchanging of commodities—especially the precious metal "latinum"—dominate the relations between the Federation, the Ferengis, the Cardassians, and most other species depicted in the series. The Federation in particular uses strategies of cooptation in attracting new members to the overall economic picture. Through Starfleet's "regime," new civilizations are encouraged to become members of the Federation if they in some way affect the Federation's vital interests. In *TNG*, the "greater good" is definitely that which is greater for the Federation, or as Security Chief Lt. Tasha Yar exhorts in "Encounter at Farpoint" during Q's show trial, "This court should get down on its knees to what Starfleet is, to what it represents!"

An additional, crucial element of the trilateralist ideology is its interpretation of the role of democracy in the future world. In 1975, the Trilateral Commission published a book-length study entitled *The Crisis of Democracy*, which examines the trilateralists' concern that "too much" democracy is jeopardizing the "governability" of society. The report states, *"The vulnerability of democratic government* in the United States comes not primarily from external threats ... but rather *from the internal dynamics of democracy itself in a highly educated, mobilized, and participant society"* (quoted in Sklar 1980, 3). According to the report, an increase of democracy in the 1960s led to a direct decrease in the governmental authority, a correlation that ultimately threatens trilateralist economic and ideological policies: The solution is "a greater degree of moderation in democracy" (Huntington 1975, 113). Predictably, considering the commission's prior support of representative government, such a publicly blunt attack on the institution of democracy raised great controversy in the commission's membership, with some calls for the group to repudiate its own study (Wolfe 1980, 299–300). Nevertheless, the arguments of the study have become integral to the trilateralist ideology. As sociologist Alan Wolfe (1980) argues:

> despite the evident sincerity of those within the Trilateral Commission who have objected to the [*Crisis of Democracy*] analysis, one cannot escape the feeling that their commitment to democracy is as much tactical as it is principled. ... The seriousness with which *The Crisis of Democracy* has been discussed, even by those who object to it, confers upon its ideas a certain legitimacy, making reasonable what only ... years ago would have seemed an outrageously extremist position. (300)

The inherent contradiction of the trilateralist position rests in the fact that tri-lateralism defines "democracy" as "capitalism," a particularly *un*democratic economic philosophy. Challenges to the capitalist system therefore get trans-lated in trilateralist terms into threats to democracy—a contradiction that is exposed when challenges demand more democracy than the system will allow.

> At the present time, a significant challenge [to democracy] comes from the intellectuals and related groups who assert their disgust with the corruption, materialism, and inefficiency of democracy and with the subservience of democratic government to "monopoly capitalism." ... [T]his development constitutes a challenge to democratic government which is, potentially at least, as serious as those posed in the past by aristocratic cliques, fascist movements, and communist parties. ... The more democratic a system is, indeed, the more likely it is to be endangered by intrinsic interests. (Crozier et al. 1975, 6–8)

The near-fatal consequences brought about by the breakdown of authority structures in "The Naked Now" hint toward a larger claim that "the crisis of democracy" is an ideological theme in *TNG*. A later episode, "Journey's End," specifically situates "the crisis of democracy" in a plot that cogently demonstrates the trilateralist ideology that the hegemonic interests of the Federation and Starfleet assume. Indeed, "The Naked Now" and "Journey's End" allegorically represent "the decay in the social base of democracy manifested in the rise of oppositionist intellectuals and privatis-tic youth" (Crozier, Huntington, and Watanuki 1975, 9), characteristic of the social movements of the 1960s and responsible for the trilateralist-defined "crisis."

In "Journey's End," Picard is informed by Admiral Lucheyev of a treaty recently agreed to by the Federation and the Cardassians that establishes a new border between the two powers. When Picard protests that the new border places some Federation colonies in Cardassian space, and vice versa, Lucheyev rationalizes the decision in the following exchange:

L: This agreement is far from perfect. Neither side got everything they wanted, but every side got something. And as someone once said, "diplo-macy is the art of the possible." Those colonies finding themselves on the wrong side of the border will have to be moved.

P: Well, the colonists are not going to be happy about that. Some of them have been there for decades.

L: It won't be easy, but it's a reasonable price for peace.

Picard becomes especially concerned when he finds that the duty of the Enterprise is to move a colony of Native American Indians from their planet; he is disturbed by the parallels between his mission and the forced removal of Native Americans to reservations in the nineteenth and twentieth centuries. To this, Lucheyev explains that "some concessions had to be made"; if the Native Americans refuse, Picard must remove them "by any means necessary." Lucheyev concludes, "I don't envy you this task, but I do believe it is for the greater good." In other words, Lucheyev echoes the oxymoronic trilateralist claim that in order to protect democracy it is necessary to suppress democracy.

Sklar (1980) argues that "The trilateral goal is to reorient efforts to *redistribute* global resources into promotion of a so-called 'new order for mutual gain.' . . . Trilateralists caution that '*in many cases,* the support for human rights will have to be balanced against other important goals of world order'" (26–30). As with trilateralist ideology, the interests of the overall order in "Journey's End" are more important than any rights to self-determination of the colonists. "The greater good" is clearly defined only in terms of the Federation hegemony. "Every side got something," save for the colonists themselves who are being forced to relocate. Indeed, the Federation considers its values to be universal to all its members, and even to those who are not (yet) members.

Picard, whose personal mission on many episodes is to find fault with Starfleet, here consents to what is figured as the dominant ideology with almost casual ease. Resigning himself to "duty," he tells the Native Americans, "There is very little I can do. The decision was reached at the very highest levels of Starfleet." But the Native Americans refuse to leave, citing deep spiritual ties to the planet they chose. Thus, the supposedly actualized liberal values of free will and self-determination, embodied in the desires of the Native Americans, come into direct conflict with the hegemonic needs and interests of Starfleet. Caught at an empathetic nexus of this tension yet nevertheless acting as a Starfleet agent, Picard initially attempts to reason with Anthwara, a chieftain of the Native American colony:

P: There are times when the greater good demands that certain sacrifices be made. . . .

A: There are also times when a people have sacrificed too much—when a people must hold on to what they have, even against overwhelming opposition.

By holding firm to the localized pole of the democracy/order dichotomy, the Native American elder exposes the ruse of Starfleet's commitment to utopian liberal values. The need for hegemonic maintenance clearly takes precedence over the individualist concerns of democracy; liberalism is forced to take a back seat and is replaced with crippling oppression. Picard carries out his orders to begin removal of the colonists.

The character of Wesley Crusher, now a Starfleet cadet, is also affected by the duty of the Enterprise to relocate the Native American colonists. Befriended by Lakanta, an Indian holy man, Wesley participates alone in an ostensibly native spiritual ritual. At the end of his "vision quest," Wesley speaks with his dead father, who encourages the cadet to act according to his conscience. Wesley reaches the conclusion that he cannot support the removal of the Native Americans from their home: when Security Chief Lt. Worf orders him to assist the involuntary removal of the colonists, Wesley sabotages their transport. This action enrages Picard and forces Wesley to make a difficult choice between the "advice" of his deceased father and the authority of Picard, Wesley's (like Ro's) surrogate father figure:

P: Inexcusable! *You defied the orders of the ranking officer* on the scene, you put the lives of the entire away team in jeopardy, and you made an already tense situation worse. Your actions reflect badly *on this ship and on that uniform.* I want an explanation, Mr. Crusher, and I want it now.

W: What you are doing down there is wrong. Those people are not some random group of colonists. They're a unique culture with a history that *predates the Federation and Starfleet.*

P: That does not alter the fact that *my orders are to*—

W: [interrupting] I know Admiral Lucheyev gave you an order, and she was given an order by the Federation council. *But it's still wrong.*

P: That decision is not yours to make, Cadet. . . . While you wear that uniform you will obey every order you are given. And you will *conform to Starfleet regulations and rules of conduct.* Is that clear?

W: Yes, sir, it is. But I won't be wearing this uniform any longer. *I'm resigning from the Academy.* (emphases added)

Trapped between two ideologies, once again represented by competing father figures, Wesley's behavior is excessively indignant and childlike. However, Picard's location within the dominant ideology, as a soldier carrying out his duties, also threatens his paternal role as benevolent father when he responds with an equally petulant militarism. Wesley is forced into a polarized position, resulting in his rejection of Picard and Starfleet. Indeed, the emotional response of Picard, the stalwart of reason, threatens to usurp the entire techno-rational ideological fantasy of *TNG* with a brutally efficient authoritarianism.

Wesley represents what the Trilateral Commission decries as "a stratum of value-oriented intellectuals who often devote themselves to the derogation of leadership, the challenging of authority, and the unmasking and delegitimation of established institutions" (Crozier , Huntington, and Watanuki: 1975, 7). Through his process of self-awareness and subsequent rejection of the Starfleet hegemony, Wesley has truly become a self-actualized, autonomous being—the idealization of liberal ideology. This is not presented as a positive attribute; rather, Wesley is initially seen as being a definitive threat to the overall hegemony; difference and self-awareness may be fine for liberal theory, but, in the military those qualities interrupt the overall efficiency of the body politic. The Trilateral Commission expresses concern over what Wesley embodies: "a shift in values ... from the materialistic work-oriented, public-spirited values toward those which stress ... the need for 'belonging and intellectual and esthetic self-fulfillment.' These values are, of course, most notable in the younger generation" (Crozier, Huntington, and Watanuki: 1975, 7). The commission sees this shift in values as negative because it poses "an additional new problem for democratic government in terms of *its ability to mobilize its citizens* for the achievement of social and political goals and to *impose discipline and sacrifice upon its citizens* in order to achieve those goals" (Crozier, Huntington, and Watanuki: 1975, 7, emphases added). The commission's coded language articulates the very real threat that social movements pose to capitalist hegemony. In other words, the actualization of liberal, democratic values results in the inefficiency of democratic leaders to conduct their business; trilateralist hegemony requires "mobilized discipline and sacrifice"—that is, the control of social dissent— to achieve its capitalist goals.

As the hegemony of Starfleet (less democracy/more discipline) becomes more clear, both Wesley and the Native Americans are forced into an uncomfortable double-bind. They can assimilate into the hegemonic collective, thereby forfeiting their self-actualized states and submitting to the oppressive hegemonic structures; or they must be expelled from the hegemony, thereby giving up any benefits of security or comfort attached to it as well as relinquishing their potential to affect it positively in the future. Wesley and the Native Americans (who also decide to leave the Federation) eventually opt for the latter choice, but that is inconsequential; with assimilation or expulsion, the dominant order of the hegemony is perpetuated— resistant elements are silenced, both ideologically and physically.

Trilateralism and Cultural Imperialism

In addition to the ideological double-bind that constrains Wesley and the Native Americans in "Journey's End," the relationship between them demonstrates another aspect of trilateralist ideology—cultural imperialism through the defense of international capital. Sklar (1980) argues that "Trilateral economics dictate increasing exploitation. ... The lesson we must draw ... is that human rights trilateral style ... is never played 'in solidarity with the oppressed' but only by and for the oppressor" (31). Whereas *TNG* appears to articulate a sympathetic position with regard to Native Americans in "Journey's End," in actuality it exploits Indians by perpetuating damaging cultural stereotypes. This episode's positioning of Native Americans against the dominant ideology thematically reifies contemporary attitudes concerning their role in society. In *Fantasies of the Master Race,* Ward Churchill (1992) specifies the Indian "role" and how it occurs:

> The aversion of even the possibility of developing non-Indian opposition to what the federal government is doing is accomplished by projecting a carefully-perfected image that the system of colonial oppression no longer "really" exists. Culmination of the process will rest on inculcating the population at large with a subliminal "understanding" that the only "genuine," "authentic," "representative," and therefore "real" Indians are those who "fit in" most comfortably. (10–11)

In "Journey's End," this "understanding" is accomplished through the advent of the episode's resolution to the conflict between Starfleet and the Native American colonists. The "voluntary" expulsion of the colonists from the Federation is sweetened by a Cardassian promise of nonintervention, thereby permitting the Indians to live peacefully on their home planet. The effect of this "happy ending," thus, is to deflect attention away from the unpleasantries of ideological double binds and toward a more pleasing resolution. The implicit assumption of Starfleet in "Journey's End" is that the Native Americans should have relocated as members of the Federation; the fact that they did not is sanitized with an agreeable denouement that ostensibly grants the colonists self-determination and allows Starfleet to avoid appearing imperialistic. Such "imaginary resolutions" and "illusions of social harmony" are precisely what Jameson (1979/1980) argues perpetuate hegemony in mass culture. Therefore, "Journey's End" assists a contemporary ideological assumption that past wrongs to Native Americans have been righted: "Only a completely false creation [of Native Americans in mass culture] could be used to explain in 'positive terms' what has happened ... in centuries past" (Churchill 1992, 241).

Additionally, stereotypes of Native Americans in *TNG* legitimate the trilateralist ideology. Churchill argues that there are three major categories of Native American stereotypes projected in television and film: (1) "the American Indian as a creature of another time"; (2) "native cultures defined by Eurocentric values"; and (3) "the implied assumption that distinctions between cultural groupings of indigenous people are either nonexistent . . . or irrelevant" (232–236). "Journey's End" situates these stereotypes when the Native Americans assume a completely ahistorical form. Projected five hundred years into the future, the generic Indians appear little different from most contemporary idealizations of them: they wear ceremonial feathers, beads, even moccasins; they live in simple, adobe-like dwellings reminiscent of *National Geographic*; they construct "dolls" that represent the "spirits" that "visit" them. The colonists have no context or history apart from obvious generalizations about how they were always relocated and Wesley's vague comment that they "predate the Federation and Starfleet." In fact, the Indians no longer inhabit the Earth. The Native Americans in "Journey's End" can be said to occupy a certain temporal "reservation"; they exist somewhere "out there," voluntarily out of sight and mind. The colonists are defined solely in terms of their conflict with Starfleet and their interactions with non-Indians. Indeed, the only specific mention of the colonists' past comes when Anthwara informs Picard he is a descendant of a conquistador. As a result, "Journey's End" helps entrench a perception that Indians have historically been little more than targets of colonialization (Churchill 1992, 233). Starfleet embodies a trilateralist assumption that the relocation is not a unique or unjustified harm to the Native Americans, thereby defining human rights in the overall interests of "intra-galactic peace and security" (Joseph 1986, n. pg.).[2]

The ability of *TNG* to define the Native American protest through Wesley, who shares only superficial values with the colonists, is particularly problematic. Wesley becomes a spokesperson for the Native American cause after his participation in the "vision quest" Lakanta prepares for him. Not only is the "vision quest" ridiculously simplistic and stereotypical, but by the end of the episode we learn that Lakanta is not even an Indian. To allow Wesley his own "happy ending," Lakanta reveals himself as the "traveler," Wesley's friend from earlier episodes. Wesley learns that his destiny lies in becoming a traveler as well, a special person who can transcend time and place. Thus, Wesley's exit from Starfleet loses any negative consequences. For the Native Americans, however, the plot device serves to expose their role as nothing more than tools to advance Wesley's interests in the narrative. Wesley needs the experience with the colonists to become self-actualized; the colonists gain nothing in return. Again, the Native Americans are exploited to serve the "greater interests" defined in specifically non-Indian terms. Articulating the trilateralist favoring of capitalist security over individual liberty and self-determination, *TNG* perpetuates an imperialistic ideology responsible for the oppressive history of Native Americans and other subordinate groups.

Conclusion

I have argued that *TNG* functions to reify modern social values while ideologically privileging the interests of a dominant class. On the one hand,

TNG presents a liberal text that envisions a utopian future where such contemporary values as free will, self-determination, and self-actualization are
ostensibly realized. However, as Jameson (1979/1980,144) suggests the
utopian gestures of *TNG* serve as a "fantasy bribe" whereby societal
desires are satisfied without actually having to be fulfilled. On the other
hand, *TNG* legitimates the repressive ideology espoused by a trilateralism
that favors hegemonic security over individual autonomy, a suppression of
democracy over an "excess" of it, and capitalist profit over social justice.
Trilateralism succeeds as a dominant ideology of *TNG*, I argue, in that contradictions that occur when liberal ideals conflict with capitalist realities
force ideological double-binds that are inevitably resolved in favor of the
dominant hegemony. Thus, the hegemony of trilateralism, and its requisite
"sacrifice" of liberal rights and desires, becomes "recognized as the prevailing, common-sense view" (White 1987, 139) of *TNG*.

My Norwegian student had difficulty comprehending who could create or
enjoy a television series like *TNG*. An examination of reification and utopia,
however, demonstrates the appeal of *TNG* in the context of U.S. society.
Although Gene Roddenberry was not, and Paramount Pictures is not, a member of the Trilateral Commission, the fact that *TNG* so forcefully assumes a
trilateralist posture testifies to the insidious power of hegemony in mass culture. *TNG* seduces by desiring the future; it entrenches by reifying the present.

Notes

This chapter began as an essay for a *Star Trek*–oriented class in rhetoric and popular culture taught by Professor Dana Cloud at the University of Texas. The author
wishes to thank Dana Cloud and the editors of this anthology for their invaluable
suggestions and help in editing the various drafts of the manuscript. This chapter is
dedicated to Frank Collins and Carole Blair.

1. *Star Trek* creator and executive producer Gene Roddenberry (1991) demonstrates the reifying characteristic of technology in *TNG*: "The Enterprise is also a
symbol of the vast promise of technology in the service of humankind. On *Star
Trek*, we've tried to show technology not as important in itself, but *as a tool with
which we humans can better reach for our dreams*" (v, emphasis added).

2. Another ahistorical stereotype of Native Americans removes Indian action from
any specific cultural grounding or explanation (Churchill 1992, 235). The colonists in
"Journey's End" are seen solely through the eyes of the Enterprise crew, through meetings and social functions, and finally through Wesley Crusher. There is never any in-
depth investigation into the Indian culture, nor is the representation of the culture in
any way complex. Instead, the Native American colony is presented as a "relic" of sim-
pler times, technologically inferior and therefore "primitive." In terms of the greater
hegemony, the relocation of the colony is in step with its "evolution" toward the
assumed superiority of Federation interests. Finally, the focus of "Journey's End" on
one, seemingly homogenous, Indian colony reinforces stereotypes that all Native
Americans are one-in-the-same. The traits of the Native American individuals are

those common to the myth of the "noble savage": silent yet strong, dignified, in concert with nature, and respectful of tribal tradition. Churchill states, "All native values and beliefs appear to be lumped together into a single homogeneous and consistent whole, regardless of actual variances and distinctions. . . . [I]t is inevitable that the native be reduced from reality to a strange amalgamation of dress, speech, custom and belief. All vestiges of truth . . . give way . . . before the onslaught of movieland's mythic creation" (236–237). Native Americans in *TNG* remain objects rather than subjects.

References

Barr, Marleen S. 1987. *Alien to Femininity: Speculative Fiction and Feminist Theory.* New York: Greenwood P.

Churchill, Ward. 1992. *Fantasies of the Master Race: Literature, Cinema and the Colonization of American Indians.* Ed. Annette Jaimes. Monroe, ME: Common Courage P.

Crozier, Michel, Samuel P. Huntington, and Joji Watanuki. 1975. "Introduction." In *The Crisis of Democracy: Report on the Governability of Democracies to the Trilateral Commission.* New York: New York U P. 1–9.

Gill, Stephen. 1990. *American Hegemony and the Trilateral Commission.* Cambridge: Cambridge U P.

Huntington, Samuel P. 1975. "The United States." In *The Crisis of Democracy: Report on the Governability of Democracies to the Trilateral Commission.* Ed. Michel Crozier, Samuel P. Huntington, and Joji Watanuki. New York: New York U P. 59–118.

Jameson, Fredric. 1979/1980. "Reification and Utopia in Mass Culture." *Social Text* 1: 130–148.

Joseph, Franz. 1986. *Star Trek Starfleet Technical Manual.* 20th anniversary ed. New York: Ballantine.

Mander, Jerry. 1991. *In the Absence of the Sacred: The Failure of Technology and the Survival of the Indian Nations.* San Francisco: Sierra Club Books.

McGee, Michael Calvin. 1980. "The 'Ideograph': A Link between Rhetoric and Ideology." *Quarterly Journal of Speech* 66.1: 1–16.

Norton, Anne. 1993. *Republic of Signs: Liberal Theory and American Popular Culture.* Chicago: U of Chicago P.

Peck, Janice. 1994. "Talk about Racism: Framing a Popular Discourse of Race on Oprah Winfrey." *Cultural Critique* 27: 89–125.

Roddenberry, Gene. 1991. "Introduction." In *Star Trek: The Next Generation Technical Manual.* Rick Sternback and Michael Okuda. New York: Pocket.

Sklar, Holly. 1980. "Trilateralism: Managing Dependence and Democracy." In *Trilateralism.* Ed. Holly Sklar. Montrèal: Black Rose Books. 1–57.

White, Mimi. 1987. "Ideological Analysis and Television." In *Channels of Discourse.* Ed. Robert Allen. Chapel Hill, NC: U of North Carolina P. 134–171.

Wolfe, Alan. 1980. "Capitalism Shows Its Face: Giving Up on Democracy." In *Trilateralism.* Ed. Holly Sklar. Montrèal: Black Rose Books. 295–307.

8

Domesticating Terrorism

A Neocolonial Economy of *Différance*

KENT A. ONO

In the prologue to each *Star Trek: The Next Generation (TNG)* episode, Captain Jean-Luc Picard announces: "Space, the final frontier. These are the voyages of the starship Enterprise, its continuing mission to explore strange new worlds, to seek out new life and new civilizations, to boldly go where no one has gone before." The triumphant music following these words signals the beginning of a dramatic, neocolonialist narrative—a patriotic reveille for today's couch potato. Whenever I hear Picard utter this manifesto, I wonder: "Who seeks?" "Who explores?" "Strange, to whom?" and "New, to whom?" As part of the larger dynamic of the show, and perhaps of television itself, a third-season episode titled "The High Ground" draws viewers' attention into the dramatic action of the characters and takes attention away from the overall narrative design hinted at in Picard's prologue. The episode's complex story relies on women's nurturing and obeisant role within the family; the maintenance of masculine, patriarchal superiority; and the Other's familiar submission to the superiority of the show's heroes. This focus accompanies *TNG*'s raw celebration of technology, space, power, and geography and creates the basis of a colonialist narrative.

In this chapter I argue that *TNG* produces a unique space wherein viewers may imagine the continuous recreation of empire through the simultaneous articulation and elimination of difference—a move similar to what Jacques Derrida (1982) calls *différance*. *TNG* imagines a space where colonial power finds, controls, and eliminates difference, specifically, in this case, race and gender differences. *Star Trek* produces these systems of difference to coordinate and articulate hegemonic relations through which future differences can be understood, assimilated, and reconstituted within a narcissistic narrative framework. *TNG* produces a carnival of differences in order to help us imagine what successful systems of knowledge/power might look like in the future. But this is not a nonhierarchical system; the

post-oppression world in which the crew operates depicts colonizers successfully integrating those they colonize into the Federation system and
teaching other colonizers similar *tactics of containment*.[1] Thus, the text
produces colonialism in order to forget it. As Paul Abbott (1979) notes
about discriminatory systems:

> Whereas repression banishes its object into the unconscious, forgets
> and attempts to forget the forgetting, discrimination must con-
> stantly invite its representations into consciousness, reinforcing the
> crucial recognition of difference which they embody and revitaliz-
> ing them for the perception on which its effectivity depends. . . . [I]t
> must sustain itself on the *presence* of the very difference which is
> also its object. (15–16)[2]

On *TNG*, seemingly endless versions of bipedal human facsimiles, infinite android/cyborg combinations, and microcellular life forms—or what
we might call bio-power—populate space. *TNG* makes a significant investment in the "vestments" of characters, a continuous strategy of reproducing, ornamenting, and dressing, through mask and masquerade, new
species for televisual display.[3] The show, however, does not depict the ideology of a true democratic pluralism. As I will argue in this chapter, the show
produces difference for self-justificatory purposes, for continuation and
preservation of the Self. *Star Trek* produces differences in order to make the
world appear to be postcolonial. In order to accept this premise, audiences
must necessarily forget the history of colonialism.

TNG is itself a *neocolonialist* world, a world in which colonial relations
still operate but do so despite having amnesia about colonialist history.
TNG works on contemporary social and political issues within the safe,
domestic sphere of futuristic television while simultaneously offering viewers the chance to reimagine the glories of past colonial power. Once the
show eliminates social problems, people of color and European and
European American women recognize the wisdom and beneficence of their
European and European American masculine counterparts. The show
beckons viewers to imagine the possibility of a colonialist system that
works perfectly, without the troublesome resistance and protest that ordi-
narily accompanies domination of differences. Not unlike how Benedict
Anderson (1983) defines a "nation" as an "imagined community," *TNG*
constructs a "limit-text," an imaginary frontier in space where rationalization of colonialist practices takes place. *TNG* pretends colonialism is a
product of the past, not a continuing present condition[4]. The text may forget racism, sexism, and economic oppression on board the ship; however,
it remembers only selectively the elimination of those awful events. In
short, it remembers that oppression is bad but thinks that protest of that

oppression is oppressive; then, it can forget that the world of *Star Trek* is itself oppressive.[5]

In order to forget, the text maintains a faith in technological progress—a belief that through the use of more advanced technological equipment, Federation (read: U.S.) society stays on a linear path toward ultimate perfection. Greater technological proficiency, which humans always attain and the Federation always possesses, will resolve contemporary and future social and political problems. Through the neocolonialist narrative, ideal viewers have to assume that a perfect mixture of scientific rationality and nationalism will result in a utopic future.[6] The show conditions viewers to believe in the Enterprise, the Federation, and their purpose—the Prime Directive—in order to understand the entertaining quality of the show. Therefore, ideal viewers also have to have faith in the authority and power of European and European American men so that the "best of both worlds"—fictional television and television that addresses social/political issues—is possible.

As a result, ideal viewers of the colonialist *TNG* signifying system also understand that when the Enterprise crew encounters Others, either those Others will have to submit to the logic, rationality, and culture of the Federation, or they will die.[7] *Différance* must fit neatly into the structure of Federation authority. Enterprise crewmembers let Others know that they are inherently inferior and that they should act more like Enterprise crewmembers, who embody ideal human potential.

As much as the show tries to make oppression part of the past, the science fiction text persistently relies on a system of difference in order to organize its message for maximum communicability.[8] Therefore, *TNG*, as a neocolonial text, selectively remembers and forgets resistance, protest, and oppression. With scientific progress as its *telos,* it faithfully adheres to technological rationality, nationalist consciousness, and military authority as mechanisms for achieving the ultimate good. Finally, *TNG* assumes all people are equal—but only on the Enterprise, where crewmembers fertilize and sow an absolutely perfect logical ideology. Elsewhere, the supremacy of Federation logic continuously has to be retaught.

Television is the perfect vehicle for this lesson because the historical truth that television shows like *Leave It to Beaver* and *Father Knows Best* create—landmark narratives in which families repeatedly realize the superior wisdom of the father before the episode ends—allows for the kind of paternalism *TNG* continues to construct.[9] In addition to the larger Enterprise family, the family unit provides a kind of pedagogical space in which to learn how to have ideal social relations. *TNG* encourages viewers to be comforted by the power they see the family-like crew successfully employ.[10] Television reproduces paternalistic, neocolonialist narratives to sustain power relations and to ensure that things are fine, even while social and political exigencies outside of living rooms abound.

We may begin this study by asking: What system of power relations best explains how *Star Trek* operates within a U.S. economy? What specific interests are served by this representational system? How are television shows embedded in logics that precede them? And how are narrative, ideology, and character systematically aligned to produce a particular system of signification? By asking these questions, we can perhaps begin to understand how ideological systems underlie the surface narrative of the show.

Power Relations on "The High Ground"

We can understand *TNG*'s administration of narrative effects by analyzing the trials and tribulations of characters within the neocolonialist episode "The High Ground." "The High Ground" is the first *TNG* episode to address directly the issue of terrorism.[11] This episode highlights the terrorist's resistance to state power, authority, and control, which makes it a particularly appropriate text to study.[12] "He" metaphorically represents the native who captures the colonizer's property, woman, and successfully evades capture, until the finale.[13] Nonetheless, because the colonialist narrative wants the Other to accept Western rationality, this episode portrays the terrorist as "rationalizable"—having the potential to be made rational. Importantly, however, the only reason this rationality is possible within the Other is because the Other can be portrayed as white (read: Western) in the first place. "The High Ground" operates via a traditional colonialist narrative even while it entertains the possibility of "native" rationality. This is important because as a result of this episode's depiction, the native need no longer be irrational to warrant elimination.

The episode begins with a series of establishing shots of a sanitized building on Rutia IV, not unlike a suburban mall with high ceilings, painted air ducts, and the like. We see Chief Medical Officer Commander Beverly Crusher, Security Chief Lt. Worf, and Lt. Commander Data on the surface before a bomb goes off. Crusher rushes to the aid of injured people, but an Ansata resistance-fighter suddenly appears, takes her hostage, and, with other Ansata, holds her in the caverns below Rutia for the rest of the episode, while (all) men on the ship fashion rescue attempts.

The episode operates via a series of dialectical oppositions and contrasts among three main ideological groups on the show: the Rutians (above ground), the Ansata (below ground), and the Enterprise crew (in space— "The High Ground").

ENTERPRISE
Transport Vessel

ANSATA	RUTIANS
Terrorists	*Legitimate Power*

These relationships reconstruct the starship as a utopic locus through the desire of others to have, control, and administer it. All of these comparisons construct the power relationships through which we are able to view the captive-woman narrative. Recovering the white woman captive through a complex set of identificatory matrices legitimates colonialist (Federation) entry into the Rutian and Ansata world. Therefore, distinctions among those maintaining patriarchal power operate together with marked gender distinctions; the episode contrasts Crusher to the female Rutian leader, and the episode revolves around a complex heterosexual economy of men fighting for women.

Enterprise

Before the credit sequence to each episode, a series of opening shots establish and organize the story to follow. Each *TNG* episode necessarily begins *in medias res*. Hence the "The High Ground" begins with a low-angle establishing shot of the bottom of the Enterprise moving away from the camera. We see the massive ship lumbering along and hear what sounds like static as it approaches the planet ahead. In his voice-over, Picard is matter-of-fact—a stenographer of sound space dictating an historical account of each episode. Unlike the original series, where an efficient female "yeoman" would often transcribe Captain James T. Kirk's notes onto her techno-steno-pad, in *TNG*, the New Age captain always records his own messages. His entry provides information about the episode. Picard says:

> Captain's log. Stardate 43510.7. The Enterprise has put in at Rutia IV to deliver medical supplies following an outbreak of violent protests. Although nonaligned, the planet has enjoyed a long trading relationship with the Federation. Now, a generation of peace has ended with terrorist attacks by Ansata separatists who are demanding autonomy and self-determination for their homeland on the western continent. Recreational shore leave has been prohibited and all away teams have been instructed to beam down armed.

References to Reaganesque discourse about terrorism and Israeli-Palestinian relations surface through the voice-over narration of Picard, the man in charge.[14] Although the act of carrying goods may appear to be a neutral act in relation to a "nonaligned" nation, the text's ideological positioning of Picard is not. Picard authorizes a specific version of historical relations even as he makes his log entry.

While Picard speaks in the opening sequence, the ship, which is the moving visual object in the prologue, serves several purposes. First, the Columbian vessel will transport the crew to the planet in the background. Second, the ship reinforces the main purpose of the larger narrative "to seek out new life and new civilizations" as the vehicle with which to conduct this scientific exploration. Moreover, the spectator's perspective below the ship emphasizes the awesome power of both military and communications technology. The Enterprise hails the spectator to pay close attention to the opening sequence that foregrounds the entire episode and also cues the viewer to her own privileged viewing position, perhaps in her own spaceship from which to observe impending events—an ethnographic perch from which to document "native" life.[15] The cinematographic structure of this initial sequence emphasizes the content of what we later find out to be the name of the episode, "The [moral] High Ground."

Right from the beginning, the episode constructs the Enterprise crew as technologically advanced, immensely powerful, and in control. We learn, for instance, that the Enterprise is technologically superior to the Ansata terrorists the Enterprise attempts to locate. The Enterprise crew sees Ansata technology as inferior. Rutians use technology rationally, whereas Ansata misuse inferior technology. Their immaturity creates anxiety. The Enterprise crew, like the ideal viewer, seeks to uncover the transportation theory the Ansata are using to counter Rutian military strength, locate the Ansata through surveillance technology, eliminate the source of anxiety (naïve, primitive power), and bring Crusher back to the ship. The power of the ship to control necessitates flexible technology and the freedom to operate in space.

The Enterprise is organizationally and structurally superior. The crew wears uniforms with pips that designate hierarchical power and rank. Each main character plays a specific role within the narrative and serves a specific function in the story (e.g., doctor, captain, adviser, information specialist, counselor, or weapons operator).

Rutians

The Rutians, whose name legitimates their dominion over the planet, Rutia, resemble the Enterprise crew. They too live in an architecturally advanced civilization, have control over surveillance technology, are technologically developed (although of course less so than the Federation), organized, rational, and pragmatic, and strive for freedom from terror and domination.

Because of this resemblance, while attempting to remain "neutral," Picard and First Officer Commander William Riker nonetheless go down to the planet to enter into talks with the unnamed Rutian leader. As their meeting is about to end, the Rutian leader says to Picard, "Perhaps if we found ourselves in possession of some of that advanced Federation weaponry of yours it would shift the balance of power back to our favor." Picard refuses by saying, "Of course, you know that is out of the question." And, so as not to disrupt the rigid narrative design and in order to point to the "common" sense Picard speaks, the Rutian leader replies, "Yes, of course."

In order to try to rescue Crusher, Picard goes back to the seat of power (the ship) while Riker remains on the planet with the Rutian leader. In a conversation with Riker in the dark Rutian control room, where surveillance technology—ostensibly useful for tracking Ansata movement—practically fills the entire wall behind them, the impassioned Rutian leader tells a story of horror to Riker, who begins to understand the gravity of Rutian politics. She says:

> [Shot/countershot from Riker's point of view] The event that really opened my eyes took place only a few days after my arrival. [Shot/countershot—Rutian point of view] A terrorist bomb destroyed a shuttle bus. Sixty children. There were no survivors. [She stands up and pauses. Medium shot.] The Ansata claim that it was a mistake. That their intended target was a police transport. [She walks toward the camera. Cut to a close-up on her with Riker visible in the background.] As if that made everything all right. [Cut to low-angle, medium close-up from behind. She turns to face Riker.] That day I vowed that I would put an end to terrorism in this city, and I will.

The Rutian leader moves from sitting to standing in a low-angle shot; in effect, she moves from moral low ground to moral high ground in this scene. As a woman, she gains moral authority by speaking about the death of children. What this signifies is not only that she can perform the subject position of military officer properly but that she simultaneously recognizes and defers to the subject position of woman-as-mother, a position in which she is held prisoner throughout the episode. While she is an officer, her femininity hobbles her. She is preoccupied with her emotional relationship to terrorism, which she says makes her continuously aware that she might be in danger. She has ingested a patently "feminine" fear of the social sphere, which limits her ability to be a competent leader. When Riker meets with the Rutian leader again, this time she justifies Rutian fear of, and hence, military operations against, the Ansata. As they both watch Rutian police arrest two Ansata boys, the Rutian leader says: "That shuttle bus I told you about, the bomb was set by a teenager. In a world where children blow up children, everyone's a threat."

Both scenes establish Rutian moral superiority over the Ansata but social and strategic inferiority to the Federation. While cinematography constructs the preferred viewing position, the narrative suggests the Rutians have a legitimate reason for rounding up Ansata and arresting them. The text asks no questions about right and wrong, innocence and guilt, only about the emphatic rationalization of punishment. The fear that terrorists will cross boundaries and threaten the citizenry is enough to justify their capture and imprisonment. The post–Cold War terrorist lurks within a high-tech world of electronic surveillance and communication. The text defines him as an Arab on a mission, like the terrorists who killed 241 U.S. allied military personnel in Lebanon in 1983. Even while "The High Ground" might be a pre–post–Cold War text, it recuperates Cold War anxiety. The show references U.S. political rhetoric in order to depict the terrorist in contradictory ways: to be feared (as Arab terrorists are) and to be considered rational (which necessitates the whiteness the episode provides, as we shall see).

Like the crew of the Enterprise, Rutian organization emphasizes power. Although not as complex as that of the Enterprise, Rutian hierarchy is ordered. Uniforms signify leaders, police, and civilians. Nonetheless, Rutian technology is inferior to that of the Enterprise. Because the Rutians do not have equipment as advanced as the Enterprise, they cannot invade the Ansata tunnels or identify their flawed transport technology; alone, the Rutians cannot stop the Ansata.

Ansata/Terrorists

The entire episode depicts the terrorist as different from all other characters on the show. Unlike the construction of the Rutians as a weaker version of the Enterprise crew and as students of their more experienced Enterprise tutors, conceptually, the text neither complicates nor elaborates on the terrorist. We see the terrorist as a type, or kind, a species of Other. There are not multiple kinds of terrorists with multiple ideological positions. The text gives us one kind of terrorist, the Ansata, with one kind of concern and one set of characteristics. The Ansata protest Rutian domination alone. They struggle by themselves, which ultimately (after the narrative accomplishes its goals) makes them easy to defeat.[16] Additionally, because they fight alone, the narrative controls them more easily; the text makes them conceptually easy to identify, understand, and observe. For instance, Kyral Finn embodies Ansata subjectivity and utters the universal terrorist ideology.[17] Synecdochically,

Finn exemplifies all Ansata people. Except for Katik Shaw, an Ansata scout, no other adult Ansata utters a line of dialogue. Most often, the text represents the Ansata as silent; Rutians experience no resistance as they take Ansata away during mass arrests.

Finn exhibits the general characteristics of Ansata people. Neither the Enterprise crew nor the Rutians can predict his next move. Therefore, he threatens all Enterprise members and Rutians alike. The terrorist makes unexpected attacks on "innocent civilians." His enemies experience anxiety as they attempt to predict and anticipate his next move. Unpredictability justifies continuous Federation/Rutian surveillance. That children could bomb civilians demonstrates the Ansata's fanaticism. As Picard says to Crusher after Ansata capture him, "Without provocation, he and his little band of outlaws have attacked my ship."[18] The generic terrorist, Finn, symbolizes a special kind of foreign agent who short-circuits attempts to eradicate him. He evades capture, avoids detection, and stealthfully undermines technology made specifically to locate him. He is, in a word, unstoppable. As in popular discourse, generally, the terrorist in this episode is inherently hostile, aggressive, irrational, insidious, and dangerous.

Nonetheless, the text does not simply villainize the terrorist. At times, the show represents Finn as a sympathetic Other. He draws pictures and reads about history—U.S. history, no less. He even shows some emotions (e.g., bitterness when he tells Crusher about the death of his son). And as I have suggested, the Enterprise crew entertains the possibility that terrorists act rationally. Nonetheless, in most instances, Picard, as judge, pronounces the Ansata to be an "irrational people." After Data realizes that dimensional transport, the means by which Ansata transport without being detected, has deleterious effects on the body of a person who uses it, he says: "But it was proven to be fatal. To use this technology would be an irrational act." As Data speaks, out of nowhere the captain enters the screen, stands behind Data, then upstages him and says, "We may be dealing with irrational people, Data." Though he misses the entire conversation, Picard enters in time to deliver its concluding line. This indicates that authorities, like Picard, can diagnose "irrationality" without context and without having to think about it. Although it is important that Picard says the Ansata "may" be irrational—which appears to be a thoughtful consideration of the point—the rest of the narrative proves this is feigned objectivity. In a conversation with Picard and Riker, the Rutian leader says:

> These are not people we're dealing with here; they're animals, fanatics who kill without remorse or conscience, who think nothing of murdering innocent people. . . . How do I combat an enemy that fails to register on any scanner until they're literally standing in front of you pointing a phaser at your head?

Speaking with Picard on the bridge, Data expresses confusion about terrorist ideology historically. He says:

D: Sir, I am finding it difficult to understand many aspects of Ansata conduct. Much of their behavioral norm would be defined by my program as unnecessary and unacceptable.

P: By my program as well, Data.

D: But if that is so, Captain, why are their methods so often successful? I have been reviewing the history of armed rebellion, and it appears that terrorism is an effective way to promote political change.

P: Yes it can be, but I have never subscribed to the theory that political power flows from the barrel of a gun.[19]

D: Yet there are numerous examples when it was successful: the independence of the Mexican state from Spain, the Irish unification of 2024, and the Kensey rebellion.

P: Yes, I am aware of them.

D: Then would it be accurate to say that terrorism is acceptable when all options for peaceful settlement have been foreclosed?

P: [Breathes out heavily.] Data, these are questions that mankind has been struggling with throughout history. Your confusion is [brief pause] only human.

Here, Data entertains the possibility that terrorism is rational. But Picard, through characteristic frustration with Data's obsession with rationality, dismisses Data's potentially narrative-threatening logic and reminds him of his honorary "human" status. Thus, Picard adjudicates rationality. The text reinforces the power relations among Data, Picard, and the Ansata through this representation. As the dialogue suggests, the Ansata are "mad," and Starfleet personnel (sans Data in this instance) are rational; rationality makes them human.

In addition to defining terrorism as irrational, the show depicts terrorists as colonized bodies. The Ansata already exhibit signs of bodily wear and fatigue—side effects of using inferior transport technology. The bodies of Finn and the other Ansata deteriorate further each time they transport, as if their bodies carry some kind of disease. The body itself exhibits signs of already being colonized by the ailment caused by inferior technology. Indeed, the dimensional shift is the only way Ansata can get back to their homeland. Colonization always necessitates rebellion, and in this case, the bodies of terrorists mark the signs of that struggle.[20] The narrative deprives their bodies of light, which makes their skin pallid and frail and establishes their need for a doctor. The body destroys itself, which makes the Enterprise's mission of colonizing the body somewhat irrelevant. Because the terrorists are already dying from use of inferior transport technology, the goal of the crew and Rutians is to stop now what will inevitably end anyway, thus naturalizing colonialism. The disease is a map of and record of narrative progress; we actually see Finn and other Ansata suffer each time they use the technology. Therefore, the battle to reclaim supremacy takes place on the terrorist's body and the body of a woman, when the Ansata capture Crusher. The body is a metaphor for land; rather than the planet disintegrating, the body deteriorates. The deteriorating body of the terrorist works in contradiction: it creates melodramatic sympathy for the terrorist while simultaneously distancing us from them in that they knowingly choose this self-destructive, futile strategy, which we know to be antihumanist sentiment.

Even while signs of inferior technology show up in the Ansata bodies, the show represents them as invisible creatures, a ravished emblem of the Cold War threat. The terrorist is a traitor or infiltrator, a stealthy enemy—invisible and undetectable. The terrorist hides out in dormancy until he regains strength. Radar screens cannot detect him. He has limited means of attack and approaches only to enter, destroy, or capture. Whenever the show depicts the terrorist as having intent, we see the strategic, insidious, unpredictable, stealthy, and uncontrollable behavior underlying the surface of the terrorist's body. Terrorism symbolizes an uncontrollable world, a continuous physical threat, and a constant fear of mortality. The terrorist lives beneath the ground and remains invisible, but is potentially omnipresent. He represents the world as a hostile and uncontrollable space. The terrorist inhabits a marginal space, works at the boundaries or seams, or on the periphery.[21]

The terrorist lives below ground, a foreigner caught beneath the city in the caverns. The terrorist clogs the bowels of city life. The city experiences constipation as a result of him; we see him only during bodily attack. The tunnels below metaphorically suggest veins, arteries, which are contrasted with the open mall-like setting of the Rutians and the light-filled free-flowing space of the Enterprise.[22] The battle takes place in a postmodern geographical space where security guards watch over the interior spaces. The tunnels evoke the mythology of the tunnels of Cu Chi in Vietnam, where surprise attacks were made against South Vietnamese soldiers and allies. Because of the lack of exterior establishing shots on the planet, the entire narrative weaves through interior settings.

And finally, the terrorist poses an ideological threat. The terrorist creates a disinformation campaign. He produces a barrage of propaganda. In fact, he is very much a televised infiltrator—not a vicious infiltrator, but an insidious one. His masculinity, not his otherness, makes him evil. The only victim of the terrorist's disinformation campaign is the feminine Crusher. Analogous to Patricia Hearst, Crusher is vulnerable to Ansata persuasion, which Picard can see right through. The show uses her vulnerability to depict a battle between two men in order to recuperate knowledge within the realm of patriarchal power.[23]

Terrorism/Femininity

In order for this neocolonialist narrative about the capture and rescue of a Federation woman to operate properly, the status of terrorism and femininity have to be conjoined. The narrative does this by comparing the threat of rape Picard represents to Crusher to the one Finn represents to her. Although neither man actually rapes her and we never see overt sexual relations, the power relations parallel a rape narrative among the three characters in several ways. First, men coerce women into consent; and if women do not consent, men harass them, order them, take them physically, or chastise them for not consenting. Second, the military narrative teaches women the effects of rape by socializing them to endure such encounters as inevitable parts of war.[24] Within the neocolonialist narrative, the threat of rape justifies military intervention and the rescue of women. Rape does not have to be overt in order for rape relations to regulate narrative progression. Even the oblique threat of rape is enough to warrant remasculinization and reracialization of the text. That is, in this particular episode, the text has to blame Crusher for (almost) "sleeping with the enemy," even while it feminizes the terrorist by giving him faulty technology. The paternalistic, patriarchal text needs a relationship between terrorism and femininity in order to signify an Other against which to pose and employ rationality. The text has to discipline both terrorists and women appropriately in order to preserve the needs of the father at the center of the narrative. That is, because rationality is the sole province of the patriarch, the central quest of this episode is to display patriarchal relations on television disciplining those whose actions deviate from predictable, rational actions. Crusher and Finn are aligned, made parallel, combined.

Crusher descends into the tunnels under Rutia, where the Ansata hold her captive.[25] The Ansata operatives live in tunnels, symbolically a sexual locus. The tunnels enable the Ansata to pose a masculine sexual threat to Crusher's femininity—the threat of miscegenation, the mixing of blood between the primitive terrorist and the advanced Federation doctor. The text essentializes Crusher by drawing parallels between her womanhood and the tunnels and by highlighting her central role as a caretaker and nurturing doctor. After the bomb explosion, she crouches down low to the ground to aid the woman lying on the floor. Later, she descends into the tunnels, where she stays throughout most of the episode. The episode defines woman as fetish, whom men transform into an object, steal, use, and ultimately own once again. The text connects women, land, and descent in order to justify domination of women by men. Though Crusher figuratively stoops to the level of the terrorists, both she (as woman) and the Ansata (as terrorist) play subservient roles within the narrative.

The first rescue attempt, fear of the alien taking women as tokens of warfare, and a second botched rescue attempt that leads to the death of the Ansata leader, Finn, all make up a fairly conventional colonialist narrative: woman taken, rescue attempt, captain taken, surgical mission conducted, terrorist killed. Crusher's capture establishes the need for insurgency and elimination of the alien. Her capture represents a break from Acting Ensign Wesley Crusher, her son, and a need to return her to the family. Her capture represents the exigency, or challenge, preceding the fight. The theft of a woman poses the greatest threat to colonialist masculinity; it symbolizes the lapse in patriarchal power's ability to discipline subjects. Women's capture justifies a counterinsurgency as a means of reestablishing patriarchal order and control. Women's capture leads to the destruction of the native and, perhaps, to his extinction. The age-old colonialist narrative operates via a simple plot: men fight men for women. Thus, while the episode operates via the traditional colonialist narrative, the military/warfare component that drives the series complicates the old save-the-woman-from-the-scheming-evil-dark-man story.

Crusher recognizes Picard as her friend after the Ansata capture him:

C: I don't know any more. The difference between a mad man and a committed man willing to die for a cause—it's all become blurred over the last few days.

P: Beverly, I don't have to remind you of the psychological impact of being a hostage.

C: I know. I understand that. But their leader, Finn, is not what you'd expect.

The text sacrifices her body for preservation of the masculine ego by telling us that if the terrorist rapes her, we must blame her. We must not mourn her violation; we must hope the narrative successfully protects the masculine ego. Moreover, her capture justifies the murder of the terrorist. The text blames both woman and terrorist. One is blamed for her capture, the other is blamed for his death. This episode's narrative is not the one described by Susan Jeffords (1991), which is "an exercise in masculine enmity: the evil, psychotic rapist versus the gentle, paternal lover" (107). Finn is no demon; he poses the threat of the gentle, compassionate, misunderstood, and artistic rapist. Nonetheless, the show constructs Finn and Picard as foes for sexual rights and control over Crusher's body. Finn's feminization is necessary to render Picard the ultimate victor. Therefore, the outcome of the rescue attempt helps reposition the father at the helm of patriarchy, back at the center of television's voice of authority, and simultaneously reaffirms the need for technological rationality as the solution to social and political problems. Thus, the subject of politics, so often the province of masculine culture, takes precedence over relationships.[26] Moreover, both stepchildren, the Rutians and the Ansata, listen to counsel of the parent ship and vie for its attention. As in the original *Star Trek (ST)* episodes "Plato's Stepchildren," "Who Mourns for Adonais," and "The Squire of Gothos," "The High Ground" represents alien cultures as immature creatures in need of parental guidance.[27] The Enterprise crew must parent those who do not see the significance of their own power so that they might learn to wield that power more appropriately.[28]

At the beginning of the episode, Crusher says she will not be taken, which becomes the *fait accompli* for the rest of the narrative action. The Ansata capture her and take her into the caverns below. The caverns are a site of melodramatic and sexual tension and produce a secondary effect—rendering standard Enterprise surveillance technology useless. Women's stubbornness and assertiveness render men impotent. The role of impotence here shows specifically how determination and perseverence on the part of the Enterprise crew, even when superior technological capabilities fail in the short run, will overcome those who have used technology for illicit purposes. The text makes Crusher's body central to the narrative. Her body's capture instigates the quest narrative, or *bildungsroman*.

After the explosion, the Ansata hold Crusher against her will in the caverns while the rest (sans Picard) of the Enterprise crew (all men) actively use their bodies and technology to move freely across space. The woman and terrorist interact within the caverns, become consubstantial, and form a relationship of power below that of the men in the orbiting ship. Then, in a surprising turn of events for the characters whose reaction shots we see, the Ansata capture Picard. After Picard's capture, Crusher tries to talk to him ostensibly about their own romantic relationship, fearing both will not escape. But the lights go out and interrupt the relational talk, a recognizable theme on *TNG*—heterosexual *coitus interruptus*. Picard says the interruption is a signal they will be rescued. Picard's goal to figure out a way to get them out of captivity, a scheme that includes using Finn's feelings for Crusher, hierarchically places the science fictional, colonialist narrative above that of the melodramic narrative. The text submerges melodrama below that of action/adventure, stressing the importance of rationality and order over the excess of emotion.

In a conversation about the first scene of the show, Crusher apologizes for saying no—for refusing to return to the ship before being captured. The following dialogue takes place:

C: I'm sorry. If I'd only gone back to the ship.

P: Should have beamed you up.

C: You wouldn't dare.

P: Oh yes I would and should.

C: Without my permission?

P: If you don't follow orders.

C: If you'd give reasonable orders I'd obey.

P: Doctor, I'll be the judge of what is reasonable. [Shot/countershot. End of conversation.]

The dialogue, though ostensibly about the quest for Crusher's rescue, functions here as a dual allegory of coercion and consent to rape and to terrorism, which allows for control over the province of rationality. Picard, in a fit of masculine frustration and anxiety, speaks through the language of Finn, the terrorist, who takes both Crusher and Picard against their wills. Crusher attempts to discern, between the two men, who is the friend and who is the enemy, a puzzle that occupies her from her capture on. Picard reverses his earlier decision to abide Crusher's will, thereby positioning the quest (masculine ego) above heterosexual romance (feminine desire). Moreover, by grasping the mantle of rationality as the guarantor of men's rights to act against women's will, Picard's dialogue ironically ruptures the depiction of terrorism as irrational and rape and terrorist narratives as rational.

The text hides the link between rape and terrorism; yet, the text relies on their equivalence. In a later scene, Crusher compares Picard's decision not to beam her up against her will to Finn's taking her hostage. Crusher says to Finn, "He [Picard] would never forcibly abduct you or play games with your life. He would treat you with respect." Yet, Picard's own capture ostensibly could/would justify, in retrospect, his having taken this action. In obverse relationship to the colonialist narrative, capture makes one into a woman. Picard replaces his desire to free Crusher with a need for his own freedom, condemns Finn for capturing him, yet regrets not having captured Crusher himself when he had the chance. In this instance, Picard acknowledges but fails to recognize how he would have taken Crusher without her consent, how he would have become what the episode defines as a terrorist.

The episode ends with a paternal handslap. By refusing to be transported, Crusher opts for her own jeopardy. The text exposes her attempts to make friends with Finn as a mistake. This, of course, is not her first mistake. Her first mistake, to challenge Picard's authority to "beam her aboard," costs her dearly. The narrative disciplines Crusher for daring to make decisions about her own body. What Jeffords (1991) says about

Lieutenant Becker, the rapist in the film *Opposing Force* (1986), applies here: Picard "must help her overcome any anxiety she might have about rape by desensitizing her to it, so that in an actual torture scenario, she would be less affected" (103). Crusher fails to recognize just how important her body is to the narrative. Unlike all of the men who work on the bridge, she fails to see her own body as a sexual commodity, as a reproductive body necessary for producing much-needed (Federation) labor (109). In fact, Picard recognizes Crusher as commodity when he asks her if she has Finn's confidence. Crusher responds by showing Picard Finn's drawings (including striking sketches of her eyes), to which Picard responds that, indeed, she does have his confidence.

At the end of the episode, of course, the family reunites. Crusher returns to her protected feminine subject position, and Picard regains his patriarchal power. The final scene demonstrates the convergence of issues (extinguishing Finn, rescuing Crusher, reclaiming Rutian power) through reunification of the family under patriarchal rule. As Crusher steps in and hugs Wesley on the bridge, right between Picard and his viewscreen, Picard says, "At your convenience, Ensign." We see Crusher's reaction shot. Crusher is visibly startled, if not shocked. Wesley moves naturally back to his post where, with a kind of recognized legitimacy, he belongs. Crusher, however, realizes she belongs nowhere (not even as direct subject of Picard's address) and looks around to find an appropriate seat. How will she get off of our television screen and allow us an unobstructed view of our captain's seated body? How will she stop interfering with Picard's view of the ship's viewscreen? She sits down on the only place left for her—the bridge's second tier next to, and below, Riker.

The *plan américain* shot that closes the episode makes Crusher almost invisible and centers the grand patriarch, Picard. He has successfully interrupted the emotional moment between mother and son. The text, once again, displaces and decenters woman. This interruption signifies the end of the quest for woman, her reappropriation, and the reinscription of the supremacy of the patriarchal military narrative. Picard's order reestablishes the clear-cut divisions between career and relationship. Crusher's duty as doctor supercedes her role as mother. Not only do emotional displays on the bridge threaten efficient military operations, but motherhood moves offscreen. Her work is done. No need to return to sickbay. For now, a stoop on the bridge will suffice. Picard takes up the stereotypically masculine position as "master" of the house. He sits with the remote control in hand to change the channel on the television set. Picard's words control the action on the bridge and reassure the viewer that emotions in the military will continue to be forbidden so that the colonialist system of relations can continue next week.

Masculinity is awarded to the one who wins regardless of whether or not he is the one who rapes. Finn represents the rape threat because he poses the danger of the stranger, thereby relying on the cultural mythology about "real rape": that acquaintance, date, and marital rapes (and nonconsensual beam-ups) are privileges of patriarchal power (which knows what women really want), not objectification, degradation, abuse, and humiliation of women. This final scene relegitimates Picard's point of view. The show decenters Crusher in order to recenter Picard. As Jeffords (1991) suggests: "As viewers, we are asked to watch the performance of rape from the point of view of the man who is not raping, the 'friend,' and to sanction his, not the woman's, view of rape" (113). So, the text positions Picard as friend precisely because he originally heeds Crusher's will at the beginning; and, as a result of having her best interests in mind, he disciplines her for not heeding his authority at the correct moment. Throughout the episode, especially when he says he should have "beamed her up," we know we are supposed to see him through his good—not bad—side. As Jeffords (1991) argues, "The camera has ingested this point of view as the view of rape and asks the viewer to take the position of the man who does not rape, reinforcing a scenario in which the man who rapes is 'other,' is the 'enemy,' is not, in other words, the man sitting in the movie theater" (113). Television appropriates the systematic threat of rape in order to give Picard an unoccluded view of his screen. The text justifies both men's coercion of Crusher by nonexplicitly representing rape relations. The text expects the spectator to breathe the same sigh of relief Picard does when Crusher stops hugging her son and gets out of the way.

The text recuperates this centrality and authority of patriarchal power in order for the ritual, televisual, colonial performance to continue. Because television wants viewers to forget historical information from other episodes in order to receive the reward of understanding the text at hand, television requires *différance*—the articulation and elimination of differences. Colonial relations cannot be reproduced anew without continually reproducing and reinventing *différance,* which contains, through its very inscription, metonymies of death.[29] The primary way *différance* functions is through death, through a silence that cannot be heard (Derrida 1982, 3). The point of differentiation and of deferral (14), of forgetting the moment of demise where what was once present is now absent, disappears through the reproduction of the relations of opposition. In order to be forgotten, what once was a presence disappears and through the act of disappearing, *différance* takes its place. While the viewer forgets the act of deferring, the text forever reproduces the site of deferral. The text does not constitute *différance* from some-thing; *différance* constitutes its own derivative features. If nothing else, *différance* signifies a location, "a spacing and a temporization, a play of traces" (15) that establishes a narcissistic effect where "the same and the entirely other, etc., cannot be thought *together*" (19).[30] Thus, while television sublimates the moment of deferral, television sticks *différance* in its place as the burial site for that to which it refers. It is no wonder that *différance* is crucial to understanding the way colonialist domination functions by reproducing systems of signs that negate the fact that people died at the hands of colonialism. Without *différance,* viewers could not forget the moment of conquest—of death, or more specifically, of dying.

What I am arguing is that the neocolonialist narrative depicts a future colonial world where colonial power is rational and effective, not only by forgetting that other narratives have made this argument previously but by forgetting about colonialism altogether. By the end of the episode, the ideal viewer forgets Finn's death and the colonialist system responsible for it. Homi Bhabha (1990) suggests that the colonialist narrative operates similarly when he writes: "Colonial fantasy is the continual dramatization of emergence—of difference, freedom—as the beginning of a history which is repetitively denied. Such a denial is the clearly voiced demand of colonial discourse as the legitimization in a form of rule that is facilitated by the racist fetish" (86). In this particular episode, both gender and race play a part of the system of enablements and constraints. In order for the Enterprise crew to recuperate the high ground, Crusher has to wear the mantle of knowledge and ultimately reject it; the viewer's pleasure rests on seeing her strive and fail. Thus, the text produces the entire scenario as a fetish of *différance.* But once the text produces a threat to patriarchal military power, the narrative hurries to recuperate the power of the colonizer within familial relations. Thus, in the end, the show restores the family to its original condition. Crusher is less visible, more on the periphery, and lacks a chair at the family table. In contrast, Picard is centered in his chair, in control of the family, waiting to engage, fully committed to the military project of the *bildungsroman,* which is the ethnographic, neocolonialist quest narrative structure. Without too much difficulty, analysis of this final shot provides evidence of the recuperation of the nuclear, heterosexual family, the centerpiece of the neocolonialist narrative, something television would tell you to hang above your fireplace.

Domesticating Terrorism

TNG constructs a colonialist system, not primarily through the representation of overt domination of peoples inhabiting the "final frontier," visual representations of conquest and of military force, destruction of evil civilizations, or ritual performances of physical power in space (although all of these are part of the construction) but through an ethnographic project that pivots on the desire for knowledge of and power over the Other. As the prologue suggests, "Its continuing mission [is] to explore strange new worlds, to seek out new life and new civilizations." In this prologue, the colonizers no longer exert physical control over the land. Instead, the contemporary form of colonization, neocolonization, entails ideological/peda-gogical control over the visual space of representation.[31]

Whereas the episode reestablishes the power of patriarchy within the tele-visual domestic sphere, the text has to make terrorism palatable as a subject for audiences afraid of terrorism's effects. Therefore, the show domesticates terrorism for television. Television produces terrorism as an experiment for viewers to imagine what would happen if terrorists actually were to take over, to envision strategies to address terrorism, and constantly to deny the terrorist as Self. Ironically, viewers can also practice being terrorists them-selves. This is television's domestication of the issue. Television announces the terrorist as something we should fear, even though the text inevitably will destroy him. Several things happen to terrorism in the process. First, television makes terrorism familiar. It creates the terrorist as a counter to the viewer's Self. As Marita Sturken (1992) suggests, "Recognition evokes familiarity. The other is not an unidentified, foreign element, but an aspect of oneself" (361). The terrorist represents the colonialist's fear of the perfect invader, the invader so much ourselves that we must fear his mimetic excel-lence, our body turning in on itself for purposes of self-destruction. This show describes Crusher as vulnerable to terrorist persuasion; in order to read the text appropriately, the viewer must fear the terrorist will succeed in persuading her that terrorists have humanity. We fear her becoming a terror-ist, par excellence, a threat to her own humanity. Domesticating the terrorist entails recognizing him as a kind of benevolent, yet traitorous, anomaly willing to kill humans for self-preservation. As Sturken writes, "This horror, like *horror autotoxicus,* is the horror of turning upon oneself, of a contami-nation of the notion of self, and an inability to separate self from non-self, friend from enemy" (369).

In this economy of *différance,* television produces the threat to and by the Other for narcissistic purposes. As Bhabha (1990) suggests, "There is in such readings a will to power and knowledge that, in failing to specify the limits of their own field of enunciation and effectivity, proceed to individu-alize otherness as the discovery of their own assumptions" (75). Those in power construct otherness within their own limited system of discourse in order to rationalize the status quo system of relations as they exist.

The narcissistic terrorist narrative can only function mimetically by standing in for a Self that is white. For example, the parameters of *TNG* texts would not have allowed an Arab or Arab American to play the part of Finn. Television domesticates the terrorist through e(race)ure of that from which white differs. In this case, television wants the viewer to forget that a person of color does not play Finn, making way for the newly constructed narrative. Finn does not look like the stereotypical, news program Arab ter-rorist that Edward Said (1988) describes. By replacing the Arab terrorist, the show does not simply elide historical terrorist depictions. The name, Finn, after all, maintains references to Irish identity, which may register as a trace reference to the IRA. Thus mere first-order signification that sees simple relations between characters and news discourse fails to address the complex way television organizes the discourse of terrorism. The system of substitution—Palestinian for Irish, Israeli for British—reinforces the license of science fiction.

Finn's whiteness allows Crusher and Data to consider Finn's terrorism a rational and legitimate form of political protest; he speaks with no accent and affirms the language of democracy. The primitive form of Finn's democratic belief structure legitimizes the history of the Enterprise/Starfleet/Federation itself. His model of democracy, though primitive, is a necessary precursor, once destroyed, to democracy's present superior condition. *TNG* functions through desire/fear of the terrorist by mirroring the centrality of that democratic ideology. Thus, Finn embodies a transitional subject position on the road to a more sophisticated and therefore more understandable and caring—hence domestic—democratic subject. And because the narrative logic of the show defines terrorism as an ideology, not as a struggle against racial oppression, imperialism, and totalitarianism, the episode lays a narrative foundation from which to eliminate the terrorist entirely. The text includes the terrorist as member of the ideological system of the narrative, but it "others" terrorism because of terrorism's primitive, infantile state. This immature state of ideological evolution—predemocracy—functions as fear of the unpredictable. The following scene between Crusher and Finn about the relative legitimacy of terrorism provides evidence of the way television begins to domesticate terrorism within the Western, rational framework. Finn is drawing pictures of Crusher:

C: How can you have such a casual attitude toward killing?

F: I take my killing very seriously, Doctor. You are an idealist.

C: [Walks away.] I live in an ideal culture. There's no need for your kind of violence; we've proven that.

F: Your origins on Earth are from the American continent, are they not?

C: North America.

F: Yes, I've read your history books. This is a war for independence, and I'm no different than your own George Washington.

C: Washington was a military general, not a terrorist.

F: The difference between generals and terrorists, Doctor, is only the difference between winner and losers. You win, you're called a general; you lose. . . .

C: [Interrupting.] You are killing innocent people. Can't you see the immorality of what you're doing, or have you killed so much you've become blind to it?

F: How much innocent blood has been spilled for the cause of freedom in the history of your Federation, Doctor? How many good and noble societies have bombed civilians in war, have wiped out whole cities, and now that you enjoy the comfort that has come from their battles, their killings, you frown on my immorality? I'm willing to die for my freedom, Doctor. [Music begins. Finn stands up.] And in the finest tradition of your own great civilization, I'm willing to kill for it too. [End of scene. Commercial break.]

In this exchange, even though Crusher interrupts him, Finn gets the last word, yet not before Crusher articulates the ideological position of the Federation she represents. She articulates the preferred ideology of the show, which is that violence is an irrational form of protest, that it is not needed to solve problems, and that terrorists, above all people, should not be allowed to use it. Therefore, terrorists cannot be trusted with power, which means they have to be placed under constant surveillance; their power frightens. Crusher argues that violence is a primitive form, that the Federation is beyond violence as a way to solve problems. Crusher, as doctor, portrays violence as an inferior way to solve problems, which reproduces the relationships among the ideological structures of medicine, government, and philosophy. This ambivalence over the ideological rationality of the position of the terrorist helps to drive the narrative.

Television produces the terrorist as an imaginary possibility, as a safe threat, so that the audience can determine the best way to eliminate the terrorist. The show structures audience pleasure so that one obtains joy from the text by imagining the final elimination of the terrorist as the conclusion to the narrative. Television produces the terrorist as not the Self by depicting it as having a false ideology but also by toying with its potential rationality. For the legitimacy of colonialism and imperialism to persist, they must continually be questioned. What Abdul R. JanMohamed (1985) sees in colonialist literature is, to some degree, amended within a neocolonialist context. Texts no longer need to conceive of civilizations completely prior to ideology. The science fictional, ethnographic, neocolonialist text instructs contemporary society about terrorism. Via the construction of the *image-nation,* the show educates present viewers about an understanding of contemporary social relations as they can be found within other, usually televisual, discourses. Thus, television does not need to depict the terrorist as prior to democratic ideology. In fact, the neocolonial text needs only the student of contemporary society, the object of pedagogical instruction, to view it.

Ultimately, television eliminates the terrorist because he signifies an inferior, primitive ideology. His inferiority and primitivity justify imperialist domination, which is maintained through better and more efficient systems of surveillance. The narrative considers the logic of terrorism before rejecting it. The show has to domesticate Finn, the terrorist. Although he may live in the caverns below, out of the reach of the Enterprise, he nonetheless espouses democratic ideology that the crew recognizes as primitive, democratic doctrine. Once the text entertains terrorist ideology as a potentially rational belief system (by portraying Crusher as having been feminized by the ease with which she falls into an empathetic relationship with the terrorist), Picard (feminized by his capture, the ultimate blow to white masculinity) and crew gain license to use violence to effect the escape. The text warrants its own self-justification of military action to return the power relations back to the original position whereby the white male ethnographer has the capacity to conduct affairs uninhibited throughout all space. The capture/revenge/return structure of the *bildungsroman* makes clear the underlying fear that terrorism will capture man himself. The narrative rationalizes invasion. The need to sustain power supplants the Federation's search for its object. Bhabha (1990) writes:

> [Colonial discourse] seeks authorization for its strategies by the production of knowledges of colonizer and colonized which are stereotypical but antithetically evaluated. The objective of colonial discourse is to construe the colonized as a population of degenerate types on the basis of racial origin, in order to justify conquest and to establish systems of administration and instruction. (75)

Moreover, in this episode, the colonized speak the historical ideology of power better than the colonist. The colonist no longer needs primary knowledge of principles of democracy, only the desire to impose those principles and protect them militarily, thereby preempting the method of ideological/pedagogical indoctrination normally associated with *TNG*. The Enterprise crew no longer needs firsthand access to democratic ideology; it can rely on the terrorist to provide that before he is killed. The terrorist and doctor speak *différance* precisely through the dominant ideology that allows them to become the Other in the first place. Thus, the show domesticates race and gender, initially, and then delegitimates positions of otherness.

Conclusion

In the introduction to *Culture and Imperialism*, Said (1993) comments on the aporia of criticism addressing colonization and imperialism. He writes: "A great deal of recent criticism has concentrated on narrative fiction, yet very little attention has been paid to its position in the history and world of empire" (xii). As we can see through this analysis of "The High Ground," contemporary colonialist narratives sustain empire by reimagining and then representing *différance*, the site where power relations between patriarch and women/terrorists are sustained and reproduced and where the moment of difference and deferral is forgotten.

Television's production of difference is not unique. Television provides a space for continuous reflection on how society maintains neocolonialism within a complex historical moment. Vast changes in information technology complicate the nature of media narratives and ensure the survival of nationalism; complexity feeds the supply-side, narrative market. The ability to imagine a nation and to envision that nation acting is central to television's socialization and ideological recruitment of subjects. As Anderson (1983) argues in *Imagined Communities*:

> Such considerations serve to underline the fact that since World War II every successful revolution has defined itself in *national* terms—The People's Republic of China, the Socialist Republic of Vietnam, and so forth—and, in so doing, has grounded itself firmly in a territorial and social space inherited from the prerevolutionary past. (12)

TNG necessarily extends the colonialist narrative. Because U.S. culture cannot integrate others into the normative system of relations, it reduces them to the level of "productive capacity" (Bhabha 1990, 76). Thus, depictions of women and terrorists come to complement the narrative of the colonizer. Additionally, the Other functions as a site of production for the Western narrative, something that can be scripted, played, created, and conceived. Bhabha argues that this construction of Other as productive capacity has another effect. "This sets up the native subject as a site of productive power, both subservient and always potentially seditious. The visibility of the subject as an object of surveillance, tabulation, enumeration, and indeed, paranoia and fantasy" increases (76). JanMohamed (1985) further explains why colonialism needs control over this administration of *différance*. The terrorist occupies the position of the colonized, the *always already not yet domesticated*. He writes:

> Colonialist literature is an exploration and a representation of a world at the boundaries of "civilization," a world that has not (yet) been domesticated by European signification or codified in detail by its ideology. That world is therefore perceived as uncontrollable, chaotic, unattainable, and ultimately evil. (83)

In "The High Ground," the desire to locate the object of surveillance, the Ansata, and therefore to employ the surveillance technology, becomes the overall strategic flaw within the narrative. This flaw gives the camera a reason to document Crusher's life with the natives in the tunnels. By virtue of the power granted to it to *observe* and *create* the fictional narrative scene, the camera justifiably seizes upon the ethnographic space.

Though the focus of "The High Ground" illuminates the ways contemporary technologies can be used toward colonizing ends, the show deviates little from traditional colonialist narratives. As Bhabha (1990) suggests, "For the scene of fetishism is also the scene of the reactivation and repetition of primal fantasy—the subject's desire for a pure origin that is always threatened by its division" (80). Such racial fantasies contribute to the ocularcentric relationship between spectators in the era of television and colonial narrative. While still talking about colonial texts, Bhabha says, "Such dramas are enacted *every day* in colonial societies . . . employing a theatrical metaphor—the scene—which emphasizes the visible—the seen" (81).

The show delegitimates women and terrorists and legitimates western patriarchal logic through this neocolonialist mode of instruction. Bhabha (1990) says that

> denying the colonized capacities of self-government, independence, western modes of civility, [narrative] lends authority to the official version and mission of colonial power. . . . By knowing the native population in these terms, discriminatory and authoritarian forms of political control are considered appropriate. (85–86)

TNG constructs narratives in order to enable the act of forgetting, which neocolonialization necessitates. One has to forget past injustices, past slaughters, past discriminations in order to gain pleasure from viewing colonialist texts about domesticity and patriarchal control. Narrativizing both gender and race, in this example, contributes to the overall function of the text to help audiences envision the perpetuation of relations of power. As part of an overall economy, *TNG* ritually depicts gender and race in order to master them by means of televisual, narrative rationality. Such a world, the world of *Star Trek*, hails a new age, an era of television, in which physical westward expansion is complete but new forms of justification and scenarios of success are needed to convince viewers that there is such a thing as an idealized nation to be, a future nation and new frontier in space. This neocolonialist nation endures no matter what obstacles lie in its path. The limit of land does not last forever. Television creates new characters to conquer and gives instructions for how to do so.

Notes

This chapter is a significant revision of a paper delivered at the Popular Culture Association Twenty-Third Annual Meeting, New Orleans, LA, April 9, 1993, called *"Star Trek, The Next Generation,* Terrorism, and E[Race]ing Racial Difference." I would like to thank Carole Blair, Ramona Liera Schwichtenberg, and my coeditors for reading drafts and making helpful suggestions at various stages during the writing process.

1. "Post-oppression" *Star Trek* relies on the narcissistic belief that the world is post-racism, post-feminism, post-exploitation, and post-suffering. Even though Security Chief Lt. Worf, Chief Medical Officer Commander Beverly Crusher, Counselor Lt. Commander Deanna Troi, Chief Engineer Lt. Commander Geordi La Forge, and Guinan, the bartender, have fewer lines than their European and European American male counterparts, the show goes to great lengths to tell us that their fellow *characters* do not discriminate against them.

2. See also Peter Stallybrass and Allon White (1986), *The Politics and Poetics of Transgression.*

3. Marjorie Garber (1992) offers the metaphor of the "scene of construction" (134), which seems to capture quite well how the entire *Star Trek* narrative is an invented, symbolic system constantly in a state of production.

4. See bell hooks (1992), "Eating the Other," for a discussion of the refiguring of history through the celebration of difference.

5. History often forgets colonialist oppression. According to Ward Churchill (1992), military force and ideological commitment could not ensure the longevity of colonialist domination. Colonists needed more than mere force and a passion for a country of their own; they needed narratives to soothe their guilt and to establish ways of seeing the world they had built as pleasurable.

6. See Stuart Hall's (1980) "Encoding/Decoding" for distinctions among resistant, negotiated, and preferred (ideal/dominant) reading positions. I use the concept of an ideal viewer in this context throughout this chapter.

7. See Charles Ramirez Berg (1989), "Immigrants, Aliens, and Extraterrestrials," for a fuller discussion of these two types of aliens in recent U.S. science fiction and how they function as metaphors for three standard U.S. responses to immigration: assimilate, go home, or die.

8. And the very notion of difference relies on ordinary representations that difference exists, as Judith Butler (1993) argues in *Bodies that Matter.* Once difference is articulated, once a difference is known or seen (produced), it is repeated, or as she suggests, cited.

9. See Bonnie J. Dow (1990), "Hegemony, Feminist Criticism, and *The Mary Tyler Moore Show,*" for a discussion of this paternalism in 1970s television.

10. As Mimi White (1992) suggests, television is uniquely positioned within the domestic space of daily life to cultivate a therapeutic narrative that absolves its audience of guilt and provides for a soothing, if not relaxing, means of addressing political exigencies.

11. The second terrorism episode on *TNG,* "Ensign Ro," tells a story about the Enterprise helping to liberate the Bajorans from the Cardassians. Although the

Enterprise crew shows skepticism about Ensign Ro Laren becoming part of the *TNG* crew, they become more open-minded by entertaining her ideology seriously. "The High Ground" tells us more about terrorism than this episode, however, and while remaining skeptical, appears to entertain it as a possible, if not logical and understandable, ideological practice. The story of terrorism continues on *Star Trek: Deep Space Nine (DS9)* in the episode "Past Prologue," in which Bajor has been freed from Cardassia, even though the more radical, "terrorist" part of Bajor, the Kon Ma, continue to terrorize. The Enterprise distinguishes between good and bad Bajorans, some of whom are terrorists but the majority of whom are not, even though the *DS9* crew see Major Kira Nerys as a possible Kon Ma sympathizer. Finally, in the fourth of a sequence of terrorist *TNG* episodes, "Starship Mine," Picard either executes terrorists or lets them die by their own devices. Throughout later episodes of *DS9*, the fight for Bajor becomes a Cold War fight against Cardassians, and Bajorans come to resemble Israel more than they do Palestine. The show domesticates Kira; the fear of her Kon Ma sympathies gradually disappears. Near the end of the *TNG* series, on "Preemptive Strike," Ro becomes a terrorist. She defects from Starfleet, an action that makes Picard furious.

12. Terrorism, as defined by western media, means the immoral use of force by unpopular and otherwise unpowerful dissident groups. As Edward Said (1988) suggests, terrorism is almost always synonymous with being (Arabic). Terrorists attack governments that have state power to back their ideological struggle. States, like the United States, do not, according to media, terrorize. In order to be a terrorist, one cannot have the backing of the military industrial complex.

13. Susan Jeffords (1991) argues that the threat of rape by the enemy is part of a larger strategy to exclude women from combat duty (103). I use "he" throughout the chapter to describe the terrorist in order to emphasize the narrative's fear of native masculine power and to suggest that whether female or male, the terrorist's subject position is primarily a masculine position to be tamed, conquered, and thus feminized.

14. References to Reagan and Bush administration discourse are particularly significant in "The High Ground." In his opening monologue, Picard describes Rutia as a "nonaligned planet." The Ansata, a thinly veiled reference to the Intifada, are "demanding autonomy." Similar to Palestinians, the Ansata want "self-determination." But, unlike Palestine, the Ansata's "homeland" is the "western continent." In reality, Israel was created as a colony after World War II; Israel took Palestine and made Palestinians live in the Gaza Strip and the West Bank. The Intifada fought to regain all colonized land, not just the West Bank. Ansata are portrayed as "mad." When the Ansata take Crusher hostage, Picard tells Acting Ensign Wesley Crusher and Troi that Crusher might be used as a "bargaining chip." Those caught within the "irrational" project of "terrorists" have "become pawns." The Rutian leader wants technology from the Federation that might "shift the balance of power." She describes the Ansata as "animals." She says, "These are not people we're dealing with;" they are instead "fanatics" who will do anything to get what they want. Picard sees Ansata as "irrational" people; some Ansata are really children. As the Rutian leader says, "In a world where children blow up children, everyone's a threat."

15. This opening is not unlike that of *The Love Boat*, in which the spectator enters the ship through the porthole (Schwichtenberg 1984).

16. Thus, as Homi Bhabha (1990) suggests, the "colonial power produces the colonized as a fixed reality which is at once an 'other' and yet entirely knowable and visible" (76).

17. His name, Kyral Finn, is perhaps a reference to a mythological Gaelic hero.

18. The reference to "little band of" may suggest another way in which the terrorist within this episode stands in for indigenous peoples.

19. A not-too-veiled reference to Mao Tse Tung.

20. Said (1993) suggests that stories of colonization often overlook rebellions and resistances, usually long-standing, that accompany colonization, which is what allows for postcolonialism in most instances.

21. I can't help but note that my description of the terrorist here parallels that of much discourse about people with AIDS (Sturken 1992).

22. All settings are enclosed, which is the show's (and much science fiction's, such as the film *Logan's Run* [1976]) comment on what the future will be like as a result of human misuse of "natural" resources.

23. The Symbionese Liberation Army allegedly brainwashed Hearst. Television, as a medium, was the masculine entity that knew better.

24. See Jeffords's (1991) discussion of the military narrative in the film *Opposing Force* (1986).

25. Janice Hocker Rushing (1989) sees the descent of woman, as in the film *Aliens* (1986), as necessary to this kind of science fiction text.

26. The presence of families disrupts the austerity of the standard military/warfare show in *TNG*. Sexual tension between men and women constantly threatens to upend the military control, uniformity, and austerity of ideological relations on the ship. Emotions and relationships threaten the decorum of military authority.

27. "Plato's Stepchildren" presents a race of superbeings who adopt a Greek social system and manipulate people like toys. It is best known for the famous Kirk-Uhura interracial (non-)kiss scene. "The Squire of Gothos" concerns an alien child who takes human form to play with human beings on a planet/playhouse. He may be a precursor to Q in *TNG*. At the end of the episode, when it looks as if Kirk and crew are about to die, Trelaine's parents yell at him and say that if he can't take better care of his toys, he can't have any, and they take him home while he whines, "I never get to have any fun." "Who Mourns for Adonais?" presents Kirk and crew on an alien planet encountering Apollo, who, we learn, is an alien but was also the Greek god Apollo (all the Greek gods were aliens who left planet Earth when humans stopped worshipping them). Apollo appears because he thinks humans are capable of worshipping him again, but he's wrong. Only one blonde woman loves him and worships him in the episode, but this ends when Kirk "orders" her to disobey and turn against Apollo so they can all escape.

28. "The High Ground" most closely parallels the *ST* episode "The Cloudminders."

29. In my reading of Derrida's (1982) essay *"Différance,"* I depend heavily on Taylor Harrison's discussion of death, forgetting, and mourning in her chapter "Weaving the Cyborg Shroud" in this volume.

30. It is important to suggest here that the idea of play is necessary specifically within the neocolonialist context of science fiction. Bhabha (1990) suggests that "the play in the colonial system . . . is crucial to its exercise of power" (75). In other

words, the ostensibly free system multiplies subjects, increases relational associations, and enhances possible narrative strategies, which allows for maximum control and administration of narrative effects, so much so that the potential for polysemy given by the text functions ideally to sell packaged variety to the consumer. This is the function of the science fiction text, to sell the imaginary as a package of variety, even across standard tropological conventions. The only thing different from its fictional equivalent is the projection of fantasy into the realm of the imaginary, temporally dislocated from the present.

Perhaps the best example of the play of *différance* to which Derrida (1982) "refers" is his 1986 book *Glas,* where two columns of writing on the page force the reader (or, if we disinvest the author of inventional status, the writer) between discourses that are simultaneously one and the same thing. When reading *Glas,* am I reading in between, through, over, across, or around? Am I reading at all?

31. Whereas history books might argue that Native Americans made peace with their oppressors, Churchill (1992) reminds us all that colonialism continues. He writes, "Things have come full circle on the literary front. Where, in the beginning, it was necessary to alter indigenous realities in order to assuage the invading colonial conscience, so it seems necessary today to alter these realities to assure the maintenance of empire" (38).

References

Abbott, Paul. 1979. "Authority." *Screen* 20.2: 11–64.

Anderson, Benedict. 1983. *Imagined Communities: Reflections on the Origin and Spread of Nationalism.* London: Verso.

Bhabha, Homi. 1990. "The Other Question: Difference, Discrimination and the Discourse of Colonialism." In *Out There: Marginalization and Contemporary Cultures.* Ed. Russell Ferguson, Martha Gever, Trinh T. Minh-ha, and Cornel West. Cambridge, MA: MIT P. 71–87.

Butler, Judith. 1993. *Bodies That Matter: On the Discursive Limits of "Sex."* New York: Routledge.

Churchill, Ward. 1992. *Fantasies of the Master Race: Literature, Cinema and the Colonization of American Indians.* Ed. Annette Jaimes. Monroe, ME: Common Courage P.

Derrida, Jacques. 1982. *"Différance."* In *Margins of Philosophy.* Ed. and Trans. Alan Bass. Chicago: U of Chicago P. 1–27.

———. 1986. *Glas.* Trans. John P. Leavey, Jr. and Richard Rand. Lincoln: U of Nebraska P.

Dow, Bonnie J. 1990. "Hegemony, Feminist Criticism, and *The Mary Tyler Moore Show.*" *Critical Studies in Mass Communication* 7: 261–274.

Garber, Marjorie. 1992. *Vested Interests: Cross Dressing and Cultural Anxiety.* New York: HarperPerennial.

Hall, Stuart. 1980. "Encoding/Decoding." In *Culture, Media, Language.* Ed. Stuart Hall, Dorothy Hobson, Andrew Lowe, and Paul Willis. London: Hutchinson/CCCs. 128–138.

hooks, bell. 1992. "Eating the Other." *Black Looks: Race and Representation.* Boston: South End P. 21–39.

JanMohamed, Abdul R. 1985. "The Economy of Manichean Allegory: The Function of Racial Difference in Colonialist Literature." In *Race, Writing, and Difference.* Ed. Henry Louis Gates, Jr. Chicago: U of Chicago P. 78–106.

Jeffords, Susan. 1991. "Performative Masculinities, or 'After a Few Times You Won't Be Afraid of Rape at All.'" *Discourse* 13: 102–118.

Ramirez Berg, Charles. 1989. "Immigrants, Aliens, and Extraterrestrials: Science Fiction's Alien 'Other' as (Among *Other* Things) New Hispanic Imagery." *CineAction!* 18:3–17.

Rushing, Janice Hocker. 1989. "Evolution of 'The New Frontier' in *Alien* and *Aliens*: Patriarchal Cooptation of the Feminine Archetype." *Quarterly Journal of Speech* 75: 1–24.

Said, Edward. Sept./Oct. 1988. "Identity, Negation and Violence." *New Left Review* 171: 46–60.

———.1993. *Culture and Imperialism.* New York: Knopf.

Schwichtenberg, Cathy. 1984. "*The Love Boat:* The Packaging and Selling of Love, Heterosexual Romance, and Family." *Media, Culture, and Society* 6: 301–311.

Stallybrass, Peter, and Allon White. 1986. *The Politics and Poetics of Transgression.* Ithaca, NY: Cornell U P.

Sturken, Marita. 1992. "Cultural Memory and Identity Politics: The Vietnam War, AIDS, and Technologies of Memory." Disseration. University of California, Santa Cruz.

White, Mimi. 1992. *Tele-Advising: Therapeutic Discourse in American Television.* Chapel Hill, NC: U of North Carolina P.

Part Three

<*>

Producing Pleasures

9

Boys in Space

Star Trek, Latency, and the Neverending Story

ILSA J. BICK

Close friends become family and family is the true
center of the universe.
—Dave Marinaccio, *All I Really Need to Know I
Learned from Watching* Star Trek

Dubbed a "phenomenon" by popular media and critics alike, the original
Star Trek's (*ST*) appeal is undoubtedly overdetermined, simultaneously dic-
tated and reified by the self-referential nature of television, cinema, and
commentaries upon these media. This orchestrated commodification of *Star
Trek* has elevated the narrative to a cultural centerpiece while providing the
basis for a theoretical template. In his exploration of *ST* fandom, Henry
Jenkins (1988, 1992) unapologetically invokes his institutional authority to
lend legitimacy to his "fan" status and confronts popular stereotypes of
"Trekkies" as "nerdy guys with glasses and rubber Vulcan ears, 'I Grok
Spock' T-shirts stretched over their bulging stomachs" (1992, 9). Jenkins
thus recuperates fandom, transmuting it to the more academic rubric of
"textual poachers," a critical paradigm resting on a Marxist critique in
which fans, institutionally marginalized and socially decentered, become
participants in a rich, nomadic, subversive subculture defying the limitations
of the manifest narratives and the capitalist regimes that control them.

Although the breadth of Jenkins's work is impressive and resists homoge-
nization of the diverse facets of fan culture, he may be exaggerating the
fans' independence. Whether one is a poacher or not, surely it escapes no
one's notice that these fans, reinvoking authoritarian institutional hierar-
chies in their own organizations,[1] are being actively courted by an entertainment industry mindful of the consumer dollars in their bulging pockets.
Speaking at the formal reception of a retrospective exhibition on the original series at the National Air and Space Museum in Washington, D.C., on

February 26, 1992, a Paramount Pictures representative, flanked on either side by *Star Trek* actors, congratulated the enthusiastic reception attendees (most of whom were parents with their latency-aged children in tow) for their unfailing vision and faithful participation in the *Star Trek* "phenomenon," appealing to them to pass on this legacy to their children. Three days later, Robert Justman, *ST*'s original associate producer and supervising producer for *Star Trek: The Next Generation*'s (*TNG*) first season, spoke at a special day-long seminar on *Star Trek* sponsored by the Smithsonian Resident Associate Program, pronouncing to the delight of the sold-out crowd that they were *Star Trek*'s true heroes.

Star Trek's critics have not yet considered the developmental premises structuring what I call the *ST* "master" narrative, the set of unconscious and conscious propositions inherent in the original series. My insistence upon delineating these propositions should not be construed as diminishing the importance of the insightful and cogent work done by such notables as Constance Penley (1991), whose groundbreaking critique on K/S homoerotica (fan fiction that depicts Kirk and Spock as lovers) paved the way for Jenkins and many others, myself included. And my use of the term "master" narrative, with all the pejorative associations the adjective conjures up, is self-conscious in the extreme. What I wish to suggest is that not only is this "master" template the mold from which all future texts surrounding *ST* are formed, these texts must pay homage to these implicit constructions just as every new show must continually reference and revere Gene Roddenberry, the "Great Bird of the Galaxy," assuring its viewers that the series remains true to Roddenberry's original "vision."

Furthermore, a careful analysis of this master narrative reveals that it actually fosters this plethora of *Star Trek* offshoots and supportive substrata, inclusive of fiction produced by the poachers. Regardless of subject matter, these offshoots do not drastically deviate from this master text. As only one example, K/S homoerotica is not really new and radical: It is already present in the narratives and is in fact controlled by overarching corporate structures with their shrewd approach to fan culture. Fans and textual poachers alike may more reasonably be termed textual "voyeurs" because their activities and thematic concerns correspond well to the unconscious tasks of childhood development in which the *Star Trek* series of television shows and films remain consistently entrenched.

This analysis will focus on a psychoanalytic investigation of the developmental structure known as latency—that period in a child's life spanning the ages of seven to eleven—as the primary foundation for the original series and the six *Star Trek* films featuring the original ensemble of actors.[2] Although I could easily continue on with discussions of the almost limitless examples of nearly identical phenomena in *TNG, Star Trek: Deep Space Nine (DS9), Star Trek: Voyager (Voyager)* and the movie *Star Trek: Generations* (1994; hereafter *STG*), in the interest of Brevity I will limit myself to truncated remarks about *TNG* and *STG*.

ST's persistent focus upon latency-age concerns provides the container in which unconscious fantasies both informing and echoing these structures reside.[3] In other words, the form and content of *ST* mutually affirm one another. One of *ST*'s preeminent and most pervasive fantasies, both central to the master narrative's format and implicit in the ensuing series's narrative structures, revolves around discovery of home and wishes for reunion. Specifically, this fantasy involves an intense curiosity about one's origins, the desire to investigate the beginnings and source of life, and the insistent press toward an ambivalent, fantasied wish-fulfillment of reunion with the primal mother.[4] Obviously not every episode of the original series was devoted exclusively or even manifestly to this thematic concern; however, this fantasy permeates the psychological landscape of the original series and spin-off films, is consistently articulated in *TNG*, continues in many of *DS9*'s episodes, and provides the premise for *Voyager*'s entire narrative in that crew's continual and fruitless search for a way (and an all-powerful [female] entity) to return (them) home.

In addition, these fantasies may provide the lattice-structure supporting a media-defined and perpetuated alternative history. Reunion fantasies implicitly promise the undoing, denial, and circumvention of "real" history and the tyranny of time in much the same way that the continuation of the master narrative in endless films and spinoff series provides the illusion of continuity and timeless perpetuation. *ST* becomes a neverending, seamless story—a static and self-contained universe resistant to the exigencies of time and impervious to most intrusions of external reality. Inevitably, and most ironically, age may be the one reality to which the narrative must submit (as demonstrated by the passing of the torch in *STG*). Lastly, the seamlessness inherent and promulgated in the *Star Trek* phenomenon may provide us with insight into the interface of commercialism with culture in the media-generated circulation of personal and cultural realities.

ST's Developmental Narrative

At the end of the movie *Star Trek VI: The Undiscovered Country* (1991; hereafter *STVI*), Admiral James T. Kirk specifies the Enterprise's course as "second star to the right and straight on 'til morning." Like the Lost Boys of Never Neverland in James M. Barrie's *Peter Pan, ST*'s principal characters and narrative structure never really grow up. A large portion of *ST*'s psychological agenda is invested in the maintenance of sameness, most explicitly manifest in the fact that the starship Enterprise, as symbolic of this self-enclosed, hermetic *stasis,* opens and closes every episode of the original series except one. Although this type of closure reflects traditional television narrative conventions, the image of the Enterprise is crucial to *Star Trek*'s reveries of home as unblemished, ever-available, and immutable.

It is also telling that the one exception, "A Private Little War," is the only episode to address explicitly the then-raging Vietnam War. The elision of the Enterprise, so crucial to the series's perpetuation of *stasis* and seamlessness, is striking, suggesting that for the veterans of this particular war, symbolized by the "tired" and battered Kirk and Senior Medical Officer Lt. Commander Leonard McCoy as well as the inhabitants of Neural, whose lives they have irrevocably altered and forever tainted by the "serpent" of bloodshed, there may be no easy return home. This near-fatal dislocation of blissful continuity is further reemphasized by the fact that this is the only episode where each of the principal male leads is wounded: McCoy and First Officer/Science Officer Commander Spock by gunfire and Kirk by a savage Mugatu.

Yet echoing this obsessive insistence upon sameness, much of *ST*'s developmental structure hinges upon recapitulations of latency-aged struggles. In his formulations of children's science fiction, Perry Nodelman (1985) noted that latency-age narratives are characterized by their protagonists' adventures in and eventual retreats from "nature," the primitive world outside civilization, usually represented by domed enclosures or self-contained societies. The developmental task for the latency-age protagonist is to leave civilization (read "family" and "mother/womb"), reenter the primitive world "outside" home in order to rediscover a personal sense of historical continuity, and then reintegrate into his or her family structure. This is quite different from the developmental structure of an adolescent narrative where an encounter with the primitive leads not only to a rediscovery but to the creation of a "new" self, usually synonymous and synchronous with the emergence of genital sexuality. These adolescent narratives focus on change, not on the maintenance of sameness; and regardless of their stated age, these "adolescent" protagonists frequently return home only in order to effect such change.

A case in point would be to contrast the differences between a latency-age narrative such as *The Wizard of Oz* (1939) with the more developmentally advanced, adolescent narrative *Logan's Run* (1976). Escaping from the drudgery and persecution of her home and borne aloft on a tornado representative of her fury, Dorothy (Judy Garland) wanders in the primitive, mystical wilderness of Oz, meeting and eventually reconciling her disparate, split, and contradictory images of mother, father, and self only to conclude that home is best. Her mantra of return, "There's no place like home," underscores that for the latency-age child home is always there, something permanent and unchanging to be left and to which one must and can inevitably return. In Dorothy's case, she proves resistant to further change, vowing never to leave home again.

Conversely, the adult protagonist Logan (Michael York), identified with the police-brotherhood of Sandmen, defies both the Law of the City and his circle of male friends, latency-age chums all, when he discovers forbidden knowledge and engages in mutually pleasurable sexuality and long-term commitment, both offered through the body of a woman. Armed with his knowledge and bound in marriage, Logan kills his best (male) friend and returns with an aged "father" (Peter Ustinov) in tow to effect change upon the City, literally causing the City "Mother" Computer to self-destruct as it is unable to reconcile Logan's discovery that there is no Sanctuary. In effect, there is no Oz and no advantage to remaining disenfranchised from civilization, however flawed. Like the Odysseus myth (to which *ST* has been consistently compared[5]), the presence of the father-figure in *Logan's Run* is essential to preserving individuality in the face of reunion with the powerful, primal mother realized in the Mother Computer's attempts to probe Logan's mind and empty it of knowledge. Celebratory of challenge and fierce individualism, such adolescent narratives hinge upon the protagonist's capacity for, and accommodation to, change.

Unlike adolescence, the latency period is one invested in the preservation of sameness, in a core sense of wholeness and bodily integrity, communal "fair play," the consolidation of discrete categorical niches, and obsessive ritualization in activities such as coin, stamp, sports card, or rock collecting or POG competitions. For latency-age boys in particular, this emphasis on commonality and narcissistic mirroring involves an almost ritualized shunning of girls, regarded by these boys as disease-riddled vessels of contaminants (such as "cooties") and malevolent, seductive interlopers intent on the destruction of the solidarity of male chums.

The original series—and hence the master narrative for all subsequent spin-offs—shares in many of these preoccupations, with its insistence upon sameness, forays into the primitive—as the crewmembers journey from planet to planet but always return to the comforting womb of civilization (the Mother Enterprise)—and the exclusivity of a company of boys. The basic storyline involves the oscillating comings and goings and heroic adventures of a band of (essentially male) space travellers, a group of functional orphans without family or ties save their intense loyalty to one another. As Amanda, Spock's mother, notes of her son in "Journey to Babel," he and his friends are "at home nowhere except Starfleet." Kirk later elaborates on this point in *Star Trek V: The Final Frontier* (1989; hereafter *STV*) where he acknowledges that McCoy and Spock form the very fabric of his family. More importantly, their continued presence by his side sustains him; in the same film Kirk says to McCoy, "I knew I wouldn't die because the two of you were with me. I've always known—I'll die alone" (a premise that is fulfilled in *STG*). After saving Kirk's life at the end of the fifth film, Spock reminds him that, contrary to Kirk's expectations, Kirk could not have died because he was never alone.

Demonstrated repetitively and in ways that regularly involve intense self-sacrifice, these men endure because of the solidarity and unchanging nature of their union and the resistance of that union to disruptive outside influences, including family. Regarded as encumbrances, family members are virtually nonexistent in the original series, or family members and their surrogates actually die off. Some representative examples include Kirk's loss of his brother and sister-in-law in "Operation, Annihilate," a wife and unborn child in "The Paradise Syndrome," and a son in *Star Trek III: The Search for Spock* (1984; hereafter *STIII*). There are also references to family members of Kirk's murdered by Kodos the Executioner on Tarsus IV in "The Conscience of the King." McCoy marries only to lose his wife to her greater duty as a priestess in "For the World Is Hollow and I Have Touched the Sky" and relives his father's death in *STV*; Spock's half-brother Sybok is killed in the same film.

This uneasy vacillation between the wish to integrate into a surrogate family structure versus the need to deny that such a wish exists is consistently replayed in *ST*'s cooptation of two synchronous fantasies: the family romance and the hero myth. As articulated by Sigmund Freud (1909) and Otto Rank (1959), the family romance and the many versions of hero myths are closely related. Given away or cast out of his original family structure, the idealized figure of the hero is invariably the descendant of exalted parents but is perceived as a potential challenger to his father's power and authority. Rescued by people of lowly birth or by animals, the hero is raised in ignorance of his true origins until such time as he embarks on some journey of discovery that leads him not only to recognize his true lineage but to return to his home, where he revenges himself upon his father (or disguises his aggression by rescuing him) and takes his rightful place of honor. Elaborations of this fantasy are evident in children's idealization and identification with superheroes such as Superman or Batman (or of adults' with Spock or Kirk). Most importantly, the fantasy has two forms, as articulated by Martin E. Widzer (1977). One is the *asexual* stage, where the child (or adult) is essentially in ignorance or denial of sexuality and thus disavows *both* parents. The second is the *sexual* or Oedipal stage, where only one parent, usually the father, is disavowed.

Since Spock is the most alien and therefore the most safely disguised and displaced transference figure, he is the only character in the original series allowed to have an intact family of "high birth" from whom he is conspicuously alienated. Although Spock's parents, Sarek and Amanda, appear in subsequent *Star Trek* films, Spock leaves his mother behind on Vulcan along with Saavik (his half-Vulcan, half-Romulan protégé introduced in *Star Trek II: The Wrath of Khan* (1982; hereafter *STII*).[6] Consistent with *ST*'s emphasis on male solidarity, Spock's relationship with his father, Sarek, is preserved; however, this bond is strained, distant, and formal, leaving Spock no alternative but to return to Kirk's side. This is underscored as Sarek and Spock go their separate ways at the end of *Star Trek IV*, a film astutely subtitled *The Voyage Home* (1986; hereafter *STIV*).

The hero myth is articulated most clearly in the heroic figure of Kirk, a man who is consistently and conspicuously exceptional (the youngest captain in Starfleet, the only one to beat the Kobayashi Maru scenario, and so on). He is daring, charismatic, and filled with a sense of duty and sexual bravado—clearly, the Oedipal-age hero constantly in need of redirection and superego restraints. Yet his defiance of and uneasy identification with patriarchy (as distilled into the rules and regulations of Starfleet and the Federation) become much more evident after the first season. Coincident with this is a palpable shift in the tenor and tone of the series toward the more aggressively militaristic and pugilistic stance of the second and third television seasons, with their numerous hand-to-hand combats and plethora of evil aliens and potential conquerors. Kirk no longer functions so much as a diplomat as the staunch defender and rival of patriarchal order (tellingly synchronous with the U.S. military escalation in Vietnam). For example, Kirk continually becomes enamored with seductive, usually alien, and frequently naïve women. If she is a crewmember, then Kirk is either bound by duty not to accept her in this essentially incestuous guise (e.g., Yeoman Janice Rand) or becomes involved with her only when she is "possessed" by an alien life form, such as Dr. Anne Mulhall in "Return to Tomorrow." Kirk eventually abdicates any claim to these women, returning to the security of his isolation and duty.

This inability to negotiate sexuality successfully, coupled with an insistence upon woman's "otherness" and retreats away from change, resembles the structure of latency-age narratives. Much of *ST* devolves from this developmental "stuckness." Not only are there repetitive returns to the same developmental preoccupations but there are also no efforts directed toward discovering or working out a solution. None of the crew's encounters with the primitive change them in any way and, as I have noted, the protected world/womb of the Enterprise resists such change. Though the *Star Trek* films manifestly focus on change in their emphases upon the passage of time and inevitability of aging, their conclusion is that change is neither desirable nor necessary. Except for the original *Star Trek: The Motion Picture* (1979; hereafter *STMP*), the other films' referencing back to one another in an historical chain establishes the semblance of time's passing yet presents a seamless continuity in the films' tenacious insistence that despite "forward" time and events, things may remain much the same.[7]

ST and the Search for Lost Origins

Given the fact that *ST*'s master narrative relies on a developmental structure emphasizing resistance to change and seamless continuity, it follows that many of the core fantasies *ST* elaborates must echo these concerns in a sort of endless feedback loop. The fantasies support the structure, and latency proves to be the receptacle capable of containing these fantasies that then reconfirm the solidity of the structure, *ad infinitum*. Were this not the case, this supportive lattice of latency would be hard-pressed to contain what might erupt just as the city in *Logan's Run* proves unable to adapt to changes antithetical to the perpetuation of sameness.

ST's recurrent thematic elements of return—to home, to Mother Enterprise, to the unchanging solidarity and narcissistic mirroring of the men—would suggest that primitive and primal reunion fantasies consistently ripple through the narrative. By definition, if the Enterprise's "mission" is to seek out new life and new civilizations, then the mission must encompass the fantasy of discovering how life is created in its articulation in the primal scenario and ultimately incorporate the discovery of the source of all life in the mother's body, a place Jacob Arlow (1982) describes as "[T]he site of creation, the locale of true reality . . . the mother's genitalia, where in fact life did begin" (189). Wandering the cosmos, a great black void, can be metaphorically taken as synonymous with the wanderings in the womb; E. P. Bernabeu (1957) points out that this quest is "reopened on a cosmic level, *denying the female as mother and conferring on the male the exclusive processes of direct reproduction*" (532, emphasis added). Furthermore, theories of creation that focus on cataclysms, explosions, and collisions all reveal their roots in "the child's concept, sadomasochistically distorted, of sexual intercourse" (Arlow 1982, 190). Arlow points to the prominence with which lightning and storms figure in the creation mythologies, postulating in the dichotomy of primary-process thought a link between initiating lightning or fire and the semen emanating from the penis, the "fructifying role of the phallus" (191).

In *Star Trek* generally and in *ST* specifically, these preoccupations with the primal scene, birth imagery, the primal mother, and the conferring of her functions onto male figures are continually replayed. These many examples include the shimmering streams of the transporter beams, which become human beings; the leap from darkness to light through a portal to be "reborn" in another place and time both in "The City on the Edge of Forever" and "All Our Yesterdays"; the creation of Nomad in the merging of this space "probe," whose mission coincidentally is to study soil samples—that is, fertility—as prelude to "seeding"/colonization with Tan-Ru after some sort of catastrophic "accident" in "The Changeling"; M-5's "birth," accomplished by the almost literal merging of man with machine through the impression of his creator's mental engrams in "The Ultimate Computer"; and the draining of energy or blood from the crew as prelude to reproduction in "The Immunity Syndrome" and "Obsession."

This preoccupation continues in the film series with a blatant construction of sexual intercourse in *STMP,* in which the whole project revolves around V'ger, itself a melded creation, and its quest to seek out its "creator" on the Mother Earth, the source of all beginnings. V'ger wishes for reunion and a joining of the machine with its creator in an intercourse signified by the merging of Commander Decker and Lt. Ilia. Tellingly, this sequence is void of words, focusing instead on alternating close-ups of Decker and Ilia, their intense, blissful gazing at one another, and the transformation of Decker's erect, upright body into a radiant, painfully brilliant column of light. The endpoint of their merger is accompanied by shimmering streams of light shooting from the heart of the machine, the cataclysmic destruction of the V'ger probe, and the emergence of a new life form: the birth of a star from whose glowing center the Enterprise emerges.

In *ST*'s lexicon, similar discoveries of sexual knowledge and attendant birth imagery are almost always portrayed in terms of loss of self in the other, the merging and effacement of individual identities, death, and rapturous ecstasy. In some cases, characters complain that they have "lost" themselves in some way through this contact, or in the merging, threaten to become the other. One graphic illustration is Spock's orgiastic mind-meld with the Ilia probe in *STMP*. Rocketed through a pulsating orifice that is strikingly reminiscent of a cervix, Spock as spermatozoa threads his way through corridors and tunnels into a womb-like cavern where he discovers V'ger's gargantuan replication of Ilia. Having earlier become a spiritual recluse on Vulcan, Spock seeks the ultimate answer to all existence and, believing he shall find it in V'ger, elects to meld with a fiery, throbbing sensor in the replicant's neck. (Earlier Ilia has been swallowed up in a pillar of light and then reborn as the replicant in a scalding hot shower.) As currents of energy surge through his body, Spock screams in pained ecstasy; Ilia's face is superimposed on his in a rapidly alternating sequence with other images; and Spock is ejected from the contact.

In other instances, this merging is initially portrayed as intoxicatingly appealing. For example, in "Metamorphosis," the Companion, a "female" alien cloud, literally envelops Zefram Cochrane. A figure from the past, Cochrane is the ultimate "father" since he is credited with inventing warp drive. Communication between him and the Companion occurs on a totally empathic/telepathic level. The Companion is the perfect mother: she is all-giving, infinitely loving, totally intuitive, and perfectly attuned to Cochrane's needs. Yet openly manifest sexuality as the wish for sexual union with the perfect mother is felt to be repugnant. The solution that *ST* offers to sidestep this dilemma is another merger that separates mothering and sexual functions: the Companion loses her powers when she becomes human.[8] "Love" is almost entirely sexualized, yet it is a fundamentally mothering, all-encompassing, and smothering love against which defenses must be erected when the enraged Companion envelops and begins choking Kirk and Spock as they attempt an escape. Whereas the Companion's transformation into another woman serves as a veil for disguising the wish to possess and be possessed by the mother sexually (particularly since Cochrane finds the idea of "sexual" love with the Companion in her alien mother form "disgusting"), Cochrane's "parochial attitude" and repugnance might better be understood as reactive against taboo and merger, not just sexuality per se. What is threatening is the loss of self in merger, which is as potentially destructive and deadly as it is rapturous.[9]

Thus, one of *ST*'s unconscious fantasies appears to be a continual, ambivalent yearning for and struggle against reunion with the idealized, preoedipal, preverbal mother. *ST* longs to return to an earlier developmental epoch when words are unnecessary, when one is perfectly attuned to and in tune with a more "natural," primal world signified in the body, the voice, and the look of the mother. This concern reverberates throughout *ST*'s narrative structure, consonant with and bolstering the "external" container of a latency-age narrative whose manifest concern is to insist upon the perpetuation of sameness and narcissistic mirroring. Another example is Gem, the mute empath in the *ST* episode of the same name, who is so perfectly attuned that her mere touch allows for total union—without words or voice; the fundamental test she must pass is whether she, the "mother" of her race, will offer her own life to save another. Indeed, the whole episode is built on the continual tension and ambivalence surrounding this merger/death as the men and Gem struggle with their fear over such total surrender.

This play of ambivalence is pointedly manifest in Kirk's relationship to the mother/ship Enterprise. The Enterprise is consistently portrayed as a nurturing woman demanding total obeisance and sacrifice from her favored son, as graphically illustrated in "The Naked Time." In this episode, Kirk, under the influence of an alien "disease," is torn by his desire to escape the smothering responsibilities of a ship that "takes and takes. . . . She won't permit me my life," just as he vows he will "never lose you [the Enterprise] . . . never." As if to reinforce this, the very doors of the turbolift admonish him with the blood-red graffiti "Sinner Repent!"

Kirk's sacrifice of self for mother-ship most frequently arises when another woman—specified as a sexual threat—threatens this continuity. In "The Naked Time," this preoccupation is focused on Rand; in "Elaan of Troyius," the antidote to the disruptive woman *is* the Enterprise; and so on. Thus, beneath Kirk's almost rapturously obsessive devotion to duty lies the wish to be swallowed up by the mother and remain perfectly united.

This wish is cloaked beneath *ST*'s focus on this consistently disruptive feminine threat, her womanly "otherness," and recapitulations of castration threats. For the principal characters of the original series, and Kirk in particular, sexual love of woman is often followed by loss of strength, sanity, or memory (see "Elaan of Troyius," "Is There in Truth No Beauty?" and "The Paradise Syndrome" as representative examples). The Enterprise's grip on Kirk, however, seems more that of a greedy, smothering mother, with the erotic implications of this surrender split off to other female characters, effectively dividing the maternal into two, disparate images. These good/chaste and bad/sexual mothers and their representatives predominate in *ST*.

Another recurrent derivative of the same theme—the push toward union as synonymous with stagnation and death—is over the achievement of or return to Paradise and the ambivalent desire to succumb versus the struggle to free oneself from such union. Paradise is invariably associated with the feminine and revealed ultimately as stultifying and controlling: a literal dead end (exactly what Kirk and Captain Jean-Luc Picard discover in *STG*). As Kirk himself expresses in "This Side of Paradise," "Maybe we weren't meant for Paradise, Bones [McCoy]. Maybe none of us were. Maybe we're meant to fight our way through. Struggle. Claw our way up, scratch for every inch. Maybe we can't stroll to the music of lutes, Bones. We must march to the sound of drums." Overblown as this may be, the way out of Paradise and blissful union is literally a life-or-death struggle.

In *ST*, Paradise is viewed as inimical to man, although not necessarily to woman, since women are usually the inhabitants of Paradise or offer Paradise through themselves. I have already discussed the ambivalent wish for perfect union in *ST*, what Freud (1930) would have called a wish for the bliss of an "oceanic feeling" (72)—a sense of merging and timelessness and a fundamental state of being realized in the paradigm of the "togetherness" of mother and infant in a bubble of potential and protected space filled by the looking, touching, smelling, vocalizing, and tasting of primal experience. This is the manifest fantasy in virtually every episode of *ST* in which the crew encounters a paradise eventually destroyed, contends with a woman with whom Kirk becomes enamored, struggles with being drained of energy or life, or faces threats realized in the merging of man and machine. Some variation of this fantasy remains integral to the latent structure in episodes that focus on time travel, such as "The City on the Edge of Forever" and "All Our Yesterdays." Despite their apparent disparities, all these types of episodes (from "This Side of Paradise" to "The Naked Time" or "The Paradise Syndrome" and "For the World Is Hollow and I Have Touched the Sky") share a situation in which one or more of the principal characters face death or suffer a loss of self-control, self, or memory. In other words, the more imminent the realization of the fantasy and the closer the men approach this merger with the idealized mother, the stronger the sense of loss of self and identity. In many, if not most, of these episodes, there is a "cloaking" layer of sexuality over this fantasy, just as the female Companion peers through her multicolored veil in order to recapture the experience of merger with Cochrane. For example, Kirk falls in love with Edith and marries and impregnates Miramanee, Spock sleeps with Zarabeth, McCoy marries Yolanda, and Chief Engineer Lt. Commander Montgomery Scott (Scotty) is enamored of Mira Romaine. This "veil" of sexuality highlights the proposition that subsequent structures echo the fantasies supporting them while displacing these fantasies to more "acceptable" alternatives. In similar fashion, what passes as sexuality in *ST* is merely the vehicle, a means to an end, which fundamentally obscures this desire for merger.

The time-travel romances and the episodes concerning the expulsion from Paradise contain archetypal elements representative of this fantasy while illustrative of this sexual "veil." In his consideration of fifty-one films, Wyn Wachhorst (1984) notes that "the fundamental components of the time-travel romance are 1) a male time traveler who encounters 2) a female inhabitant from another time. . . . Archetypal to the time-travel romance . . . is an innocent, feminine world invaded by the omnipotent male time traveler" (341). Wachhorst also equates the past with the primordial mother, pointing out that the female figure is invariably portrayed as transcendent and intuitive: "To go home again—to seek unconditional love—is to deny the reality of conflict, compromise, and limits on the self. . . . To return to Paradise, in other words, is to annihilate the uniqueness of self; it is the very image by which we conceive of death" (345).

In another context, I note that *Back to the Future* (1985), a film that continually tests the immutability of Time as symbolic of the Father, belies the facade of cheery optimism with which the first film closes by virtue of the leap back across reality-based generational and genital boundaries (Bick 1990). Specifically, in the realization of fantasied wish-fulfillment and the superimposition of fantasy, *Back to the Future* depicts what Janine Chasseguet-Smirgel (1984) would term the "anal universe," a manipulated, rewritten universe in which the exigencies of generational and genital distinctions are no longer applicable. Following her formulations regarding creativity and perversions, Chasseguet-Smirgel asserts that perversions represent an attempt to obliterate the reality-based differences separating the child from the mother—who is the child's desired object. The fetish represents just such a device in the re-creation of a new or alternative reality out of chaos. This fetish is manifest in the "anal phallus," a condensation of "all the elements separating the son from his mother. Genitality represents the major obstacle between the son and his mother because of the differences it includes between the sexes and the generations, that is, reality itself" (11). For example, in *Back to the Future Part II* (1989), the reconstructed world is darker, more violent, dirtier, and grimmer than its predecessor, and this violence is most often blatantly constructed around sexuality (Bick, forthcoming).

This evocation of chaos is just as applicable to *ST* episodes such as "Amok Time," in which Spock, suffering from *pon farr* (the Vulcan mating urge), returns home because of his telepathic link with his betrothed, T'Pring, only to lose control of himself in *plak tow* (blood fever). Erupting in a deadly, calculating, murderous rage, Spock is "cleansed" only after he believes he has killed Kirk, a paternal stand-in, in combat for T'Pring. In "This Side of Paradise," loss of self is the precondition for entry into Paradise, and the crew degenerates into violence and chaos before normalcy is restored. In an analogous situation, the character Lawrence Marvick takes the Enterprise into an alternative, directionless, chaotic universe in a fit of murderous insanity in the episode "Is There in Truth No Beauty?" The films *STIII* and *STIV* also postulate this link between Paradise and chaos as first the Genesis planet and then Earth degenerate into chaos; the beginnings of this chaos are ultimately signified and presaged in the destruction of the Enterprise, as the structuring container of civilization, in *STIII*.

Violence, death, sexuality, Paradise, returning to the mother in a loss of self: If we apply the same notions to *ST*, particularly to an episode such as "The City on the Edge of Forever," we see that derivatives of this ambivalently invested fantasy for merger and reunion are integral to its structure. "City" is a particularly good example because so many of these elements are present in fairly undisguised form. For example, a time "storm" rocks the ship, and a terrible accident where McCoy accidentally injects himself with a drug places the doctor on the opposite end of the fantasy of penetration and seeding. As the receptacle for chaos, McCoy is ripped from the continuity of the men, "losing" himself in paranoid delusions. Following McCoy down to the planet, Kirk and his party encounter the Guardian of Forever, a sentient machine that controls the time portal through which they will eventually pass. Conspicuously posited as a "male" presence (the control of "real" time being synonymous with the paternal/genital/Oedipal universe of the father), the Guardian reaffirms that the flow of the past cannot be altered. This sentiment is echoed by Spock as the very incarnation of Logos/reality. Yet McCoy, who has "escaped" from reality, is represented as the agent of chaos and violence. For example, he "arrives" in the past at night, all of his scenes are set in darkness, and he engages in several fights while repeatedly screaming, "Assassins! Murderers!" His circumvention of reality and paternal order in his reunion with the past sets chaos in motion. McCoy even appears to serve as Kirk's agent, since immediately preceding McCoy's escape through the Guardian, Kirk speaks of an almost mystical pull for reunion with the past, a "strangely compelling" urge to leap across time to "lose oneself." The present "reality" for those left behind ceases to exist and is replaced by a chaotic, re-created universe much in the same way that the perverse solution, in its ceaseless aim at reparation of the rift between idealized mother and self, seeks to re-create new realities.

When Kirk and Spock enter the past, their cross is pointedly made from darkness into light (an appropriate metaphor for rebirth, particularly since they leap through a circular orifice). They almost immediately confront another "law" in the form of a police officer, and their escape, much like the circumvention of paternal law, leads them straight to the character Edith Keeler's basement. This is a particularly interesting touch given the fact that a reunion with the past also implies the derepression of subterranean/unconscious/"basement" memories and fantasies. Figured as the idealized woman, Edith Keeler is the focal point of time and aim of reunion. (She even wears a watch around her neck!) In keeping with the strategies of the time-travel romance, Edith is portrayed as a chaste, resourceful, prescient visionary, and though her realm is not Paradise, she is Mother Earth herself, feeding and clothing the itinerant men who gather at her mission while she spouts fantasies about the future and world peace. Fittingly, she is framed almost exclusively in extreme close-ups, as if the camera itself were attempting to imply this close approach to the idealized maternal object. What is sought is the face and the reaffirming look of the mother.

Kirk's "falling in love" with the idealized mother is a displacement, obscuring this wish to return to the maternal in the reenactment of a child's first love story. Kirk's love story is twofold. On the one hand, there is the wish to reclaim the mother sexually, thus sidestepping paternal law to claim an Oedipal victory. On the other hand, this act of reclamation involves a restoration of a lost past just as the entire narrative takes place in the literal past. The chastity of the mother is preserved; for example, the one bum who references sexual desire toward Edith is killed when he activates McCoy's phaser, and Kirk is never shown kissing or embracing Edith. Both of the moments when sexuality is implied are bracketed by the eye of Logos, the representative of "real" time and paternal law embodied in Spock. In the first instance, the camera cuts away to a parallel scene with Spock who, in his insistence upon finding truth/reality, foresees Edith's death. In the second, there is a cutaway to Spock from a kiss taking place, significantly, on a staircase as a metaphor for instability and uncertainty. His is the defining look, identified with the father watching the mother-infant pair. He is the very embodiment of logic and law as he reminds Kirk that to save Edith and to "do as your heart tells you to do" is to allow for the millions who "will die who did not die before": chaos.

Even though Kirk does what is "right" and allows Edith to die, his grief reflects the more poignant and irrevocable loss of the maternal. However, for Edith to die so violently is perhaps both the expression of rage at this separation and a highly disguised articulation of the reason why the mother is lost to Oedipal law and the "forward" push of time. Time, the Father, and paternal Logos enforce the child's exclusion from the primal scenario. The narcissistic mortification of such exclusion is frequently symbolized in vengeful, violent, or destructive imagery (Arlow 1982). For example, Edith shrieks at the moment she is killed, yet this occurs offscreen, and the only witnesses are Spock and McCoy. Clasping McCoy in a bearhug and reconstituting the continuity of the circle of men, Kirk faces the opposite direction, his eyes tightly closed. By preventing McCoy from rescuing Edith, Kirk has essentially enforced his own exclusion, returning Edith to the Father in the continuing, forward movement of paternal Law and Time. While ostensibly a noble, courageous act of self-sacrifice, Kirk's sacrifice is doubled back upon itself: He destroys his own alternative time, what he himself might have become, and the mother as well.

Lastly, no discussion of this reunion fantasy would be complete without a consideration of its expression as the stratagem of the Vulcan mindmeld. The hetero- and homoerotic implications of this type of surrender and merging are only dimly hinted at in the original series, with Spock's more searingly personal contacts occurring with aliens or machines and directed in efforts to protect the rest of the crew from danger or, in a penetratingly phallic way, to extract information (from Lt. Valeris in *STVI* or from McCoy in "Mirror, Mirror"—McCoy even looks a little dazed at the end).

The homoerotic implications of this surrender reverberate through *ST*'s master narrative just as this homoeroticism serves to bind the men defensively together. K/S fanzine homoerotica might be better understood as a "logical" extension of this romantic quest: if the most important task of the latency period is the discovery of one's mirroring chum and the preservation of the same-sex peer group, then the accompanying fantasy is predicated, at least partially, on seeking perfect merger in one's mirror-image. For example, the idea of finding God in *STV* lies in discovering one's reflection. This is only a dyslexic step away from finding oneself in the reflection of the mother's eye, and in the majority of this fanzine homoerotica, close-ups of eyes, gazing, and the men's looking at one another in *ST* episodes are read as synonymous with intimacy (Bacon-Smith 1992).

My emphases upon latency-age constructions or these attendant fantasies should not be taken as synonymous with an endorsement of developmental fixation as etiological to homosexuality; the point is that every developmental phase builds on and retains vestiges of those that precede it. These fantasies are the bedrock upon which subsequent levels of development are layered. Thus, when Kirk and Spock turn to one another for comfort and support in "The Naked Time," theirs is a highly conventional, socially acceptable display of "male bonding" predicated upon homosocial constructions articulated in latency. The fact that the men must resort to violence, each literally beating the other, indicates that this is the only way in the master narrative that homoerotic elements can be consciously expressed. In addition, this violence follows on the most heartfelt expressions of Spock's friendship for Kirk and his "shame" over that. This shame, the violence, and the ambivalence associated with this homoeroticism are then displaced *defensively* to the more primitive fears of merger with the mother. Their fist-fight is followed by Kirk's anguished ruminations on the demands of his duty and his desire to have a woman "to touch, to hold." This skillfully deflects attention from the fact that the "disease"—and therefore Kirk's longing—has been precipitated by touching and holding Spock.

The only other instance in the entire lexicon where Spock and Kirk openly touch in quite this way takes place in *STMP*. Here they wordlessly express their feelings for one another, engage in an intense few minutes of mutually affirming looks, and then profess that the touch of their hands, this "simple feeling," is more important than all the knowledge V'ger possesses. Union with V'ger is "cold, sterile, barren, empty"; Spock's turn to Kirk at this point in the narrative can be interpreted as a defensive one designed to redress the terror of merger. In other words, the prospect of blissful reunion may be ecstatic, but the obverse to this oneness is the obliteration of difference and individuality. This merger threatens to empty Spock of his uniqueness as he breaks down later in the film and weeps in his identification with V'ger's longing and relentless search for reunion. Perhaps it is not accidental that this film, the one most clearly associated with an irrevocable change in Spock, which would then entail an irreversible shift in this never-changing circle of men, is so consistently elided and obliterated from the *Star Trek* lexicon. Quite simply, the film is treated as if it does not exist.

The Neverending Story

Perhaps it is fitting that *TNG*'s series finale, "All Good Things . . . ," blatantly announces in its ellipsis that an "end" is not in *Star Trek*'s vocabulary. *ST*'s master narrative promotes unchangeability even as it circulates between times, probing its own origins and insisting on seamless continuity. The "last" *TNG* episode is circular, returning its crew to its literal and metaphysical beginnings. "Encounter at Farpoint" gave birth to the series by referencing a familiar *ST* preoccupation—that of the seeking of blissful union in one's perfect mate. In its last episode, *TNG* returns to the moments of its conception. Through Q, Picard revisits the primordial Mother Earth, fulfilling the fantasy only to be denied inclusion as the moment of creation never arrives. Similar to many other episodes in *TNG*, Picard must eliminate the dislocated element in order to set in motion the "forward" flow of time.[10] Although excluded from the moment of conception, Picard finds himself included in the never-changing circle of friends at episode's and series's end, discovering at last what the latency-age child has known all along: Friends are the center of the universe.

This preoccupation with historical continuity, returns to lost origins, and confrontations with and remakings of histories seems to partake of a phenomenon unique to the past decade, one most invested in the rewriting of history. In my analysis of *E.T.* (1982; Bick 1992), a film that, like the thematically related *Close Encounters of the Third Kind* (1977), unabashedly incorporates *ST* imagery, I note that references to *ST, Star Wars* (1977), and other cultural mythologies appear to be attempts to persuade the audience that *E.T.* is a clearer, more faithful representation of reality. For example, when one of the film's characters asks why E.T. cannot just "beam up" to his ship, Elliot retorts, "This is reality, Greg."

In a similar fashion, *ST*'s master narrative presents its viewers with the opportunity to manipulate time through images, placing these images into whatever order or with whatever accompaniment (as in fan filking) they desire while still insisting that there is only one, true *ST* reality. For example, in the two-part *TNG* episode "Unification," Spock references events that are "past" for *TNG* but in the "future" in "real" time. At the time of the episode's original broadcast, they had not "happened" for the viewer.

The title ostensibly refers to the plot, but it also points to the linkages of histories past and present. Yet it is not Spock who becomes the focal point for history but Picard who, by virtue of his mindmeld with Sarek, carries past, present, and future. What is so intriguing is the reassertion of history within the body of a *man,* as if the arbiter of reunion must remain the province of paternal law and order and the masculine (cf. the "Guardian of Forever"). Presumably, too, Spock's continued presence, implied both in the fact that Picard carries Sarek's thoughts of him and Spock's choice to remain on Romulus (but in hiding/in the unconscious), constitutes a "hope" and expectation for a revisitation of multiple pasts.

Following on the heels of "Unification," the times were still, appropriately for *STVI,* "out of joint." Not only was the temporal "future" of the film known, it had become a fixture of the viewer's past. Characters such as Sarek, whose death occurred in the viewers' past of "real" time, were presented as still living in a habitation of the conflation of present/future. What this emphasizes, however, is the fact that this fictional reality is predicated on fiction. For Jean Baudrillard (1989), such a reality is composed of simulacra, a hyper-reality layered upon what is real. The fictive is presented as representational, "concealing the fact that the real is no longer real" (171). Robert Eberwein (1990) expands on this conjecture, observing that sequelization offers the opportunity for a "universe of recurrence" and "smoothly flowing temporalities."

The same holds true for *Star Trek,* and particularly for the recent film *STG,* which is both sequel to and continuation of the master narrative. This "bridging" film labors to reassure its viewers that regardless of "change" and the fires of time in which we burn, things will remain much the same. Summoning familiar devices used in its predecessors, *STG* hearkens back to and recalls these "past" plot lines and recurrent fantasies, suturing the film into place in this unbroken and neverending story. Some of these strategies are more jarring than others. For example, playful banter and verbal repartee are never prominent in *TNG;* the "play" between the "boys" so central to *ST* is absent, and interpersonal tensions amongst *TNG*'s characters are usually muted to the point of nonexistence. In *STG,* however, there is a strained attempt at this "play," designed to hearken back to the more light-hearted, if ascerbic, moments of *ST.*

Other linkages are more obvious. For example, just as the Enterprise is destroyed and then resurrected in *STIII* and *STIV,* respectively, so *STG* recalls this by destroying the Enterprise-D while reassuring its viewers at film's end that there will always be a ship called Enterprise. The holosuite scene early in the film highlights an ancient clipper ship named Enterprise, thereby inserting the ship and its crew into an historical, canonical chain; Picard mouths, almost verbatim, dialogue spoken by Kirk, who also yearned for the "wind at his back" in "The Ultimate Computer." Like Kirk, Picard suddenly feels the burdens of command, yet this was rarely manifest nor a true difficulty in *TNG*. In *STII*, Kirk discovers and reconciles with his son, David, only to lose him in the next film. In recompense, Kirk resurrects Spock from the dead, a device that both reconstitutes their neverchanging circle of family and obliterates alternative history. Not surprisingly, *STG* echoes this by having Picard lose his brother and nephew. Orphaned like Kirk before him, Picard is the "end" of his line, and this sets up the conditions by which Picard then struggles with what amounts to a reunion with the past in his discovery of bliss (i.e., the natural/maternal) in the Nexus. Picard's wished-for family is rooted in the "naturalness" of the nineteenth century; when prodded to return to his own time, Picard must also tear Kirk, a figure from his own temporal past, away from his blissful fantasy (again set in rustic, naturalized surroundings offered through the body of a woman, Antonia).[11] Like Kirk, Picard loses his ship and entire crew but resurrects them.

Similarly, *STG* attempts to displace Kirk and Spock's relationship to Picard and Lt. Commander Data's relationship.[12] What appears to be a radical change—Data's acquisition of an emotion chip—can be read as nothing more than a reverberation of Spock's continual war with his emotions. Kirk functioned both as their focus and anchor, just as Picard and Data's relationship is similarly altered. They have a deeper, more emotional connection; a brief moment of physical contact occurs when Picard places a comforting hand on Data's shoulder, reminiscent of similar episodes between Kirk and Spock (cf. "The Naked Time," "Plato's Stepchildren," *STMP*, etc.). Not only does Data confide in Picard in his distress as Spock always did with Kirk, but Picard, ever the figure of superego control, insists in true Kirk-like style that Data "get a grip."

Finally, as with everything else in *ST*, nothing is permanent. Kirk might be dead—sort of—but *STG* assures us that his "echo" resides in the Nexus, awaiting resurrection.

Far from a fire, time in *Star Trek* is reduced to a mere passing flicker. In fact, Pocketbooks, publisher of the various *Star Trek* franchise novels, stipulates in its instructions to authors that whatever the scenario or whatever "changes" occur, the characters must return to the status quo and the sanctity of their union. Nothing must really change.

Congruous with this effort to perpetuate a universal text, the movies and spin-off series continually allude to canonical texts such as Dickens, Twain, Doyle, and, the most canonical and doctrinaire of all, Shakespeare's entire *oeuvre*, to legitimate and elevate its narrative to immutable *mythos*. Thus, *Star Trek*'s universe seeks to stretch across times just as these same fictional characters traverse the boundaries between simulacra and reality, calling upon collective memory and cultural doctrines to suture them, immutably, into place. Hence, in a 1993 MCI commercial advertising "Family and Friends," Nichelle Nichols can call upon her alter, Communications Officer Lt. Uhura, for maintaining "communication"; Shatner can capitalize on his

reputation for egoism without sacrificing Kirk; Nimoy may arch an eyebrow; and their audience, represented by the crowd of telephone operators
looking at the characters' larger-than-life images, can be "in" on the joke
while reassured through their identification with and associations to these
simulacra that time may pass without the sacrifice of a sense of cohesive
union. They share common memories. They are family. They are
immutable. They are static.

In a way, this rewriting of new and yet unchangeable histories opens a
window into one perspective of the cult phenomenon that is *Star Trek*, consistent with Jenkins's (1988, 1992) proposition that poachers act in defense
of the original text.[13] By superimposing a new hyper-reality, the ability to
enter into an historical continuity becomes part of prevailing cultural
mythology realized in the collapse and conflations of time (for example, the
bringing together of past, present, and future through multiple series and
films as well as the reentry into the past made possible through repetition
and re-viewing). The ability to reside in a parallel history that is still part of
"history" but that is reified in the interrelated self-referencing of the technological media of cinema and television and their attendant technologies,
reinforces that these are the consciously articulated and culturally sanctioned manifestations of the intrapsychic agendas implicit in these
"reunion" films (or the illusory, temporal seamlessness of sequels). Slipping
into the substance of these simulacra and this timeless, mirroring, mutually
affirming realm, one unites in a common fabric. Resistant to change, *ST*'s
neverending story becomes the means to its own end, returning always to
itself, echoing the self-regenerative, self-perpetuating, ruminative fantasies
that inform its structure. *ST* takes us forward into the past, and indeed we
find that to go where no one has gone before is to rediscover where we all
have been.

Notes

This chapter was presented in a much abridged form under the title "The Final
Frontier: The Search for Lost Origins" as part of the Smithsonian Resident
Associate Program on *Star Trek* cosponsored by the Smithsonian's National Air
and Space Museum, Washington, D.C., on February 29, 1992, and for the Society
for Cinema Studies Annual Meeting, SUNY-Syracuse, Syracuse, NY, on March 2,
1994. I wish to thank Mary Henderson, art curator at the Smithsonian National
Air and Space Museum, and Margaret Delvecchio, coordinator for the
Smithsonian Resident Associate Program, for soliciting my participation in the
1992 symposium. Thanks are also due Constance Penley at UC–Santa Barbara for
her illuminating discussion with me about K/S homoerotica. My deepest thanks go
to Krin Gabbard at SUNY-Stonybrook for his insightful comments and helpful,
collegial criticisms.

1. See Camille Bacon-Smith (1992).

2. When I invoke "psychoanalysis," I am not referencing mainstream academic theoretical permutations of Lacanian analyses but rather psychoanalytic inquiries as being first and foremost methods of inquiry into developmental schemata.

3. For a good overview of latency see Charles A. Sarnoff (1976).

4. For an excellent discussion of these fantasies as well as a good developmental critique of infantile separation-individuation see Kenneth Wright (1991).

5. While debunking explanations that were too "intellectual," William Shatner (1991) stated that *ST* represented the contemporary equivalent of a cultural mythology, paralleling the adventures of Odysseus in the first half of The Odyssey "as he wandered in search of home—[*ST* is about] an intrepid group of individuals constantly on a journey, searching" (D4).

6. Saavik has presumably been Spock's one-time lover during a "regrettable" lapse in *STIII* when Spock was undergoing an adolescent surge of *plak tow* (blood fever). After her brief reintroduction in *STIV*, Saavik is conveniently dropped from further storylines, and in keeping with *Star Trek*'s narrative strategy, Spock does not remember their one sexual encounter anyway.

7. For example, not only does Spock never really have to die, but in *STIV*, when Kirk is forced to sell his eyeglasses for money, Spock queries, "Weren't those a present from Dr. McCoy?" alluding to an event in *STII*. Kirk responds, "That's the beauty of it. If this works out, they will be again." In *STVI*, Spock quips, "I've been dead before," referencing his own death and subsequent resurrection in *STII* and *STIII,* respectively.

8. Another interesting twist is the introduction of language as prelude to separation. The mother of primordial fantasy envelops her child; as Wright (1991) notes of early infantile experience, the *nucleus of the real* is articulated through "touch, skin contact, being held, the firm pressure of the mother's body" (56). Vision and, later, language add layers of separation. In "Metamorphosis," first the Companion is "heard" and denoted as separate through the imposition of language (the universal translator). Next, the Companion assumes a shape in her coalescence into the "real" body of Assistant Federation Commissioner Nancy Hedford, who then speaks as a separate entity and yet, at one point, wistfully gazes at Cochrane through her veil as if to recapture some earlier experience while forcefully articulating how very separate and separated they now are. In the end, Cochrane's knowledge of his love for the Companion is made possible through this looking and touching. I would suggest that this final articulation of the two as a sexual (mother/father) couple is perceived through the gaze of the triangulated child, signified in the looks of Kirk, Spock, and McCoy, a child who, Wright asserts, looks at "what the other two are doing . . . [encompassed within] a space, the boundaries of which must not be broached, a NO ENTRY space, within which objects can only be looked at or observed, but never touched" (12). Following on this latter point, it is significant that Cochrane exhorts Kirk not to tell anyone about him. In essence, Cochrane secures a NO ENTRY space, a Paradise complete with a fig tree.

9. Even an episode as disarming and lightly humorous as "The Trouble with Tribbles" involves the attendant anxiety of "too much" love signified in the cooing, soothing trilling of the tribbles. Significantly, the tribbles are brought aboard the ship by a woman, Communications Officer Lt. Uhura, and run rampant, voraciously "eating up" and threatening to smother with too much mothering.

10. Of the thematic concerns most consonant with and reminiscent of *ST*'s master narrative, preoccupations with mutability, the negation of time, the search for origins, and fantasies of return endure as the most pressing and acute in *TNG*. Many *TNG* episodes center on the very same infantile fears of and desire for symbiosis and fusion with which the original series was riddled. An especially interesting character is Picard, since he is the one crewmember in whom the tensions of the fantasies of the negation of time and explorations of the past are articulated most clearly and without the overlay of sexual bravado. Picard's character is precariously placed on the border between the pull of the past and the push toward the future. A case in point is the two-part episode "The Best of Both Worlds," ostensibly the top-rated episode of the series, and its continuation in the subsequent episode, "Family." The Borg represent the loss of self through fusion of mind and machine into an anonymous collective. Particularly appropriate is the Borg's search for the "origins" of humanity—Mother Earth, Sector 001—as the place to effect this fusion as V'ger had earlier sought out Earth in *STMP*. The fact that Picard is "absorbed" and powerless to avoid this loss of self represents a narcissistic assault upon paternal order and omnipotent control and reveals the terror of merger. Furthermore, Picard remembers "everything" that has happened, and subsequent to this failure of repression he goes back in memory and reality to his family. Consonant with Nodelman's (1985) characterization regarding children's science fiction and Wachhorst's (1984) points referencing the time travel romance, Picard's older brother, Robert, insists upon living in less "civilized" surroundings, drinks "real" wine, eschews technology, and the like. In essence, Picard returns to the natural to regain and incorporate a sense of self in an historical continuity that he presumably carries back to civilization/the Enterprise. As the paternal agent promulgating separation, Robert's continual bullying provokes Picard to the point where they actually come to blows. During this sequence, Picard breaks down, admits his weakness, is accepted by his brother in this weakness, and then pushed/enabled to leave. Just as Spock serves as the arbiter of paternal order for Kirk in "The City on the Edge of Forever," so Picard's brother as displaced paternal object insists upon the boundaries of time and development, thrusting Picard back into his own time and place. Picard leaves Earth with a renewed sense of continuity, symbolized by Picard's nephew who gazes at the stars at the episode's close.

11. As a friend wryly pointed out to me, our discovery that Kirk lives in the woods, splits logs, and raises horses fits very well with the all-encompassing nature of hyper-reality. Quite simply, Kirk's fantasy is to become William Shatner.

12. There is even a stab at reconstituting the troika of Kirk, Spock, and McCoy, if only briefly, by literally sandwiching Kirk between Ensign Pavel Chekov and Scott, having the three men engage in playful banter, and overall seem much more involved with and caring of one another than in any other *ST* narrative.

13. A case in point is the amalgamated novel by Alexis Fagen-Black (1994), *The 25th Year*. While manifestly celebratory of "infinite diversity," the book is fashioned as a collaborative K/S narrative and attempts to link together all the disparate stories in the K/S "canon" into one master narrative.

References

Arlow, Jacob. 1982. "Scientific Cosmogony, Mythology, and Immortality." *Psychoanalytic Quarterly* 51: 177–195.

Bacon-Smith, Camille. 1992. *Enterprising Women: Television Fandom and the Creation of Popular Myth.* Philadelphia: U of Pennsylvania P.

Baudrillard, Jean. 1989. *America.* Trans. Chris Turner. London: Verso.

Bernabeu, E. P. 1957. "Science Fiction: A New Mythos." *Psychoanalytic Quarterly* 26.4: 527–535.

Bick, Ilsa J. 1990. "OUTATIME: ReCreationism and the Adolescent Experience in *Back to the Future.*" *Psychoanalytic Review* 77.4: 587–608.

———. 1992. "The Look Back in *E.T.*" *Cinema Journal* 31.4: 25–41.

———. Forthcoming. "*Back to the Future* I and II: Re-Creationism, Repetition, and Perversity in the Time Travel Romance." *Psychoanalytic Review.*

Chassegeut-Smirgel, Janine. 1984. *Creativity and Perversion.* New York: Norton.

Eberwein, Robert. 1990. "Sequels, Film History, and Simulacra." Florida State University Conference of Literature and Film, Tallahassee, FL.

Fagen-Black, Alexis. 1994. *The 25th Year.* N.P.

Freud, Sigmund. 1909. "Family Romances." *The Standard Edition of the Complete Psychological Works.* Trans. James Strachey. London: Hogarth Press, 1953. Vol. 9: 237–241.

———. 1930. "Civilization and Its Discontents." *The Standard Edition.* Vol. 21: 59–148.

Jenkins, Henry, III. 1988. "*Star Trek* Rerun, Reread, Rewritten: Fan Writing as Textual Poaching." *Critical Studies in Mass Communication* 5.2: 85–107.

———. 1992. *Textual Poachers: Television Fans and Participatory Culture.* New York: Routledge.

Marinaccio, Dave. 1994. *All I Really Need to Know I Learned from Watching* Star Trek. New York: Crown.

Nodelman, Perry. 1985. "Out There in Children's Science Fiction: Forward into the Past." *Science-Fiction Studies* 12: 285–296.

Penley, Constance. 1991. "Brownian Motion: Women, Tactics, and Technology." In *Technoculture.* Ed. Constance Penley and Andrew Ross. Minneapolis: U of Minnesota P. 135–161.

Rank, Otto. 1959. *The Myth of the Birth of the Hero and Other Writings.* New York: Vintage Books.

Sarnoff, Charles A. 1976. *Latency.* Northvale, NJ: Jason Aronson.

Shatner, William. 6 Dec. 1991. "The Many Phasers of William Shatner." *The Washington Post*: D4.

Wachhorst, Wyn. 1984. "Time-Travel Romance on Film: Archetypes and Structures." *Extrapolation* 25: 339–352.

Widzer, Martin E. 1977. "The Comic-Book Superhero: A Study of the Family Romance Fantasy." *The Psychoanalytic Study of the Child* 32: 565–603.

Wright, Kenneth. 1991. *Vision and Separation: Between Mother and Baby.* Northvale, NJ: Jason Aronson.

10

Enjoyment (in) Between Fathers

General Chang as Homoerotic Enablement in *Star Trek VI: The Undiscovered Country*

EVAN HAFFNER

What if Kirk and Spock really were gay?, or, What if Kirk and Spock *really were* gay? It is interesting to note how much information is packed in the two italicized words in this question. The second form of the question could easily be read as asking, in a hegemonic context that normalizes heterosexuality, what if, despite the heterosexuality that seemed so certain, Kirk and Spock were actually homosexual? This question implies that up until some time before its being posed, Kirk and Spock's heterosexuality—indeed, heterosexuality *as such*—had been obvious, that is, invisible as an issue. It implies further that, subsequently, homosexuality became a general possibility, though disallowed for Kirk and Spock. The italicization of the two words connotes the cathected state of denying the possibility that the formerly impossible, now the prohibited, might always have been the case. What if Kirk and Spock *really were* gay? What if Kirk and Spock's formerly unthinkable, but now surmised and rejected, homosexuality turned out to have been the case all along?

The first question reads differently: What if Kirk and Spock were not heterosexual, but homosexual? The form of the answer it delineates implies a mutual exclusion of the two categories of sexuality thus far allowed:

- "Ah, they're actually queer; *now* I've got it straight" and

- "No, no, they're indeed straight. An interesting speculation, their homoerotic relationship, but just not true"

do not jibe as coincident opinions. The second question is more paradoxical insofar as it implies a synchronicity of two supposedly mutually exclusive categories: "What if those two heterosexuals, Kirk and Spock, were homosexual all along?" This hypothetical speaker's surprise implies a certain disavowal, as opposed to an overwhelming shock: "I know very well that they're heterosexual, but what if they were homosexual anyway?" The first clause is not countermanded by the second, but is somehow its enablement, or perhaps its result—I do not want to stake out the priority of either just yet. What we have here is not a paradoxical simultaneity that we could commend for exceeding Logic, and then go on to read carefully instead of simply dismissing it. Such a parataxis of the two categorizations (they're heterosexual; they're homosexual) would lose all sense of movement from and toward; or perhaps it would be a dialectic, or an anxious oscillation between two poles, two quantum states, neither wholly stable but that may only be occupied stochastically, conditioned by some relentless Uncertainty Principle. We could consider *différance* (Derrida 1973) to be that conditioning principle (though of course *différance* is not a principle, nor even a concept—but still), and the two specified paradigmatic poles of sexuality to be two of many, though this many is not a plurality of equal positions, a homogeneous potential field. Truly, some unknown number of paradigms remains unspecified here, and there too may remain other paradigms of sexuality that have yet to be specified. This theoretical grid can be made finer, but that is not to say that its coarseness could not be exploited. The problem with the rhetoric of strategic exploitation is that it smacks of that anti-theoretical theory called pragmatism. I do not want to imply here the mastery and critical distancing that the term "strategic" connotes, but point instead to the fetishistic, anti-differantial logic that the above "but still" implies.

The "presence" of *différance* depends on the perdurance of a differential system of relationships without positive terms, that is, without empirically verifiable, undifferentiable, undeferrable presences (Derrida 1973). That "homosexuality" and "heterosexuality" are not positive terms is evidenced by their contestedness and interior differentiation.[1] Their constant renegotiation (and the persistent renegotiations of the social terrain they, in part, manifest and that make their appearance possible) points up their historical contingency. Such contingency further undermines positivity. And yet there is something so darn positive about these terms: In any synchronic slice of the social, we necessarily lose all the contingency that comes along with historicity. So there is a certain (temporally) localized plenitude whose movement due to the forces of contingency is, for a time, frozen, stamped.[2] I would like to call these partial solidities the *nodal points* (Laclau and Mouffe 1985, 112) of sexuality whose temporary privilege is the partial fixity that attempts to impede the differantial flux.

What then is the relation of *différance* to nodality? I am not trying to engage here in a critique of Derrida's notion of *différance* that aims to prove in some way its falsity or illusoriness. *Différance,* however, immediately upon its employment as a critical category, cannot *not* be conceptualized, and though it may overflow all possible conceptualizations—for that is Derrida's point—the experience of any such overflowing cannot be conceptually differentiated from some mode of those-who-experience-such-overflow's conceptualization of *différance.* Otherwise *différance* becomes absolute, unconditioned by the anti-*différance* figured in fetishization, reification, abstraction, and conceptualization. *Différance,* in that case, becomes some ultimate fact of the matter, everything's condition of possibility, the ground for all skepticism in the face of claims to positivity. Such a Cartesian grounding in doubt would symptomatize the modernist skeptical position. Nodality answers the question of how *différance* gets abstracted (i.e., conceptualized) away; losing *différance* is the condition of possibility of having a world, having nodality or positivity, regardless of how negative or "illusory" that positivity might be.

Indeed, the positivity of these nodal points is a result of their own radical negativity and takes its rise from their constitutive, antagonistic, and differential character; they are positive insofar as they are able to differ from the other points in the field—that is, insofar as they are radically negative (to differ is to *not* be something), insofar as they are identified with the notness that makes nodality possible: their unconceptualized, unrationalized places of inscription. Negativity thus becomes constitutive and foundational, and sexuality can never be fully constituted or objectively ordered since such an attempt would be to strive to pose sexuality as *merely* positive.[3] If we consider sexuality to be the social field of nodal points (sexual identities), then we can turn to Ernesto Laclau's (1990) analysis of the social as illustrating the logic of negativity and antagonism I want to make use of here:

> The antagonizing force fulfills two crucial and contradictory roles at the same time. On the one hand, it "blocks" the full constitution of the identity to which it is opposed and thus shows its contingency. But on the other hand, given that this latter identity, like all identities, is merely relational and would therefore not be what it is outside the relationship with the force antagonizing it, the latter is also part of the conditions of existence of that identity. (21)

In fact, we could let Sexuality designate the totalization of this field of contingent identities, where the signifier Sexuality would not effect its totalization by subsuming all contingent moments under some absolute One but would act as the impossible horizon, the final marker of that field's inability to constitute itself objectively. Thus sexuality becomes a nonobjective totality that is, in the manner of Slavoj Žižek's (1991) totalization of society, "'held together' by the very antagonism, split, that forever prevents its closure in a harmonious, transparent, rational Whole—by the very impediment that undermines every rational totalization" (100). I do not want to render totality in a utopian way that seeks to ontologize, from the Žižek example, society's self-undermining seeds, since such a rendering would logically necessitate some sort of revolutionary guarantee. The ultimate unsubsumability of *différance* would, in a like manner, reify radical contingency into Cartesian doubt-as-ground. Rather, I want to figure society (and sexuality) as a *self-exceeding* (not self-destroying) totality whose excess is up for grabs, even as it is always already grabbed and may very well be grabbed in the negative sense (i.e., hegemonically excluded). The notion of *différance* that "remains intact" is *différance*'s status as the reminder that the necessity of having a world—some identity or suite of identities—in no way implies the necessity of the world that is had. The resulting position does not clear away the Cartesian doubt mentioned above; by removing such doubt *qua* ground, however, it carries doubt even further than Cartesian skepticism by admitting the contingency and possibility of loss of any world, of any ultimate fact of the matter. Since it is thus anti-epistemological, such a position is irreducible to modernism and so not committed to that historical form of critical blindness.

Positivity, if it is not to be dismissed as a mere foolishness that is better off forgotten, stands to be redefined—as historically experienced—as that which exerts its necessary effects from a point of residuality that is as originary (because *différance* has necessarily been abstracted away) as the putative origin under which it cannot be subsumed (since *différance* cannot merely be erased by abstract negation). I would then like to employ the term "sexuality" in a manner that might otherwise appear essentialist, except for the fact that each occurrence invokes this antiessentialist take on positivity, on plenitude. "The analysis must therefore begin with the explicit 'objective' identities of the social agents—those making up their 'fullness'—and then go on to emphasize the dislocations adulterating that fullness" (Laclau 1990, 36).

With regard to sexuality my aim will be to answer the question, How is heterosexuality constituted, and to what extent, in the movie *Star Trek VI: The Undiscovered Country* (1991; *STVI*)?[4] How is homosexuality abstracted away in order to enable such constitutedness? But I also want to go beyond any logic of heterosexuality as what always appears and homosexuality as that which is always erased. To do this without some celebratory reversal that roots figures of homosexuality out of their hiddenness—to do this without simply moving Starfleet headquarters from the Presidio to the Castro—I will also ask how the constitution of homosexuality's positivity makes its exclusion possible. That is, how does Chief of Staff General Chang's presence, in all its complex figuration, adumbrate a homoerotic economy? How does heterosexuality emerge and function as a nodal point that does not simply exclude homosexuality, but excludes its own nodality? Such a reification of what has hitherto been contingent *is* heterosexuality's instituting repudiation, the constitutive repression that is indistinguishable from the return of the repressed. That economy is antagonistic to the normative one that in turn *needs* the former in order to perform its constituting repudiation. Yet hegemonic normativity, which directly follows Chang's obliteration, cannot simply be identical with itself (naturalized) because of this very need. As Laclau (1990) says in the above quotation (21), its full constitution is blocked by its need for that which antagonizes it. Chang's obliteration is the repression that cannot be distinguished from the return of the repressed. His visibility, as that which needs to disappear in order for things to be "normal," symptomatizes hegemonic normativity's identity, its compulsion to repeat what it takes to be itself. Nodality's naturalization *is* what repetition compulsion repeats.

Sexuality's experienced positivities must be staged in their moment of immediacy before analyzing the constitutive displacements. Identity, at any rate, is *at the very least* sexual identity, so I would at least like to remain consistent with this ontologization of identity, since this *psychic différance* does not impede the postulate that sociality goes all the way down—that is, that *différance* is conditioned and psychic registration is always already mediated. If *STVI* is about the repetition of normativity, the Name of the Father, then such repetition is also fully mediated, mediated by sociality, by enjoyment, an enjoyment *between* fathers.

Despite my apparent limitation here to two kinds of enjoyment—my reifying the heterosexual/homosexual binary that risks retroactively fixing meaning on what hitherto might have been contingent—it is imperative not to be seduced into yet another master narrative. It is not a matter of getting to "the real story" or of deconstructing anything purporting to be a real story, but of seeing how the various real stories are mutually enabling and how the space where meaning and identities emerge is constituted. This distinguishes a modernist symptomal reading that purports to uncover "the actual level" of agency from the obscuring symptoms, from a postmodern one in which the relationship between the "actual" agency and the obscuring symptoms is one of antagonism, of mutual enabling, constitution, and necessity. In other words, we cannot, in a modernist manner, separate the (sexual) symbolic practices of *STVI* from the (impossible totality of) cinematic experience of the film. A postmodern logic still does, in some sense, reinscribe a necessary correlation of practices, but the difference from modernism lies in the nature of the relation: it is not one of determination or *transparent* mediation, but the one's necessity of the Other as medium because it is itself not a reifiable thing that has been clouded over by mediation, but is, rather, universalized mediation. Postmodernism is characterized not by modernism's evaporation but by modernist distinctions that have broken down.[5] Hence critique must stage the historical distinctions in their reified moments before pushing on—in a

mode of inquiry fully conditioned by, but not reducible to, those distinctions—before pushing on into, if you will, the philosophy of the broken
down, of the urge: "The subjective Idea is in the first instance an *urge*. The
specific nature of this urge is therefore to sublate its own subjectivity, to
make its first abstract reality into a concrete one and to fill it with the *content* of the world presupposed by its subjectivity" (Hegel 1989, 783–784).[6]
That urge and breaking down is enjoyment and what prevents a pure differantial interstitiality; its figure in *STVI* is Chang and his obliteration.
Chang is the figure of enjoyment's essentialization—and essential instability. That is, Chang's presence is precisely what enables Admiral James T.
Kirk's and First Officer/Science Officer Captain Spock's mutual enjoyment
in rooting out the conspiracy and vanquishing him, while at the same time
such enjoyment is itself grounded in the relentless, even desperate, pursuit
of Chang's destruction and the consequent return to normativity. As a conditioning in-betweenness, Chang figures a differantial idealized contingency (modernist grounding in doubt); as presence, as one who does not
just make enjoyment possible but embodies it, makes it appear, makes it
present, he is an antidifferantial Father *in* whom enjoyment *is* (a postmodern avatar who even ungrounds Cartesian skepticism). This appearance of
différance's becoming-dialectical destroys all claim to its pure polysemy,
dissemination, and general economy. The postmodern difference is that
neither is this postmodern economy restricted in the Derridean sense; it is,
rather, finite, but indefinite.

This context in which (1) the collapse of clearly demarcated distinctions
between levels and (2) the radical interpenetration of what get designated
"cause" and "effect" both hold sway is the context in which I hope to
intervene. In *STVI,* one can view two kinds of enjoyment as implicating,
enabling, even figuring the other in the radical interpenetration of levels
that is the mark of a postmodernist reading rather than the modernist
symptomatic one. Such readings will avoid privileging or reifying any particular paradigm, beyond the locality of the status of a nodal point—for
example, the Oedipal scenario. Once again the efficacy of a *différance* of
interpretive paradigms, of psychoanalytic paradigms, exerts its interstitial
self, but, further, subjectivity is the economy of the intersticed zone (the "I"
that is a "we" that is historically conditioned) as opposed to subjects that
emerge from any given point of accumulation (a society, a "we" that would
be rationalizable into constituent "I's").

Does such a postmodern turn merely smuggle substance back into subject, subordinating objectivity to subjectivity by the subject's master narrative? No. Every subjectively constitutive substantiality's provisional status
marks the subject's partiality. Subjectivity is now formalized as not fully
locatable since it is relational, that is, it is partially located away from itself,
hence its location is *uncertain* (recall *différance* as relentless Uncertainty

Principle). And *différance*'s "deferrence" forecloses on any notion of arriving at a fixity, thereby formalizing the historicity of any (psychic, interpellative) component of the subject. But that temporal and spatial uncertainty, in a most undifferantial manner, *is itself uncertain,* that is, cannot account for the appearance of immediacy, of Substance. History's substantiality is itself historically conditioned, but nevertheless substantial. Subject must then be approached indirectly, by reading its manifestations and oscillations from node to node, not by taking a direct route that deconstructs each node or claim to nodality. This critical position, at least until the brightness of the particular constellation fades into some other, makes movement imperative. The maintenance of such a locomotive possibility is, right now, critique's *sine qua non.*

They Are

The rule of law, in the sense of the economy of demands from diegetically legitimate authority, has a curious status in *STVI*. Not only are Federation law and protocol—presumably the ruling order for all Starfleet crews—frequently ignored by the officers of the Enterprise, but they are treated as a downright nuisance. With the notable exception of "helmsman" Lieutenant Valeris's[7] jumping to attention when Kirk walks onto the bridge for the first time [0:12:12], the film is filled with such serious and not-so-serious transgressions as follows.

- The Enterprise leaves the space dock at high speed merely for the visual thrill of the officers, who then produce Valeris's social incompetence as an Enterprise officer when she points out to Kirk that this is a violation by (1) Commander Uhura clucking her tongue, (2) Spock's "ahem," and (3) Kirk's patronizing bemusement [0:13:25].

- Kirk has contraband Romulan ale served to the Klingon diplomats, which wins a certain amount of their admiration [0:22:04].

- Valeris instructs Uhura and Commander Pavel Chekov to pretend that communications are down so that Starfleet orders can plausibly be disobeyed [0:41:00]. Spock goes along when informed [0:44:23].

- Spock instructs Valeris to report the warp drive inoperative so that Starfleet orders can plausibly be disobeyed [1:02:35].

- Captain Hikaru Sulu reports that he does not know the location of the Enterprise when he in fact does; this allows the Enterprise to carry out its illegal rescue operation without being accountable to Starfleet [1:08:40].

And this exchange between Kirk and Sulu:

K: Sulu, you realize that by even *talking* to us you're violating regulations.

S : [Deadpan.] I'm sorry, Captain, your message is breaking up.

K: Bless you, Sulu. [1:30:30]

What serves diegetically as one avatar of the symbolic order is greatly diminished for the officers of the Enterprise. This is nothing new to *Star Trek*—while being cross-examined at his Klingon show trial, Kirk readily admits his penchant for violating orders—but the Jonah-like annoyance with Federation law as inconvenient nuisance, as opposed to a more strident and guilt-ridden antipathy (the sense of transgression is null here), marks a diminishing of the symbolic order, the paternal metaphor, that itself is the dead and deadening force *par excellence*. The most salient example of this is Klingon Chancellor Gorkon's daughter, Azetbur's, ascent to the chancellorship at the death of her father. From that moment on, all her public speeches invoke the name of her father, the Name of the Father in whose name she commands. For example, when negotiating with the Federation president: "Mr. President, I've been named Chancellor by the High Council in my father's place" [0:41:20]; "Mr. President, let us come to the point: you wanted this conference to go on, and so did my father. I will attend in one week" [0:41:38]. When consulting with her own staff:

Adviser: Better to die on our feet than live on our knees.

Az: That wasn't what my father wanted.

Chang: Your father was killed for what he wanted.

Az: The process will go forward. Kirk will pay for my father's death. [0:42:35]

And when addressing the peace conference, her speech begins by invoking her father's memory. But she is now deadened to the presence of the conspiracy that surrounds her (her top advisor is the traitor, conspirator to her father's murder), and her obliviousness persists to the very end of the movie. In the final melee when all is exposed, Azetbur is reduced to merely asking, "What's happened? What is the meaning of all of this?" [1:42:50]. This is a sharp difference from the more criticizing role she plays before joining the corps of officially sanctioned (symbolically ordered), and exclusively male, diplomats. Before her father's death she responds to the Federation's humanist universalization of "inalienable human rights": "'Human' rights. Why the very name is racist. The Federation is no more than a *Homo sapiens* only club" [0:24:15]. I must quickly add that reading the paternal metaphor's ability to castrate Azetbur (cut her off from her castrating power—Chekov is completely silenced, unmanned, after her above comment) as a reinscription of its centrality would be completely misleading since her role is truly minimal compared to that of the murderous, all-enjoying, debauched General Chang.

This quick turn away from what would amount to a modernist critique of patriarchy as that which obscures the "more authentic" level of masculinist gender oppression is precisely the afore-mentioned postmodern turn. This is not to say gender oppression is false, but that to inscribe it as more than a mediated moment would be to ignore much of the masculinist economy that is advertising for investors, or, worse, to set up a radical outside that could critique such a dominant[8] masculinism and thinks itself free of masculinity's dominating effects. The place from which modernist feminism passes critical judgment is conditioned by what it criticizes, and such a feminism now appears undermined by blindness to this, its own "extimacy." Postmodern feminism would then be a refiguration of what constitutes gender oppression; such a critical feminism would take masculinist economies rather than "men" for its object. Hence, the emergence of a father figure that exerts a destabilizing effect on the Name of the Father is no longer paradoxical:

> This postmodern shift affects radically the status of paternal authority: modernism endeavors to assert the subversive potential of the margins which undermine the Father's authority, of the enjoyments which elude the Father's grasp, whereas postmodernism *focuses on the father himself and conceives him as "alive," in his obscene dimension.* (Žižek 1992, 124)

Federation law and enjoyment are no longer mutually exclusive.

What there is of the big Other is peripheral and oblivious to the situation in which Kirk, Spock, Chang, Chief Engineer Montgomery Scott (Scotty), and Valeris find themselves. Instead of the law and its Kantian, modernist father, we get a father whose capacity for evil enjoyment is limitless and monstrously beyond the Enterprise's control. The ultimate figure for this is Chang's ship, which is able to fire its weapons while operating a cloaking device so that it eludes detection despite its proximity—a monstrous capability:

K: There's a Bird of Prey [a Romulan warship presumably on loan to the Klingons] on the lookout for us, and she can fire while cloaked.

Su: Surely not!

[1:30:57]

Sp: A Bird of Prey.

C: [Incredulous.] Cloaked?

Sc: A Bird of Prey cannot fire when she's cloaked!

Sp: All things being equal, Mr. Scott, I would agree. However, things are not equal: this one can.

V: We must inform Starfleet command.

Sc: [Shouting.] Inform them of what?! A new weapon that is invisible? Raving lunatics, that's what they'll call us! They'll say we're so desperate to exonerate the captain, we'll say *anything*.

Sp: And they would be correct. [0:54:51]

Out of this postmodern matrix emerges Father-Enjoyment, the reverse of the now submerging Name of the Father who:

> is not the agency of symbolic Law, its "repression," which hinders the sexual relationship (according to a Lacanian commonplace, the role of the Name of the Father is precisely to *enable* the semblance of a sexual relationship), its stumbling block is on the contrary a certain excessive "sprout of enjoyment" materialized in the obscene figure of the "anal father." (Žižek 1992, 125)

Would it be too extravagant to view the short ponytail that shoots out of the back of Chang's otherwise bald head as his "sprout of enjoyment"?

To leave it at that would be to sustain the ponytail as *merely* exotic and leave that which renders it legible as such unthought. Such a physical detail does not simply coincide with the other ways the Klingons are coded Asian (such as Chang's name), stereotypically Middle Eastern/North African Islamic (such as their infighting and swift, hard "desert" justice), or Asian/Islamic (the name Azetbur). Racial and cultural/religious otherness become economies that can then mediate a host of social relations—sexuality not the least among them—and make nodality possible. The Klingons have strong class encodings as well. Upon first beaming onto the Enterprise they are staged as a haughty crew in bikers' studded leathers and boots. Chang's ponytail resonates here too, not just in its racial exoticization. The Klingons are, to this extent, what the evil, scheming General Cartwright refers to as "trash": "To offer the Klingons safe haven within Federation space is suicide. The Klingons would become the alien trash of the galaxy" [0:09:07]. There is a resonance here with white trash. Cartwright, however, is one of the villains, and as the response shot of Senior Medical Officer Leonard McCoy's indignant raised eyebrow look of chastising consternation corroborates: this overt bigotry is eschewed in favor of a liberal tolerance. For the Federation officers, the Klingons, despite being a vulgar bunch who quote Shakespeare but "in the original Klingon"[9] (i.e., have redeeming features that need a little polishing), are a people to be *tolerated* in the interests of galactic peace. The Klingons are lower class, but that's okay: They're still on the same scale as we are; they are just less evolved forms of us. And though they can never become us, thank God, (the Klingons' bodily differences—ridged foreheads, etc.— mark them indelibly), we know darn well that *they want to.*

This is not "simple" racism, by which I mean a rhetoric of violence directed at some essentialized "them," and so it is precisely here that any liberal pluralist rhetoric can only miss the postmodern point: race in complex, nondeterministic relation to sexuality. *STVI stages* the liberal pluralist utopia in relativizing Klingon otherness without falling into a romanticizing orientalism, simple racism's strategically naïve flip side. It is imperative to recognize liberal pluralism's good intentions qua good intentions, that is, in their moment of immediacy. For example, upon the Klingons' beaming back to their ship after the formal dinner, the Enterprise crewmembers shed their formal, but courteous, politeness and literally proceed to breathe freely after the bad-smelling Klingons have left. The comic aspect of this breath of fresh air as acknowledgment of the objectionable quality of our own (as Starfleet officers) disgust is a sign that this Klingon distastefulness neither orientalizes them nor makes them the target of a simple racist attack. They disgust us; our disgust is reprehensible, and that is the reflective comprehension of the long way we have to go to meet our pluralistic ideal with which faith is, ultimately, kept, and which is hence left unconditioned, uninterrogated.[10]

Such a movement is a critique of orientalism: the Other is not simply assimilated as exotic and desirable. It is not simple racism either: Klingons may disgust us Starfleet officers, with their body odor and their unseemly eating habits, but we also recognize that disgust as saying something about *us.* It is our own enjoyment in insulting the Klingons behind their backs that is being called on the carpet, and, via this economy of enjoyment, sexuality reenters the problematic as mediator of the racial and class language that articulates it. Race and class, in this moment, become sexuality's instruments.

Instrumentality toward the Other is modernist, utilitarian logic's reinscription, racism taking the form of the fight against racism. This "metaracism" (Balibar 1991) mediates the good intentions mentioned earlier. It is crucial that instrumentality toward the Other[11] appears to its fullest when we consider *STVI's* sexual economy: a suite of instrumentalized othernesses—a psychoanalytic toolbox of otherness, if you will—is *used* to construct the normativity that occludes (represses) the traumatic relation to our own enjoyment, and thereby to stage the trauma[12] in the only way such nonidentity can be staged: via its occlusions.[13]

If heterosexuality is as hegemonic in the twenty-third century as it is in ours, and we take the symbolic order, in the Lacanian manner, to be what commands heterosexual enjoyment,[14] then the receding of the symbolic order threatens the effacement of the imperative to heterosexual enjoyment. And to the extent that heterosexuality is the effacement of homosexuality, the emergence of the anal father, General Chang, negates this homosexual repression. This negation of homosexual repression is the emergence of homosexuality as a viable subject position, its "elementary matrix of signification" (Žižek 1991, 42), and is localized in the main character relationship in *STVI*, that of Kirk and Spock.

Chang, then, does not block a heterosexual relationship—though there is no heterosexual couple produced at the end of the film—but, as negation of the negation, he is the figure of the repression, or sublimation, of homosexuality, producing the couple Kirk and Spock in this mode once again.[15] *The obliteration of the anal father is the condition of heterosexuality's enablement and the beginning of its naturalization, the forgetting of its contingency.* Chang is sadistically cruel, debauched and perverted, yet a figure of total mastery: He never loses control, always dissimulating his rage; for example, his laughing, ironic banter with Kirk before and during the dinner scene is much more malevolent than noisy rage. Indeed, he organizes his most violent act (ordering torpedoes to be fired at the Enterprise—the Enterprise's violation) with the merest of hand gestures, whose framing in extreme close-up belies this very mereness.

He knows no limits: Chang is responsible for his commander's murder, the father of his new master, Azetbur, who trusts him with the prosecution of her father's murderers and retains him as chief of staff. He is cruel to the extreme, yet at the same time he knows who is here to kill him, and is resigned to it. "The 'primordial father' is not a primitive figure of pure, presymbolic, brute force, but a *father who knows*" (Žižek 1992, 159). Chang knows that Kirk has come to kill him before Kirk knows it:

C: From one warrior to another.

K: [Ironically.] Right. [0:21:14]

And later, when Chang says to Kirk, "There's no need to mince words. In space, all warriors are cold warriors" [0:23:55], Kirk smiles politely, but does not respond, unable to fathom what Chang is really getting at. There is a similar sort of exchange when the Klingons leave the Enterprise and Chang says, "Parting is such sweet sorrow, Captain. [Laughs.] Have we not heard the chimes at midnight?" [0:25:40], and Kirk just shakes his head as if to wonder whether or not Chang is simply mad. Kirk's unreflective relationship to his own status as cold warrior against "Klingonism" is Rick Worland's (1988) point in his "Captain Kirk: Cold Warrior." Worland reads the Enterprise's diplomatic battle against the Klingons for the hearts and minds of "Third World" planets as an allegory for the Cold War U.S. politics of the 1960s. I would disagree with Worland's point only inasmuch as the Cold War brinksmanship in *Star Trek (ST)* does lead, sometimes, to an exchange of blows, though certainly never the all-out warfare for which both sides repress the desire (the Federation) and fear (the Klingons). The difference now is that what has been Cold War in the guise of *sotto voce* hot war has now become substantially colder: What was *sotto voce* is now *sub rosa,* narrowed down and conducted with a kind of nudge-and-wink confidentiality and secretiveness (Chang's attitude toward Kirk)—so secret that Kirk does not yet know he is in on it. But he is soon to find out; Chang's enjoyment is a public one. Chang, as persistent threat to make what was cold hot, is a figure of war's desire—a forbidden enjoyment— and, by persistently drawing attention to the Cold War aspect of their relationship, can thus be read as alienating Kirk and the *Star Trek* universe *from* that coldness.

Much later, however, Chang's hitherto *sub rosa* comments regarding their confrontation's fatality come home to Kirk as their relationship's unavoidable truth. From his cloaked ship via a communication link, about to fire his first torpedo at the Enterprise, Chang says, "Oh, now, be honest, Captain. Warrior to warrior. You do prefer it this way, don't you. As it was meant to be. No peace in our time [nor Cold War *détente*]. Once more unto the breach, dear friends" [1:35:58]. Due to his ability to fire while cloaked, Chang wields unlimited power in this confrontation; he knows and enjoys this, spinning in his chair and yelling "Cry havoc! and let slip the dogs of war!" [1:39:47]. Yet this monstrous threat proves to be utterly unstable: Chang is impotent, brought down by a most errant torpedo that zigzags fecklessly but manages somehow to zero in on Chang's ship's waste products, its "gaseous anomalies" [1:37:00]. As soon as the Enterprise's lone adapted torpedo is fired, Chang is paralyzed and can do nothing but watch it wander in, the explosion revealing his location, enabling Kirk and Sulu to obliterate him in an instant. This is the evacuation of enjoyment around which the Name of the Father can emerge, along with its normative heterosexuality, in the form of Kirk and Spock's soon-to-be-prohibited anti-heteronormative mutual enjoyment—the Enterprise will be decommissioned after this mission.

The anal father's obliteration is not enough: Normativity must iterate itself so that its own contingency can be forgotten. The anal father's death cannot be mourned since doing so would commemorate the prohibition he de-prohibited, the prohibited enjoyment he enjoyed. But neither must that which is prohibited be rendered impossible: The Name of the Father makes what was impossible prohibited. The repressed returns, but mere remembrance of Chang would be a persistent reminder that there has been a prohibition.[16] Kirk and Spock, in the last scene, do the normalized thing by disobeying Starfleet and warping off together.

The Kirk/Spock pair, though not figuratively gendered in a simple way, is not symmetrical either. Spock is figured as (normatively) feminine in a number of ways. Traditionally, the periodicity of Spock's sexual receptiveness *(pon farr,* a recurrent theme in K/S fiction [Penley 1991, 158]) figures him as a female mammal in heat. Secondly, even his notorious logic is diminished, when need be, in favor of a more intuitive wisdom:

S: You must have faith.

Valeris: Faith?

S: That the universe will unfold as it should.

V: But is that logical? Surely, we must . . .

S: Logic, logic, logic. Logic is the *beginning* of wisdom, Valeris, not the end. [0:16:30]

and sometimes even opposed to the phallic, as Kirk implies when he says "You're a great one for logic. I'm a great one for rushing in where angels fear to tread" [1:32:21]. It is not that logic is necessarily feminine, which would be, to be sure, an extravagant claim. The point is that despite Kirk's invocation of logic's active, interventionary aspect, it is still hypostasized, for such exchanges, as that which opposes a certain (irrational! [because not logical]) phallicism via a castrating power.

Then there is Spock's mysticism tinged with Asian/African influence (also, see the decor of his cabin [0:16:30]) in the context of a Judeo-Christian (read: European) ethic. Such a stereotypically mystical conception of Asia/Africa is more than a generalized exoticization due to the feminizing history of that generalization.[17] This is not *only* exoticization that essentializes the exotic other; it is, rather, the culmination of a history of exoticization that narrativizes both gender difference's becoming *the model for* hierarchical difference and the (political) exclusion of other kinds of difference.[18] In other words, feminist critique—the investment in the masculine/feminine gender binary that also represses its simultaneous investment in a hierarchically higher masculine—takes as its object masculinism, which emerges historically by marking one side as special, nonnormative, or exotic, and then forgetting that history. The heteronormative economy has a great stake in dehistoricizing exoticization: If exotic difference is unhierarchical, differentiation within that which is exoticized cannot be, for that economy, sexual difference. This erases the possibility of multiple symbolics within the exoticized, in this case the feminine. Such erasure produces the essentialized gender economy's nodal points: Man, Woman. Erasure reifies the blindness to the masculine/feminine distinction's ordering power, grounding the symbolic order of gender in a particular, hierarchical distinction.

Interestingly, however, if the presence of the anal father inhibits the symbolic order and its normative heterosexuality, and, by extension, the heterosexual male fantasy of the *femme fatale,* then we have a kind of localized Name of the Father in Spock's cabin where he is the dominating father figure for Valeris (he was her sponsor at Starfleet Academy and has "followed her career with satisfaction" [0:15:32]). Valeris turns out to be a *femme fatale* for Spock to the extent that she is his agent of (near) destruction, to which he is attracted beyond any "logical" justification: "I was prejudiced by her accomplishments as a Vulcan," Spock declares [1:33:10]. Whatever component of *femme fatale*ness we read in Valeris, I think it is greatly overshadowed by the figure of the primordial father. After all, she is in conspiracy with Chang and others, but there is never a sense of hierarchy among the conspirators—they never interact in any way whatsoever—and so Valeris is less *femme fatale* than anal father herself. Perhaps Spock can be read the same way vis-à-vis Kirk. Valeris partakes of the same ferocity as Chang (though we see only evidence of her brutality, not the act itself) and is equally murderous and fully informed (except, notably, for the location of the peace conference, which information would be difficult to obtain without giving away her role in the conspiracy). If knowledge is her power, then she is reduced to impotence (though not as easily as Chang) during the rape scene on the bridge—the violation of her mind via Spock's Vulcan mindmeld.

In this sense, Kirk and Spock consummate their relationship, Valeris mediating what Chang de-prohibits. Kirk orders the mindmeld with the merest of (masterful) linguistic gestures: he merely says "Spock" and Spock understands completely and complies without hesitation [1:28:00]. Spock probes Valeris's mind, the Vulcan organ of enjoyment, for her desire to invoke all-out war with the Klingons and the secret stored there—her secret horrific enjoyment—while Kirk acts as the interrogating voice (only Spock and Valeris are in frame and in focus throughout the scene). Valeris is the medium of this, the most libidinally cathected sequence in the film, complete with Valeris's sexual groans and the camera panning full circle around the mindmelding pair. This rape is Valeris's effacement, thus the destruction of what there is of primordial father in her figure (she is silent and submissive the rest of the film). Kirk and Spock's mutual enjoyment of this eradication of an enemy of the order is their homoerotic enjoyment and at the same time the production of its impossibility, since it leads to the conspiracy's failure, Chang's destruction, and the end of this joint venture. The hegemonic economy reproduces itself, stamping out its nodal points, but this reproduction can only be thought of as iteration. The forgetting of the symbolic order's mediacy and contingency shores up its naturalness. Valeris has, nonetheless, mediated the consummation on the bridge in front of the whole Enterprise "family" and in this sense is a malefactor become vanishing mediator via her sacrifice.

> In this final reversal the agent previously identified as malefactor
> suddenly changes into donator, i.e., into a "mediator" who, by
> means of his sacrifice, enables the hero's salvation. And it is perhaps
> the very experience of this reversal of the "condition of impossibil-
> ity" into a "condition of possibility"—the experience of how "only
> the spear that smote you/can heal your wound" (to quote from
> Wagner's *Parsifal*)—which constitutes the core of what we call
> "dialectics." (Žižek 1992, 128)

The vanishing mediator (Žižek 1991, 180–189) is not some unsubstantial
merely formal structural necessity; there is a violent logic to being "disappeared" in such a manner, and this is not coincidental. The observation that
homoerotics are figured as a libidinalized violation is indeed disturbing—that
is the point—in that it risks being complicit in policing normativity's boundaries. Anything less leaves us in pursuit of a position from which to speak
with, as it were, clean hands, and such an endeavor is liberal pluralism's characteristic good intention, as well as its well-intentioned crime. But pushing
farther on from within this complicitous mode, this telling scene demonstrates the mainstream film *STVI*'s figuration of homosexuality in the hegemonic, heteronormal economy, as a forbidden enjoyment, thereby removing
it from the realm of the impossible. The repressed appears—is normatively
structured; that is, its appearance conditioned by that to which it is heterogeneous—and has causal efficacy as the return of the repressed. What appears
is forbidden because it threatens the hegemonic identificatory economy's dis-
solution along with all those subjective identities invested in it.

The film concludes with Azetbur declaring to Kirk that the Name of the
Father is reconstituted: "You've restored my father's faith" [1:43:25].
Homosexuality is occluded, but again, going further, it is *staged* in the only
manner possible here: via its occlusions. It is not just forbidden but always
already proscribed, hence *impossible* for this economy, an economy of the
possible. If homosexuality cannot be bared, denuded, then it is that which
denudes or, more properly, *de-nodes* nodal points, in the sense that it
threatens to restore the repressed nodality, contingency. Homosexuality is,
in this economy, neither a nodal point nor that which merely appears as
effaced, but *is* effacement, or more accurately, that which persistently
threatens effacement. *Therein lies the occlusion:* Homosexuality is never
figured as having *been* effaced since threat extinguished would be altogether something other than effacement's (read, now: homosexuality's) persistent threat. The threat's persistence is no guarantee, however, that
homosexuality's possibility cannot disappear.

In the most extreme, abstract version of repression—a nodal point that is
fully naturalized—the very naturalness of what appears as such *is* the
symptom of what has completely disappeared and of a wholly unnatural
exclusion. That thought, however, is exterior to what is now natural—

though this is the most unstable of naturals since the slightest deviation becomes the greatest possible qualitative perturbation of what had hitherto taken itself to be a Whole. This preservation of the points' nodality, their provisional status, draws attention to the violence that compels and constitutes the hegemonic order's citational repetitions.[19] After this staging, in order "to ameliorate and rework this violence, it is necessary to learn a double movement: to invoke the category and, hence, provisionally to institute as identity and at the same time to open the category as a site of permanent political contest" (Butler 1993, 221–222). Recognizing political contestation—antagonism—as something that makes identity possible, rather than as an effect of subjective agency, maintains critique's locomotive possibility. Thus, the truth of any historical social formation's critical judgments—which it *must* make in order to *be* a historical formation—is figured as historical and not transcendental.

Having enjoyed once, Kirk and Spock are to return to base and the Enterprise is to be decommissioned. At this horrifying call to duty, Kirk hesitates, and Spock fills in the indecisive moment:

[Upon Sulu's taking his leave.]

Chekov: So. This is good-bye.

K: I think it's about time we got underway ourselves.

Uhura: Captain, I have orders from Starfleet command. We're to put back to space dock immediately. To be decommissioned.

[15-second silence]

S: If I were human, I believe my response would be "Go to hell." *If* I were human. [1:45:12]

But if they do venture out again, they know they are on borrowed time. Will they go out in search of more anal fathers so that they can enjoy again, or will they pass on the baton, lose it, to the next generation?

S: But, Captain, we both know that I am not human.

K: Spock, you want to know something? Everybody's human.

S: I find that remark . . . insulting.

K: Come on, I need you. [1:34:00]

Notes

1. I am thinking here of popular discourses that root gayness in biological necessity as well as those that locate this and other constitutive aspects of the subject, to varying degrees, in socialization.

2. "To stamp Becoming with the character of Being—that is the supreme will to power . . . high point of the meditation" (Nietzsche 1967, 330).

3. This negativity is not characteristic solely of sexuality but of any element that emerges historically to fix the partial, multiply situated subject.

4. All subsequent references to this film are in the form [hour: minute: second] and reference the timecode on my videotape copy; timecodes on other copies may vary somewhat.

5. Joanna Hodge (1991) characterizes Adorno's apparently modernist elitism regarding "background music" as a postmodern mode insofar as it pushes its "own enquiries and concepts to the point at which distinctions between different kinds of enquiry, between metaphysics and ethics, between epistemology and aesthetics begin to break down, and this break down is a sign rather of a postmodern mode of philosophizing than of the modern, which seeks to maintain a detached control over such distinctions and conceptual boundaries" (96).

6. Cf. Hegel (1989, 770). Dialectics, as philosophy of the urge, then, keeps faith with the logic of *différance* insofar as they are both committed to the impossibility of *prima philosophia*. Dialectics is not ur-philosophy, but *urge-philosophy.*

7. *She* is the murderous traitor, so her scrupulousness conceals its opposite. But this moment is retroactively quilted by her unmasking, the establishing of that nodal point of her subjectivity.

8. In such critiques "dominant" hegemonizes "hegemony."

9. Compare this with Chekov's ascribing Russian lineage, in the original television program, to much that is revered or pleasurable. Spock in contrast, "properly" acknowledges origins. He admires and uses the Chagall in his quarters, for example, as a source of inspiration to muse upon humanity and its grounding mythologies' representations.

10. Perhaps it is worth noting Sulu's figuration as an upwardly mobile Starfleet officer; he is Captain of the *Excelsior* and completely capable and effective in his normative roles. Sulu is also clearly of Asian descent, but not exoticized (in *this* film) and, for the most part, a "regular guy" in a supporting role. Though his Asianness is certainly not coincidental, it is not really a saliency in this film relative to Chang's. This is liberal pluralism's utopianism hypostasized, and its *intentions* must always be thought in their moment of immediacy. Simple racism—Asianness as an *essential* marker of social position—would be much more univocal since it could never take Asianness to be, as it is regarding Sulu in this movie, a matter of indifference. Failing to discern pluralism's intentions here would risk identifying the Categorical Imperative with Evil and would preempt critical reflection upon those intentions and all they criticize and make possible and impossible. Sulu's Asianness is not a nonissue because of Federation pluralism; rather, the liberal pluralistic order sees Sulu as sufficiently evolved. In liberal pluralism's utopia, *everyone,* without prejudice, is free to submit, that is, is forced to be free.

11. Such instrumentality is, for both Hegel (1977, 359–360) and Adorno (1973, 15–18), Enlightened modernity's lone, but subsuming, crime.

12. Where trauma's staging is the return of the repressed.

13. Note that this logic of occlusion does not, for example, reify gayness as effacement and thereupon proceed to act merely as an accomplice to that violence. The claim is, more properly, that nonidentity (and so identity, the inside that nonidentity supplements) is only known via its occlusions, its distortions, its fictions. As Judith Butler (1993) puts it regarding the phallus, "The phallus has no existence separable from the occasions of its symbolization; it cannot symbolize without its occasion" (90).

14. We could make this the definition of the hegemonic: that which the symbolic order commands. This does not preclude multiple symbolics, but does require that there be a locally dominant one.

15. We can see a precedent for this anal father figure in such classic *film noir* as *The Glass Key* (1942) and *Gilda* (1946).

16. In the same way any figure of liberation must also be a figure of the unfree state.

17. An early case in point is Carthage's Dido's relation to Rome's Aeneas in the *Aeneid*. Dido's Africa (i.e., Aeneas's) is savage, irrational, fecund, and seductive. Dido, who diverts the hero Aeneas from realizing his destiny, is herself destroyed by that most feminine of gods, Rumor. Interestingly, Dido's destruction points to the contingency of even the Roman emperor's power. To that extent, Vergil's epic can be read as serving a warning to his patron Augustus: the rabble has a power—gossip and rumor—that you cannot control even if you contain it within the feminine.

18. I owe this last observation to a conversation with Leslie Minot.

19. For Butler (1993), this is what would constitute the nodal points: "'to be constituted' means 'to be compelled to cite or repeat or mime'" (220).

References

Adorno, T. W. 1973. *Negative Dialectics*. Trans. E. B. Ashton. New York: Continuum.

Balibar, Etienne. 1991. "Is There a 'Neo-Racism'?" In *Race, Nation, Class: Ambiguous Identities*. Ed. Etienne Balibar and Immanuel Wallerstein. London: Verso. 17–27.

Butler, Judith. 1993. *Bodies That Matter*. New York: Routledge.

Derrida, Jacques. 1973. *"Différance." Speech and Phenomena*. Trans. David B. Allison. Evanston, IL: Northwestern U P. 129–160.

Hegel, G. W. F. 1977. *Phenomenology of Spirit*. Trans. A. V. Miller. New York: Oxford U P.

———. 1989. *Science of Logic*. Trans. A. V. Miller. Atlantic Highlands, NJ: Humanities P International.

Hodge, Joanna. 1991. "Feminism and Postmodernism: Misleading Divisions Imposed by the Opposition between Modernism and Postmodernism." In *The Problems of Modernity: Adorno and Benjamin*. Ed. Andrew Benjamin. New York: Routledge. 86–111.

Laclau, Ernesto. 1990. *New Reflections on the Revolution of Our Time*. New York: Verso.

Laclau, Ernesto, and Chantal Mouffe. 1985. *Hegemony and Socialist Strategy: Towards a Radical Democratic Politics.* London: Verso.

Nietzsche, Friedrich. 1967. *The Will to Power.* Trans. Walter Kaufman. New York: Random House.

Penley, Constance. 1991. "Brownian Motion: Women, Tactics, and Technology." In *Technoculture.* Ed. Constance Penley and Andrew Ross. Minneapolis: U of Minnesota P. 135–161.

Worland, Rick. 1988. "Captain Kirk: Cold Warrior." *Journal of Popular Film and Television* 16.3: 109–117.

Žižek, Slavoj. 1991. *For They Know Not What They Do.* New York: Verso.

———. 1992. *Enjoy Your Symptom!* New York: Routledge.

11

"All Good Things ... "

The End of *Star Trek: The Next Generation,* The End of Camelot—The End of the Tale About Woman as Handmaid to Patriarchy as Superman

MARLEEN S. BARR

On May 23, 1994, U.S. television carried the endings to two cultural lega-cies: Jacqueline Kennedy Onassis's funeral, which marks the end of the Camelot era, and "All Good Things ... ," the final episode of *Star Trek: The Next Generation (TNG),* which marks the end of part of a popular cultural phenomenon. Both these endings concern rewriting the cultural tale about Woman as talented, powerless handmaid to patriarchy as Superman. In this chapter I explain that the demise of Camelot and *TNG* epitomizes the struggle within U.S. culture to conclude a pervasive story about women who function as appendages to all-powerful men.

Beauty and wealth alone do not explain why U.S. popular culture was so moved by the passing of a book editor, mother, and wife. Other wealthy and beautiful women have died without evoking the deep feelings Jackie's death elicited. Marilyn Monroe, for example, was not given a nationally televised funeral. People revere Jackie, I think, because in addition to acting as a powerless appendage to two Supermen, a role typical of Woman in U.S. popular culture, she approached the role of Superman herself. She boarded Air Force One clad in her pink blood-stained uniform, flew over the country, and functioned as the Wife of Steel—a superhero(ine) leading a mourning nation. But because U.S. culture has no place for Woman-as-Superman, Jackie attached herself to a Superman II, Aristotle Onassis. Empowered by the Kennedy name and the Onassis wealth, Jackie, in a sin-gle bound, leaped to the top of the tall building at 1040 Fifth Avenue. She was accompanied by Maurice Tempelsman who, as a Jewish man, cannot assume Superman status. Jackie's death evokes emotion because she repre-sents truth, justice, and the white Christian "American" way. Yet, of course, wielding governmental power did not cause this courageous and talented woman to become a national myth.

Now that JFK's infidelities have made him something less than fully
Superman, people might believe that Jackie, a paragon of mothering and
nurturing who held the national family together, was something more than
a handmaid. *TNG* reflects such a desire to represent competent women, to
see women as something more than handmaids. This chapter, in part, looks
at the representation of that desire in the final episode of the series. "All
Good Things . . . "—which places Captain Jean-Luc Picard in the past, present, and future—reflects U.S. culture's readiness to recognize that patriarchy, though a good thing for men, should come to an end.

Star Trek, *Camelot,* and *Superman*

During the utopian time of Camelot, a militarily and economically power-
ful United States applauded a White House that welcomed arts, humanities,
and European culture. The country had two saviors ensconced in the White
House: JFK, who saved the United States from the Communists in Cuba
and their flying nuclear phalluses; and Jackie, who provided the United
States with cultural values and subjective taste. She was a powerless
Superman who came to our rescue. She turned the White House into a *Star
Trek* holodeck, whose programmed vision championed artistic expression
and historical reclamation. The nation emulated Jackie's style, her White
House as holodeck. Jackie, who neither held public office nor repelled a
single missile, constructed a cultural reality to be emulated and idealized.

The unmanly respect and responsibility for art and cultural diversity
characterizes another White House, the starship Enterprise commanded by
Picard. He breaks with some traditional representations of the "all-
American hero": he is an Englishman playing a captain of French heritage;
he quotes Shakespeare; and he even sometimes leaves the action of away
missions to his second-in-command. His Enterprise is no penile rocket.
Continuing the legacy of the last generation, positioned like breasts, two
thrusters propel his round, "feminine" ship, which houses authorized
Others. A racist nation even tolerates a Klingon security chief on the
bridge, Lt. Worf, played by an African American man. Perhaps the United
States is ready to empower some versions of the outside Other (even if he
has few lines), including a white woman (*Star Trek: Voyager*'s Captain
Kathryn Janeway) and an African American man (*Star Trek: Deep Space
Nine*'s Commander, now Captain, Benjamin Sisko).

Worf (a Klingon Starfleet officer) exemplifies Linda Hutcheon's (1988)
notion of the postmodern acceptance of the "ex-centric." (The same holds
true for the Kennedy family's recent doings. A Jew and an Austrian have
both become Kennedys. Despite their own wealth and achievements, when
Schlossberg, Tempelsman, and Schwarzenegger penetrated the Kennedy
family inner circle, they became male appendages to Kennedy women. They

became sidekicks—"wives." Schwarzenegger's Hollywood fame does not outclass Maria Shriver.) In the Kennedy White House, as on Picard's Enterprise, nurturing and artistic pursuits receive comparable airtime to militaristic power displays. On trips abroad, Jackie was often more visible than JFK; on the Bridge, Counselor Lt. Commander Deanna Troi is often more visible than Picard, albeit because these women have been presented as heterosexualized objects for the U.S. public's gaze. In Camelot and on the Enterprise, the patriarchal institution known as marriage does not engender people's best selves. All (but one) of the Enterprise officers are single; Jackie was her best self sans husbands.

TNG and Camelot exemplify postmodern reclassifications of fixed definitions. JFK deconstructed cultural stereotypes when he showed that someone other than Eisenhower—someone other than an elderly Protestant—could be president, as long as this Other was still white and male. As captain of a ship that generally hovers light years from Starfleet range, Picard is at once a part of and outside the reach of Starfleet Command. As a white Catholic male, JFK was at once a part of and outside the U.S. political hegemony. Picard's Enterprise and Kennedy's Camelot battle a similar enemy: the definition of an objectified and fixed Other. Picard confronts the Borg, the single-minded mechanistic communal entity, and JFK confronted the Soviets, the emblem of single-minded Communist ideology. As Picard and crew "seek out new life and new civilizations" ("discovering" and inflicting their own worldview onto alien cultures), they both affirm and counter Starfleet's Prime Directive as grand narrative. As JFK, Jackie, and their empowered compatriots challenged U.S. cultural isolation (while maintaining military and economic dominance), they both affirmed and countered expansionist imperatives to spread capitalism across the globe.

Picard, the blatantly not macho man, is empowered; JFK, the outsider Catholic, is empowered. But what about other Others, such as talented white women? What about Troi, Chief Medical Officer Commander Beverly Crusher, and Jackie? As we are all aware, these women are neither captain nor president. And even though the body of the ship is feminized, the seat of power is not. The Enterprise is Superman. The White House is Superman. U.S. culture has not yet allowed white women either to be or to control Superman. But the Superman that constitutes the White House and the Enterprise is not unitary. These institutions function via power ensconced in mergers of dynamic duos. The White House and the President are a fused cyborg juxtaposition of governmental machine and individual. The Enterprise and the crew are a fused cyborg juxtaposition of technological devices and individuals. Superman is no man; Superman transcends the power of one man possessing a penis. Superman's power is ubiquitous.

Many of Picard's crewmembers have proto-cyborg or nonhuman bodies. Chief Engineer Lt. Commander Geordi La Forge's human body is supplemented by a mechanical visual device. Lt. Commander Data is an android who craves human emotions. Troi's empathic abilities are Betazoid, not human. Worf has a back-up spine. Even Picard has an artificial heart. And now, at the end of Camelot, both JFK and Jackie have transcended their bodies to become superhuman myths. "In death, our princess has been returned to us. Now she will be buried next to our prince, and when the television cameras make their periodic respectful visits to the Kennedy grave, the eternal flame will be the powerfully telegenic symbol for them both" (Blair 1994, 25). The U.S. culture that valorizes cyborg *Star Trek* characters and writes mythology about deceased male and female White House inhabitants seems to be asking the question Ursula Le Guin articulated: Is gender necessary? The fact that JFK and Jackie are receiving equal prestige as myths in contemporary America sets the stage for a white woman president. *TNG*'s world of cyborg imagery and reality constructed at will sets the stage for a white woman captain. "All Good Things . . ." functions as this stage. "All Good Things . . ." articulates the Prime Directive of *TNG*: to separate the he-man from the captain, to jettison U.S. manhood, to characterize First Officer Commander William Riker and Picard as two distinct entities in order to proclaim that someone Other than Captain James T. Kirk can be Superman. And *TNG* boldly goes beyond Riker's Island, beyond the prison house of patriarchal language and patriarchal reality. *TNG* implies that some white women can be Superman.

Who, Appropriately, Is Superman?

This question presently pervades U.S. culture. It is, for example, at the heart of Ted Kennedy's recent political life. A May 23, 1994, *New Yorker* article, "We're Not in Camelot Anymore," proclaims that Ted Kennedy is definitely not Superman: "[F]or the first time in thirty years, Ted Kennedy is campaigning in a Senate race whose outcome is not already certain" (Boyer 1994, 39, 40). Far from being Superman, Ted Kennedy himself needs to be saved from the tarnished image of Kennedy manhood. Chappaquiddick and the rape trial of Kennedy's nephew, William Kennedy Smith, can be understood to transform Ted Kennedy into Lois Lane. None other than a white woman appears to rescue Ted/Lois: his new wife, Victoria Reggie, who "became the centerpiece of Ted Kennedy's rehabilitation by marrying him" (44). Peter J. Boyer continues:

> Vicki Reggie Kennedy is often referred to as "the asset," and one meeting with her explains why. She is attractive, gracious, and smart, and her presence beside Kennedy inspires approval. . . . Alone on the campaign trail, without Vicki, Kennedy might seem nothing but spectacle, all bloat and tremor; with her one senses a

flash of new energy. . . . Her visibility may, in fact, be her greatest contribution to her husband's campaign. She is a direct answer to the character issue, living evidence that Kennedy's raucous bachelorhood is over. (44, 45)

Kennedy as a tremorous bloat epitomizes the literature of exhaustion—the tired male hero story—revitalized by a trope of replenishment—the presence of a savvy woman. Victoria is Ted's Superman. But despite her success as his rescuer, she is not running for the Senate.

The question "Who is appropriately Superman?" also applies to a more powerful female half of a prominent couple: Hillary Rodham Clinton. The United States absolutely accepts the idea that although Jackie could never become president, the same does not hold true for Hillary. In fact, the May 23, 1994, cover of the *New York Post,* which shows pictures of both Jackie and Hillary, announces this recognition. The headline "Final Farewell to Jackie" is directly above "Pals: Hillary for Prez." The *Post* article "Hillary for Prez? Friends Want First Lady in Office" proclaims: "Friends of First Lady Hillary Rodham Clinton are plotting for her to become the next commander-in-chief once President Clinton's two-term limit runs out, *New Yorker* magazine says" (Rauber 1994, 2). Hillary's plotting friends have replaced Cold War plots generated by Communist enemies. The anxiety that the Russians are coming, the Russians are coming, has been replaced by a new anxiety: A powerful woman is coming, a powerful woman is coming. This can also be seen in the popularity of bumper stickers demanding "Impeach Hillary." Bill is described by a comfortable title—"President"; Hillary is called something more threatening—"commander-in-chief." The *Post* headline and article reflect the fear that Jackie's current White House counterpart is a woman who can become Superman. Here is what the *New Yorker* has to say about her potential:

The notion of Hillary Clinton as a Presidential candidate is an interesting one. She is almost an icon for many women today. . . . Hillary is, of course, attempting the feat on a singularly elevated platform in full public view. . . . What seems plain, to me watching Hillary Clinton as First Lady, is that she is always learning, and that the makeover never stops. And, notwithstanding the President's denial, if her goal is, as friends have suggested, to fashion her own place in history, or to become President herself, then that means that for the first time since she decided to throw her lot in with Bill Clinton she is no longer merely an adjunct. There are vestiges of such a role, since at this moment her power is still dependent on and largely protected by his. But the bedrock premise of their partnership may be altered, for what is best for him politically is no longer necessarily best for her. (Bruck 1994, 94)

The United States is now poised to empower a brilliant woman, as long as she is white. Ironically, she might attain power at the expense of someone who is a dead ringer for Superman. President Clinton denies that Hillary Rodham Clinton would even think of upstaging Al Gore: "But I also think she didn't think about that sort of thing, in no small measure because she has an enormous regard for Al Gore, and for what he's done here, and how much of a difference he's made to our common endeavors" (Bruck 1994, 93–94).

Hence, U.S. popular culture now stages the question of who, appropriately, is Superman with regard to the power position of the Other in hegemony. For example, Richard Goldstein (1994), writing in the *Village Voice*, positions Oskar Schindler as Superman: "And then there is the question of the righteous Christian in the movie [*Schindler's List*], the Superman figure, who flies in and saves Lois Lane, the Jew" (27). As I have explained, like Oskar Schindler, Victoria Reggie is Superman; Ted Kennedy and Schindler Jews are Lois Lane. Victoria and Ted, Schindler and Schindler Jews, and Hillary and Bill are teams who benefit from each other's presence. Although Superman does not need Lois, these pairs need each other—and the Camelot myth needs Jackie. ("But what put JFK over the top on television—and arguably won him the election—was his wife" [Blair 1994, 25]). Hence, heterosexual teamwork between the empowered and the relatively disempowered, between the powerful white man and the talented Other, is currently a pervasive cultural topic. We have President Hillary Clinton. We have a Jewish Kennedy family member. Negative comments are not made about Schlossberg or Tempelsman. The point is that Lois/Jew is currently often positive, influential, and no longer distinct from Superman.

Lois is always a single career woman rescued by Superman when she bravely goes beyond her professional call of duty. And she is now a woman of the nineties. The new series is called *Lois and Clark: The New Adventures of Superman*; Lois is given top billing. Lois and Clark support my conception of the cyborgian heterosexual pair as Superman. Lois and Clark are the new adventures of Superman; Lois and Clark are Superman. Another current television show, *Dr. Quinn, Medicine Woman,* portrays a brilliant, traditionally feminine white woman who becomes Superman via her scientific expertise. Sully, Dr. Quinn's he-man lover/husband, does rescue her from the woods. But Sully, when he is sometimes ill, also becomes Lois rescued by Dr. Quinn/Superman. If Lois and Clark reflect Hillary and Bill as First Lady and President, Dr. Quinn reflects the Hillary the United States contemplates electing to the presidency, rewriting the tale of the talented woman acting as handmaid to a man.

TNG—and "All Good Things . . ." in particular—signals that neither Reagan nor Bush were ever Superman. *TNG* points out that the United States is tired of the lone he-man individualist Superman and wants women and men to work together as a team. The nation wants women and men to behave like Lois and Clark. Bush and Reagan have given way to Bill Clinton. Kirk has given way to Picard. And "All Good Things . . ." tells us that even Picard is not Superman. The last *TNG* episode seems to ask this question: What do talented white women who are forced to act as hand-maids to Superman want? The episode's answer: These women want a new tale, an alternative to the patriarchal story about who has the right stuff to be Superman. "All Good Things . . ." even retrieves Security Chief Lt. Tasha Yar—the white woman ejected from *TNG* because she was too pow-erful.

Patriarchy Is Not a Good Thing

"All Good Things . . ." convinces me that Troi represents Jackie Kennedy and that Crusher represents Hillary Clinton. Troi is a dark-haired charis-matic beauty, a sexy and elegant possessor of superhuman emotional insight, the respected bringer of decorum to the Enterprise. Like Jackie, Troi is "fascinating, not competitive; gracious, not ambitious; poised, not strategic . . . graceful, sympathetic, a marvelous listener. All of which Jacqueline Kennedy [and Troi] did better than anyone else ever" (Blair 1994, 1). In "All Good Things . . ." Troi/Jackie, the love object of two powerful men (Riker/Kennedy and Worf/Onassis), dies prematurely, ending her role in the future.

Crusher, in comparison, commands in that future. Hillary might become President Clinton; Beverly does become Captain Picard. When I saw Crusher answer to the name "Captain Picard," I reacted as if I were hit by a photon torpedo. "Dr." Crusher, the former Mrs. Picard who becomes Captain Picard, gives the aged Jean-Luc the command seat "for old times' sake." When Riker and Worf refuse to help Jean-Luc, Beverly provides the ship he needs. For the benefit of humanity, the white woman captain coop-erates with the formerly powerful white man. The good-old-boys network no longer works; only Beverly and Jean-Luc's teamwork is effective. "All Good Things . . ." shows that male supremacy and solidarity can come to an end—or, at least may lose some political efficacy. The final *TNG* episode is a postmodern, rewritten "A Christmas Carol"—a vision of Picard's past, present, and future that asserts that patriarchy is Scrooge.

Crewmembers' language enables this reading. A female officer calls Captain Beverly Picard "sir." Crusher informs Picard that she will state that even though he is her ex-husband and ex-captain, he is verbally out of line. Yar echoes Beverly's assertiveness. When these women question male authority, they reflect the current cultural penchant to act in kind. The aged Jean-Luc's word choice, too, underscores his lack of credibility: charged with diffusing an anomaly that threatens human existence, the former cap-tain, who might be suffering from a brain-impairing illness, refers to the threat as "my mommy." Beverly rightly treats the infantalized Jean-Luc like a child. Jean-Luc now appears in colorless loose-fitting pajamas as opposed to the sleek, pajama-like Starfleet uniform that connotes power; Shakespearean actor Patrick Stewart seems to be playing King Lear. The man whose competence and verbal utterances were never questioned is reduced to saying, "I'm not stupid." He is told to go back to bed. Jean-Luc represents patriarchy as passé and childish.

But even a future in which Beverly becomes captain and Jean-Luc becomes Lear on the heath fails to keep a woman in command. Captain Beverly Picard, who upbraids and sedates the former Captain Jean-Luc Picard, commands a ship that is about to explode. Beverly immediately goes from commanding to becoming Lois Lane rescued by Superman (in the form of the Enterprise commanded by Admiral Riker). Beverly was Superman for one brief shining moment. But her exploding ship burns brighter than her time as a captain.

"All Good Things . . ." conveys mixed messages; it simultaneously questions patriarchal power and yet is unable to depict a woman continuing to wield power. After Beverly's ship explodes, however, the critique of patriarchy does continue. Jean-Luc's nemesis Q judges him while seated on an ornate chair that has two outstretched protuberances appropriate to a gynecologist's office. Q, who proclaims that the human race is an inferior entity, examines and judges humanity in the manner that patriarchy examines and judges women. Q sounds like a woman who has just spent the day listening to the Hill/Thomas Senate hearings. "You don't get it, Jean-Luc," he says. He challenges Picard to expand his mind, to chart unknown possibilities of existence instead of mapping stars. Q critiques patriarchy by advocating alternatives to the white male-oriented science responsible for the Enterprise itself. Q would seem to have more respect for Troi, a pioneer of inner existence, than for Kirk, he-man star mapper. Q would have more respect for Jackie, a pioneer of aesthetic space, than for JFK, launcher of Sputnik, repeller of missiles. Picard responds to Q's verbal challenge by saying, "I'll get back to bed. I can use some sleep." This former male commander is extremely tired; Q articulates the need for new possibilities—albeit within specific prescribed boundaries of race and sexual orientation—to replace the male commander-as-exhausted story.

An image of a precursor to rebirth also communicates this need. In order to nullify the anomaly threatening the continuation of life in "All Good Things . . . ," Enterprises from the three time periods meet and create a "stellar warp shell" that can accomplish the "disengagement of a tachyon pulse." The three Enterprises, in the manner of sperm, gather to penetrate a round anomaly. Picard fathers a method in which starships/sperm nullify a pulse that makes it possible for the anomaly's threat to humanity to exist. The future Picard, then, is a good nurturing father rather than a dead father who perpetuates patriarchal imperatives. The anomaly—the "antitime" that is larger in the past—might represent patriarchy itself. The starships/sperm that nullify the anomaly and, hence, nurture humanity represent new uses of masculine bravado and the current decline of the he-man's prestige. The decline creates space for talented women effectively to wield power, although only white heterosexual women are suggested as likely participants.

Male power games, after all, have changed; some women can now play, sometimes. In the manner of George Bush's friendly relationship with Mikhail Gorbachev, two male antagonists of differing cultural heritages, Riker and Worf, cast aside their he-man stance to give each other a cooperative "hand." They sit down at a card table with Troi, Crusher, Data, and La Forge to play "five card stud, nothing wild, and the sky's the limit." He-man, disabled black man, white woman, sexualized half-Betazoid, cyborg, and Klingon play a new game in which the "stud" is tamed, in which those who are Other to "all-American" manhood vastly outnumber the he-man.

Like the ship/sperm surrounding the round anomaly, the crewmembers—sperm-like entities about to create a new something—surround the round card table. The new something is a sense of an ending, the sense that patriarchal power can be terminated. The present Captain Picard, the non-macho male authority figure, finally sits at the table to play with his subordinates. This card game depicts an end to patriarchal power games. The round card table is the Round Table. In the postmodern United States, Camelot and *Star Trek* never end. The same does not hold true for the patriarchal story that demands that talented women serve as handmaids to male Supermen. Dr. Crusher and Dr. Quinn, women who have been Superman, pave the way for *Voyager*'s Captain Janeway and President Hillary Clinton.

The Kennedys: The Next Generation

Star Trek never ends. And neither does the Kennedy family. Unfortunately, *Kennedy: The Next Generation* is not as progressive as *Star Trek: The Next Generation*. John, not Caroline, stood at the entrance of 1040 Fifth Avenue to describe Jackie's death. After his announcement, television news commentators called John, not Caroline, the next President Kennedy. A clone of the Cold War heroic he-man does not emanate from the site of the dead mother. Yet, the particular examples of popular culture that I have been discussing indicate that the next generation of U.S. citizens does not wish to resurrect the dead father, the Cold War presidential hero.

U.S. citizens are, instead, ready to follow Q's injunction to expand our minds, in terms of gender if not race. The next generation can accept a new possibility. Instead of repeating the past, instead of electing another President John Kennedy, we might opt for President Caroline Kennedy. Perhaps the concluding episode of *Voyager* will not involve its white female captain being rescued by a white he-man admiral. Perhaps this last episode will not involve an intuitive feminine crew member who dies because of the actions of he-men who vie for her attentions. There is hope for creating a new grand narrative, an alternative to the predominating social story about women acting as handmaids to white male Supermen. Jackie changed. Tempelsman, the last man in her life, was an invisible man and, in the discourse of her funeral, Aristotle Onassis was an invisible man too. Jackie "became less identified with the man she was with. [M]uch of America learned about him [Tempelsman] only when she died. . . . Aristotle Onassis, the wicked intruder in our national fairy tale, has been nearly erased. In network coverage of her funeral . . . commentators barely mentioned her second husband's name" (Blair 1994, 25). The he-man is passé; the Other is at the heart of the present and the future. As JFK symbolized, some Others can be president.

And it is the Other who respects the alternative to public prominence Jackie epitomized. When I went to Grand Central Station to sign the book the Municipal Art Society placed there to commemorate Jackie, I noticed that those standing on line were predominantly white women and black men and women. The white men in business suits who routinely rush through Grand Central Station were not clamoring to sign. Perhaps the white women, the black men and women, and the casually dressed young white men were standing in line to sign a declaration of independence from white men in business suits. My observation about the Grand Central Station line also holds true for the picture of the crowd standing outside 1040 Fifth Avenue that appeared on the front page of the *New York Times* on May 21, 1994. Again, white women, black men and women, informal young white men (and a lone Jewish American feminist science fiction critic) are in evidence. The men in business suits, Jackie's neighbors, were not paying their respects outside their front door. The Others gathered to mourn someone who despite her great wealth is, in relation to presidential power politics, one of their own.

As we are all aware, men in business suits also do not appear on the starship Enterprise. Anna Quindlan (1992), however, comments that the 1992 Democratic National Convention looks like the Enterprise: "Late at night, bleached by the street lights, Madison Square Garden looked like the Starship Enterprise, the satellite dishes pale moons at its perimeter" (17). The starship Enterprise crew represents an idealized multicultural U.S. society. May the U.S. government act like the Enterprise crew playing cards at the Round Table. In the near future, may the U.S. president look like Beverly Crusher, Geordi La Forge, or even Maurice Tempelsman. For the moment, we, at least, realize that the Russians are not Klingons—and Hillary's cookie-baking is an anomaly from the past.

As Captain Janeway and the next version of the Starship Enterprise/ Superman flies across television screens in America, we can rest assured that all good things do not necessarily come to an end. On May 23, 1994, two Rose Kennedys were living in America. One of them, Caroline's daughter, can become president of the United States—and, while ensconced in the White House, the younger Rose Kennedy can watch a version of the *Star Trek* myth that speaks to her generation's cultural reality. While sitting in a room Jackie decorated, President Rose Kennedy might watch a *Star Trek* episode about Admiral Tasha Yar.

Moving Beyond "All Good Things . . .": The End of Racism and Homophobia

Caroline's daughter Rose, like the women I have discussed in this chapter, is considered a "good thing" in regard to appropriate women's roles: the child is young, white, privileged, and pretty. And as long as no whisper of lesbianism is heard, she will also conform to "proper" sexual behavior. My point is that although Hillary no longer casts herself as a cookie baker, the women who can become Superman are cut from a cookie-cutter mold. Jackie, Hillary, Lois, Dr. Quinn, et al. are not Roseanne. Colin Powell, who could arguably be a viable future Presidential candidate, has no black female counterpart. Karen Burstein, the out lesbian who in 1994 lost the race for New York State attorney general, plays no part in the national political stage. Black women and homosexuals are still not considered "good things" to place on Presidential tickets.

Black women do become presidents of colleges, however. In his article about Smith College's decision to name Ruth Simmons as its new president, *New York Times* reporter William H. Honan (1994) states that "Karen Webster, chairwoman of Smith's board and a member of the search committee, said that race became an issue after Dr. Simmons became the leading candidate. 'The unanimous belief was that, given the opportunity to show who she is, what she can do, and the style with which she can accomplish things, she will allay any concerns,' Ms. Webster said" (A32). Webster's comments show that Simmons is suspect merely because she is a black woman. Even if she is, like Simmons, a Harvard graduate and a Princeton vice provost, a black woman must show what she can do—allay concerns, jump through additional hoops.

When Simmons speaks in favor of women's colleges, she herself does not mention race and sexuality:

> It is not true that all barriers to women have come down. . . . We all imagine that someday we will live in a society that does not impede women. But will that happen in my lifetime? I doubt it. And so, for now, the best way to deal with it is to separate women so that they

can achieve—especially in fields like physics, chemistry and economics. (quoted in Honan 1994, A32)

In terms of Simmons's remarks, my chapter implies that women positioned to break down barriers in the political field are women who, in
order to achieve, have been separated from other women (rather than from
men): privileged, white, thin, heterosexual women have been separated
from women who are not described by these adjectives. Hillary can become
president. The same cannot be said for Karen Burstein and Jocelyn Elders.
The potential woman president looks more like Lois Lane than Oprah
Winfrey.

Although politically prominent black women are unlikely to become
president, they have become "queen." When commenting on Elders and
her discussion of masturbation, Frank Rich (1994) explains that the
"cashiered Surgeon General was fated for a fall in Washington, where black
women who speak their minds are now routinely vilified with racial epi-
thets spun off from that popular coinage of the Reagan era, 'welfare
queen.' As Lani Guinier was the 'quota queen,' so, inevitably, Dr. Elders, a
proselytizer for preventative measures in an age of rampant teen-age pregnancy and AIDS, was the 'condom queen'" (15). Black women in politics
become queen for a day; their white counterparts, in order to become queen
(in the sense of political consort), spend their days trying to adhere to the
beauty queen role. Jackie, like all of *TNG*'s white female protagonists, was
a beauty queen. Hillary, in the attempt to become such a queen, routinely
changes her image. When confronting the issue of women and political
power, people who were shocked by the public articulation of the word
"masturbation" happily play with female self-representation. Simply
stated, the possibility of Elders becoming president—or of Queen Latifah
playing the captain on *Voyager*—is as remote as warp drives, holodecks,
and transporter rooms appearing on Air Force One.

To move beyond "all good things," to move beyond the requirement that
potential female wielders of political power must adhere to particular racial
and sexual rubrics, it is necessary to present the 1960s Camelot myth as a
very different retold tale. Or, Quota Queens and Condom Queens should
boldly go where no Quota and Condom Queens have gone before: to the
White House. Perhaps *Voyager* will present an episode in which the crew
beams down to an alternative United States whose president is a *zaftig* out-
spoken black lesbian.

According to Wayne Koestenbaum (1995a), author of the book *Jackie
under My Skin: Interpreting an Icon,* Jackie would approve of using the
transporter room to encounter the new Camelot myth I describe.
Koestenbaum's Jackie "will never condemn a dreamer's transports. Her
motto is motion" (41). Jackie moved as far beyond "all good things" as
possible for herself and her era. Jackie Onassis, no consort, embraced scan-

dal and extravagance. Jackie the icon merges with science fiction myth: "Someone once called Jackie 'spacy.' If she was spacy, bless her for it. Only a spacy icon has the space for every worshipper. Jackie's spacious duration is still expanding, still permitting imaginary voyage, still providing buoyancy and steam and wind for any flight or cruise the contemplator wants to take" (Koestenbaum 1995a, 42). Jackie has become an entity that is at once a holodeck and an ever-expanding black hole. She is an icon that provides space for an enterprise about seeking out new life, new U.S. civilization that is the end of the Camelot we knew.

References

Blair, Linda. 29 May 1994. "Jackie O, Who Lived a Mini-Series." *New York Times*: 1, 25.

Boyer, Peter J. 23 May 1994. "We're Not in Camelot Anymore." *New Yorker*: 39–45.

Bruck, Connie. 30 May 1994. "Hillary the Pol." *New Yorker*: 58–96.

Goldstein, Richard. 29 Mar. 1994. "*Schindler's List*: Myth, Movie and Memory." *Village Voice*: 24–31.

Honan, William H. 16 Dec. 1994. "Smith College Makes History in Naming Its Next President." *New York Times*: A32.

Hutcheon, Linda. 1988. *A Poetics of Postmodernism: History, Theory, Fiction.* New York: Routledge.

Koestenbaum, Wayne. 1 Jan. 1995a. "Her Bouffant Magnificence." *New York Times Magazine*: 40–41.

———. 1995b. "*Jackie under My Skin: Interpreting an Icon*." New York: Farrar, Straus, and Giroux.

Quindlan, Anna. 19 July 1992. "The Fourth Wall." *New York Times*: 17.

Rauber, Marilyn. 23 May 1994. "Hillary for Prez? Friends Want First Lady in Office." *New York Post*: 2.

Rich, Frank. 18 Dec. 1994. "The Last Taboo." *New York Times*: 15.

Next Generation (TNG). Close examination of such a trope and the complex of meanings it occasions slows the text, placing a drag on its freedom and power of movement, articulating a space in which to linger over moments from which the text seems to have a vested interest in hurrying away. Textual speed is a consistent feature of *TNG* in particular; the show disallows potentially revealing connections through the often breathless quality of its action-adventure narratives. An examination of the cyborg themes that permeate the text occasions a complex collection of reflections upon the nature of the cultural moment in which *Star Trek* currently functions but is ill-equipped to confront, or even to participate in productively (rather than reductively).

The problem is not that *Star Trek* does not pay serious attention to the complexities of its cultural moment. Indeed, this text may, with all its power, be able to suggest the places where cultural anxiety lodges most securely, and thus where cultural critics may best focus their attention. The insistent presence of cyborgs on *TNG* functions as a starting point for a reading of such anxiety, for the cyborg embodies particularly fraught collisions and contradictions. The very word "cyborg" brings together "cybernetic" and "organism"; similarly, the cyborg as a textual figure points to and stands in for other fusions. Such a strategy is not one of masking, but of replacing— prosthetizing, one might say. Indeed, *TNG* itself may be understood as a prosthetic replacement for a wide variety of cultural strategies.

The objection could be raised at this point that it is unfair to ask a television text to bear such weight. Such an objection is misguided, for it suggests that there are some texts that deserve serious consideration and some that do not; further, that texts that *could* stand such scrutiny are somehow less prosthetic— less artificial—than is a television show about adventure in space. *TNG* both stands in for and *does* the cultural work of which it speaks and as a result functions as a prosthetic cultural site; no text could function otherwise or could do more. The critical task at issue thus becomes the *recognition* of the cultural work done by the text; as I have suggested, this recognition cannot occur in the absence of that which the text seems to wish we would forget. To understand the work done, then, we must be able to remember, to make connections, to retain the images and sounds that hurry by.

Such a project first requires recognizing surfaces to which the text returns. In their most arresting and visible form, cyborgs appear on *TNG* as the aptly named Borg (a shortened, speeded-up version of "cyborg"), the master villains of the series's second, third, and fourth seasons. *TNG* characterizes the Borg's villainous actions as purely threatening, purely evil. In "Q Who?" the episode that introduces the Borg, the Enterprise's mysteriously knowledgeable bartender, Guinan, describes them: They are made up of organic and artificial life. . . . My people encountered them a century ago . . . they destroyed our cities, scattered my people throughout

12

Weaving the Cyborg Shrou(

Mourning and Deferral in *Star Trek: The Next Generation*

TAYLOR HARRISON

> To psychologists mourning is a great riddle, one of
> those phenomena which cannot themselves be
> explained but to which other obscurities can be
> traced back.
> —Freud, "On Transience"

> *mourn* (morn), v.i. 1. to feel or express sorrow or
> grief. 2. to grieve or lament for the dead. 3. to dis-
> play the conventional tokens of sorrow after a per-
> son's death.
> —*The American College Dictionary*

The continually expanding *Star Trek* universe constitutes a
powerful intertextual space. In the proliferation of texts, howe\
thing happens: in their very multiplicity, the texts cease to \
another except in the most monotonic inflections; they move
quickly, blending to form one big text that speaks with a sing
a commercial television text may hurry over potentially troul
comes as no surprise; casting the strategy of such texts in t
however, clarify the task of the academic observer who mu
them as part of the media landscape she or he seeks to descrit
The critical task must be the slowing of the process of te
whether by paying close attention to small segments of suc
phenomena as those that comprise *Star Trek* or by listening
ways in which various texts' voices blend.

I take both of these movements as my objectives in this
traces the figure of the cyborg as it makes its way throug!

the galaxy. . . . They swarmed through our system, and when they left, there was little or nothing left of my people." The Borg are pure totalitarian power incarnate; they inflict diaspora, destruction, death—yet their constitutive features and characteristics reveal, paradoxically, their *im*purity. The Borg are, for example, a collective consciousness, with the individual bodies constituting the collective, all telepathically linked. Thus they confuse the distinction between individual and collective social forms and indeed bring the nature of subjectivity itself into question.

The Borg's appearance further emphasizes its/their paradoxical fusions. They are "enhanced" humanoids who wear black leather suits and have mysterious tubes running in and out of their bodies as well as detachable limbs, gears, claws, lights. In fact, what is perhaps most striking about them is their lack of clean machine lines; their costumes seem at once to celebrate the distinctions between their organic and cybernetic components and to indicate the contamination of each by the other. The black leather, for instance, clothes bodies that have lost their color—their presumably organic skin is gray, drained of recognizable pigmentation; the "organic" is thus made artificial. Similarly, the leather in which they are clothed may or may not be "real" leather (which, of course, would be someone else's [organic] skin); its very envelopment of Borg bodies suggests its questionable material origins.

Intriguingly, it is precisely the material of the Enterprise in which the Borg initially show interest. They wish to consume the machine itself and begin their consumption by simply slicing a section from its hull, killing eighteen people in the process. The reactions of the captain and crew to the deaths are indicative and constitutive of the text's relation to the cyborgs: the crewmembers are to forget the deaths and do the job at hand—that is, deal with the Borg as continuing threat rather than with the results of their actions. Mourning is deferred. When Captain Jean-Luc Picard is informed of the deaths, his response is, "We'll deal with that later."

Mourning Becomes Deferral

> The age of the Photograph is also the age of revolu-
> tions, contestations, assassinations, explosions, in
> short, of everything which denies ripening.
> —Barthes, *Camera Lucida*

Deferral is a temporal displacement, an implied re-placing of an action or process at some point in the future. Deferral is, one might say, waiting— and waiting may seem to imply allowing for adequate time to confront a potentially disturbing process or activity. The question remains, however, what are the text and characters of *TNG* waiting for? What response to death does the text offer? Where does mourning, a primary cultural response to death, fit here, and what does its presence (or lack thereof) on *TNG* suggest? What, ultimately, *is* mourning?

For Freud, mourning is the progress of the detachment of libido from its investment in an object that no longer exists. This is a process of reverse-cathexis, with the persistent force of the original cathexis lending mourning its particular character. The work of mourning is neither easy nor quick; "in mourning," Freud (1916) says, "time is needed" (100). The unlacing of the libido from the beloved object is ultimately temporally unpredictable for, as he writes, "Mourning, as we know, however painful it may be, comes to a spontaneous end. When it has renounced everything that has been lost, then it has consumed itself, and our libido is free (in so far as we are still young and active) to replace the lost objects by fresh ones equally or still more precious" (101–102). Thus mourning in Freud's view requires a certain reversibility of time, for what is renunciation but an attempt to return to a moment *before*? Yet perhaps permutations of "before" and "after" are not the most important terms here, for they obscure the qualification Freud offers for the subject newly able to cathect (again): "in so far as we are still young and active." The endpoint of mourning, then, requires the potential not only for cathexis but also for movement: the freedom to move forward temporally—"young"—and the power to effect such movement—"active."

Is such movement possible? *TNG*'s insistence on speed suggests that it is, and further, its deferral of mourning allows the text, in a sense, to have it both ways. It holds out the possibility of the ideal, successful completion of mourning, and implies, furthermore, that there will eventually be time during which mourning may take place. The waiting is frictionless, for the voyages of the Enterprise continue despite the complete lack of narrative attention to the consequences of the death toll that increases with each adventure. The surviving members of the Enterprise crew are always "young and active."

I do not wish to argue that *TNG* is an inadequate cultural text simply because it does not have a history of depicting onscreen the individual, affective responses of its characters to death. The deferral of mourning that this text practices may be read as a symptom of its larger strategies, for mourning itself carries far greater implications than Freud's rather clinical account may suggest; recent commentators have argued that grief and mourning are constitutive features of both the postmodern and the poststructural worldviews. Kathleen Woodward (1990–1991), in particular, writes that she has "wished for a discourse about mourning more *expressive* than that provided by psychoanalysis, a discourse that would combine the affective dimension of the experience of mourning with theoretical descriptions of mourning as a process" (94).

Woodward examines several texts, both fictional and nonfictional, in her search for an expressive discourse about mourning; she settles most significantly on Barthes's (1981) *Camera Lucida* as an example of how Freud's approach may be modified and complicated in the writing-through, or the performance, of Barthes's "interminable grief" over his mother's death. She writes, "The book itself embodies a resistance to mourning, a resistance which entails a kind of willed refusal to relinquish pain" (1990-91, 97). This resistance to mourning differs significantly from the tendency of the *TNG* narratives to defer; deferral is, as I have suggested, a way of avoiding mourning while still holding out its possibility, whereas resistance entails a holding off of mourning's completion in order to prolong the pain—and work—and memory—of fractured cathexis. Barthes, says Woodward, "has come to a dead stop" (98). Resistance entails a refusal to move; "for the rest everything has remained motionless" (Barthes, quoted in Woodward 1990–1991, 98).

The point of Barthes's immobility in the face of mourning the loss of his mother is to retain her place in his memory. He refuses to retrace his love for her in order to allow her place to be taken by another object. Yet need such refusal always be willful? Derrida suggests not. For Freud, mourning consumes itself; in *Cinders*, Derrida (1991) qualifies this approach, taking as a premise the notion that such self-consumption can never be complete, that some trace, some ashes, must remain. As Ned Lukacher (1991) suggests, "Derrida is interested in what persists within the 'enigma' of mourning, of what still 'clings,' what still continues to burn and cannot be consumed" (12). For Derrida (1991), no subject could ever be "young and active" enough to freely begin again; the cinders of mourning drag on the freedom and power of movement that its completion ideally entails. No aggrieved subjectivity exists unencumbered—the place of Barthes's mother in his memory is painfully assured. Indeed, the loss of the object through death occasions pain because it signals the object's taking up of residence in the memory alone; elsewhere, Derrida (1986) argues, "We weep *precisely* over what happens to us when everything is entrusted to the sole memory that is 'in me' or 'in us'" (33).

In the postmodern world, however, memory no longer resides in "the sole memory that is 'in me' or 'in us.'" In "Cyborgs, Postmodern Phantasms of Body and Mind," Gabriele Schwab (1987) follows Jean Baudrillard in reading "the totalization of memory through archives and computer memories" (78) as an indication that memory is no longer an individual, internal element of subjectivity but has become a *systemic* feature of postmodernity. For Schwab, systemic memory is not shared memory; it leads not to collective practices of mourning but to unmournable death. On *TNG*, the Borg as collective consciousness—and thus as necessarily systemic rememberers—would seem at first glance to perpetuate this inability to mourn. Yet the role played by prosthetic memory in the mourning process is not as simple as Schwab (or

TNG) suggests. Collective, non-individuated memory might do the work of removing—or reminding us of the nonexistence of—Freud's endpoint of mourning, for computers do not forget . . . but equally, it would obviate cathexis in the first place, for computers privilege no one object over any other. But let us again consider that the distinction may lie not in the difference between remembering and forgetting, but in Freud's qualification, "in so far as we are still young and active." Is it that the older we get, the more memory accrues and the harder it becomes to retrace and erase our attachments? The more irreversible is time, then, the more impossible is Freud's successful completion of mourning. Woodward, Barthes, and Derrida may all be understood as articulating the necessity for a reconsideration of the role played by time, and its relation to individual subjectivity, in the mourning process. Stand still, or move slowly, if you move at all. Thus the cyborg, altered so as to enjoy a different relationship to time, to last longer, may serve as the privileged rememberer.

Cy/borgs and Prosthetics

> Now what does the *Critique of Pure Reason* tell us?
> That examples are the wheelchairs of judgment. . . .
> The wheelchairs, however, do not replace judgment.
> . . . The exemplary wheelchairs are thus prostheses
> which replace nothing. But like all examples, as
> Hegel will have pointed out, they play, there is play
> in them, they give room to play. . . .
> —Derrida, "Parergon"

Reading the replacement of individual memory by technologically supported memory is to read the prostheticization of memory, and a certain logic of the prosthetic in general adheres to discussions of the cyborg. In *TNG*, the introduction of the Borg in "Q Who?" is directly followed by the episode "Samaritan Snare," which babbles an incoherent response to the Borg-posed problematic of the prosthesis: Picard, we discover, has an artificial heart. He is, in fact, a cyborg, but his status is hidden within his apparently fully organic outer body. Whereas the Borg wear their fusion and confusion of boundaries, Picard aggressively internalizes his, dissembling to keep his crew from finding out about his prosthesis. The plot complication of the episode is that the heart is malfunctioning and must be replaced—thus the divide separating Picard from the Borg is made clear: the Borg are invincible and never malfunction, whereas Picard is hardly that; his implant is faulty. The fusion of organic and mechanical is thus not productive but destructive—in the same way that the Borg represent an externalized version of this fear, so Picard internalizes it.

Unarticulated, though no less important, is a certain fear of what Picard's prosthesis replaces. We learn of how Picard received the implant in the context of his recommendations to Acting Ensign Wesley Crusher for success in Starfleet: Picard warns the young man: "For ambitious Starfleet officers, there are certain costs involved. You must be cautious of long-term commitments." This is an interesting comment, for it seems outwardly to embrace a politics of temporary coalition—could this be an embrace of progressive politics, giving reason to celebrate the revelation of this patriarch as cyborg? Regrettably, the text does not sustain such a reading; rather than speaking of political commitments, Picard is here referring to affective ties. Such ties must be disavowed—or misremembered—in order for mourning, among other affective responses, to be deferred.

Picard reiterates this disavowal of affect by explaining to Wesley that a lack of self-discipline led to his heart replacement after he was knifed through the back during a barroom brawl. He implies that if he had been more disciplined from the outset—that is, *had he behaved more like a machine*—he would not have been individually prosthetized, would not have been made into a cyborg. Humans, then, have the capacity to remake themselves in the cyborg's image. Picard's artificial heart foregrounds this shift but replaces nothing, since the ability to accomplish the remaking is inherent; indeed, it is a prerequisite for serving in Starfleet, as evidenced not only by this conversation with Wesley but also by the imposition of discipline on the minds of those who would otherwise succumb to individual, affective responses to death. Picard and his compatriots *aspire* to an inability to subject themselves to being moved, to do the work of mourning. As Barthes aspires to the pain of remembrance and the maintenance of affect, so *TNG*, in diametrically opposed fashion, requires the ease of forgetfulness and the disavowal of affect.

Just as Picard's artificial heart replaces nothing but rather functions as an example, a figuration, of an inherent capacity for artificiality, so his abduction and further cybernetification by the Borg in a three-episode arc ("The Best of Both Worlds: Part I," "The Best of Both Worlds: Part II," and "Family") act as a prosthetic example of the death of the non-cyborg subject.

In "The Best of Both Worlds," Picard, the patriarchal leader and a primary ideological voice of both the Enterprise and *TNG*, is taken over by the Borg and made one of them. The Borg cause the death of Picard "as we know him"; this suggestion comes at first metaphorically: an away team goes to the Borg ship to rescue him, but they find only his uniform and communicator in a drawer in a room that resembles a morgue. In strangely cybernetic fashion, it is Picard's uniform that makes him what he is; that detachable piece of him is not merely a marker of his status but a second, prosthetic skin that enables him to perform his duties. The ability to command is not contained in a uniform—just as, perhaps, the ability to remember is not contained in a computer bank—yet a uniform is more than a symbol of such ability.[1]

The characterization of the Borg themselves has changed significantly (this is the end of the third season, eighteen months after "Q Who?"): where before they were only interested in the technology of the Enterprise, now, as they explain to Picard after his abduction, "Resistance is futile. We wish to improve ourselves. We will add your biological *and* technological distinctiveness to our own. Your culture will adapt to service ours." Thus the Borg once again evince a willingness, or possibly a compulsion, to mix the organic and the mechanical.

Picard responds indignantly: "Impossible! My culture is based on freedom and self-determination." Picard here disavows the way in which his culture, as represented on *TNG*, wishes to improve itself, and so adds the biological and technological distinctiveness of the cultures it encounters to its own ("to explore strange new worlds . . . to seek out new life and new civilizations"), forcing them ever-so-benevolently to service Starfleet and the Federation. In this exchange, the Borg have articulated quite clearly the prevailing ideology of the show while Picard disavows it—just as they display and revel in their mechanical enhancements while Picard hides his. Thus they dismiss his objection: "Freedom is irrelevant. Self-determination is irrelevant. You must comply. . . . It has been decided that a human voice will speak for us in all communications. You have been chosen to be that voice."

To read Picard simply as a mediator here, the figure whom we have come to know as cyborg and therefore an appropriate conduit for cybernetic messages, is attractive, though perhaps too easy. First, he makes no simple step into his new role; he must be further cyberneticized. The shedding of his Starfleet uniform constitutes the necessary first step of this process. When next we see him, he wears the Borg uniform. Where his Starfleet suit *figured* prosthetic skin, the black leather has become part of his body; the integrity of his skin has been breached. The fear here of the self's permeability speaks to the text's unwillingness to deal with the crisis of individual subjectivity that the technologization of memory—and its symbolization in/as the Borg collective—entails; if subjectivity is no longer dependent on individual history and memory, how can it be maintained? If memory becomes collective, how can one maintain one's subjective boundaries? Indeed, how can one recognize oneself as "one" at all? The Borg do not make such distinctions; the Borg collective, speaking through various spatially separate bodies, always refers to itself with the pronoun "we."

The *TNG* text resonates with viral logic here in its wrestling with questions of the self and its permeability, and it focuses a certain amount of anxiety currently circulating around such ways of thinking. With regard to the AIDS crisis, Lee Edelman (1989) finds, that "the human immunodeficiency virus . . . attacks the mechanism whereby the body is able . . . to distinguish between 'Self and Not-Self'" (313–314). Picard as the Borg have altered him is no longer Picard; he has become part of the Borg collective, for which there is no distinguishing between "Self and Not-Self"; the entire collective is "we." In AIDS discourses, this indistinguishability allows the damaging viruses to invade; the body, unable to understand that the invaders are not part of the Self, has no reason to dispel them. The Borg function as a large body, endeavoring to make everything they encounter part of the Self. The idea that there might be a Not-Self is not part of their collective imaginary—rather, they seem to operate on the principle that there are only Self and Not-Yet-Self. They are separated from Not-Self not by a spatial, but by a temporal, boundary.

Picard's response, when told of the Borg's plans for humanity, is to declare, "We would rather die." Note the structure of his answer: he speaks for humanity as a collective, using the pronoun that indicates a blending of selves. This pronoun brings out the connection between human and Borg, a connection that the expected assessment of Picard = good and Borg = bad would seem to disallow; humanity has already been infected by practices and beliefs that set it on the road to collective consciousness. "We would rather die." Rather die? Rather than what? Rather than become part of an extant collective in which individual subjectivities would be lost, absorbed, blended. Thus, according to Picard, we would rather risk relying on each other's individual memories of (and deferred mourning of) us than acknowledge that the technologization of memory has already begun, that our relation to memory, time, and history is already well on its way to resembling the Borg's.

"Death is irrelevant," respond the Borg to Picard's impassioned claim. Here they appear to participate in Schwab's (1987) unmournable death; if no one object is accorded pride of place over any other, then death certainly becomes irrelevant. But Picard, too, indicates that death is irrelevant by declaring his willingness to embrace it merely as a way of disavowing a set of relations in which he already participates.

Blurring the focus on Picard for a moment leads one to question the relevance of death in a different way. Death becomes the preeminent topic of conversation for those left on the Enterprise as they attempt to deal with Picard's abduction. He is declared a casualty of war, and Guinan, the character who offered the first information concerning the Borg, also gives the definitive statement of Picard's liminal status: "Picard is still here with us in this room. If he'd died it would have been easier . . . but he didn't. They took him from us, a piece at a time." Yes, it would have been much easier if he had died; then the text would know what to do: defer. Instead, it must fumble for a way of relating to a now-declared cyborg. The AIDS allegory is strong here: Picard is out as a cyborg now that he has been infected by the Borg, now that he wears his cyborg status on his body. Death would be easier. Douglas Crimp (1989), writing in "Mourning and Militancy" of the connection between AIDS-related deaths and activism, suggests "We must recognize that our memories and our resolve also entail the more painful feelings of survivor's guilt, often exacerbated by our secret wishes, during our lovers' and friends' protracted illnesses, that they would just die and let us get on with our lives" (10). Mourning cannot begin until the object is lost, but neither can its deferral. The Enterprise crew must forcibly detach themselves from Picard, disavowing any connection with this now-infected body that does not even know itself as a body, and they must forget—not retrace so as to mourn, but *forget*—whatever individual, affective ties they may have had to Picard as a recognizable object. "We would rather die." We do not have that option, Picard. Death is irrelevant. If you are forgotten, you have not died. You have ceased to exist.

Ultimately, these textual machinations remain in the realm of the figural, for Picard returns to the Enterprise and the Borg are defeated. But can Picard retreat into the cyborg closet? The visible evidence of his revelation can be and is removed, but damage has been done. *TNG* devotes the following episode, "Family," to repairing this damage. "Family" tells three stories, all of which trade in memory, cathexis, and death, building to a climactic moment in which Picard confesses to his brother[2] his own culpability: "They [the Borg] took everything I was. They used me to destroy, to kill. I couldn't stop them. I should have been able to stop them. I tried. I tried so hard, but I wasn't strong enough, I wasn't good enough." He has been, until this point in the narrative, unable to function—unable to make decisions, to act as the subject he was before. He must prove himself to be "young and active" once again, and he does this precisely by proving he can do the work of mourning. But he mourns not those he killed in his incarnation as Borg. He mourns his own subjectivity and self-image, retracing not his affective ties to other humans but his attachment to his own selfhood. His brother's response is to place a sort of artificial Derridean drag on Picard's renewed freedom of movement: "So . . . my brother is a human being after all. This is going to be with you a long time, Jean-Luc. A long time. You have to learn to live with it."

Picard mourns as a survivor rather than as a perpetrator.[3] Ideally, of course, he should mourn as both survivor and perpetrator, yet how might one negotiate that boundary? Surely it is the most impure of all fusions, the most fraught with the complications of memory. Donna Haraway (1985) writes, in the context of a discussion of the implications of cyborg technology, "We have all been injured, profoundly" (100); I would add that we have all caused injury as well. Eric L. Santner (1990) carries a similar observation a step farther as he discusses survivors' and perpetrators' attempts to come to terms with the impossible, yet essential, mourning of the Holocaust: "The task of integrating damage, loss, disorientation, decenteredness into a transformed structure of identity, whether it be that of an individual, a culture, or an individual as a member of a cultural group, is . . . one of the central tasks of what Freud called Trauerarbeit, or the 'work of mourning'" (xiii). Santner goes on to call for a new mode of being-in-the-world, a new relation between memory and history in which each individual subject retraces and thus faces the capacity for, and the actuality of, suffering and inflicting damage. For Santner, as for Barthes and Derrida, this necessary task is the work of mourning—a mourning that cries for lost potential but does not immediately result in political paralyzation. This task Santner rightly refers to as integration; that is, a taking-in for the purpose of making something new. And this, ultimately, is the point on which TNG's representation of the work of mourning breaks down: Picard does not integrate his perpetrator and survivor selves; he differentiates them by insisting on (remembering) one at the expense of the other. This is as far as TNG can go, it seems; it can point to the complexity of subjectivity and the power relations it occasions, but cannot—or will not—renegotiate them.

Death Is Irrelevant

> That is what mourning is, the history of its refusal,
> the narrative of your revolution, your rebellion, my
> angel, when it enters into history and at midnight
> you marry a prince. . . . And do not lie, you well
> know how solid a sentence is. By its very disappear-
> ance it resists so very many eclipses, it always has a
> chance of returning, it "incenses" itself to infinity. . . .
> The sentence is adorned with all of its dead.
> — Derrida, *Cinders*

Picard's brother suggests that he will "have to learn to live with" his survivor status. The way Picard lives with it becomes all too clear in "I, Borg," the episode in which the Borg return. "I, Borg" is a curious narrative in which the crew of the Enterprise capture an injured young Borg and proceed to make an individual of him. The episode is anticlimactic, for it shows just how far under control are the anxieties occasioned by the figure of the cyborg. The Borg are no longer a threat, for now the humans have discovered a way to infect them with humanity. Humanity itself has become the virus; Self will infect that which cannot distinguish Self from Other. All concerned exhibit extreme disavowal (there is much talk of how the young Borg just doesn't *look* like a collective consciousness), and Picard disavows more strenuously than anyone. In addressing Picard's abduction, Counselor Lt. Commander Deanna Troi speaks the language of rape: "Sometimes, even when the victim has dealt with his assault, there are residual effects of the event that linger. You were treated violently by the Borg, kidnapped, assaulted, mutilated. . . ." Picard cuts her off with "Counselor. I very much appreciate your concern, but I assure you, it is quite misplaced." Troi's articulation allows Picard to disavow a certain *feminization* rather than cyberneticization. Further, what he must deal with—has dealt with—is an assault, a mutilation of self, *not* that self's perpetration of atrocities. These are the "effects" that will linger. And yet

Troi is not simply wrong; her concern is *misplaced*. In this very small gap, Picard continues to live with it.

To forget damage, to forget pain, to forget loss—to forget cathexis, the root of all these—such is the work of the text. Yet to mourn the loss of what the text cannot fail to silence is to reconnect with its cinders, its trace. By insisting on the importance of this television text, I insist on what Woodward (1992–1993) calls "the efficacy of affect—without which discursive procedures (critical writing on literature, for example) in the face of a loss real to us are meaningless, doomed to repeat themselves endlessly, to rehearse the same scene of representation over and over to no effect" (110). My own affective response to the text(s) of *TNG* adorns this chapter, yet drives it too. I offer that response not as a way of filling in the text's gaps, of investing it with things that are not there, but in order to provide a prosthetic replacement for something that was there all along but that the show has a vested interest in not articulating—the drag on its freedom and power of movement that one may glimpse by tracing its treatment of the figure of the cyborg.'

Notes

This chapter was first presented at the 1993 Console-ing Passions: Television, Video, and Feminism Conference in Los Angeles, California. It has survived multiple revisions, and I thank my coeditors for their insightful (and sometimes painful) suggestions for change. The chapter exists here in debt to Gates McFadden, Abby Hayhurst, Doug Johnson, and Marnie Schroer.

1. Markers of rank and status are curiously implicated and maintained in cybernetics. In the virtual world, their equivalent might be the password or code key, another sort of marker that allows access and command. Picard's four pips on his collar indicating the rank of captain, and his communicator, which connects him to every part of his ship and every member of his crew, make him, in a sense, the nexus of a network of power and information. Interestingly, a subplot of "The Best of Both Worlds" features First Officer Commander William Riker's inability to decide whether to accept a command of his own on another ship—his competence is characterized in terms of his willingness to accept and wear the insignia of command.

2. Until this episode, Picard's brother did not exist; he was not a presence in the series, either embodied or in anyone's memory—that is, his existence was not an issue. This is the usual role of objects for/with whom any character might have affective ties; they are brought in when they are narratively useful, then forgotten—until, of course, they become narratively useful again. Picard's family, in fact, reappears in the feature film *Star Trek: Generations* (1994), only to be immediately disposed of as a way of setting certain aspects of the film's plot into motion.

I wish to argue not for *TNG*'s uniqueness in this narratively convenient use of objects but for this strategy's particular visibility on the show—and its particular significance in the context of *this* narrative.

3. In the opening episode of *TNG*'s spin-off series, *Star Trek: Deep Space Nine (DS9)*, Picard is portrayed solely as a perpetrator. *DS9*'s commander, Benjamin Sisko, has lost his wife in an attack directed by Picard in his incarnation as Borg and spends the episode attempting to deal with both that loss and the confrontation with Picard that his transfer to *DS9* entails. In a fashion previously unheard of for *Star Trek*, Sisko faces the consequences of his wife's death because of the way in which the prolongation of his mourning holds him in one place, unable to move forward or backward in time. Interestingly, Sisko's rehearsal of trauma takes place at the behest of an alien consciousness, one wishing to understand the functioning of linear time. Sisko attempts to explain the concept by retracing the significant moments in his emotional attachment to his wife; in this way, he is able to complete the work of mourning while maintaining through explanation the "natural" human relationship to time and temporality. Although this depiction did not—does not—satisfy me completely, it does indicate a certain amount of representational potential. That *DS9* has not realized this potential to date does seem to suggest that episodic television as a venue cannot push these concepts much beyond the limits I've indicated in this chapter.

References

Barthes, Roland. 1981. *Camera Lucida: Reflections on Photography*. Trans. Richard Howard. New York: Hill and Wang.

Crimp, Douglas. 1989. "Mourning and Militancy." *October* 51: 3–18.

Derrida, Jacques. 1986. "Mnemosyne." *Memoires for Paul de Man*. Trans. Cecile Lindsay. New York: Columbia U P. 3–43.

———. 1987. "Parergon." *The Truth in Painting*. Trans. Geoff Bennington and Ian McLeod. Chicago: U of Chicago P.

———. 1991. *Cinders*. Trans. and ed. Ned Lukacher. Lincoln: U of Nebraska P.

Edelman, Lee. 1989. "The Plague of Discourse: Politics, Literary Theory, and AIDS." *South Atlantic Quarterly* 88.1: 301–317.

Freud, Sigmund. 1916. "On Transience." *The Standard Edition of the Complete Psychological Works of Sigmund Freud*. Vol. 14. Trans. and ed. James Strachey. 24 vols. London: Hogarth, 1953–1974. 303–307.

Haraway, Donna. 1985. "A Manifesto for Cyborgs: Science, Technology and Socialist Feminism in the 1980s." *Socialist Review* 80: 65–107.

Lukacher, Ned. 1991. "Mourning Becomes Telepathy." In *Cinders*. Jacques Derrida. Lincoln: U of Nebraska P. 3–18.

Santner, Eric L. 1990. *Stranded Objects: Mourning, Memory, and Film in Postwar Germany*. Ithaca: Cornell U P.

Schwab, Gabriele. 1987. "Cyborgs, Postmodern Phantasms of Body and Mind." *Discourse* 9: 64–84.

Woodward, Kathleen. 1990–1991. "Freud and Barthes: Theorizing Mourning, Sustaining Grief." *Discourse* 13.1: 93–110.

———. 1992–1993. "Grief-Work in Contemporary American Cultural Criticism." *Discourse* 15.2: 94–112.

Appendix A

Interview with Henry Jenkins

Taylor Harrison: *Textual Poachers* (1992) treats *Star Trek* as only one part of a much larger media fandom environment. Do you read *Star Trek* as a baseline for other kinds of media fandoms?

Henry Jenkins: That is a complicated question. On the one hand, the media fandom that I talk about in *Textual Poachers* grew out of *Star Trek* fandom, to a large degree. Historically, it was one of the first places where women got actively involved with the science fiction fan community and began to take on the task of publishing zines,[1] which had been predominantly male activities since the 1920s. *Star Trek* fandom, and its heavy female participation, set the model for subsequent developments in media fandoms. *Star Trek,* conventions set the model for subsequent fan cons. *Star Trek* zines set the model for subsequent fanzines. And the *Star Trek* letter-writing campaign to keep the series on the air set the model for subsequent fan activism. Many fans came into fandom via *Star Trek,* but not all fans do, not anymore. Each new fannish show has produced new waves of fans. *Beauty and the Beast* has fans who are not necessarily connected to *Star Trek,* or someone might come in as a fan of *The Professionals* or *X-Files* without coming through *Star Trek.* So, "media fandom" came out of *Star Trek* in a very real sense. But, on the other hand, *Star Trek* is not the only model for media fandoms. Historically, one could look at female fans of movie stars as establishing a very different kind of relationship to the media, or soap opera fandom has been another important space for women, or Chad Dell is doing interesting work on women wrestling fans in the 1950s. One of the ambiguities I struggled with in writing *Textual Poachers* is that I knew people would take it as a book on fans as a broadly constituted social category, and I wanted it to be a book about a *particular* fan community, with an understanding that, of course, its concepts could be broadened and used to talk about other kinds of fandom, but they would have to be tested against fieldwork. The concepts have to be examined in relation to the specifics of individual fan communities, not taken as a theory that can be generalized to account for all fan behavior.

Harrison: So *Textual Poachers* would not account for fan behavior but would provide a vocabulary for talking about how fans, not only in this context but in various contexts, might function or think of their own activities?

Jenkins: Part of what troubles me is that *Textual Poachers* is still read as a book about *Star Trek* fandom without recognizing that it is about a group of women who have constituted their own community by nomadically pulling together a range of texts that are important to them. One crucial text is *Star Trek*, but they are not a *Star Trek* fan community. They are not "Trekkies" or "Trekkers." They are a part of media fandom. On the other hand, *Star Trek* fandom is much larger than this one community. A recent Harris Poll tells us that something like 53 percent of the U.S. public defines themselves as *Star Trek* "fans." Now, that statistic has to include a tremendous range of different relations to the television program; not all of these "fans" are tied to the group in *Textual Poachers*. Some people read *Poachers* as saying that most *Star Trek* fans are women. I wouldn't say that at all. Most of the *Star Trek* fans who write zines and are part of the subculture I described in the book are women. But there are many other ways of relating to *Star Trek* that that book does not begin to talk about.

Harrison: Part of the problem may be using the word "fan" as a kind of catch-all term for all kinds of activities by all kinds of people who function in different social contexts and have different relations to texts.

Jenkins: Absolutely. You know, it is used broadly and I think the Harris Poll must include people who watch the show occasionally, who, for example, say they once bought a *Star Trek* novel. Of course, the *Star Trek* novels are almost all on the *New York Times* bestseller list the week or two after they come out. So that's a large public.

Harrison: Yeah, somebody is buying these things, and some of the people buying these things must not be fans in the sense of the kind of ethnographic look you want to take.

Jenkins: Sure. The work that I have been doing with John Tulloch (Tulloch and Jenkins 1995) talks about at least three different *Star Trek* fan communities, and I could have talked about many more. A male MIT student logged onto the net talking about the technology and nit-picking about the various scientific flaws in the series has a totally different relationship to the text than the women who are writing fanzines or the Gaylaxians who are a gay-lesbian-bisexual organization lobbying for the inclusion of a queer character on the show. Their politics are different, their interpretive strategies are different and their modes of engagement with the text are different. Going beyond that book, we might include the Klingon organizations, which have gotten some visibility lately. That is a very different point of entry for understanding *Star Trek*. Even if we take committed fans as a model, then that is still describing a range of reading practices and different values, and there are constant sources of tension between those different communities. Some of the computer nets refer to the women who write slash as FUBS ("fat ugly bitches").[2] That term suggests real antagonism within *Star Trek* fan culture. The same group often leveled homophobic blasts at the notion of including a queer character, so the Gaylaxians also had fights with the male computer net culture. On the other hand, when I did interviews for that book, there were people whom I could have interviewed who would have belonged to all three groups. There were women at MIT who were lesbians and belonged to the Gaylaxians, who read the series in technological terms, and who wrote and read slash stories, so we cannot see them as totally separate groups either. *Star Trek* fandom is a fairly complex cultural space.

Harrison: One of the questions that would then arise is, "Can these different kinds of communities who have these different relationships continue to exist side by side, or are the aims of one going to eliminate the need for the other or the possibility of another existing and functioning in the same space or around the same text?" And, as you say, if there are people who can negotiate their positions in multiple groups, the situation becomes even more complicated.

Jenkins: It does. There are neither simply opposed readings nor are there interconnected readings, but there are a range of possible identities or subject positions vis-à-vis *Star Trek*. To use academic language, people can float between and choose to move within those groups. And they may maintain separate and discrete identities in relation to these multiple interpretive communities. I discovered several women whom I met one place early on in my research for *Poachers* whom I then encountered again when I did the Gaylaxian chapter. When I interviewed them for *Poachers,* I had no idea whether they were queer because in that space, they were not out and they were not functioning as queer readers and they were involved fully in a romantic reading of the text that would seem to depend on heterosexual assumptions. And then, as Gaylaxians, they were reading, within a very queer political space, in terms of queer politics and fantasies. All of us in our heads are many different audiences, and fans can, in fact, belong to many different social groups.

Harrison: This drives home the point that the idea of shifting subject positions, combined with each individual wanting to see him or herself as a coherent subject, is not simply *theoretically* important. . . .

Jenkins: These shifting subject positions are lived in people's experiences—fandom really illustrates this in a phenomenal way both by having people flip between texts within a single fandom and flip between fandoms in regard to the same text. I see both kinds of behavior on a fairly routine basis. For these fans, that theoretical problem is lived out.

Harrison: I suggested that *Star Trek* is an essential textual location from which to discover or locate fandom. And in a sense it seems to be, in that you can fix certain things in this kind of study. You can say, "Okay, we're going to look at the different subject positions that line up around *Star Trek*," or "Here's a type of fan, let's look at the different texts around which this type of fan tends to circulate."

Jenkins: And between the two books that I have written on science fiction audiences, one looks at a fan community that pulls in many texts and the other takes the position that *Star Trek* is an important text which generates many communities. I am trying, in my own work, to go back and forth between these two notions of the nomadic. Unfortunately, *Textual Poachers,* as I said, continually gets read as a book about *Star Trek* fans, and one of the hesitancies I had about writing the new book was, "Am I going to reinforce that?" After all, I began by writing "*Star Trek* Rerun, Reread, Rewritten" (1988), which was about *Star Trek* specifically, and now I'm back talking about *Trek* again. To read *Poachers* that way totally forecloses this understanding of nomadic reading I'm talking about. When I do radio interviews, for example, which I do fairly often, I am told before I go on the air, "We only want you to talk about *Star Trek* because *Star Trek* is something our audiences will recognize and know." And then, I get on the program and they say, "Well, why is it that it is only a show like *Star Trek* that has generated this kind of fan response?" And then what do I say without breaking the agreement? There are thirty, forty, fifty shows I know of that generate this kind of fannish engagement in one way or another. It is not just *Star Trek*. To define it as just *Star Trek* is to put all the power back into the text again and not in the audience to construct their own relationships. In the same way, within the academy, it is easier to talk about *Star Trek* fans than to talk about any other group. The point of reference is so much easier to explain. If I wanted to give a talk about *Blake's 7* fandom, which at its peak was tremendously active, I would have to spend most of my time giving background on the show, rather than talking about the reading practices. I feel constrained by the fact that fans read a broader range of programs than academics do. *Star Trek* is a central text—from the point of view of the academy—but not necessarily from the point of view of any one fan. Academics seem to be compelled to see *Star Trek* as this powerful text that has created some "unique" audience phenomenon, rather than understanding it as one text that has had a lot of resonance with fans and that fans, for a variety of reasons, have chosen to engage with it—as one text among many.

Harrison: That actually was my follow-up portion of this question—whether you have to cater to the mainstream popularity of these originating texts—and it seems to me very clear that in fact, you do. You can get something published on *Star Trek* or *Twin Peaks* rather than on *Blake's 7*.

Jenkins: It is absolutely the case and I think that is a real problem. On the other hand, *Star Trek* is such a rich example! I do believe that, early on, Gene Roddenberry had a conception of a polysemic audience and that shaped his conception of *Star Trek*. His main selling point to the networks was that science fiction was a kind of "grab bag genre" that attracted many different kinds of audiences.

Harrison: But what Roddenberry was never willing to do was let the fans, or fan desire, invade the text.

Jenkins: Well, it invades the text in at least two ways, or three ways actually, but none of them are very significant, it seems to me. It invades the text of *Star Trek* in terms of winking jokes like "Please, Captain, not in front of the Klingons" at the end of *Star Trek III: The Search for Spock* (1984), a joke many people read as a nod to slash. Or the passage in the novelization of *Star Trek: The Motion Picture* (1979) where they talk about rumors that Kirk and Spock might be lovers. Those sorts of throwaway gestures are usually there precisely to dismiss the fans' desires. Secondly, Roddenberry literally incorporated fans as extras in *Star Trek: The Motion Picture*. There's one boardroom scene where a number of individual longtime fans are incorporated into the text and get to see themselves on the screen. Again, that does not strike me as a significant response to the fan community, except in a kind of individual payback level. It did not give fans any power. It just let them dress up in costumes and parade in front of the camera and say to their friends, "Look, that's me in *Star Trek*." That's not what fans want, by and large.

Harrison: Yes, which is why the word "desire" isn't used to talk about that.

Jenkins: The desires that fans expressed were often politically difficult ones for Roddenberry, who pretended to be a great liberal but who in fact was a relatively conservative force in the production of the show. He never was really willing to give fans space in the text, to play out the sorts of stories or the sort of politics that fan communities were committed to.

Harrison: Let's move on. Your approach is frankly ethnographic. You are in some sense the classic participant-observer in terms of the way you set yourself up as both fan and academic.

Jenkins: [Lying back on the couch.] I'll do this couch thing.

Harrison: That's very nice. Yes, confess to me here. You'll feel much better when this is over. How do you reconcile this traditional way of doing business with what you have said is one of the purposes of your work, that is, to reorient the academic project of subcultural theorization and description?

Jenkins: I think I disagree with the premise of your question. I think if you want to talk about traditional participant-observer approaches, Camille Bacon-Smith's (1992) book *Enterprising Women* follows that model much more closely than mine does, because the traditional participant-observer in ethnography, as it has been practiced over a hundred years or more, is someone who comes in from the outside and seeks to be integrated into the community, and who sees, but neither touches nor is touched by, the community. They are a participant but in a relatively trivial way. As Bacon-Smith frames her book, she describes her own migration as "The Ethnographer" into the tribal culture of the exotic where she gradually gets integrated, step-by-step, into the heart of the community. She learns the secret rituals, she learns to get along with her mentors and the village leaders, and finally, she finds the "heart of darkness" at the center of fandom—which for Bacon-Smith is "hurt/comfort"—but, at the same time, as she participates within and writes about fandom, she preserves this status of the outside observer, the objective and impersonal Ethnographer. My work comes out of a newer tradition of ethnography that has emerged from feminist and queer ethnographic practice. In fact, identity politics has strongly influenced the process of ethnography, where the person who is writing writes from a position of proximity or closeness, writes from a position of their own lived subjectivity. I wrote *Textual Poachers* only after being part of a fan community for fifteen years. There is no suggestion there that I'm coming into fandom from the outside and I am observing this so I can bring it to the outside, nor do I preserve a clear separation between my authority as an ethnographer and the authority of the community I am writing about.

The practice of writing the book involved sending out copies of the manuscript to large numbers of fans, getting their feedback (and they wrote extensive feedback), and then rewriting in accordance with it, sitting in the fans' living rooms and listening to them critique my work and trying to be responsive to it. Now, I think we can't delude ourselves. Of course I wrote it. Of course my name is on it. Of course my career is being shaped by the reputation it builds. And of course I am staking out a position here, but it is a position that is engaged with a community and involved them in rewriting the construction of their own image. I think that differs from traditional participant/observation in terms of the ways that we break down the authority structure of ethnography and the desire to neither touch nor be touched by the experience of the field. And it is tied to the notion of situated knowledge, the idea that we can only know from a social space. For me, in writing this book, my knowledge comes from being a fan, which to me is a real, lived identity. There is no insurmountable break between the academic and the fan here. I was a fan, I am still a fan. Being an academic is one way of being a fan for me.

Harrison: This is actually two points. One is the way in which work like this starts to blur the distinction between academic and fan and creates another problem in that even if you say, "I'm a fan and an academic," people who read your work can preserve the distinction for themselves. They can say, "Okay, he can say all that, but *I'm* still an academic and *I* don't have to acknowledge my own investment in the texts I work with." The second thing is that while I totally agree that you write from a position of someone who is, in fact, a fan, who has lived that position, on the other hand, you haven't. You cannot have lived the same position as many of your subjects—especially, say, the female *Beauty and the Beast* group. Do you feel like that makes you more of an ethnographer in those sorts of circumstances?

Jenkins: Probably—that is the case. Boy, those are two complicated questions. Let me take the first one and you may have to remind me of the second if I get carried away here. Rhetorically, what I tried to do when writing the book was to gradually shift the center of gravity from addressing academics to addressing fans. The most theoretically dense chapters are at the beginning of the work, and as the academic becomes more accommodated to the fans' points of reference, the book's rhetoric becomes more governed by fan references and fan discourse and fan examples. So, the last chapter cites many more shows than the earlier chapters. The fan video chapter moves much more heavily into fan knowledge and further away from the space of academic competence, so that my goal was for the academic readers to become more integrated into the fan community as they moved through the book. Now, what happens when people read it—and my primary basis of evidence is the reviews of the book—is that they pull back from that proximity as they read the book. Many of them are not seeing the connection to their own lives and, in fact, what happens is that all of those stereotypes about fans that I talk about early on in the book get mapped onto me as the writer of the book. I am variously described as nerdy, as preoccupied with trivia, as taking it all too seriously, as forgetting that it is only a television show, as being humorless in relation to details, as being overly exacting in my focus on particulars. All of these stereotypes come even in positive reviews. I have yet to read a review of the book that did not feel compelled to signal to the reader, "Jenkins is a fan and I am not. The author's objectivity is in question because he is a fan, but I am not, since I am writing this review and I have to mark that space away from it." I think that the academic's relationship to fandom is so vexed still that people are not willing to take on that space, and I am not sure what one could do to challenge it more fully, because the history of academia in media studies has been the desire to squash or deny our own relationship to the fan. We had to justify ourselves in the academy by saying, "Look! We are not just fans or movie buffs. We are serious academics." And we did just that and it seems to me that the price for admission to the academy was twofold. First, we had to prove that popular works were authored. If we were going to be taken seriously alongside music or literature or drama, we had to create the author. And the ability to have *auteur* theory on the one hand and art cinema on the other allowed us admission and allowed us to talk about media from an intellectual position that was totally removed from the affective space of the fan. Fan/buff discourse had governed writing about film up until that point and shaped the best writing, I think, with people like Parker Tyler, Robert Warshow, and Gilbert Seldes. We had to move away from all of that and adopt a dryer, more impersonal, more theoretical language for writing about popular culture, and that was the second price we paid for admission into the academy.

Harrison: That totally misses what it is that's important about studying film or television: these texts *move* people and that seems to me one of the only reasons to try to understand them. It completely escapes me what, at least in this moment, is the importance of retreating back to a structuralist position or an auteurist position or anything like that. What good will that do, other than maintaining academic credibility, which is obviously always going to be a concern? But I don't know if there is space for that or not.

Jenkins: I would say that the defining characteristic of popular culture is its emotional intensity, its ability to make us proximate to it, to be close to it, to be involved with it. If we pull back to a traditional academic distance, we cannot understand it at all. We cannot acknowledge the degree that we are linked to the mechanisms of pleasure and desire which constitute the text. I was told when I started as a graduate student that I should only write about texts that I hated because it is only when you hate a text that you get sufficient distance from it to be able to talk about its ideological structures "accurately" and "objectively." That sick linkage of hate and objectivity, I bet, governs a lot of writing in our field, still.

Harrison: That's amazing. That's it! Isn't hate one of the most invested relationships you can possibly have with a text? You would think that indifference would be the most "objective" relationship you could have with a text.

Jenkins: What does it mean that many people in our field spend their lives writing about things they hate rather than about things they love, other than this need for us to reaffirm continually the validity of our discipline? Stating that you write as a fan throws all of that into crisis. The other side of the policed divide is that the need for admission into the academy meant high theory. It meant we had to define ourselves, as structuralism was coming in, as just as theoretically rigorous as any other field, announcing our rigor by the ability to use academic jargon and complex theoretical formulations. That also pulled us away from being fans because it meant our work on popular culture could not be read by popular audiences. It is not part of popular debates about media, and the price tag for that today is that Neil Postman can be talked about in *TV Guide* and we cannot. How many people at this conference or in the Society for Cinema Studies can get access to the mass-circulated publications? We are not choosing to engage with that audience. We are losing the larger battle in our political struggles over popular culture by refusing to talk to the popular, by refusing to be accessible, and what is important about the move towards the fan-academic has been the willingness to write to communities that are not within the academy, that are in the general public that will read such books. *Textual Poachers* has been read by, and been important to, large numbers of people who are not tied to the academy and who, you know, are interested in and committed to popular culture. Fans were circulating fliers for the book through the underground fan networks so that they got large numbers of mail orders for this book from places where all they have access to is the local B. Dalton's. I've gotten phone calls from high school students who have read this book and really wanted to talk about what it meant to them and I'm very moved by that because I've succeeded, on one level, in breaking down some of those barriers. Now, I don't mean to be self-congratulatory about it. The title itself, *Textual Poachers,* puts some people at a distance; my dependence on de Certeau (1984) is problematic for large numbers of popular readers who do not understand these obtuse formulations. I didn't totally succeed, and I think the struggle for authenticity and authorization in the academy shaped *Textual Poachers* as much as any other book, but it has pointed out to me the need for us to rethink the relationship between the fan world and the academic community. It is a question central to our attempts to change the politics of the popular and to understand what popular culture is.

Harrison: Are you still invested in the poaching metaphor as a way of describing and/or valorizing fan activity? This has a lot to do with the audiences you can speak to or the audiences that you *want* to speak to and how you go about explaining these kinds of relationships.

Jenkins: The poaching metaphor is tremendously convenient because it had resonance within the academy, particularly within a leftist academy that wants to identify things as guerrilla semiotics, underground, subversive, resistant, and so forth, and because once it was fully understood, it had resonance in the fan community, which also wanted to see itself in those terms and could link the metaphor "poaching" to Robin Hood. Almost all of these women who were part of media fandom read Robin Hood stories or were interested in Robin Hood growing up. It's one of the texts they have in common, so that that sense of stealing from the rich and giving to the poor, of being a poacher on the king's domain, had tremendous power for them. It was an image they were comfortable with, by and large. Now, some fans were critical of it and said, "That poaching metaphor implies we hurt the text, that we take from the owners something that belongs to them." They said, "The text already belongs to us; we are not taking anything other than our own fantasies, so therefore we are not stealing anything at all. We're simply constructing our own space and our own culture and our own life that happens to exist alongside a commercial text and does not do it damage." They're a little uncomfortable with the aggressive conflictual nature of the metaphor since they felt it gave too much power to the media producers; and there is, of course, a segment of fandom that values its closeness with the producers and their interests. The other criticism I've heard, and I think it's perhaps a valid one, is that poaching is a masculinized metaphor. That is, it's a military metaphor—and that's a problematic issue I have been spending a lot of time trying to rethink. It is a problem if we see struggle and specifically *aggressive* struggle as a masculine domain, but these women, in fact, in their Robin Hood fantasies, had already constructed that guerrilla metaphor as potentially open for women. Aggression or taking over territory or asserting power is feminine from their point of view, and so they did not seem particularly uncomfortable with that masculinized notion of it. They see themselves as powerful women and they are comfortable talking about power. By and large, only academic feminists posed that challenge to me, and I want to think through the implications of their suggestion that women cannot be tacticians, women cannot be guerrillas. Certainly if we look in the real world, hell, they have always been. You know, the history of poaching has always included women going back to the early peasant uprisings that E. P. Thompson (1979) talks about, which is what I always thought about when thinking about the poaching metaphor.

Harrison: That just reemphasizes the point that you're speaking to very different audiences with the book. The interpreting audiences for the book itself are just not thinking in the same ways.

Jenkins: But the power of poaching as a metaphor was that it spoke, said what needed to be said, to both groups in a term that could be shared with both groups but meant something different in the two spaces. Now, where the book has problems is with words like "heteroglossia," which I used to talk about fan music videos. That's a word that the fan community can't get a purchase on, that they haven't known what to do with, and just shrug off as "academic bullshit." But "poaching" as a term has been important to them and has been picked up by computer groups, for instance, to talk about their relation to the computer corporations. It is getting a wider space as the book has become better known. Poaching seems to be a word that many groups can share, meaning slightly different things, and so I probably would not repudiate the term. If I did it today, I might not have a title that had "textual" in it, because the textual part is also a kind of academic marker that makes fans and other general public people say, "Well, that's not for us." It keeps getting garbled into "textile" or "textural." What negotiates them into the book is the cover art, right? Jean Kluge's beautiful cover which everyone, both academics and fans, loves, attracts them to the book. She's very user friendly from the fans' point of view. They recognize Kluge as an important fan artist and they are drawn to the book by that and they are willing to say, "All right, it may be called *Textual Poachers* but it is also clearly tied to our fan community and our fan aesthetics." So, it gives mixed signals and, to some degree, as I wrote it, I was very painfully aware of the fact that I am writing as a fan to academics and as an academic to fans, that I am trying to create some dialogue across those spaces; and that is structurally built into the book, even into the design of the book, in ways that may not be fully visible to someone who is simply on the academic side of that divide.

Harrison: That's very interesting because it makes "book" itself a different kind of commodity than it normally is in academic circles. A lot of people don't buy books simply because they look cool. Well, they do buy books because they look cool, but they don't say that they're doing it because of that.

Jenkins: Yes, that's right. That cover art has now been turned into a T-shirt design in fandom. The fans are buying the cover art, not *Textual Poachers,* on their shirt, but it clearly marks textual poaching in the fans' space—you know, where that is a statement of identification with the textual poaching metaphor to a large degree.

Harrison: But doesn't that in a sense preserve the divide between fans and academics? Because academics aren't wearing the T-shirts. Additionally, even if you do manage to speak to some academics in the ways that you want to, aren't you preaching to the choir? These are people who are already on the road to, if not already in, a place where they acknowledge this very complicated shifting fan-academic relation within themselves and in relation to the texts that they write about and think about.

Jenkins: Perhaps, and that's a potential problem, but it's important to build a community. It is also important to gain some solidarity and understanding among ourselves—as fan-academics—before we tackle some larger space. What's interesting is that so far, the logical next move, which is to bring this discussion back to the academic convention circuit, is being resisted. I have proposed panels to several conventions on the question of academics-as-fans and vice-versa and they have been rejected with no explanation. I don't think they want to talk about that in the academic space yet. I think people are really threatened by breaking that divide down because it has been so central to the institutionalization of media studies. At a time of economic retrenchment, when film studies is under attack, people do not necessarily want to take the next step I am pushing them towards, which is to say, all right, let's be up front about the fact that we are emotionally committed, we are fans, we are part of fannish politics, and let's break down those barriers. Because to break down those barriers is to acknowledge a potential trivialization of your field at a moment when the credibility of your discipline is again under fire. I understand the resistance. I think the resistance is wrong. I see the fan-academic as a public intellectual who moves back to the popular or participates in popular debates, works in the grass roots with communities of people, talks about what we have learned as academics, and shares it with a broader public. At the same time, I do not just want to learn *about* fans, I want to learn *from* fans. I want to learn *as* a fan. Those relationships are very complex. So far most of the work on fannishness, most of the academic discussion of fans, has been learning about fans, maybe as a fan (in the case of Constance Penley and myself and many of the younger graduate students who are doing that work or are learning as fans about fandom). What I want to see next is learning from fans certain modes of writing, certain modes of criticism, certain modes of interpretation that may liberate us as academics in our relation to popular culture and allow us to be better at what we do. I think that fandom's got a hell of a lot to teach us about the media and about media studies and we have not really listened yet.

Harrison: Are we poaching the fans, then?

Jenkins: Sure! But I would say we are *poaching* them. We are not appropriating them or co-opting them. Maybe something like slash provides a model for criticism that allows for thinking through the characters from the inside out, having the playful ability to rethink or write around the ending, etc. To think about revising and rewriting the text as part of the process of ideological criticism, for example, is a strategy I have seen more and more within the academy. It is not just coming from fandom, but I think there is a moment now in which what the academy wants to do, particularly in queer studies, and what fans have been doing, are coming together. I would say that Alex Doty or Eve Sedgwick or Cathy Griggers are slashers. They are writing academic slash in the ways in which they are reading the text and constructing these relationships that other readers are reluctant to see. They are pulling them to the surface and writing them out and envisioning, as Cathy Griggers (1993) does in her piece on *Thelma and Louise (1991),* other scenes that might have been there but were not. Many of us can learn how to do that as a more creative, playful, pleasurable, proximate, and, yes, powerful way of engaging with the text.

Harrison: What I find intriguing about the whole relationship is that on the one hand we, the academics, are supposed to be "objective" and look at the text in these very stilted ways, and on the other hand, if you *do* make the kind of investment that seems required in other fields, then suddenly you are accused of being invested in a text that is not worthy of that kind of scrutiny. The charge that gets leveled at me all the time is that these texts cannot bear the weight of what I want them to talk about, that they are not sufficient to let me talk about all the things that I think are important, all the affective dimensions that I don't have any other text to use to talk about. Now maybe that's just because of who I am as a person, but the texts that have any kind of resonance for me are precisely the popular texts. It isn't that they completely jibe with my experience in the world, but, in their very inadequacy, I negotiate my relation to affect. I say, "Gosh, this text doesn't look right," and an understanding of that gap lies precisely in understanding the details of how the entire setup works together and creates a social world. And yet I am told that it cannot stand up to this kind of—tension.

Jenkins: And you get told that by people in television studies and film studies, not just people outside. It is really telling that we have this anxiety about our status as a discipline which means that, on the one hand, we are demanding to be taken seriously because we can talk about authors or ideology or poststructuralist theory, too. On the other hand, we are caving in to an anxiety that our object of study is not worthy of serious study, that when we actually engage with the object of study we suddenly fear that it is too trivial, that it is not worth talking about after all, that we cannot take it seriously on its own terms. That is anxiety number one. Anxiety number two that I hear is that we still, despite all the theory about textuality and intertextuality and all of that, get anxious if the meaning is not found in the text. We do not allow ourselves to be readers in the sense that we talk about our ethnographic subjects as readers. We do not allow ourselves the freedom to appropriate, speculate, engage with the text beyond what's there, you know, what can be found, nailed down in textual terms. We do not even allow ourselves to imagine a mode of criticism that is more speculative and fanciful, which allows you, as you said, to deal with the incompleteness of the text and to think through it and to use it as a starting point for thinking about other issues or thinking about our identities or our politics, as fans frequently have, and to work through the text in a new way. We do not allow ourselves the creative freedom that the fans allow themselves in the ways in which we engage with text, and I think that is painfully sad.

Harrison: This gets back to the question of ethnography. How has your thinking about your position in relation to media fandom changed since the writing of *Textual Poachers*? For example, in your paper last year at the Console-ing Passions: Television, Video, and Feminist Studies Conference, you came out as bisexual. Does this alter the position from which you can speak as a commentator on fan groups? And what does such a positioning of yourself and your own subjectivity do to, say, your reading of the *Beauty and the Beast* group you relied on in *Textual Poachers*?

Jenkins: Part of the argument I would make throughout the book is that fantasy is not as anchored as we would like to think. The fantasy, the sexual fantasies, the romantic fantasies that fans construct, either as straight women envisioning Kirk and Spock as lovers or as lesbian women envisioning Catherine and Vincent as lovers, are more fluid than our simple categories for talking about sexuality would allow us to get at. On one level, my new openness about my bisexuality does not change anything. As a participant in the community it may complicate my own personal identity, my sense of myself, but I'm not sure that it changes anything that I say specifically in the *Beauty and the Beast* chapter, other than the fact that if I were to write it today I might feel more compelled to dig in further to those experiences of the lesbian and bisexual women in fandom. But I am not sure that I would in any case, because my interest is more in terms of how the community as a whole forms collective fantasies than on the personal identifications and goals of individual fans. I think that is one way we might differentiate my approach from Camille Bacon-Smith's, say.

Harrison: It is ultimately a question, and this goes back to what we were saying about ethnography before, about how you, as a man, in the first place, on this very biologically essentialist level, fit yourself into this predominantly female fan community. How far can you be a participant in that community, and does a change in your centrality or marginality as a social actor alter how you can participate?

Jenkins: I think this is an important question. In some senses, I am marginal in fandom, in some senses there are barriers set up. In some senses, and this is difficult to talk about, I am more powerless in fandom than I am in the general society. Fandom is a female-constructed space; the power within fandom is held by women and it acts as a countervailing pressure on some of the power that I bring in from the outside as a male academic. If I sit in a room full of women fans as a man, my subjectivity is in question at that point in a way that it is not if I sit in the room full of academics as a man. That room full of women can challenge me and ascribe to me, "Well, you're just a man; you don't understand this" and confront me, and they collectively have a source of power in relation to me that is very important—very important to them and very important to me. Yes, as an academic and as a man, I am in a privileged position in the larger culture, but I would also say that a social space takes up its norms of interpretation and values of interaction based on the dominant members of that group. Fandom is predominantly female. It is a female-centered space—but not a female-only space. Its mode of interpretation comes out of female, feminist, and feminine experiences, however socially constructed all of that may be. So, when I move into that space, if I am going to be accepted as a participant, I have to participate on the level of discourse that space has set up, and I have worked through that as a male fan in a predominantly female fandom for fifteen years. I have learned to read according to their interpretive norms. I have learned to participate in the discussion on their terms. I have given up certain privileges I might enjoy elsewhere in order to participate. Now, that's somewhat utopian and I'm not trying to say I have been totally successful in that, but I think there is a way in which it exerts countervailing pressure on my participation; and insofar as the women that I have talked to in the study are concerned, the most important fact was not my gender but the fact that I declared myself to be a fan, that I was part of the group. That was the most important defining characteristic. I did get a few letters when I sent out the chapter on slash from women who did not know me and they said that they were suspicious when they saw it was written by a man, but when they were through reading, they felt that I had gotten it right, that I had understood and communicated what slash meant to them, and I consider that a high compliment.

Harrison: Maybe one of the things that feminist academics are looking for in *Textual Poachers*—at least I know that I'm looking for this—is a sense not of the end result, the conclusions that you come to and the readings that you give, but of how that process of confrontation happens, how the women, say, in the *Beauty and the Beast* group, come up to you and say, "Henry, you're just not getting it because you're a man." What did you think before that point, how does the evolution happen? How do you get to a later point?

Jenkins: If I wrote that book today, that process would be much more important. I do acknowledge the process in multiple places in the book; I do spell out the methodology and the sending out of manuscripts at the beginning. Because I was getting conflicting responses from the community, I do specifically stop in the *Beauty and the Beast* chapter and lay out what the criticisms were, what the conflicts were, and why I was doing what I was doing. I don't do enough of that. There is an anxiety I have as an ethnographer about to what degree I should listen to the community and represent what they are saying and to what degree I should be examining my own subjectivity. I have seen certain ethnographers who, in the reflexive ethnographic tradition, swamp the community, become so obsessed with their own methodological anxieties and subjective positions that the autobiographical overwhelms the social, the cultural. I did not want to do that, and I thought that was particularly important not to do as a male ethnographer writing about a predominantly female fan community—to let my male problems swamp the experience of these women. But in not doing that, I left myself open to the charge of making it seem too transparent, of making it seem too easy and natural. Frankly, when I was writing, I didn't know how to talk about it. I didn't know what language to discuss it with. People kept saying, "Situate yourself, situate yourself." How exactly do I situate myself as a white male in relation to a predominantly feminine culture? Everything I say would seem self-serving, rationalizing; it would only make things worse. The risk I am taking right now in this interview is that whatever I say can be potentially read as self-serving and self-congratulatory in some ways as a male talking about my relationship to this community, and I think in some ways that would be even more false to the kinds of relationships I have established there.

Harrison: One of the things that I like best about what Constance Penley (1992) has done is that statement she makes at the end of the article in *Cultural Studies,* during the question and answer period. She says that her work on *Star Trek* and psychoanalysis are both really important to her, and that the important thing about the *Star Trek* work is that it has meant she cannot think psychoanalysis in the same way that she did before, and psychoanalysis means she thinks *Star Trek* differently. So, you get this constant sense of interplay that is not always foregrounded in her work—I don't want to say that she is predominantly focusing on process, but that kind of situatedness is useful to see. It's not in the sense of "Oh, my subjectivity is in crisis; what am I going to do now?" but the sense that one's thinking does change and that it is precisely the process of "Here I am in a situation that is challenging the academic precepts that I came into it with."

Jenkins: Maybe this is the point to pull back to the questions of my bisexuality in relation to fandom, which I only started to answer. On one level, it does not matter in fandom. On another level, it matters a lot. What I should say is that fandom and writing about fandom have allowed me to come out as bi—that it is part of my experience of thinking through fandom that has allowed me fianally to conceptualize my sexuality in those terms after twenty years of struggling with who I am and what my sexuality is and how I relate to the world, of hiding from a lot of my queer feelings and my queer desires and my queer fantasies and pretending they did not exist, or masquerading as fully straight and passing myself off. It was when I confronted slash, when I read slash and found out that I really was getting turned on by this—

that this was not just a simple academic object of study—and as I began to rethink fantasy in relation to slash and what it meant to have erotic fantasies and how one relates to one's erotic fantasies, that I began to move away from a theoretical and abstract proposition—that everyone is basically bisexual but culture shapes our sense of our sexuality into narrower terms, that for social and cultural reasons we are constructed in certain ways but that there is an underlying amorphous perversity that allows us to be more fluid in our object choices. I could talk that intellectual game until I was blue in the face but never come out and say, "I am bisexual," never pull back to the personal and say, "I am a bisexual. That means me." Moving to talking about the Gaylaxians pulled me into contact with a community of queers more intimately than I had been up to that point. For them, it was a question of this word, "queer," which I had to think through, because I am living in a long-term, monogamous, heterosexual relationship. Did I have the right to speak of myself as queer? What does that word mean? Does that include me? Is it one of those words like "nigger" that you can say if you're black, but if you're white, it is an exercise of power against that community? I felt empowered to speak as queer and about queerness as I became implicated in my own fantasies in relation to the texts of slash. The first time I ever came out to anyone other than my wife was in a room full of two hundred or so fans at the Gaylaxicon where I said publicly for the first time that I am a bisexual and I am proud of who I am. It was at that point that I felt the community of support that allowed me to say who I was. Since then, I have moved toward being acting director of Gay and Lesbian Studies at MIT, to talking about it here. My involvement in fandom provoked me to think about my sexuality in a different way and subsequently it shaped every other piece of criticism that I have written. I am not only a fan when I write about fans; in that same way, I am not just queer when I write about the Gaylaxians. I am queer when I write about *Dennis the Menace* and permissive parenting, and all of those subjectivities—queer, fan, and parent—shape how I write, how I respond, how I do my business as an academic. But, for all the reasons we have talked about so far, it is hard in the academy to pull back to that level of personal confession, to focus on yourself and your growth rather than on a subcultural community or a text, and I am struggling with whether my personal growth should even be that important or interesting to readers.

Harrison: Do you feel that you foreground that kind of complexity in the writing that you do?

Jenkins: In various ways, to various degrees. When I write about WWF Wrestling, for example, I do talk a great deal about the homoerotics of the relation between the men and the degree to which it plays and flirts with Eve Sedgwick's (1985, 1990) notion of the continuum between homosocial and homoerotic desire. It is a queer reading of WWF Wrestling in the midst of an essay that is, at that very moment, also talking about my relation to my son, which is, of course, a marker of my lived heterosexual experiences. They both exist side-by-side there. Still, I struggle with how autobiographical I want my writing to become. I want to acknowledge my pleasures, my social situatedness. I do know from a very concrete social space, but I do not want an essay to just become about me, because frankly, the lifestyle of a male academic is not that compelling or interesting to anyone other than male academics. Maybe I am resisting too much examining my own pleasure, even as I am challenging others to look more closely at their own, but it seems to me that there is a thin line here between proximate epistemology and sheer narcissism that is hard to negotiate much of the time and that a lot of confessional criticism crosses too far, in my opinion.

Harrison: One criticism leveled at your work is that it constructs fandom as a kind of utopic space. Do you agree with this criticism or see it as justified? Do fans themselves construct fandom as utopic?

Jenkins: The conclusion of *Textual Poachers,* where I talk about utopianism, was intended to represent what is very hard to talk about but is very real—the material way that fandom *is* a utopian space. I see utopianism not as escapism but as a very political thing. Utopianism is, by its nature, a critique of, an alternative to, the established order. To think of a world that is different allows you to recognize why the world is not the way you would like it to be. It poses a question, but it also forces us to envision an alternative space and what it would look like. It is not sufficient within utopian discourse to be merely critical. You have to propose another world. You have to propose another kind of space and try to create the social structures that allow it to exist. In that sense, I think fandom is utopian—and the academy is not. We do not challenge ourselves to imagine an alternative reality and in many ways we are often terrified to acknowledge our own successes. Academics have such a hard time understanding the concept of utopia because the academy is not a very utopian place as a rule.

Now, there's another sense in which the criticism of utopianism in *Poachers* gets raised which is very different: it's said that I am only affirming the positive side of fandom. Even fans come to me and say, "Look, you don't talk about things like the feuds disrupting fandom. You don't talk about some of the tensions and rivalries there. You don't talk about the fact that this is a predominantly white space. You don't talk about the class issues that are involved." I think those are valid criticisms, but at the moment in which I wrote the book, academic discourse on fandom was predominantly negative. The negative stereotypes were so strongly in place that I didn't feel comfortable attacking fans. I did not think it was my task to go out there, find this group, and expose them to the public view so that I could berate them for what was wrong with their culture. Raising the negative in that space would have been destructive to them, destructive to the creation of a dialogue that makes us rethink what fandom is. So, yes, I soft-pedaled. I chose to tell a story that accented the positive rather than the negative, but I think it was tactically necessary at that point and I stand behind that. I also respected the wishes of the community not to talk about certain things. If I had violated that trust, I would have lost the respect of the community. I would have committed an abuse of my ethnographic authority by pulling back to the academic and abusing the group I was working with. I felt they had a say in their self-representation and if they asked me not to talk about certain dimensions of their culture in a public space, I respected them in the same way I would respect some of the questions about closeting or not closeting in the queer community when we are writing about it. It would not have been appropriate and I did not do it.

Harrison: Do you have a sense of how you would go about starting to think those issues, at a moment when it might be more appropriate? Can you envision a moment at which you would be able to explore confrontational issues of race or sexuality?

Jenkins: It's something I'm still struggling with, to be honest. I think if I did it I would do it in cooperation with the fan community. I would do it by including in the public space some of the internal debates that fans themselves have around these questions. I would explore it in the context of fans struggling with these issues. These are not just academic radicals coming to say, "Look at those people. They're so naïve that they don't think through this side of slash and they don't think through homophobia and they don't think through the racism of their own practices." These are concerns that fans have, too, though they articulate them in different ways, and it might be refreshing to find alternative terms to think through these debates. I have tried to address this in a new essay I have coming out on slash, homophobia, and queerness, and I will be eager to see what people think of the results. The article, which pulls together many fans, straight and queer, talking about their pleasures in slash, has been controversial among fans, since there is inevitably a question of whose voice gets heard, whose voice gets accessed, especially because it touches on a lot of hot topics in slash fandom; but I think it was an important risk to take, because I get tired of listening to academics who assume that the fans themselves never take up these questions or have nothing of relevance to say about them.

Harrison: This brings up the whole question of the interface between fans and texts. It's not just the fans that are important but also the texts that they are responding to or reacting to or remaking, reworking. Fandoms, all kinds of media fandoms, are not odd, aberrant spaces. They have their connections to other kinds of social spaces.

Jenkins: On the one hand, I think that people have exaggerated the gap between audience studies and textual analysis. I do not see a potential conflict between the two. For example, in my section on ten ways to rewrite a television show, I continually show how structures like hurt-comfort are in the text and are then explored and rewritten by fans in more elaborate ways. That section moves back and forth between textual structures and fannish reading practices. In my own work, I have actually written more about texts than I have written about audiences, but those things are thought of as so separate that there are people who read my work on audiences and other people who read my work on texts. They are not being connected and that is troubling to me.

The texts of *Star Trek* have not exactly been ignored. If you look at the bibliography, there is a lot more work out there on *Star Trek* as a text than there has been on *Star Trek* audiences; it's just that in the last few years that work on the audience has started to come together. And textual analysis has been shaped by implicit assumptions about the audience, often very critical or negative assumptions about the audience. Robert Jewett and John Lawrence's (1977) work on the "monomyth" of *Star Trek* talks about fans as inarticulate, or unable to explain their relationship with the text; the critic has to step in and justify it—to its fans. Textual critics often begin from the assumption that textual analysis can explain why *Star Trek* is popular and then proceed to choose episodes that are looked down upon by the audience. The ignorance about the audience has shaped textual criticism, and one of the problems in a lot of purely textual analysis is that the authors do not own up to the assumptions about the audience they are making, nor do they test those assumptions against anything other than introspection or theoretical citation or the text itself.

I think the time is right to merge the political economy of institutions, audience research, and textual analysis in various complex ways, and I do not think we can understand fandom without understanding all three. It isn't that I chose to write about fans instead of the text, or that I ignore the text. I had to understand fans, and the text became secondary to the task of understanding fans at the time I was writing *Textual Poachers*. The *Beauty and the Beast* chapter talks about the text a fair amount, because there the text was central to understanding the fans. There I have all three: the properties of the texts that enabled fan interpretation, the production decisions that alienated the fans, and an analysis of the fans' responses. That comes closer to the model of what I would like to see criticism doing. I think I also achieved that synthesis in my discussion of the Gaylaxians in *Science Fiction Audiences* (Jenkins 1995).

Harrison: It's only now that we seem to be in a moment where we could conceivably start to think these things together. There does seem to be both an academic and a theoretical climate in which that would be possible—a climate of vocabulary as well, of words that we could use.

Jenkins: I think that the time is right to break down those barriers. I am excited by an ideological critic such as Jackie Byars and a political economist such as Eileen Meehan (1994–1995) collaborating on the Lifetime Network: When a political economist can collaborate with an audience researcher then we really have a breakthrough. Both sides have been historically suspicious of each other's theoretical paradigms, the top-down versus bottom-up models of the audience. From my point of view, you cannot understand fans unless you recognize the issues of media ownership and media access. You cannot understand why fandom is necessary as a social practice unless you recognize that most of us are excluded from any access to the modes of production and unable to tell the stories that matter to us through television as a medium. We are stuck, as audience members, in a system that does not allow us to tell our own stories and that will not tell the stories we want most to see told, and therefore, the predominant materials we have to construct our narratives are imperfect media materials. We have to use materials that do not belong to us. We have to poach; we have to work in relation to a field that is defined as someone else's intellectual property. If we lived in a climate where culture belonged to the people, where everyone had access to the dominant myths and could tell them freely as an oral culture once told the stories of Robin Hood or Br'er Rabbit or Coyote or whatever, then what fans do would not seem strange at all. What fans do is a continuation of the oral folklore tradition in a society that has now put fences around intellectual property, that is now policing the boundaries. I think the possibility of talking about political economy and audiences together is tremendously important, and it might mute the allegedly utopian or optimistic thrust of *Textual Poachers*. Poaching has to be understood as a survival mechanism within a space where fans do not own, and do not control, the telling of the story that matters to us.

Harrison: And yet we still do need to walk that fine line between love and hate, between a utopian configuration of the text itself and a constantly critical stance. We do need to acknowledge that there is a double movement of rejecting the text and at the same time embracing it intensely. I'm not quite sure we have the vocabulary to talk about that yet.

Jenkins: It's very hard, but it's what fans do. For me, fandom comes out of a fascination and a frustration and those two are interlocking: fascination with the material and the desire to engage with it, to feel creative about it, and frustration that it still is not telling the stories we want to hear. It is not telling the narratives that matter to us. It is not speaking to our experience, so we have to continue to struggle with it and rework it. If the fascination were not there, we would just walk away. If the frustration was not there and we were fully satisfied, we would walk away. It is only when there is a tension and we move back and forth, struggling with the text, that the kinds of productive work fans do becomes possible. The same is true for us as academics.

Harrison: That is precisely what academics need to learn to do. We need to understand how the frustration works, but also how the fascination works. Sometimes I despair that that is simply not going to be possible, or that it is going to be so resisted as a named central project for us to undertake that it is never going to take hold, that one or the other is always going to win: "This is a good text," or "This is a bad text."

Jenkins: At the moment, as long as we are in the business of labeling this text as progressive and that text as reactionary, then we are going to be stuck in that either/or mode. Whenever we say, "Yes, there are these progressive moments in the text, but they do not count because they have been co-opted and contained by the reactionary pressures," then we have lost the battle. We always act as if everything were resolved, one way or another, by the end, and so the process of how we got there, the progressive moments that incite our fantasies and our desires and our creative imagination and our passions disappear when we start to write. If we could talk about ideology as multivocal, we could talk about the fact that all popular culture is not "either/or" but "always and/but also" and that both progressive and reactionary elements exist simultaneously in any popular text that incites our imagination. If we could talk about the fact that all popular texts are both strongly progressive and potentially reactionary at the same time. If we as critics could struggle to move away from some easy answer to the more complex question of how all that works and how we, as fans, as academics, get pleasure from it. If we could identify those progressive potentials and then rework them, show what the text could have said but did not, show how its possibilities might be fully realized but were not. If we could talk about the mixture of fascination and frustration that we as academics share with ourselves as fans. If.

Notes

This interview was conducted by Taylor Harrison at the Console-ing Passions: Television, Video, and Feminist Studies Conference April 24, 1994, in Tucson, AZ.

1. Usually, these are fan-written, -produced, and -distributed magazines made on shoestring budgets by few people. Often, especially in relation to *Star Trek,* they are heavily associated with conventions and reading/viewing groups.

2. "Slash" refers to fan fiction that depicts sexual relationships between Kirk and Spock (K/S), as in *Star Trek,* or between other, usually homosexual, combinations, such as Starsky and Hutch (S/H).

References

Bacon-Smith, Camille. 1992. *Enterprising Women: Television Fandom and the Creation of Popular Myth.* Philadelphia: U of Pennsylvania P.

Byars, Jackie, and Eileen R. Meehan. 1994–1995. "Once in a Lifetime: Constructing 'The Working Woman' through Cable Narrowcasting." *Camera Obscura* 33/34: 13–41.

de Certeau, Michel. 1984. *The Practice of Everyday Life.* Berkeley: U of California P.

Griggers, Cathy. 1993. "*Thelma and Louise* and the Cultural Generation of the New Butch-Femme." In *Film Theory Goes to the Movies.* Ed. Jim Collins, Hilary Radner, and Ava Preacher Collins. New York: Routledge. 129–142.

Jenkins, Henry. 1988. "*Star Trek* Rerun, Reread, Rewritten: Fan Writing as Textual Poaching." *Critical Studies in Mass Communication* 5.2: 85–107.

———. 1992. *Textual Poachers: Television Fans and Participatory Culture.* New York: Routledge.

———. 1995. "'Out of the Closet and into the Universe': Queers and *Star Trek.*"Science Fiction Audiences. John Tulloch and Henry Jenkins. New York: Routledge. 237–265.

Jewett, Robert, and John Shelton Lawrence. 1977. *The American Monomyth.* Garden City, NY: Anchor P.

Penley, Constance. 1992. "Feminism, Psychoanalysis, and the Study of Popular Culture." In *Cultural Studies.* Ed. Lawrence Grossberg, Cary Nelson, and Paula Treichler. New York: Routledge. 479–500.

Sedgwick, Eve Kosofsky. 1985. *Between Men: English Literature and Male Homosocial Desire.* New York: Columbia U P.

———. 1990. *Epistemology of the Closet.* Berkeley: U of California P.

Thompson, E. P. 1979. "The Moral Economy of the English Crowd in the 18th Century." *Past and Present* 50: 76–136.

Tulloch, John, and Henry Jenkins. 1995. *Science Fiction Audiences: Watching Doctor Who and Star Trek.* New York: Routledge.

Appendix B

Selected Bibliography of Critical Work on Star Trek

Compiled by Sarah Projansky

Amesley, Cassandra. 1989. "How to Watch *Star Trek.*" *Cultural Studies* 3.3: 323–339.

Armitt, Lucy, ed. 1991. *Where No Man Has Gone Before: Women and Science Fiction.* London: Routledge.

Bacon-Smith, Camille. 1992. *Enterprising Women: Television Fandom and the Creation of Popular Myth.* Philadelphia: U of Pennsylvania P.108-1400

Barr, Marleen S. 1993. "Antipatriarchal Fabulation; or, The Green Pencils Are Coming, the Green Pencils Are Coming." In *Lost in Space: Probing Feminist Science Fiction and Beyond.* Durham: U of North Carolina P.

Berger, Arthur Asa. 1981. "A Personal Response to Whetmore's 'A Female Captain's Enterprise.'" In *Future Females: A Critical Anthology.* Ed. Marleen S. Barr. Bowling Green, OH: Bowling Green State U Popular P. 162–163.

Bernardi, Daniel. 1994. "Infinite Diversity in Infinite Combinations: Diegetic Logics and Racial Articulations in the Original *Star Trek.*" *Film and History* 24.1/2: 60–74.

Bick, Ilsa J. 1996. "Boys in Space: *Star Trek,* Latency, and the Neverending Story." *Cinema Journal* 35.2: 43–60.

Bjorklund, Edi. 1986. "Women and *Star Trek* Fandom: From SF to Sisterhood." *Minerva* 24.2: 16–65.

Blair, Karin. 1977. *Meaning in* Star Trek. Chambersburg, PA: Anima Books.

———. 1979. "The Garden in the Machine: The Why of *Star Trek.*" *Journal of Popular Culture* 13.2: 310–320.

———. 1983. "Sex and *Star Trek.*" *Science-Fiction Studies* 10.2: 292–297.

Braine, F. S. 1994. "Technological Utopias: The Future of the Next Generation." *Film and History* 24.1/2: 1–18.

Buhler, Stephen M. 1995. "'Who Calls Me Villain?': Blank Verse and the Black Hat." *Extrapolation* 36.1: 18–27.

Buxton, David. 1990. *From* The Avengers *to* Miami Vice: *Form and Ideology in Television Series.* Manchester: Manchester U P.

Byers, Thomas B. 1987. "Commodity Futures: Corporate State and Personal Style in Three Recent Science Fiction Movies." *Science-Fiction Studies* 14.3: 43, 326–339.

Casper, Monica J., and Lisa Jean Moore. 1995. "Inscribing Bodies, Inscribing the Future: Gender, Sex, and Reproduction in Outer Space." *Sociological Perspectives* 38.2: 311–333.

Claus, Peter J. 1982. "A Structuralist Appreciation of *Star Trek.*" In *Anthropology for the Eighties.* Ed. Johnnetta Cole. New York: Macmillan. 417–429.

Cranny-Francis, Anne. 1985. "Sexuality and Sex-Role Stereotyping in *Star Trek*." *Science-Fiction Studies* 12.3: 274–284.

Deegan, Mary Jo. 1986. "Sexism in Space: The Freudian Formula in *Star Trek*." In *Eros in the Mind's Eye*. Ed. Donald Palumbo. New York: Greenwood. 209–224.

Dutta, Mary Buhl. 1995. "'Very Bad Poetry, Captain': Shakespeare in *Star Trek*." *Extrapolation* 36.1: 38–45.

Ellington, Jane Elizabeth, and Joseph W. Critelli. 1983. "Analysis of a Modern Myth: The *Star Trek* Series." *Extrapolation* 24.3: 241–250.

Felner, Julie. May/June 1995. "Where No Woman Has Trekked Before." *Ms.* 5.6: 80–81.

Franklin, H. Bruce. 1994. "*Star Trek* in the Vietnam Era." *Science-Fiction Studies* 21.1: 24–34.

———. 1994. "*Star Trek* in the Vietnam Era." *Film and History* 24.1/2:36-46.

Goulding, Jay. 1985. *Empire, Aliens, and Conquest: A Critique of American Ideology in* Star Trek *and Other Science Fiction Adventures*. Toronto, Canada: Sisyphus P.

Greenberg, Harvey R. 1984. "In Search of Spock: A Psychoanalytic Inquiry." *The Journal of Popular Film and Television* 12.2: 52–65.

Grenz, Stanley J. 1 Mar. 1994. "*Star Trek* and the Next Generation: Postmodernism and the Future of Evangelical Theology." *Crux* 30.1: 24.

Hassler, Donald M. 1995. "Memories from the Golden-Age." *Extrapolation* 36.1: 3-4.

Hegarty, Emily. 1995. "Some Suspect of Ill: Shakespeare's Sonnets and 'The Perfect Mate.'" *Extrapolation* 36.1: 55–64.

Henderson, Mary. 1994. "Professional Women in *Star Trek*, 1964–1969." *Film and History* 24.1/2: 47–59.

Hines, Susan C. 1995. "What's Academic about *Trek*." *Extrapolation* 36.1: 5–9.

Hodges, Shari. 1994. "A Pedagogically Useful Comparison of *Star Trek II* and *Paradise Lost*." *CEA Forum* 24.2: 4.

Hostetter, Clyde. 1991. Star Trek *to Hawa-i'i: Mesopotamia to Polynesia*. San Luis Abispo, CA: Diamond P.

Houlahan, Mark. 1995. "Cosmic Hamlets? Contesting Shakespeare in Federation Space." *Extrapolation* 36.1: 28–37.

James, Nancy E. 1988. "Two Sides of Paradise: The Eden Myth According to Kirk and Spock." In *Spectrum of the Fantastic*. Ed. Donald Palumbo. Westport, CT: Greenwood. 219–223.

Jenkins, Henry. 1988. "*Star Trek* Rerun, Reread, Rewritten: Fan Writing as Textual Poaching." *Critical Studies in Mass Communication* 5.2: 85–107. Reprinted in *Close Encounters: Film, Feminism, and Science Fiction*. Ed. Constance Penley, Elisabeth Lyon, Lynn Spigel, and Janet Bergstrom. Minneapolis: U Minnesota P, 1991. 171–204.

———. 1990. "'If I Could Speak with Your Sound': Fan Music, Textual Proximity, and Liminal Identification." *Camera Obscura* 23: 149–175.

———. 1992a. "Strangers No More, We Sing: Filking and the Social Construction of the Science Fiction Fan Community." In *The Adoring Audience: Fan Culture and Popular Media*. Ed. Lisa Lewis. New York: Routledge. 208–236.

———. 1992b. *Textual Poachers: Television Fans and Participatory Culture*. New York: Routledge.

Jewett, Robert, and John Shelton Lawrence. 1977. *The American Monomyth*. Garden City, NY: Anchor P.

Jindra, Michael. 1994. "*Star Trek* Fandom as a Religious Phenomenon." *Sociology of Religion* 55.1: 27–51.

Joseph, Paul, and Sharon Carton. 1992. "The Law of the Federation: Images of Law, Lawyers, and the Legal System in *Star Trek: The Next Generation*." *University of Toledo Law Review* 24.1: 43–85.

Joyrich, Lynne. 1996. "Feminist Enterprise: *Star Trek: The Next Generation* and the Occupation of Femininity." *Cinema Journal* 35.2: 61–84.

Lagon, Mark P. 1993. "'We Owe It to Them to Interfere': *Star Trek* and U.S. Statecraft in the 1960s and the 1980s." *Extrapolation* 34.3: 251–264.

Lalli, Tom. 1990. "Same Sexism, Different Generation." In *The Best of TREK #15*. Ed. Walter Irwin and G. B. Love. New York: Penguin. 39–67.

Lamb, Patricia Frazer, and Diana L. Veith. 1986. "Romantic Myth, Transcendence, and *Star Trek* Zines." In *Erotic Universe: Sexuality and Fantastic Literature*. Ed. Donald Palumbo. New York: Greenwood P. 235–255.

Littleton, C. Scott. 1989. "Some Implications of the Mythology in *Star Trek*." *Keystone Folklore* 4.1: 33–42.

Marsalek, Kenneth. 1992. *(Star Trek:* Humanism of the Future." *Free Inquiry* 12.4: 53–56.

McCrone, John. 1993. *The Myth of Irrationality: The Science of Man From Plato to* Star Trek. London: MacMillan.

Palumbo, Donald. 1992. "The Monomyth in Time Travel Films." In *The Celebration of the Fantastic: Selected Papers from the Tenth Anniversary International Conference on the Fantastic in the Arts*. Ed. Donald E. Morse, Marshall B. Tymn, and Csilla Bertha. Westport, CT: Greenwood. 211–218.

Pendergast, John S. 1995. "A Nation of Hamlets: Shakespeare and Cultural Politics." *Extrapolation* 36.1: 10–17.

Penley, Constance. 1986. "Time Travel, Primal Scene, and the Critical Dystopia." *Camera Obscura* 15. Reprinted in *Close Encounters: Film, Feminism, and Science Fiction*. Ed. Constance Penley, Elisabeth Lyon, Lynn Spigel, and Janet Bergstrom. Minneapolis: U of Minnesota P, 1991. 63–80.

———. 1991. "Brownian Motion: Women, Tactics, and Technology." In *Technoculture*. Ed. Constance Penley and Andrew Ross. Minneapolis: U of Minnesota P. 135–161.

———. 1992a. "Feminism, Psychoanalysis and the Study of Popular Culture." In *Cultural Studies*. Ed. Lawrence Grossberg, Cary Nelson, and Paula Treichler. New York: Routledge. 479–500.

———. 1992b. "Spaced Out: Remembering Christa McAuliffe." *Camera Obscura* 29: 178–213.

Reid-Jeffrey, Donna. Spring 1982. "*Star Trek*: The Last Frontier in Modern American Myth." *Folklore and Mythology Studies* 6: 34–41.

Reinheimer, David. 1995. "Ontological and Ethical Allusion: Shakespeare in *The Next Generation*." *Extrapolation* 36.1: 46–54.

Rose, Pamela. 1990. "Women in the Federation." In *The Best of the Best of TREK*. Ed. Walter Irwin and G. B. Love. New York: Penguin. 21–26.

Roth, Lane. 1987. "Death and Rebirth in *Star Trek II: The Wrath of Khan*." *Extrapolation* 28.2: 159–166.

Russ, Joanna. 1985. "Pornography by Women for Women, with Love." In *Magic Mommas, Trembling Sisters, Puritans and Perverts: Feminist Essays.* Trumansburg, NY: Crossing P. 79–99.

Selley, April. 1986. "'I Have Been, and Ever Shall Be, Your Friend': *Star Trek, The Deerslayer* and the American Romance." *Journal of Popular Culture* 20.1: 89–104.

———. 1990. "Transcendentalism in *Star Trek: The Next Generation.*" *Journal of American Culture* 13.1: 31–34.

Spelling, Ian. 1995. "Voyage to a New Frontier." *Hispanic* 8.3: 14–16.

Tetreault, Mary Ann. 1984. "The Trouble with *Star Trek.*" *Minerva* 22.1: 119–129.

Tulloch, John, and Henry Jenkins. 1995. *Science Fiction Audiences: Watching Doctor Who and* Star Trek. New York: Routledge.

Tyrrell, M. Blake. 1977. "*Star Trek* as Myth and Television as Mythmaker." *Journal of Popular Culture* 10.4: 711–719.

———. 1979. "*Star Trek's* Myth of Science." *Journal of American Culture* 2.2: 288–296.

Whetmore, Edward. 1981. "A Female Captain's Enterprise: The Implications of *Star Trek's* 'Turnabout Intruder.'" In *Future Females: A Critical Anthology.* Ed. Marleen S. Barr. Bowling Green, OH: Bowling Green State U Popular P. 157–161.

Wilcox, Clyde. 1992. "To Boldly Return Where Others Have Gone Before: Cultural Change and the Old and New *Star Treks.*" *Extrapolation* 33.1: 88–100.

Wilcox, Rhonda V. 1991. "Shifting Roles and Synthetic Women in *Star Trek: The Next Generation.*" *Studies in Popular Culture* 13.2: 53–65.

———. 1993. "Dating Data: Miscegenation in *Star Trek: The Next Generation.*" *Extrapolation* 34.3: 265–277.

———.1995. "Goldberg, Guinan, and the Celestial Mother in *Star Trek: The Next Generation.*" *Mid-Atlantic Almanack* 4: 18–31.

Winegarden, Alan D., Marilyn Fuss Reineck, and Lori J. Charron. 1993. "Using *Star Trek: The Next Generation* to Teach Concepts in Persuasion, Family Communication, and Communication Ethics." *Communication Education* 42.2: 179–188.

Witwer, Julia. 1995. "The Best of Both Worlds: On *Star Trek's* Borg." In *Prosthetic Territories: Politics and Hypertechnologies.* Ed. Gabriel Brahm Jr. and Mark Driscoll. Boulder, CO: Westview Press. 270–279.

Woods, L. A. 1994. "Jung and *Star Trek* The Coincidentia-Oppositorum and Images of the Shadow." *Journal of Popular Culture* 28.2: 169–184.

Worland, Rick. 1988. "Captain Kirk: Cold Warrior." *Journal of Popular Film and Television* 16.3: 109–117.

———. 1994. "From the New Frontier to the Final Frontier: *Star Trek* from Kennedy to Gorbachev." *Film and History* 24.1/2: 19–35.

About the Book

Can you imagine a world without *Star Trek*—without warp drive, phasers, photon torpedoes, tricorders, communicators, and transporters? After six Hollywood movies and twenty-five years of nonstop television presence, *Star Trek* is, indeed, a pervasive cultural phenomenon! This is the first critical, scholarly look at the mysteries, hidden meanings, and complex issues of the text known as *Star Trek*.

Looking at the original Spock-Kirk *Star Trek*, the contributors ask and answer questions such as: What are the cultural conditions surrounding the homoerotic relationship between Kirk and Spock? How does the show depict gender relations while simultaneously recreating the cultural conditions under which women continue to experience sexual aggression and violence? They also explore *Star Trek: The Next Generation*, raising issues such as: Was Data a battlefield on which the struggle for human rights was waged? Did militarism and warring versions of masculinity intersect at Worf?

Readers will discover the unique charges of cultural studies scholarship and how it enables us to designate a powerful pop-cultural phenomenon such as *Star Trek* into a legitimate site of study. The thirteen contributors address the very real and necessary topics of hegemony, utopias, militarism, colonialism, gender, violence, race, class, sexuality, and liminality, analyzing individual episodes and overarching themes of *Star Trek* and *Star Trek: The Next Generation*. Their insights on how *Star Trek* affects what we understand our culture to be, how it represents the social and political order, and how it reproduces pleasure and pain in its televisual texts will fascinate scholars, students, and Trekkers alike.

About the Editors and Contributors

Marleen S. Barr is visiting professor of American studies at the University of Innsbruck. She is the author of *Feminist Fabulation: Space/Postmodern Fiction, Lost in Space: Probing Feminist Science Fiction and Beyond,* and other books and articles. Her current research project, a book called *Genre Seepage: Discourse as Black Hole,* deals with the breakdown of boundaries in postmodern literature and culture.

Ilsa J. Bick, MD, is a child and adolescent psychiatrist in private practice in Fairfax, VA. She is the author of numerous articles on psychoanalysis and film. She has published in both professional psychoanalytic and cinema journals, including *The Journal of American Psychoanalytic Association, American Imago, Psychoanalytic Review, Cinema Journal, Journal of Film and Video, Discourse,* and *Film Quarterly.*

Katrina G. Boyd is a Ph.D. candidate in film studies and comparative literature at Indiana University, Bloomington. She has a published article on Terry Gilliam's *Brazil* in *Cinefocus.* She is currently working on a dissertation on the relationship between utopian thought and mass culture in 1980s film and television.

Steven F. Collins is a Ph.D. candidate and assistant instructor in the Department of Speech Communication at the University of Texas, Austin. His research interests include the rhetoric of popular music, film, and television. Currently, his research includes an investigation of the city in popular film and continuing projects on the Mod Movement in mid-¡1960s Britain and the neofeminist music of Liz Phair.

Evan Haffner is a Ph.D. student in comparative literature at the University of California, Berkeley. His research and teaching interests include reading popular movies and literature that intersect with the cultural, philosophical, and psychoanalytic movement from modernity to postmodernity. *Star Trek* is of particular interest to him, since it bridges this modern/postmodern movement in the United States from the 1960s to the 1980s. He has recently published poetry and short stories in *The Minetta*

Review, The World, The Minnesota Daily, and *The National Magazine of the Lower East Side.*

Taylor Harrison is a Ph.D. candidate in film studies at the University of Iowa, where she is completing a dissertation on representations of female stars, across multiple media, of the classical Hollywood cinema. Her research investigates questions of voice and body in film, television, and radio, especially as they relate to queer and other problematic organizations of meaning. She has taught courses on media representations of history and violence, feminist theory, and film history and criticism.

Amelie Hastie is a Ph.D. candidate in the modern studies program at the University of Wisconsin, Milwaukee. Her research and teaching examine the multiple roles of women in film and television production, theory, history and narrative. She has published work in *Discourse,* and her essay "Louise Brooks, Star Witness" is forthcoming in *Cinema Journal.*

Elyce Rae Helford is assistant professor of English and women's studies at Middle Tennessee State University. Her research focuses on gender, race, and ethnicity in science fiction literature and television. She has published articles on Stanislaw Lem, Octavia Butler, and the British science fiction sitcom *Red Dwarf* and reviews of feminist science fiction theory. She is currently writing on near-future dystopias by ethnic women writers and Jewish feminist fantasy while reading underground women's comix and K/S fiction.

Henry Jenkins is associate professor of literature and director of film and media studies at MIT. His most recent works include *Science Fiction Audiences: Watching* Doctor Who *and* Star Trek (coauthored with John Tulloch), *Classical Hollywood Comedy* (coedited with Kristine Brunovska Karnick), and *What Made Pistachio Nuts? Early Sound Comedy and the Vaudeville Aesthetic.*

Kent A. Ono is assistant professor of American studies and Asian American studies at the University of California, Davis. His research focuses on representations of race and gender in television and film. He has contributed essays to *Communication Monographs, Amerasia Journal,* and several collected volumes. He is presently working on two books: one on politics within poststructural theory and a second on film and video representations of the incarceration of Japanese Americans during World War II.

Sarah Projansky is assistant professor of women's studies at the University of California, Davis. She is currently revising a manuscript on contemporary film and television rape narratives and postfeminist discourse. She is also working on a project that explores the relationship between teenage women actors' bodies and their characters' subjectivity and has published an essay about *Dr. Quinn: Medicine Woman* on the subject. She teaches courses on popular culture; media representations of gender, race, and feminism; film theory and criticism; media cultural history; and feminist theory.

Leah R. Vande Berg is professor of communication studies at California State University, Sacramento, where she teaches courses in television criticism, media studies, and women's studies. Her research interests include television criticism, media and cultural values, and images of women in media and arts. She is coauthor (with Nick Trujillo) of *Organizational Life on Television* and coeditor (with Lawrence Wenner and Bruce Gronbeck) of the forthcoming *Television Criticism* book. She has also published articles in *Communication Monographs, Critical Studies in Mass Communication, Journalism Quarterly,* and other journals.

Rhonda V. Wilcox is associate professor of English at Gordon College. She has published essays on *Northern Exposure, Moonlighting, Remington Steele,* and three essays on *Star Trek: The Next Generation* for *Extrapolation, Humanities in the South, Pynchon Notes, The Mid-Atlantic Almanack,* and *Studies in Popular Culture* (which awarded her the 1993 Whatley Award for her essay). She has a forthcoming article on *Lois and Clark: The New Adventures of Superman* in *Journal of Popular Film and Television* and a forthcoming essay in a critical anthology on *The X-Files.*

Index